how to murder your life

cat marnell

EBURY
PRESS

1 3 5 7 9 10 8 6 4 2

Ebury Press, an imprint of Ebury Publishing
20 Vauxhall Bridge Road
London SW1V 2SA

Ebury Press is part of the Penguin Random House group of companies whose addresses can be found at global.penguinrandomhouse.com

Copyright © Cat Marnell 2017

Cat Marnell has asserted her right to be identified as the author of this Work in accordance with the Copyright, Designs and Patents Act 1988

This edition published by Ebury Press in 2018
First published by Ebury Press in 2017
First published in the US by Simon and Shuster in 2017

www.penguin.co.uk

A CIP catalogue record for this book is available from the British Library

ISBN 9780091957360

Printed and bound in Great Britain by Clays Ltd, St Ives PLC

Penguin Random House is committed to a sustainable future for our business, our readers and our planet. This book is made from Forest Stewardship Council® certified paper.

For all the party girls.

Introduction

A BABY SEAL WALKED INTO A CLUB. Just kidding! The baby seal was *me*. And fine, I didn't walk into a club, per se—not on that night, anyway. It was the VIP tent of Cirque du Soleil—you know, the famous French Canadian circus show? They'd set up a big, white tent—it sort of looked like a peaky marshmallow—called the Grand Chapiteau on Randall's Island, which was up on the East River just off Manhattan. Earlier that evening, I'd been picked up at the Condé Nast building in midtown and chauffeured there. For "work."

It was the summer of 2009, and I was walking with a bit of a limp because I had broken glass in my foot from . . . well, I wasn't sure what from, exactly. I *think* I broke a bottle of Kiehl's Musk on my bathroom floor and then I stepped on it, I guess, and I never wound up getting the shards taken out.

"You need to go see a doctor," my boss—legendary beauty director

Jean Godfrey-June—said every day when I hobbled into her office in ballerina flats. "*Today.*"

"I will," I'd promise. But then I'd just go home, pound Froot Loops in a dark trance, or get high with my friend Marco.

Yep! I was twenty-six years old and an associate beauty editor at *Lucky,* one of the top fashion magazines in America, and that's all that most people knew about me. But beneath the surface, I was full of secrets: I was an addict, for one. A pillhead! I was also an alcoholic-in-training who drank warm Veuve Clicquot after work, alone in my boss's office with the door closed; a conniving uptown doctor shopper who haunted twenty-four-hour pharmacies while my coworkers were at home watching *True Blood* in bed with their boyfriends; a salami-and-provolone-puking bulimic who spent a hundred dollars a day on binge foods when things got bad (and they got bad often); a weepy, wobbly hallucination-prone insomniac who jumped six feet in the air à la LeBron James and gobbled Valium every time a floorboard squeaked in her apartment; a tweaky self-mutilator who sat in front of *The Tonight Show with Jay Leno*, digging gory abscesses into her bikini line with Tweezerman Satin Edge Needle Nose Tweezers; a slutty and self-loathing downtown party girl fellatrix rushing to ruin; and—perhaps most of all—a lonely weirdo who felt like she was underwater all of the time. My brains were so scrambled you could've ordered them for brunch at Sarabeth's; I let art-world guys choke me out during unprotected sex; I only had one friend, a Dash Snow–wannabe named Marco who tried to stick syringes in my neck and once slurped from my nostrils when I got a cocaine nosebleed; my roommate, Nev "Catfish" Schulman, wanted me out of our East Village two-bedroom; my parents weren't talking to me ever since I'd stuck my dad with a thirty-thousand-dollar rehab bill. I took baths every morning because I was too weak to stand in the shower; I wrote rent checks in highlighter; I had three prescribing psychiatrists and zero ob-gyns or dentists; I kept such insane hours that I never knew whether to put on day cream or night cream; and I never, ever called my grandma.

I was also a liar. My boss—I was her assistant at the time—had been incredibly supportive and given me six weeks off to go to rehab. I'd been telling Jean that I was clean ever since I got back, even though I wasn't. And then she promoted me.

So now I was a beauty editor. In some ways, I looked the part of Condé Nast hotshot—or at least I tried to. I wore fab Dior slap bracelets and yellow plastic Marni dresses, and I carried a three-thousand-dollar black patent leather Lanvin tote that Jean had plunked down on my desk one afternoon. ("This is . . . too shiny for me," she'd explained.) My highlights were by Marie Robinson at Sally Hershberger Salon in the Meatpacking District; I had a chic lavender pedicure—Versace Heat Nail Lacquer V2008—and I smelled obscure and expensive, like Susanne Lang Midnight Orchid and Colette Black Musk Oil.

But look closer. I was five-four and ninety-seven pounds. The aforementioned Lanvin tote was full of orange plastic bottles from Rite Aid; if you looked at my hands digging for them, you'd see that my fingernails were dirty, and that the knuckle on my right hand was split from scraping against my front teeth. My chin was broken out from the vomiting. My self-tanner was uneven because I always applied it when I was strung out and exhausted—to *conceal* the exhaustion, you see—and my skin underneath the faux-glow was full-on *Corpse Bride*. A stylist had snipped out golf-ball-size knots that had formed at the back of my neck when I was blotto on tranquilizers for months and stopped combing my hair. My under-eye bags were big enough to send down the runway at Mercedes-Benz Fashion Week: I hadn't slept in days. I hadn't slept for more than a few hours at a time in months. And I hadn't slept without pills in *years*. So even though I wrote articles about how to take care of yourself—your hair, your skin, your nails—I was falling apart.

I'd never been in the VIP section of a circus tent before. There was an open bar and colossal flower arrangements, and waiters in black tie swishing around with trays of minicheeseburgers and all that. Maybe little shotties of vichyssoise. You know how it is! Anyway, I was at the fucking Cirque du Soleil not by choice, but as the guest of a major "personal care" brand—one of *Lucky*'s biggest advertisers. As associate beauty editor, it was my job to represent the magazine at get-togethers like these: to rub elbows and be pleasant and professional. Seriously, it was the easiest gig in the world! And yet it wasn't always so easy for me.

"I'll take one of those." I stopped a dude with a tray of champagne. "Thanks, honey."

"Hi, Cat!" a beauty publicist with a clipboard said. "Thanks so much for coming!"

"Good to see you," I lied. Thunder clapped outside.

"The gang's over there," she said.

The publicist was referring to the usual group of beauty editors— my colleagues. They were from every title you've ever heard of: *Teen Vogue*, *Glamour*, *Elle*, *Vogue*, *W*, *Harper's Bazaar*, *InStyle*, *O*, *Shape*, *Self*. I attended events alongside them every day, and yet I never felt like I belonged. I'd spent years trying to get into their world: interning, studying mastheads, interviewing all over town. But now that I *was* one of them, I felt defective—self-conscious and out of place in the dreamy career I'd worked so hard for, and unable to connect with these chic women I'd idolized. I could barely make small talk with them! It probably didn't help that I was always strung out on Adderall, an amphetamine pill prescribed for the treatment of attention deficit disorder. (How *much* Adderall was I always strung out on, you ask? *Lots* of Adderall. Enough Adderall to furnish four hundred Damien Hirst *Pharmacy* installations! Enough Adderall to suppress all the appetites of all the starving children in all the world! Enough—well, you get the idea.)

I set down my empty glass and approached "the gang" with the same vague dread I always felt. A few women nodded hello.

"How are things at *Good Housekeeping*?" I asked an editor with a Hitchcock-blond bob.

"*Cosmo*," she corrected politely.

"Champagne?" It was the same waiter.

"No thanks," *Cosmo* Editor said.

"Sure!" As I helped myself, a woman standing with her back to me turned around. It was the person I'd dreaded seeing all night: the Vice President of Marketing for this (major—*major*) beauty brand. Oh, no.

Now my bosses at *Lucky* had essentially sent me here tonight to kiss up to this powerful, advertising-budget-controlling woman—the Vice President of Marketing, who not only detested me, but had recently seen me on drugs and in my underwear. It all went down on a weekend press trip to the Mayflower Spa in Connecticut, one of the most luxurious retreats on the East Coast. Other beauty editors and I were there for two nights as a guest of Vice President of Marketing and the beauty brand. The first night, there was a fancy dinner. I ate nothing. Then I wobbled back to my deluxe cottage, stripped off my clothes, popped a Xannie bar, boosted it with a strawberry-flavored clonazepam wafer I'd found stuck to a tobacco flake–covered Scooby-Doo fruit snack at the bottom of my grimy Balenciaga, and blacked out on top of the antique four-poster feather-top bed.

When I woke up, sunlight was streaming through the windows in my suite. There was a lipstick-smeared drool stain on the Frette linens. And someone was . . . shouting. Wait, what? I turned my heavy head.

The Vice President of Marketing was in my room—yelling at me!

"AHHHHH!" I was nearly naked! I fumbled for the duvet.

"You missed breakfast!" The Vice President of Marketing was bugging. Behind her was a male hotel employee with a key card. "We've been calling and calling!"

"I overslept!" I cried. "Why are you in my *room*? Can you give me some fucking privacy? You can't just bust in on people!" I knew I shouldn't talk to one of *Lucky*'s biggest advertisers this way, but I was pissed. I may have been a drug addict, but I had my dignity! You know?

"Be at the spa in fifteen minutes!" the Vice President of Marketing shrieked. Then she stormed out. The hotel employee scurried after her. I sat there in my benzo-fog. Had that really happened?

The rest of the weekend was awkward, to say the goddamn least. The Vice President of Marketing glowered at me the whole time. I'd never been so happy to leave a spa.

It was the worst press trip ever! But, of course, I couldn't tell my boss that.

"How was the Mayflower?" Jean had asked first thing on Monday.

"Fantastic," I'd lied—too well, maybe. Because a month later, I was assigned *another* event with the beauty brand. And here I was—the Vice President of Marketing's guest, again—representing *Lucky* beauty at the Cirque du Soleil.

"Nice to see you." I grimaced. The Vice President of Marketing nodded stiffly, then turned away. My favorite waiter passed.

"I'll take one more," I said, taking two champagne flutes. *Glug-glug-glug.*

And then . . . *showtime!* Our group took up half of the first two rows. I was sandwiched between two other beauty editors.

Uuuuuurrrrrgghhhhhhhhhh, I thought as the house lights went down. I slid my Ray-Bans off the top of my head to cover my eyes.

You *know* what happened next. Clowns dressed like wiggers—am I allowed to say "wiggers"?—jumped out of a big box, wearing their wide pants! Or something like that.

Thirty minutes later, I was still sitting there chomping on Juicy Fruit and worrying that my self-tanner was making me smell like Ritz Crackers, when . . .

"*HIC!*"

It was the loudest hiccup I'd ever hiccupped, and I am a loud hiccupper.

"*Oof!*" a clown grunted onstage as he pushed a ball around. Otherwise, it was quiet in the theater.

"*HIC!*" I had downed that champagne *way* too fast.

"*Oof.*"

"*HIC!*"

The editor next to me shifted in her seat.

"*Oof.*"

"*HIC!*"

Finally, I could take no more.

"Excuse me," I whispered to the *Cosmo* editor. *Wow*, I was drunk.

"*HIC!*" I squished—"*HIC!*"—past the beauty editor from *Harper's Bazaar*. "*HIC!*" I squished past *Vogue*. Everyone—"*HIC!*"—got a lap dance for free, like in the N.E.R.D. song. "*HIC!*"

Finally, I was in the aisle. I turned to head up the steps and—

"AUGGGH!" I cried. *WHAM!* I hit the ground *hard*.

The audience gasped.

Oh. My. God.

"*HIC!*"

I scrambled out of the dark theater—into the VIP tent, where the waiters were prepping for intermission. I staggered up to the bar like I had a gunshot wound and ordered two glasses of champs. If there was ever a time for double fisting, it was now.

Unbelievable, right? You'll never believe what happened next.

At intermission, the VIP tent filled with people. About five minutes later, my hiccups went away. I was preparing to return to my seat for the second act when a man in a suit approached me.

"Ma'am," he said. He was speaking in a low voice. "I'm afraid I am going to have to ask you to leave."

I didn't think I'd heard him right.

"Excuse me?" I said.

"You're going to have to leave," he repeated.

"Who are you?" I said.

"I work for Cirque du Soleil." The man took my elbow. I jerked it away. "I'm going to escort you to your car."

"You're kicking me out of the *circus*?" I said.

"Yes, ma'am," he said. "I've been ordered to escort you out."

"But . . . but why?" I stammered.

He wouldn't answer.

"Ma'am—"

"I'm here with [beauty brand]!" He *had* to be mistaken. "They're corporate sponsors! They bought the entire first two rows!"

"Please, ma'am." The guy looked embarrassed. "I have to escort you out."

"Is this because I tripped?" I said. I was so confused. "I couldn't see the stairs!"

"Ma'am." He had me by the elbow again! So I jerked it away again. "Your car is out front."

"How do *you* know that?" I said. How did *he* know that? He took me by both elbows and led me through the crowd. People were staring. "Who told you to make me leave?" I looked around wildly. That's when I caught the Vice President of Marketing's eye: she was glaring at me. *Aha.*

Finally, we reached the door. "Will you get off me?" I wriggled out of the guy's grasp. I clomped out of the Grand Chapiteau. It was pouring rain. Sure enough, there it was: the same car the beauty brand had sent to pick me up at Condé Nast earlier that evening. My name was still in the window and everything. (How very *thoughtful* of the Vice President of Marketing to call it for me.) I ran twenty yards in heels on a muddy gravel path through the downpour. What did I care if I fell again?

"Where to?" my driver said as I slipped into the backseat.

"East Sixth Street," I said. "Between Avenues B and C."

We pulled away, and I took another Adderall to sober up. I looked out the window at the rain. The pill was caught in my throat; I kept swallowing and swallowing, but I couldn't get it down.

At my door, I took off my heels to climb the five flights of stairs to the apartment I shared with Ol' "Catfish" Nev. I unlocked the door, crept through the living room full of Nev's beautiful midcentury modern furniture, and went into my bedroom. My own decor was "midcentury meth lab," let's put it that way. The walls were papered practically to the ceiling with fashion magazine tear sheets—"collaging" was my favorite thing to do when I was geeked up—and makeup (so, *so* much makeup) was everywhere. The ceramic box on my desk was full of glass stems, Q-tips, my glassine dope baggie collection; my bed was covered in Sharpies and nude Clarins lip liners and wafts of blond clip-in hair, plus books—Norman Mailer's Marilyn Monroe biography and *Ooga-Booga* by Frederick Seidel—and feather coats and Tsubi jeans. I hardly ever slept there. When I did, I just pushed everything over.

Tonight I thought I'd rest. I lit a candle for ambience, then I took stuff from the mattress and threw it to the floor until I found them: two pill bottles, tucked under a pillow. My Xanax, and my Ambien.

I took one of each. Then I went to the window to light a Parliament. The rain had stopped, and Alphabet City looked pretty, shiny and wet. I tried to feel at peace, but it was impossible. I kept flashing back to the Cirque du Soleil tent—the falling down, the beauty editors turning to look at me, the angry and pointed stare of the Vice President of Marketing, the grip of the man pushing me through the crowd to the car. What was I going to tell Jean? What were other beauty editors going to tell Jean? She knew them all.

Suddenly, I needed to lie down very badly.

I stubbed out my cigarette into a seashell, closed the window, and got in bed. I rubbed some Pure Fiji coconut lotion onto my stomach, closed my smoky eyes, and waited for the curtain to fall. I hated this part. I tried to focus on my breath, just like I'd learned in rehab: *inhale, exhale.*

But I couldn't quiet my mind. Goddammit, Cat. What was wrong with me, anyway? I had more issues than *Vogue*. And things weren't getting better as I grew older. They just kept getting worse.

Inhale, exhale.

Fuck this. I sat up and took half a Roxicet I had on the bedside table.

Then I closed my eyes again. Time for some visualization exercises.

I imagined a white tiger leading me through a black jungle to a black river that would carry me away from my problems—away from the Grand Chapiteau, away from the Vice President of Marketing, away from the beauty editor gang. The black river carried me through the black jungle to the end of the island, then it dumped me out into a vast black ocean. But there were no sharks under the surface; it was just me. I was floating on my back and looking up at the black sky.

Inhale, exhale.

When the heaviness finally came it felt so nice—like the lead X-ray smock they drape over you at the dentist. I forgot all about the Red Flower candle burning on the dresser. Black waves were crashing on my bed. I slipped beneath the turbulent surface of the water. It felt so good that I wanted to sink forever. *Mmm.* My eyes rolled back, my body relaxed, and I passed out to the Britney Spears *Blackout* album always looping in my head.

Chapter One

AS FAR BACK AS I CAN REMEMBER, I always wanted to be a beauty editor. To me, being a beauty editor was better than being president of the United States! Yes, I lifted these lines directly from the opening of the movie *Goodfellas* and replaced "gangster" with "beauty editor." But they work here, in my story, too.

In front of me are two *very* rare back issues of *Beauty Queen Magazine*, the hottest title of the nineties. Full of brassy Magic Marker blondes with ballpoint pen–red lips and crudely drawn noses that look like dicks, the mag featured "the most beautiful ladies age 10–20" in the latest fashions: wedding dresses, bikinis, and what appears to be . . . snorkeling gear. As for beauty, the "Feb–June 1991" issue's cover girl, Lindsay Liner, is "[a]dvertising New Michanne Make-Up"—and we know this because there's an arrow drawn from the credit, pointing directly at Ms. Liner's face. Alternately, the "July–Sept 1991" cover model is sans fard: "Sally Smothers, an all-natrural [*sic*] girl without make-up!" the cover line reads. "Does she look right?"

"But Cat, who *published* this dope magazine?" all you print aficionados must be wondering. "Hearst? Hachette? Meredith Corp.?" No, no, and (definitely) no. *I* published *Beauty Queen Magazine*. I launched it in 1990, at seven years old. Young Caitlin Marnell was also editor in chief, art director . . . everything! If you were a blood relative, you subscribed to my magazine whether you fucking liked it or no: that was my readership. Which explains why there are still so many back issues floating around a quarter of a century later.

I hadn't seen a copy of *Beauty Queen Magazine* for fifteen years when I discovered the two issues in 2010 in one of my grandmother Mimi's keepsake drawers. I was gobsmacked as I paged through them. Had I really been tuned in to like things like advertiser relationships and beauty credits and "makeunder" stories and cover lines when I was in third grade? The evidence was right there in my hands. I'd been "playing" beauty editor almost twenty years before I actually became one.

Crazy, right?! But then again, I guess that's just how it is when you're hardwired to do something—to *be* something. And I'm sure of it: I was *born* hardwired to be a beauty editor. The thing is, I was also *born* hardwired for addiction—I believe so, anyway—and this has caused some . . . problems.

But I'm getting way ahead of myself. Let's turn back time, shall we?

Warning! If you are grossed out by "white girl privilege" (who isn't?), you might want to bail now. I am from the same town as disgraced former E! network personality Giuliana Rancic—Bethesda, Maryland, a suburb of Washington, DC, so white that you could practically snort it like a line—and there's nothing I can do about that. Believe me, I have tried to cut this chapter out twice! My editor keeps *making* me put it back in. Also, I get very bored talking about my childhood, which means *you* might get very bored reading about it. Let's just get it over with.

I was born on September 10, 1982, in the District of Columbia under a crack-rock white moon (Marion "bitch set me up" Barry *was* mayor, after all). I've got a cassette tape recording of my birth and everything. A sample:

"It's a girl!" the doctor announces.

"A *girl*?" my mother wails. "I didn't want a girl!" Aw.

When I was a kid, I had it all and then some. I grew up in a swanky neighborhood that was about "twenty minutes from the White House," as my parents always said. The houses on my street, Kachina Lane, were so far apart that no one ever had any trick-or-treaters on Halloween. Our next-door neighbor was a Pulitzer Prize–winning journalist who'd uncovered a CIA plot to assassinate Fidel Castro. He was Mormon and had about a zillion blond grandchildren and a huge, kooky storybook-looking Tudor house with a "bee problem" in the walls. This meant there was a crack over the living room sofa that oozed honey, and you could swipe the trickle and then pop your finger into your mouth. *Mmm.*

On the other side of our property was the white-clapboard Hermon Presbyterian Church. I played hide-and-seek in the pretty little cemetery with my chocolate lab, Benny the Bear. Then there were some woods, and then—two minutes down the road—there was a cream-colored mansion at 8313 Permission Tree Road. When I was about thirteen, someone put up iron gates with a cursive *T* on them. Then the boxer Mike Tyson moved in! He'd just gotten out of jail for rape. My sister and brother—Emily and Phil—and I would wave at his white limo. Sometimes we saw him grocery shopping at the Giant Foods in Potomac Village.

What did the Pulitzer Prize winner, Mike Tyson, and the Marnell family have in common? Our properties had backyards adjacent to the famous Congressional Country Club golf course.

"FORE!" we'd scream, right as a senator/golfer type was trying to focus on a crucial putt. Our backyard trampoline was practically on top of one of the holes.

When tournaments like the US Open came through, my sister and I sold soda cans and water bottles through the fence for a dollar a pop. We broke into the course in the summer to run around in the sprinklers; I was also always uprooting the strange mini–Capitol Building domes that were all over the place and smuggling them back to my yard. In the winter, we'd go sledding in Congressional, which wasn't that great. You know how golf courses are! They aren't made for children or *real* fun. You'd slide down a not-so-steep man-made incline and then—*whoop*—drop another foot into a sand trap. So that was as good as the sledding got.

Our front yard was sprawling and *green-green-green*, just like the golf course. Strangers used to picnic out there; my parents let them. We had a tennis court, and a Waldorf School–looking playground that was carved out of trees that had fallen during thunderstorms. We used the dogwood trees as soccer goals, and there were long swings hanging down from the branches of our tulip poplars. Bean pods and little pieces of fairylike fluff were always flittering down from the mimosa trees; we had a bunch of magnolia trees, too, and they had dark leaves and ultrafragrant white flowers. I used to climb them and spy on all the birds' nests. The azalea bushes bloomed sunset colors every spring: pink, orange, orangey-red, and lavender. And there were camellia bushes, too.

Seriously, it was insane. One time a woman even knocked on our front door and said that she was sorry if she seemed crazy, but ever since she was a little girl she'd dreamt of getting married at 7800 Kachina Lane—and now she was engaged! She showed us her diamond ring and everything. My parents wound up letting her have the wedding in the backyard, by the swimming pool and the rose garden. We all got to go! I hit the dance floor in a honeysuckle crown.

My brother, sister, and I were beyond lucky to live in this . . . Shangri-la for ten years. My father—not so much. Five acres is a lot to keep up with. And my dad insisted on doing the lawns himself, like he was a farmer instead of a psychiatrist. There was this cranky old red tractor that came with the property, and when we were small we always had to get on there with him—I guess to share in his misery. I mean, I can't remember *volunteering* to get on this tractor. It just jostled you *violently* in the seat. It was always spitting fire balls at my dad and breaking down. He cursed at it a lot. My grandmother wanted to buy us a llama to *eat* the lawn, but my dad said no. He thought Mimi was a birdbrain.

Then there was the house itself! God, it was so cool and good-looking—supercontemporary. Like . . . you know how Brad Pitt sort of thinks he's an architect? Brad Pitt would have *loved* this house. Mimi and my parents bought it from a movie producer in 1987, a few months before my fifth birthday. The story was that the legendary Frank Lloyd Wright designed it originally, but he wound up clashing with the producer's wife and abandoned the project to one of his students, who finished it. God knows if any of that's true. Either way, the place was sick. It was the *skinniest* house you've ever seen. From the front, it looked like a military bunker—long and one-story, with kooky rows of tiny square windows. From above, it looked like a . . . a *pinwheel*, okay? Like, there was a wand—that was the bedrooms and the den and the hall—and the roof was flat and covered in gravel. You could climb a Japanese maple tree to get up there, and then walk around and bang on the skylights and scare your nanny. And the head of the pinwheel was made up of the kitchen, the dining room, and the living room, which were wrapped around a huge stone chimney in the middle. You could run through all three spaces on a loop.

The front doors were oversize and three inches thick—dark oak, engraved. The wind always blasted them open, and my dad would lose it over the heat or AC that leaked out. The place cost a fortune in utilities every month. This was also because there were hardly any real walls. Everything was glass! When I was five, a *massive* tree fell through the glass living room during a summer storm. It was very Robert Frost:

"Such heaps of broken glass to sweep away / You'd think the inner dome of heaven had fallen." Do you know that poem? "Birches." My dad quoted it all the time. Another day a little girl was over, running in and out of the house, playing tag with her brother and Phil. Then, *SMASH!* She ran right through one of the glass walls, and it shattered all over her. The blood gushed out of her in sheets! I saw the whole thing. It looked like the movie *Carrie*; she screamed and screamed. An ambulance came to take her to the hospital.

Oh, it was *such* a special house. Surely I have not done it justice with my descriptions. I wish you could look it up on StreetEasy or somewhere, but you can't. When I was fifteen, my parents sold the house to a synagogue. I think they kept the stone chimney, but that's it. The magnificent front yard is now a very ugly parking lot. I mean, no offense to Adat Shalom or anything—but it is *exceptionally* unsightly. Then again, I guess anything would look awful compared to the beautiful memories in my mind.

I will now give you what you bought this book for: juicy gossip about my fascinating parents! I'll get right to it.

My mom had a scale and it said: *THINNER*—like the Stephen King movie. *Everything* about my mother was skinny—even her nickname for me: "Bones."

"Do these come in seven *narrow*?" she'd ask at the weird Italian shoe store at the Tysons II mall.

My dad gave my mom Shalimar perfume for Christmas, but she refused to wear it. She returned the furs and jewelry he bought her, too. All she wanted was furniture, furniture, furniture. It was all bizarre and ultramodern—to match the insane house. Her side tables looked like bicycle pumps and her living room chairs seemed like they were imported from Guantánamo Bay. Her "pieces" were always shattering or poking you with a sharp corner if you bumped into them. There were no throw pillows or curtains or dust ruffles or anything feminine.

Everything was angular. The only thing in the whole house with any curves was the baby grand piano.

My parents' master suite had a glass wall overlooking the cherry blossom grove and the forsythia bushes in the backyard, and a white-and-gold tub with Jacuzzi jets that never worked. That's where the nannies would comb out my lice while I cried in my bathing suit. My mom smoked exactly two cigarettes every morning back there, but she said she didn't. She kept the gold soft packs of Benson & Hedges in her underwear drawer alongside her flesh-toned bras and bikini panties. They matched her peachy-nude manicures that elongated her fingers, her neutral lipstick, her beige bob, and her tanned, toned arms.

My mother had diabetes, so we always had a live-in nanny.

"My blood sugar is low," my mom would say when my sister and I had one of our knock-down fights. Then she'd go back down the very long, skinny hall to her bedroom and shut the door.

When I was in nursery school, the nannies were named things like Anka, Margaret, and Anna. Then the Berlin Wall came down, and I guess all the Eastern European girls went home. After that, our nannies were from Iowa: Ruth, Debbie, Karen, and Amy. They got us ready for school while my mom sat with her coffee and her insulin, watching Katie Couric and her gleamy crisscrossed legs on the *Today* show. My mom never flinched when she pricked her finger. Her diabetes drawer was full of syringes. One time I injected water into my belly. The needle didn't hurt at all.

Mimi raised my mom in Virginia Beach. My mom's father loved golf so much that the Princess Anne Country Club flew their flag at half-mast when he died. My mom went to Norfolk Academy, then she boarded at St. Catherine's in Richmond. In college, she became anorexic. She kept a package of raw hot dogs chilled on her dorm room windowsill, and she ate one per day. She'd stopped coming out of her room, but it took the college a while to realize it. Then my mom was in the hospital for a long time. I got all this dirt from Mimi. My mother didn't talk about it.

And now she was a psychotherapist with a private practice on Forty-Second Street NW and a part-time job at the Psychiatric Institute of Washington (PIW) on Wisconsin Avenue. She wasn't home much. Sometimes she took me to Saks Fifth Avenue in Chevy Chase to see a handbag she was "thinking about."

"Hi, Stacey," the saleslady always said.

"This is my friend Jennifer," my mom would tell me.

"Hi, sweetie," Saleslady Jennifer would coo. "I've heard so much about you."

My mom shopped and shopped and shopped. She would stay at the malls until they closed. Sometimes kids got to go. One night we came home at eight thirty—a half hour past family dinner time. We'd picked up takeout from California Pizza Kitchen. My brother and I carried the bags of food from the car into the dark dining room. Phil hit the switch for the chandelier, and that's when we saw it: all six chairs were in pieces all over the floor. The mahogany table was splintered. It looked like a tornado had come in! My mother had just bought them, too.

"*Mom!*" I yowled.

She came up behind me.

"Kids," she said. Her expression was as smooth as a stone in our Japanese rock garden. "Go to your rooms."

On my way downstairs, I saw that the potted tree in the foyer had been knocked over. A picture was off the wall. Someone—I knew who—had smashed absolutely *everything*. No one ever explained why.

My dad was the chief of psychiatry at a big hospital and oversaw the adolescent unit at another. He made *Washingtonian* magazine's "Best Doctors" issue every year, but he told me it wasn't a real award.

"If you are homicidal or suicidal, please hang up and call 9-1-1," my dad's secretary chirped on his voice mail. "Otherwise, leave a message."

My dad's patients were always throwing urine on him, and things like that. Scratching him up or biting him, and he'd have to take AIDS tests. Hanging themselves. It was a lot to deal with. He left the house at 6:45 a.m. sharp and came home hungry at 7:30 p.m., Monday through Friday. After dinner, he'd be in his office for another hour. On Saturdays, he did a half day of rounds at the hospital. Sunday was his day off. But that's when he'd get on the tractor.

My dad loved history and Shakespeare and was so smart that you could watch *Jeopardy!* with him and he knew the right question for every statement. He had been a chemistry major at Duke, and then he went to medical school at Tulane. He did his residency at a hospital in London. His home office was full of books from his school days: Freud's *The Interpretation of Dreams*, Jung's *Memories, Dreams, Reflections*. But he sure never interpreted any of *my* dreams. He never seemed to think about that kind of psychiatry anymore. He was too busy, I guess. When he was home, he was "on call." The phone would ring at three o'clock in the morning and then he wouldn't be able to get back to sleep. He was always taking psych ward admissions over the phone, telling nurses to prescribe Thorazine or lithium or Geodon to all of the people who'd beat up their mothers because God was talking through the television.

My dad was such a talented physician that he could prescribe antipsychotics with his eyes closed! I'd wake him up from his Sunday afternoon nap in the backyard hammock. A book would be splayed open on his chest—*The Magic Mountain* or *Tess of the d'Urbervilles* or something. Maybe a Harold Bloom.

"Dad." He'd open his eyes. "Phone." He'd take the cordless, then he'd close his eyes again. He'd listen for a second. Then . . .

"Risperdal," he'd mumble. "Two milligrams." And he'd fall right back to sleep after he hung up.

Other weekends, my dad took me on special outings: to state fairs, to far-flung dollhouse furniture stores. Sometimes we'd have to stop at one of his psych wards first so my dad could do his rounds. The nurses would tell me how much they admired my dad. Then they'd give me a pineapple juice or something. I'd take it into the rec area and watch *Married . . . with Children* with the patients in their paper jumpsuits.

Every night after my dad finished his phone calls, he'd whistle for Benny the Bear. Sometimes I'd go out with them.

"So was I once myself a swinger of birches," my dad always said—Robert Frost again—as we wheeled trash cans down our crazy-long driveway to Kachina Lane. Under the boring Bethesda stars.

And so I dream of going back to be, I'd think.

"Never be a doctor," my father told me another time. As if he had to worry.

Why should you never marry a tennis player? Because to tennis players, love means nothing! *Mwa-ha-ha.* The only thing my parents did together, ever—as far as I could tell—was play tennis. I played secretary inside. As I said, the phone never stopped ringing. We had an unlisted number, though some of my parents' patients had access to the hotline.

"Marnell residence," I'd answer on a Sunday afternoon when my parents were out in the front yard, playing tennis.

Pant. Pant. Pant.

"*He-wrowghh*," a lady would finally . . . garble. It was a bipolar patient my mom and dad shared. Lynn had a mouthful of rotten teeth and they couldn't make her go to the dentist. She called the house all of the time. "*Ish Stashey shere?*"

"She's not available right now," I'd say politely. Mom was allowed to not take calls during tennis. My dad always had to.

Ten minutes later . . .

"Marnell residence."

"Answering service," the bored-sounding lady would say. "Is Dr. Marnell there?" I was already out the door in bare feet with the cordless. It would take a few minutes to get to the court. My parents would be playing with another couple—doubles.

"GODDAMMIT, STACE," my dad would be roaring. He'd be

wearing white Izod shorts and those wraparound sports glasses. "GO TO THE NET!"

"I'm *trying*!" my mom would wail. Mom would be in an Asics tennis dress and, underneath, those horrible underpants that you tuck balls into. *Tennis panties*, they're called. *Ugh*. I can still see her . . . *reaching* into her skirt and pulling out a ball. This disturbing visual has been *imprinted* irrevocably on my mind.

"Dad," I'd interrupt.

He'd set down his Wilson racket and wipe the sweat off his palms and take the phone.

"This is Dr. Marnell." The other couple would stand there. Then: "Give him [such and such] milligrams of Zyprexa every four hours." And I'd take the phone back.

"Five–love," someone would say. Then the *thwack* of the tennis ball. *Thwack. Thwack. Thwack.*

My mom would be weepy for approximately four hours on the days my dad shouted at her on the court. Then she'd turn to ice.

Ah. "Dysfunctional" families. If you are from one as well, I don't have to explain. If you aren't, well—think of the most toxic relationship you've ever been in. You know, the one where you and your partner were both your worst selves: yelling, smashing things, not speaking for days, making nasty comments, locking yourselves in bathrooms. *Then* imagine it was with your father, mother, older sister, and little brother instead of your ex. Then imagine that you couldn't leave that relationship for fifteen years! That was my childhood. Sure, it could have been worse—but, to quote Keith Richards on the end of his relationship with Anita Pallenberg: "It could have been better, baby."

We all played a part, but I didn't understand all that, so I blamed everything on my dad. He was such a good person, but his temper was B-A-N-A-N-A-S. You never knew when things were gonna pop off—though "at the dining room table" was a pretty good guess. Family dinner was at eight o'clock sharp, in the dining room, seven nights per week. No exceptions. More often than not, it ended disastrously.

"IF YOU THROW UP, YOU HAVE TO EAT IT," my dad roared one night while I cried and choked down the bite of fish on my plate. I was seven and a picky, dramatic eater. "GODDAMMIT!"

"AUUUUGH!" I moaned, gagging.

"EAT IT!" my dad screamed.

"No one can make you feel anything you don't want to feel," my mother told me once, a complete delusion.

He never got physical, but it sure got scary. To this day, I completely shut down when someone is yelling.

"Girls!" my mom screamed another night. We had just sat down to our filet mignon and broccoli when my dad leapt from his chair. "CALL THE POLICE!" My sister and I left our baby brother at the table. We ran all the way through the long house to my parents' suite and locked the door. My sister dialed 9-1-1.

"My mom just told us to call you!" Emily told the operator. "We're at 7800 Kachina Lane!"

We hung up with the cops and ran back through the house to see what was happening. My dad was shouting up a storm. The front door was wide open, and he didn't even care. That's when I knew it was really serious.

"THIS IS IT!" he was yelling. "I'M OUT. GODDAMMIT. I'M OUT." He whistled for the dog.

"He's taking Ben!" I cried.

"*Shh*," Emily said. My dad got in his car and drove away.

My mom would hardly let the cops in when they rang the doorbell.

"It was a misunderstanding," she said. "Everything's fine." The next night my dad was back for family dinner, so I guess it was.

"Don't say anything bad about your father," my mom would sigh when I came to her—which wasn't too often. She'd be sitting in her bedroom, watching *L.A. Law*. "Can you rub my arm?" Tennis elbow.

I had two places to escape to when things were bad at my house. The first was my Mimi's. She lived just a stone's throw from our glass house, in the guest cottage. I went over there whenever I needed to. My grandmother was my favorite person in the whole world. She was from a very old Virginia family, and her own cousin, a man named Beverly, was in love with her. She had a southern accent and called me "sugah" and "dah-lin.'"

Her living room was full of orchids and tiny sterling silver spoons and teensy demitasse cups and saucers, and peacock feathers and mother-of-pearl binoculars and *juno volupta* seashells. You could pick up her great-granddaddy's fox-hunting horn and *HONK!* into it if you so desired. And all of this was just scattered about. Her shiny black baby grand Steinway piano was in the corner. She'd play it and trill in her old-timey singing voice.

"Fox went out on a chilly night . . ."

"Prayed for the moon to give him light . . . " I'd chime in.

Mimi kept costume jewelry under her bed in plastic ice trays. All the dangly earrings were clip-on, so you could wear them even if you were only five. The stuff in her closet was even better: fake braids, turbans, glamorous hand-carved walking sticks, silk kimonos, and real minks with googly glass eyes to throw over your shoulder when you played Cruella Marnell.

At sunset, Mimi would drive me into Potomac to watch the horses at Avenel Farm. Sometimes we'd feed them carrot sticks. Then it would be time for me to go home. Mimi never ate dinner with us in the glass dining room. My dad didn't like it.

The *other* place I could always escape to was my bedroom. It was in the basement—very far from my parents' room, and from my brother's and sister's. The nanny's bedroom was next to mine, so I wasn't totally alone. Still, I'd been afraid to sleep down there when we first moved to Kachina—I was four—but there wasn't room for me upstairs with everyone else.

"You're the bravest," my mom had told me. True dat.

The lower level was huge—and a mess. Biblical floods! Pipes in the laundry room would burst in the middle of the night and water would *gush* from the ceiling; my dad would pull me out of bed at one in the morning and make me hold a bucket. Blame Frank Lloyd Wright's apprentice, I guess. The hallway stank of mold and the carpet was always wet and squishy; your socks would get soaked through. I was always *leaping* over puddles to get to my bedroom. And there were so many *bugs* downstairs: little ones with pinchers—my sister and I called them tweedlebugs—and daddy longlegs that would creep right up on your comforter while you were snuggled under the covers with a chapter book. Eventually I got bunk beds—just so I could sleep up high.

But you know what's funny? The older I got, the more I liked living in that gnarly basement. It was like my own world! No one even monitored me. My dad would come say good night and switch off my light, but ten minutes later I'd just turn it on again and read *Sweet Valley High* as long as I wanted. When I was in the fifth grade, I watched a Saturday night *Saved by the Bell* marathon on TBS in the playroom until dawn—my first all-nighter. Then slept until one in the afternoon on a Sunday, and no one even noticed! It was the craziest thing I'd ever done. I had lice for months and didn't tell my mom; I picked the bugs off my head in the basement. Then I'd pick all the fleas off Benny the Bear (I don't know where he got them, but there were *so* many). I didn't even have to brush my teeth! Or take baths or comb my hair. I snuck junk food downstairs and ate in bed; I kept my room like a swamp, but no one cared. No one ever bothered me. Seriously, I could get away with murder down there! And no one ever knew.

Chapter Two

MIDDLE SCHOOL TIME! UGH, THE WORST. Okay, so I turned twelve in September 1994. Being a teenybopper tween in this era was *pret-ty* dark. The cutest rock star, Kurt Cobain, shot himself in the head, and my friends and I were wildly interested in this. How could we not be? Murdering your life had officially gone pop! Courtney Love was reading Kurt's suicide note over a loudspeaker on MTV. "I HATE MYSELF AND I WANT TO DIE" posters were stocked alongside the usual Salt-N-Pepa and Madonna at Sam Goody at the mall. I bought one! Kurt was wearing green Converse One Star sneakers in the suicide photos, so *I* bought green Converse One Stars—and so did my friend Lauren. And then so did my friend Samara! That sort of thing. Kurt was dead, yes, but he was still dreamy: we all agreed on this. His blue eyes were just *so* pretty. And his chin-length hair on *Nirvana: Unplugged*? Omigod.

Zack and Kelly came down from my walls in the Kachina basement (Mark-Paul Gosselaar was starting to look all 'roided out, anyway—it was *The College Years*) and Kurt and Courtney went up. Not that I was home much. My squad and I convened nearly every day after school in my new best friend Shabd's hot-pink bedroom, so painted after the feathers on the cover of the *Garbage* album she always had on repeat. We'd flip through *Sassy* and *YM* magazines and watch *120 Minutes* and eat junk food from 7-Eleven. I was a big fan of Utz Salt'n Vinegar potato chips and drastically less so of doing my homework. (Is this what ADHD is? I'll never know!)

All we talked about were rock stars, rock stars, rock stars: it was, after all, what *Rolling Stone* has since called "Mainstream Alternative's Greatest Year." Lauren loved Dave Grohl and Beck; Shabd squealed about Michael Stipe, Billy Corgan, and Shannon Hoon. Samara got hot for Anthony Kiedis and Eddie Vedder; Sarah was into Perry Farrell and Scott Weiland. And me? I was all Courtney Love, all of the time. I loved her platinum hair; I loved her baby-doll clothes; I loved her music. I bought every magazine she was in—from *Sassy* (I had the Kurt and Courtney cover on my wall) to *Spin* to *Rolling Stone*. I read the profiles until I'd memorized them. She stimulated my brain. Every Courtney interview taught me thirty new things. She was so gossipy and funny— glamorous *and* a feminist! (I was getting into feminism, too—riot grrl and all that.) And her mother was a weirdo psychotherapist, too.

Shabd had been raised in some sort of . . . "community," let's say. Whatever it was, her family wasn't in it anymore. Her mom had hair down to her waist and a sort of . . . New Age accent. The whole family was vegetarian, and they lived in a tiny house full of crystals and health food and . . . I don't know. Driftwood! (Maybe not driftwood.) Anyway. I was so jealous of my friend. Her parents let her do anything she wanted to do—and Shabd wanted to do *crazy* things, like bleach her hair platinum and then dye Manic Panic stripes into it like a rainbow. I wasn't even allowed to wear black eyeliner. I did anyway, but still.

Shabd's dad had a long, brown beard and barely spoke. He took us to concerts! We were obsessed; we scoured the *City Paper* every week. The best shows were at a tiny DC club called the Black Cat. Shabd's dad would stand in the back while we maneuvered to the stage: "Excuse me, excuse me, excuse me, please." Mad squeaky. Shabd was literally four-eight and I was five feet, so people were nice. Well, until the mosh pit started—but we didn't mind a little violence. The rougher things got, the more likely it was that bouncers would lift us up and out of there and plunk us down on the stage by the speakers and the amps. That's how I saw L7—so close up that I thought a guitar neck might bash me in the face!

God, I just loved the feeling of being in that club! And Shabd and I knew a secret about the Black Cat: the bands had to exit through the front to get outside to their tour buses. So if you waited around in the club after the show—while the bartenders counted the money and the cleaning crews swept the floors—you could meet the rock stars! Normal adult fans didn't get to just linger about, but tweens are very charming, you know. Work it while you can, kids.

We met so many people: Seven Year Bitch, Tripping Daisy, Collective Soul, the Presidents of the United States of America. Radiohead! Thom (we called him "Thom-with-an-H") was cute, but it was the guitarist Jonny Greenwood we were really hot for. He was skinny and pale, with brown hair hanging in his eyes, *long* fingers, and terrible posture. We sat onstage and screamed every time he looked at us, which wasn't too often (I think he was afraid). Then, after the show . . .

"WE LOVE YOU!" we screamed in unison, as we generally did. "CAN YOU SIGN OUR POSTERS? *BWAHHHH!*" They were very sweet. Shabd and I were still crying when we left the Black Cat.

If you're young, you *must* go to as many shows as you can! You'll never regret it. My friends and I saw the Lords of Acid ("Crablouse"), R.E.M. on their *Monster* tour, Smashing Pumpkins, Silverchair, the Cranberries on the Mall in DC. We cut school for that one and it turned into a riot—no, seriously! Shabd and I got *jostled* around until a nice cop pulled us out and drove us back to Bethesda in his squad car. We held hands and giggled in the backseat.

But my biggest rock-star day was at the HFStival, when I was thirteen. Anyone who was anyone in 1995 was playing this show. My friends and I squished to the front as usual—but this was RFK Stadium, not a club. The guys thrashing around by the stage were *mental*; we were holding on to the guardrail for our lives. Screaming for each other. Garbage was onstage; it was ninety trillion degrees, and I hadn't been drinking water or anything, duh, because I was stuck in front of this stupid mosh pit. The bar was pressing so hard into my stomach that I finally blacked out.

Bouncers snatched me up and carried me to the infirmary backstage. The medics were wearing GERMS T-shirts—a nod to onetime Nirvana guitarist Pat Smear, who was playing the festival with his new band, the Foo Fighters. As a GERM checked me out, I peeked over his shoulder. Weren't those . . . the Everclear dudes? Walking right by. That's when I realized the GERMS station was set up between the dressing rooms and the main stage . . .

"You're good to go," the GERM told me.

"Can I rest here for a little while?" I said sweetly. I was wearing Shabd's minuscule X-Girl hot pants, Urban Decay nail polish, ice-blue Hard Candy glittery eyeliner, and a Bikini Kill "YEAH YEAH YEAH YEAH" T-shirt from Smash! in Georgetown. "I still don't feel good."

"Sure," the medic said. "Don't leave this cot, okay?" I nodded. And that's what I did: stayed put, and observed the celebrities from a respectful distance.

"GWENNNN!" Just kidding. The second I saw Gwen Stefani, I *levitated*—seriously—and flew directly into her arms. No Doubt had just made it big with *Tragic Kingdom*. She was wearing a crop top and approximately fifty pounds of makeup (swag). "I LOVE YOU! I LOVE YOU!"

"Aw . . . " She hugged me back. I was wailing. Weeping! Clinging to that bitch like a barnacle. "I love you, too!" Then her belly chain got caught on my necklace. Do you die?!

I accosted them all: Shirley Manson (who said she remembered me), the Presidents of the United States of America (who *also* said they remembered me), Jewel, the Lush chicks, the cuties from Goldfinger. I didn't pounce on the Gin Blossoms because . . . they were the Gin Blossoms.

Everyone was nice, but Pat Smear was the best. After I'd attacked him like a bold disturbed mistress—as they say on MediaTakeOut.com—he looped a backstage pass around my neck and took me to get a vegetarian lunch at craft services! *Then* he brought me into the Foo Fighters' dressing room to meet Dave Grohl. The three of us—you know, me and *basically half of Nirvana*—sat and talked for almost an hour! Dave told me he liked my shirt!

Then! Pat took me to the side of the stage to watch No Doubt's set. I remember looking out at the stadium crowd during "Just a Girl" and thinking . . . well, my first thought was, *Shabd is going to* hate *me*. (I was right: she didn't talk to me for two months.) My *second* thought was, *This is the happiest day of my life.*

I loved my new alterna-groupie identity, but my father was *not* feeling me. He was ultraconservative—and definitely not down with rock 'n' roll. In the seventies, he took my mom to a Rolling Stones concert at the Superdome in New Orleans, and everyone kept asking him where the bathrooms were—because he was the only guy in the place wearing a tie! And he'd never taken a drug, not even marijuana. He was from a hard-core GOP family (so I was, too): his mother had been president of Republican Women of Pennsylvania. My dad was always doing weird things like declaring the *Washington Post* to be too liberal (it's not that liberal) and canceling our subscription, or encouraging me to apply for an internship at the Heritage Foundation.

"If you're not a liberal when you're twenty, you have no heart," my dad used to quote Winston Churchill in the car after my soccer games. "If you're not a conservative at forty, you have no head." Then he'd crank up the Vivaldi.

My dad barely knew who the Cobains were, of course, but he hated my favorite couple almost as much as he hated Bill and Hillary Clinton, the other most famous couple of the nineties. He'd come down to my basement lair just to tear their pictures from the wall.

"Why does he have to be so *mean*?" I sobbed to my mother after one such . . . *desecration*. I mean, I understood his problem with Kurt—my dad treated suicidal people every day—but Courtney? She was the best! And my dad had just torn their wedding photo to bits (he'd noticed that Kurt was wearing a dress).

"Your father is just worried about you," my mom said.

Fair enough. My grades throughout this time were bad. Really, *really* bad. Unacceptable. Dismal. Gnarly. Atrocious. The pits! I'd been a straight-A student in elementary school—whatever that means to anyone—but as soon as I hit puberty . . . everything went downhill. Everyone treated this "change" like it was some huge mystery; my mom read *Reviving Ophelia* and all that. Can hormones make you stupid? Because that's what *I* think happened.

Also . . . you know what? Some people just aren't meant for the grind. I was in one of those huge public middle schools, taking seven different classes a day. I couldn't keep up. I couldn't even remember my locker combination! So I started shutting down—figuratively *and* literally, during classes. I'd been fully alert at ten years old; then I turned eleven and suddenly I couldn't keep my eyes open. I'd fall asleep right there at my desk. And not because I wasn't totally well rested; I totally was! It was so weird. And in the next class, I'd nod off again, at a different desk.

Desks, desks, desks. Six different desks a day. I felt *chained* to desks. Sometimes I'd just walk out of a class and not come back. Math class was the worst. Those fucking graphing calculators! When my teachers handed out quizzes, I didn't even try. I just handed them in blank. And homework? Forget it. I know it wasn't actually agony and torture, but it felt like agony and torture. How could any normal young person actually be expected to sit and read *Cry, the Beloved Country* after a full *day* of school? It just seemed wrong. So I just refused to do it. The brain wants what it wants! And after a long day of classes, *my* brain wanted to try on rubber dresses at Commander Salamander.

My parents brought in tutors, the whole thing. But my grades kept going down—my confidence, too. I got a D in English; I flunked ceramics. And I did not give a fuck. I just could not get down with school.

I did like one thing about junior high: it wasn't my crazy house! The situation at 7800 Kachina Lane was *no bueno*. My family's fights were *so* bad. I never brought friends over; I was too nervous. My big sister Emily was always at the center of the storm—especially after she turned fourteen.

She was always getting into it with my dad. I'd be hiding out in my room in the basement.

"GET AWAY FROM ME, ASSHOLE!" she'd be hollering, smashing things up. "OR I'LL BURN THIS WHOLE FUCKING HOUSE DOWN!"

"*GODDAMMIT, EM!*" My dad. *CRASH.* Emily's room was above mine. I never knew what was going on up there. *SMASH.* It sounded like they were throwing furniture around.

"AAAAAAUUGH!" Emily again. *CRASH. THUMP.* "FUCK YOU! FUCK YOU! I HATE THIS FUCKING FAMILY!" I did, too.

When she was fourteen and I was thirteen, Emily pulled a knife on my dad in the kitchen. My dad put my sister in a psych ward, then took her out again. I didn't ask questions—that is, until one Sunday, I came upstairs for breakfast and Emily was gone.

"Your dad's taking Emily to look at a boarding school," my mom told me. But only my father came back.

Everyone was supposed to be relieved.

"Now peace shall be restored to the family," my dad said at our family meeting (he really does talk like that).

"You left her there?" I asked.

And there was a twist: no one was allowed to contact Emily for ninety days.

"Why not?" No answer, again. Shock-a-roo.

After three months, the first letter arrived on pastel-colored stationery. It was like it was written by a very positive, peppy alien.

"I have 30 points now and I'm on Phase 2! So every 4 days I get a candy or a treat! But if you don't do your chores good enough you don't get it!"

Umm, I thought, reading this.

The letters came every single day after that. They got progressively stranger. She referred to my dad as "my precious daddy" and to me as "my favorite sis." (She never wrote my mother—or even mentioned her.)

"Today I got to phase 3. Can you believe it? That means I get to wear Birkenstocks!"

"I am working on so many things! Today it is crocheting and we are reading this excellent book called 'The Gift' by Danielle Steel!"

Eventually I understood that Emily was in a lock-up—the kind of place rebellious girls went after they'd been abducted in the night from their own bedrooms. I'd read all about them in *Seventeen* magazine.

Months passed. The letters got sadder and sadder.

"Honestly I really do feel abandoned and like I am never going to see you again!" she wrote. "I feel also that the family doesn't think about me and that my presence is not missed!" I felt so guilty: that *was* how we acted most of the time. "And it is more like a relief that I am here! I am crying writing this!"

It was awful.

My sister's fifteenth birthday came and went. We couldn't send her anything. She sent *us* gifts, though: crocheted monstrosities, made of fifteen different colors of yarn. My mother draped them over the sofas in our ultramodern house. Every time I saw one of Emily's Cross Creek blankets I felt uncomfortable.

"I got to Phase 4!" the updates continued. "Now I get later shut-downs and get to wear shoes. It's called Trust Room!"

"Write your sister," my dad told me gruffly.

"What do I say?" I protested.

Over spring break in eighth grade, we took a family vacation to La Verkin, Utah, to visit her at "boarding school." She'd been away for six months. Cross Creek Manor looked like a haunted, gloomy plantation house plunked down in the middle of the desert. It had pillars and a porch with no furniture. Then, when you went inside, there was a strange foyer with wrought-iron patio furniture: café tables and chairs. There was a fountain, and fake plants and ivy everywhere—to conceal the bars on the windows.

Jail, I thought.

Emily gave us a tour. It was one windowless, empty room after another.

"This is where we do Seminar," she said. Emily didn't tell us then that she had stripped naked in that particular room and danced to "I'm Too Sexy" while other girls—at the encouragement of a staffer—taunted her and called her a whore.

"This is where we eat," Emily said. She failed to mention the customary predinner music, the theme song from *2001: A Space Odyssey*. That was the signal to the girls to sit down and shut up. Emily also skipped the isolation or "iso" rooms in the basement where she'd spent her first three days of "school" after my dad—who'd tricked her into getting on an airplane—left her there. (You can see photos on CrossCreek.WWaspsn.org, though. While you're there, check out all of the class-action lawsuits that have been filed by former "students" against the place.)

The final stop was my sister's room. She shared it with three other girls, and there were two sets of bunk beds. Crocheted blankets were everywhere.

"There was a lice outbreak!" Emily was talking to me, but I was barely listening. I was staring at two skinny lines of hair where her thick, Elizabeth Taylor–esque eyebrows used to be. "But I didn't get it! And we get to go swimming once a week, but the pool is really dirty, Caitlin, you wouldn't like it . . ."

Emily's roommates jumped out of bed to greet us.

"*Hiii*," they purred.

"These are my roomies!" my sister said. There was something hysterical in the way she was speaking, like she was a demented cheerleader. I felt so upset. Emily was still talking. The roomies stayed gathered around her. They were like creepy, clingy monkeys. One took my sister's hand; another rested her head on Emily's shoulder. The third girl wrapped her arm around Emily's waist. And all three monkeys were *beaming* at me. Wide eyes, huge smiles. Where were their eyebrows?

When it was time for us to go, my sister looked so panicked that I almost started crying. I actually hugged her—something I hadn't done in maybe ten years. Then we left her.

My family spent the next few days crossing the desert in a rental car. I sat in the backseat next to Phil. I couldn't stop thinking about my sister. Emily was a hell-raiser and a bully, but she was also loving, maternal, and gutsy. One time she hid a kitten from my parents in the basement for a month. She was the greatest babysitter—other families loved her. When my brother was a toddler, she would lift him up and hold him on her hip. She baked cookies in the kitchen. She did all the things my mom didn't do. She taught me how to shave my legs. When Emily told my dad to go fuck himself, she was standing up for me, too. And now she couldn't do anything except pluck all of her eyebrows out.

It was nighttime when we arrived in Vegas. I'd never been there before. I pressed my head against the window and looked out at the Strip.

"What do you think, Cait?" my dad asked. But I wasn't speaking to him.

The letters resumed right when we got home.

"I'm starting the Zoloft you brought me tomorrow," Emily wrote my dad. "All the staff here thinks it's funny because I have so much."

"I am really really worried about Caitlin," a letter from my sister to my dad begins. (I have a stack of them in front of me, in case you were wondering.) "She seems so upset about things! She actually said she loved me and missed me and wanted me to come home!" It's dated September 9, 1996—the day before my fourteenth birthday.

"Upset" is right. My parents had said that Emily had to go to Utah so that peace could be restored to our family. But that's not what happened at all. My dad's stress—and therefore his temper—was worse than ever. He screamed and screamed, even though there was no one yelling back anymore (my mom, my brother, and I were *not* fighters—we just shut down). And now, with Emily gone, he screamed mostly at me.

"GODDAMMIT, CAIT!" my dad would roar when I was being "hyper"—too talkative—at dinner. He'd slam his fist on the table so hard that wineglasses would jump. Sometimes Benny the Bear would get up and leave the room. "I'M SICK OF YOUR BULLSHIT." I never talked back or anything, like my sister did—I'd just clam up.

But inside, I'd be fuming.

What . . . did I ever *do . . .* to *him?* You know?

I would lie awake at night, staring at the ceiling through the dark, thinking about this.

By then, Mimi had moved out of state, leaving the full burden of kooky 7800 Kachina Lane to my dad—and he'd decided to sell. He got a rental offer first, though, so the four of us had moved into the little guest house. My little brother slept on a cot in my parents' room. I had the other bedroom to myself, but I still felt like my family was right on top of me. I had no basement to retreat to when things got ugly. Which they still did—a lot. Any little thing would set my dad off.

One night I went to sit down for dinner and my Bikini Kill *Pussy Whipped* CD was at my place. Where did he get that? When had he even been in my room?

"You can forget about that ski trip this weekend, CATO," my dad snarled. I'd been *dying* to go on that school ski trip. I wept to my mother.

"I'm sorry," she told me. She seemed very sympathetic. "I wish there was something I could do. Your dad has his mind made up."

Then it happened again: I sat down at dinner, and my friend Cale's

Cypress Hill T-shirt was at my place. It had a pot leaf on it. Was my dad going through my closet? I was so confused.

"NO FRIENDS' HOUSES FOR A MONTH!" my dad roared.

Jesus. Couldn't he just relax?

No. It got more and more intense. I felt so trapped. My father hated how I dressed—in thrift-store slips, like Courtney and Kate Moss. I weighed eighty-five pounds; I didn't look skanky. I was trying to dress grunge! He made me start checking in with the vice principal's office every morning. It was so embarrassing, having my outfit looked over. Half the boys in the high school were wearing that "HEY HO LET'S GO" Ramones shirt. It seemed unfair.

"*I hate him*," I sobbed to my mother.

"Your dad loves you so much," she told me. But it didn't feel like love. It felt like my dad had failed to control his first daughter, and now he was obsessed with controlling me.

Think I'm exaggerating?

"NO MORE USING THE WORD 'FEMINISM' IN THIS HOUSE!" My dad stood up from the table and *screamed* this at me one night (I guess I'd been . . . talking about feminism?) His face was fucking fuchsia. He went *nuts*. "THAT WORD IS BANNED, GODDAMMIT!"

I gaped at my mother, who said nothing. Seriously?

That night I was so upset that I took my pillow and comforter into Mimi's walk-in closet, shut the door behind me, and slept on the floor. I couldn't get far enough away from my dad.

I wasn't totally blameless, don't get me wrong. My ninth-grade report cards were dismal. And now I was in high school, where it counted. This should have "motivated" me, I guess, to improve . . . but . . . I couldn't get my grades up.

What?! I couldn't!

I *tried*. I definitely tried! I am fairly certain that I tried.

I mean . . . I sat with all those stupid tutors they made me sit with. For hours! I did! I did it all! I did whatever they told me to!

"No friends' houses until your grades come up," my dad said. He'd decided Shabd—who got straight As—was a bad influence. I was destroyed, of course. My friends were my whole world. Now I wasn't even allowed to hang with them on the weekends. I went crying to my mother to help me change his mind.

"You can see your friends at soccer," my mom said. She was all blank in the eyes. I wanted to hit her. I was on a special "select" traveling team. But those girls weren't my friends. My mom knew that. Also, my dad was an assistant coach. He'd holler from the sidelines with his red yelling face. Ugh, enough!

I sat down to another "offensive" CD at my plate: *Pretty on the Inside* (featuring "Teenage Whore"). And my dad punished me *again*. No more music, in fact. My CD player was confiscated.

"Mom," I begged her. "Please. I just want to listen to *music* in my room. Do something!"

"I'll try," she sighed.

One day I came home from soccer early and walked into my bedroom. My mom was in there—snooping! She jumped a foot in the air. Then it all made sense: *she'd* been bringing things back to my father . . . and then acting all phony when I came to her. The whole situation was so nuts. I didn't even blame her. I just didn't go crying to her after that.

After my "friend privileges" were revoked, I never got them back. Every day after school, I had to come straight home . . . and sit in silence. This didn't "inspire" me to do my biology homework, though. Instead, I was starting to daydream about escaping. For once, I actually loved a novel I was reading in English class: *A Separate Peace*, which was set at a New England boarding school. (Remember how the kid bounces the tree branch just so and his more popular, athletic roommate Phineas falls off and breaks his leg? So good.) It might as well have been set at Disneyland: all teenagers, living together away from their parents. "A separate peace" indeed.

But I wasn't going anywhere. So I passed the time studying what *actually* interested me: rock stars and fashion magazines. So imagine my excitement when I opened one of my favorite magazines and saw . . . my favorite, much-maligned rock star—in couture! The stunning photographs were by Steven Meisel. Even my dad said that Courtney looked good. I was so delighted that I even wrote the magazine a thank-you note. (I was a weirdo.)

I was chilling at our new brand-new house after school one afternoon in February when the cordless rang.

"This is [so-and-so] from *Vogue* magazine," a woman said when I answered. "Is Caitlin Marnell there?" *Was* I?

Then she told me: my letter to the editor was going to appear in the magazine!

"OMIGOD!" I tried not to scream. I didn't want *Vogue* to figure out that I was only fourteen and change their minds.

The letter ran in the April issue:

> I have nothing but gratitude to express to you lovely VOGUE editors for your breathtaking piece on my eternally imperial goddess, the (no longer) infamous Courtney Love! [. . .] Thank you ever so much for exposing to the world a goddess who is charming, witty, and indeed pretty on the outside as well as to my Right wing Republican parents! [. . .] Thank you thank you, a million times thank you!
>
> **Caitlin Marnell, Bethesda, MD**

Being published (sort of) in *Vogue* was the most exciting thing that had ever, *ever* happened to me—even better than meeting all those rock stars!

When I wasn't reading magazines, I was making my own. No, not

BQM; that was kid's stuff. My *new* joint was a zine. (Teen readers, real quick: imagine if there was suddenly no Internet—forever. No e-mail, nothing. How *would* you express yourself to strangers? The answer is, you'd write your blogs and Tweets and Facebook posts on paper, and then you'd photocopy them into a homemade magazine. A paper blog! Then you'd send your paper blog out all over the world, and people would send you *their* paper blogs in return. In envelopes! Amazing, right? That is what a zine is.) Or at least it *would* be—when I finished it.

In 1997, the web was about to kill off the entire zine community, of course, but I didn't know that yet. All I knew is that I'd been blowing through my allowance mailing stamps and one-dollar bills to people who listed their zines in the *Factsheet Five*. But if I had my own, I could just trade with people—and I wanted *nothing* more.

I decided to call mine *Alterna-Teen Retard*—not the greatest title, sorry. The master copy was a stack of eight-and-a-half-by-eleven pieces of paper. I used scissors, Sharpies, glue sticks, words cut from the newspaper, construction paper, stickers, Wite-Out . . . anything and everything. Each page was stiff and heavy with cut-and-paste "layouts" covering both sides. (This way, when I eventually double-sided photo-copied them, I could then fold the papers in half and have "digest"-size zines.) Blocks of text were glued on top of the layouts: about feminism, music, rock stars, boys, my crazy family, whatever. On the cover, I'd spelled out A-L-T-E-R-N-A-T-E-E-N in mismatched cutout letters for a ransom-note effect; "Retard" was simply handwritten in cursive. Then, below that: "$1 or Trade."

I slaved over it every day in my silent bedroom: handwriting head-lines and gluing text blocks and then ungluing them, and arranging images and *re*arranging them. Getting my zine where it needed to be took two months, then three. *Alterna-Teen Retard* was *almost* ready to send to press (aka Kinko's) after four months, but it still needed tweak-ing. Then I took it to Camp Rim Rock and worked on it through the summer.

By the time I started sophomore year in September, I'd been working on *Alterna-Teen Retard* for almost seven months. The master copy was up to eighty pages, which I hid in a special Doc Martens box under my desk. While I worked, I daydreamed about X-Day: Xerox Day! I was going to make a hundred copies. Production costs would be financed by Mimi, who always gave me a hundred dollars for my birthday. I could . . . not . . . *wait*.

Later that month, I went to Mimi's for a belated fifteenth birthday celebration weekend. I came home on Sunday night with *two* hundred dollars in my pocket. I went right up to my room to stash the cash in the Doc Martens box with my master copy. But when I opened the box, my zine was gone.

No.

"*Mom!*" I raced into her room. "*Where is it?*"

"*Hmm?*" She was watching *Ally McBeal* on her chenille armchair.

"MY ZINE!"

"Your what?" my mom said without looking away from the television.

"The magazine I was making," I said shakily.

Her show went to commercial.

"Oh." She turned to me. "That."

"Please give it back!"

"There was *sexual* stuff in there." She shuddered.

"I'll take out whatever you want!" I snapped. "Just give it back!"

My mom shook her head. I could feel hysteria stirring in me.

"There was really horrible stuff about your dad—"

"I'LL TAKE OUT WHATEVER YOU WANT!" My mom looked taken aback. I was supposed to be the passive daughter. "*JUST GIVE IT BACK!*"

"Calm—"

"GIVE IT TO ME!" I wailed. "IT'S MY ONLY COPY!" I *lunged* at my mother. I wanted to beat her! But I fell on the carpet on my knees instead. "*PLEASE!*" *Screaming.* "THIS IS THE ONLY THING I CARE ABOUT! WHERE IS IT? GIVE IT BACK!"

"Caitlin . . ." my mom said.

"I'll do anything," I sobbed. I was still on my knees, pounding on the floor, trying desperately to get through to her. "Please, Mom. If you love me, you'll give it back. You don't understand. *Please. Please!*"

This went on and on. Nothing worked. I'd coaxed "obscene" CDs and things back from her before. But tonight was different. My mom had a funny expression as she watched me implode. That's how I knew it was bad.

Eventually my mom admitted that she *couldn't* give my zine back. She'd shown it to my dad, who'd destroyed it.

"I didn't know it meant that much to you," she said.

I ran out of her room, down two flights of stairs, and into the rec room in the basement of our new house.

"*AUUUUUUUGH*," I screamed into a sofa pillow.

That was it. My zine was gone. I *still* feel very teen-angsty about the whole thing, if you can't tell from this emo chapter. And so angry at my parents. Back then, it was a real watershed moment for me: I was officially done with my family. With Bethesda. With my house. With the dinner table. With it all. I was *so* fucking done. Game over. I'd lost my sister; I'd lost my "friend privileges"; I'd lost my zine. And I'd *definitely* lost any respect or affection I had for my parents. It was time for me to get lost, too.

Chapter Three

WHERE DID THE PARENTS OF THE ADHD teen send her when she was failing school? A concentration camp! Sorry, sorry; that is a *very* offensive joke. I have taken it in and out of this manuscript fifteen times. Let its presence here in the final edition be a harbinger of bad judgment to come.

Where my parents *really* sent me was . . . boarding school! Can you believe it? A *real* boarding school, too—not a "boarding school" like Cross Creek Manor. A prep school, like in *A Separate Peace*. A few weeks after the zine "incident"—the *soul murder*, let's call it—I went into my mom's bedroom with a fucking agenda.

"I need to talk to you about something important," I said.

My mom muted the television and turned to face me. She was in her chenille chair again.

"Okay . . ." she said.

I took a deep breath. My mom looked nervous.

"I was wondering," I said. "If it would be possible for me to go away to boarding school." Relief washed over my mom's face. "I think it would benefit me, my grades, and the fam—"

"I think it's a great idea," my mom said. "I'll talk to your dad." That was easy! I thought I was going to have to beg and plead. But my mom seemed all about it.

A few nights later, she called me into the dining room, where my parents were still sitting at the table with the bloody plates and steak knives from dinner.

"We've decided that you can go to boarding school," my mom said. Very serious.

"Really?!" I squealed.

"We feel that you deserve it," my dad said. "After everything you've been through with your sister." Right.

That very week, my mom and I went to a special consultant and found my new school. I flew up to Massachusetts to interview. I told the admissions woman that I wanted to turn my academic career around. I was accepted to the school.

The night before I left, my father and I took a walk under the stars just like old times. Benny the Bear limped behind us. He had a base-ball-size tumor in his snout. It was the Sunday after Thanksgiving, so it was *so* cold outside.

"Cait," my dad said, "it's time to cut the crap."

"I know," I answered. I was looking up at the moon. It was really shiny!

"It's time to make some serious changes, Cait," my dad said. "This is it."

"I understand," I replied.

"It's time to cut the crap, Cait," my dad kept repeating.

"I *know*, Dad."

At the end of our walk, he gave me a hug. *Ack.*

"You are loved," he said.

"I knooo-oowwww," I said, and deep inside I did. But by then I was in my head directing the amazing glamorous movie of my new life, and I didn't want him—or anyone else in my family, but mainly him—to have a role in it anymore.

My new home, Lawrence Academy—"LA," as students called it—was about thirty minutes outside of Boston, in a very old town call Groton, Massachusetts. It was a private school for grades nine through twelve, and there were exactly four hundred students—half boarders, half day. Everyone was really cute. I like New England guys, don't you? I mean, the sexy ones are *sexy.* The boys were named things like Austin Colby, and had red-rimmed blue eyes and holes in their sweaters. They were always cranking Phish and smoking "butts"—Groton slang for cigs—in their moms' station wagons en route to snowboarding team practice. The girls were fab, too: preppy and athletic, with long, healthy hair. (I stopped wearing my wild clothes pretty quick, let me tell you.)

Five minutes down the road was the famous Groton School, where about a zillion Roosevelts went. Lawrence was a good school, too, and very old and very beautiful. The schoolhouse, the dining hall, and the library were austere redbrick buildings with white pillars. The quad and the grounds were supergreen with old trees that turned electric red and orange and yellow in the fall. And there was piercing-blue sky everywhere you looked.

When I arrived in early December—the first day of the second trimester—the leaves were already off the trees. I rolled my suitcase over black ice to my new dorm, Pillsbury House. It was a white two-story house with black shutters. Classic New England steez. Pillsbury had seven bedrooms, two bathrooms, and one pay phone that got taken off the hook during study hall. I lived on the first floor. The window by my bed overlooked the football field and Gibbet Hill, which people said was haunted because there were public executions up there in the 1600s. Now the hill was covered in cute cows! And at the top, there was half a stone castle—it had partially burned down—with stone walls and a turret. (It was—I would discover soon enough—a very magical place to smoke weed.)

I was immediately happier, and I would stay that way for the next few years. Boarding school *was* a dreamy, no-parents-allowed teen paradise, just like I'd imagined when I read *A Separate Peace*. I ate breakfast, lunch, and dinner with teens, then went home to my house-dorm full of more teens. No parents! No yelling.

I was never homesick once that first winter. I was absolutely all good. I didn't have close friends yet, but that was okay. I loved going to Boston on Saturdays and riding the T and seeing the sunset behind the skyline. It felt so good being in a city—I was grown up! One weekend I even took my "emergencies only" Discover card into a salon on Newbury Street and bleached my hair platinum, which I so, *so* was not allowed to do. I've been blond ever since.

I stayed on campus on Sundays. My roommate, Manjari, had family nearby in Ayer, so I'd have our huge room to myself. I'd collage my walls a bit—I'd brought Marilyn Monroe and Sid Vicious photos from home—then I'd curl up in bed with candy and Doritos and Coke from the student center snack bar and reread *The Liars' Club* or Jean Stein's *Edie*. I'd eat a Hershey bar very slowly, savoring every square, and I'd pick the new peroxide scabs off my head and stare out the window at the cows. They'd be mooing on the hill, keeping me company—comforting me.

Those same cows were my friends for the next three years in Groton—or so I thought. As I was writing this chapter, I learned that my bovine friends weren't dairy cows at all! They were actually Gibbet Hill Grill's award-winning Black Angus cattle, and every August the full herd was taken to a place called Blood Farm to be "processed." I was looking at different cows every September. God, that's dark. I'm glad I didn't know better back then!

That first winter went by fast. I was never homesick once. Everything was better at boarding school. Well, except for . . . can you guess? That's right: my grades. Ugh. Grades. Oh God. *Grades*. Grades!

That first winter trimester at Lawrence I got very bad grades. Despite the small classes and roundtable seminar-style teaching (which I did really like), there were things that I just couldn't nail, especially geometry, and at the midterm of winter trimester I was placed on academic probation. I got my average up to a C-plus before finals, but it was a huge effort—with more expensive tutors. My parents were paying extra for them.

Sigh. I spent most of study hall—seven thirty to nine thirty at night—looking at my new blond hair in a mirror on my desk, anyway. Then there was half an hour of free time before dorm curfew; I'd get a Peppermint Pattie at the student center or something. After ten, it was girl time. Face masks—everyone used that Freeman Cucumber Peel-Off one—and talking about boys and all that wonderful dorm stuff. I was always bouncing in and out of people's rooms. It was like having ten sisters!

Every underclassman dorm had a token senior selected for her "role model"-ness and leadership abilities. Ellie, our proctor, had the only single in Pillsbury House. One night in spring semester, I was in there after study hall and saw Ellie swallow a pill at her desk.

"What's that?" I asked.

"Ritalin," she said. "For my ADD."

I'd heard of that: kids liked to snort it.

"It helps you study?"

"Yeah." Then: "Wanna try?" Ellie extended her open prescription bottle like a tin of Altoids.

Was Mark Wahlberg Catholic? The pill I fished out was white and round, like a little moon.

"Do I take it now?"

"If you still have homework," Ellie shrugged. I popped it.

Half an hour later, I was downstairs at my own desk when I felt my first ever stimulant kick. My heart beat a little faster. Then my brain was, like . . . *aroused*. Turned *on*. Stimulated—like Tyga in that gross song he wrote about having sex with Kylie Jenner when she turned eighteen. Just *horny* for homework. I stayed up reading *Walden* like it was a juicy Jackie Collins novel. And wasn't it fun, suddenly, to use these highlighters—to take neat little notes in the margins? Then I looked up and it was two in the morning. Geez!

I needed my own prescription, stat. And I knew just who to call.

Now—eighteen years later—my overcooked brain remembers that I ordered Ritalin from my dad and he delivered it right to my door—like a pizza! As in: I'd called my dad and told him all about Ellie and her attention deficit disorder ("I think that's what I have!" I'd said) and her medicine, how she said it had changed her life. Maybe it would help me, too! I remember *babbling* all this, as I am wont to do. And I remember that my dad didn't say much; he just listened. Then my parents arrived the following Friday for a previously scheduled visit; they stayed at the Groton Inn. On Sunday afternoon, my dad came to my dorm room to say good-bye. That's when he gave me a bottle of methylphenidate (generic for Ritalin). There were 120 ten-milligram pills, to be taken four times daily!

My parents, however, say this is completely insane. They insist that *I* came down to visit *them*; that I went to the National Institute of Health to be tested for ADHD (I do vaguely remember this); that I scored higher than I'd ever on any test in my entire life; that I then saw a DC psychiatrist, who wrote me a Ritalin prescription that we did not take to the pharmacy to fill. I returned to Lawrence with *nada*. Only weeks later, when they visited, did they bring the filled script. ("Your dad wanted time for a serious talk," my mom says.)

I vaguely remember this talk. It was right there in my freezing-cold-all-the-time dorm room in Pillsbury.

"*Blahblahblahblahblah*," my father instructed me. "*Blahblahblah*."

"Got it." I tried not to eye the narcotics on my desk. I couldn't wait for him to get out of there. "Uh-huh."

One thing's for certain. As soon as my parents drove away in their rental car, I crushed up a pill with my Discover card, rolled a slip of paper, and snorted a chunky line off my geometry textbook. It was my first time taking anything up the bracket, as the Libertines would say. *Yowza.*

After that, it was off to the races. The good news is that you will never have to read about my stupid bad grades again. The bad news is that you will now have to read the phrase "I popped a ___" approximately eighty thousand times.

If you would like some theme music, cue Britney's "Work B**ch!" on YouTube, because after I got my first bottle of Ritalin pills, that was *all* I wanted to do. The last trimester of tenth grade—that first "medicated" spring—my grades went from Ds and Cs to Bs and As: honor roll. I assure you that I did absolutely nothing different to drastically improve my GPA other than start doing huge amounts of Ritalin—up my nose *and* orally. Usually I just swallowed it. After two months, I didn't need water: I just tossed 'em back.

What can I say? Big pharma isn't *lying* to you (fine, they probably are): performance-enhancing drugs deliver, babes. In the short term, at least. I felt so ambitious! I was bright-eyed and chatty at roundtable discussions about the American Revolution; I participated eagerly in language lab. I could sit with anything for hours without getting restless. And doing homework was a blast. I even put myself in supervised study with all of the kids on academic probation, which I'd marginally avoided the semester before. Who *does* that? (Answer: speed freaks.)

And I am not making this up: I understood things that I didn't get before, like math equations. It was *wild*—like all of the letters and numbers in the alphabet-soup swamp in my head aligned themselves to spell out answers for me. Do you remember geometry proofs? I went fucking *Good Will Hunting* on that shit! I'll never forget sitting in class one day and just . . . *understanding* how the "steps" of the proof on the blackboard stacked upon one another like paragraphs in an essay—to prove a solution at the end. I began getting As on math tests. And on essays.

I never felt sleepy sitting at a desk ever again. I was always wired—hopped up. It was great. I never had an appetite. I'd already been skinny, but I got *really* skinny. My jeans were all a bit baggy, so I ordered a pair of Sergio Valente twenty-three-inch-waist jeans from the Alloy catalog (boarding school girls *live* for mail order, you know). Twenty-three inches! On my life. They had white cow skulls stitched on the back pockets.

What else? I *felt* cooler, because I was "on drugs." I never told the school I had meds or handed them to the nurse. I took my prescription with me everywhere, so I guess no one cared. Or they thought it was antibiotics or something.

"You shouldn't do that," Alistair told me when I sat down at dinner with the little orange bottle on my tray. He was a grade above me and had transferred from Cascade School in Northern California; we'd been the new kids on the same day. He was rich, druggy, and from New York City. I wanted to be just like him. "Carry your pills around for everyone to see."

But I knew what I was doing. I wanted friends—party friends. My Ritalin prescription was like a honey trap for the fast crowd: I had something everyone wanted. Soon enough, cool, druggy upperclassmen (Alistair included) started knocking on my window at Pillsbury House.

"Wanna smoke?" they'd ask.

"Sure!" I'd say. We'd walk across Powderhouse Road and puff

Marlboro reds (ugh) behind the pizza parlor Dumpster. Then the seniors would hit me up for pills on the walk back to campus. I always
gave up the goods. Back at the dorm, I'd feel pretty dope as I spritzed
myself—heavily, to cover the smoking smell—in Elizabeth Arden's
Sunflowers, a light floral.

By the end of sophomore year, I was murdering the game. Not only did
I have bomb grades, I was tight with the hottest party girls in the senior
class. I sat with them at dinner every night.

"You're our little sister," they told me all the time—you know, after
we took our walks to behind the Dumpster.

So in May, when the campus was "closed" for a long weekend
(meaning I couldn't have stayed on campus if I wanted to) and I hadn't
made arrangements to go anywhere, I didn't worry too much. I'd heard
my "big sisters" plan their hotel-party weekend, and I figured I could
tag along with them. After all, they were taking my Ritalin as much as
I was. They always wanted me around.

I split a car into Boston with the two older girls on Friday evening. I
sat up front next to the driver. The seniors were in the backseat wearing
their clubbing outfits already, smoking Camel Lights with the windows
down. When we got into the city, they asked where they could drop me
off.

"Uh," I said. "Do you guys want to grab food real quick?" They
shrugged.

My "big sisters" and I were eating salads at the Armani Café on
Newbury Street when I broke the news.

"I don't have anywhere to go," I said. "Can I hang with you guys?"

The girls made eyes at each other.

After dinner we cabbed it to the Cambridge side of the Charles
River to the Royal Sonesta hotel. They *marched* me through the lobby,
which was full of contemporary art, and into the elevator. We got out
on the eighth floor and knocked on a door.

A senior jock from school opened it. There was a hotel party going on inside. It was cigarette-smoky in there, and the music was very loud. "Déjà Vu (Uptown Baby)" was playing.

There were about ten dudes from the senior class in the room: half of the varsity hockey team (or rather—since it was May—half of the varsity baseball team).

"Cat needs a place to stay tonight," one of my big sisters said. "We don't have room at our hotel."

"Okay," the boy said.

"We're gonna stay and drink for a while," the other senior girl said.

I wandered over to check out the view. Boston Harbor was twinkly and gold and black. The varsity hockey player was sitting on a chair by the window, "puffing butts" and chilling with a bottle of Goldschläger. He was very manly looking with his beefy physique and sort-of-square head, and his eyes were bluer than a ten-milligram Adderall pill. We were both boarders, so we kind of knew each other.

"Can I bum a smoke?" I said. So cool.

"If you take another shot," he said, flirting with me. I giggled. The gold flakes glimmered in the liquor. I took a Ritalin and gave one to Varsity, who just slipped it in his pocket. Then I drank the gold.

By the time the senior girls came over to say good-bye, I was sitting on Varsity's knee like a ventriloquist's dummy.

"Cat, you're good?" one big sister asked.

"Of course," I slurred.

"We'll pick you up tomorrow to go shopping," the other said. And then: "Take good care of her, [Varsity]."

"I will," Varsity said. Then they left, and I was the only girl at the party.

"Can I have another cigarette?" I asked Varsity.

"If you take another shot."

An hour later, I got up and stumbled over to the bathroom like Keith Moon on animal tranquilizers. I peed and washed my hands— these are the details you need to know—and when I opened the bathroom door to go back into the hotel room, Varsity was standing there smiling—waiting for me. He sort of gently pushed me back inside. I went in and out of consciousness as I had sex for the first time—on a bath mat! And it wasn't rape or anything. I mean, I'm still going in and out of consciousness during sex today! I always take my sleeping pills too early.

I woke up fully clothed on Saturday morning at the edge of a bed, next to two snoring hockey players. There were three dudes on the other bed, and four conked out on the floor. Varsity was asleep in his chair by the window. I got up and sort of stepped over their hunky varsity bodies to get to the bathroom. Then I used hotel mouthwash and looked in the mirror. Fifteen is such a funny, in-between age, isn't it? It felt so weird not to be a virgin anymore.

I didn't know where I was going, but I couldn't stay there. I grabbed my stuff, took the elevator down, and hightailed it past the long wall of Andy Warhol *Flowers* in the lobby. *Pop.*

The summer between sophomore and junior years, Lilly Pharmaceuticals took my whole family to Puerto Rico! Emily was there; she was out of lockup and in a more normal boarding school called Linden Hall, which was in Amish Country. We saw the Lilly factory, where pills were made. Then we rode bareback in the rain forest. Even Mimi came along for the ride! She didn't know there wouldn't be saddles, and the horse trotted her *very* hard through that jungle (I was a tad worried about her pelvis). Later that afternoon, a pharmaceutical rep strolled with us through Old San Juan. It was really nice.

In September, I was thrilled to return to Lawrence, go onstage at the awards assembly, and collect my honor roll certificate for the previous trimester.

"Outstanding!" the assistant headmaster said, vigorously shaking my hand.

"I need more Ritalin, please!" I would ring my mom—never my

father; I knew better—from my new dorm's pay phone. "I'm out! It's an emergency! Please!"

"Caitlin," my mom would always say. "Your dad really doesn't want to be writing these prescriptions any more. You need to find a psychiatrist in Groton."

"I will, I will!" I always said. "I'm just so busy with all this schoolwork! Just one last time!" It was never the last time. "*Please* beg him for me, Mom! Please!"

"I don't think he's going to do it," my mom would always say.

"*PLEASE!*" I'd always get scared. "*I need it! My grades are going to slip again!*" My mom would sigh.

And so the FedEx packages kept arriving—month after month. Her handwriting was always on the envelopes; my dad's name was printed on the little orange bottles inside.

I *loved* my room junior year. It was a corner single in a dorm called Dr. Green, with lots of windows and trees right outside. It was great not having a roommate. I didn't have to turn the lights off and go to bed, like, ever. I took my new medicine and stayed up doing homework late in the night, hyperfocused and erasing and reprinting my math homework. Branches would bang on the glass and scare the shit out of me; there was also a stupid *owl* out there that was ridiculously loud and hooty. So I was always practically falling out of my desk chair. (Stimulants make the nerves a bit . . . *jangly*, you know. Especially at three in the morning.)

I also had a new best friend—right down the hall. Greta T. was from Hamburg. She had dirty-blond hair, light blue-gray feline eyes, huge boobs, and a tiny waist. She wore smudgy gray eye shadow and spritzed on Versace Blue Jeans perfume to cover the smell of the Camel Lights she covertly puffed all over campus like a boss.

"I'm European," she'd say with a shrug when a teacher caught a whiff of her.

What a fox! The usually cocky varsity-athlete guys just gawked at her, and she barely knew their names. She loved house music. Every night after study hall, she'd crank "Music Sounds Better with You" and "Horny" and we'd dance in her room.

She was the first real party girl I ever knew. Greta T. was also an insulin-dependent diabetic—a sinister combination if ever there was one. Talk about train wrecks! Diabetics risk going into comas every time they get loaded; still, Greta T. spent every weekend in the clubs, downing that sweet sugary booze. Hard-core. On Sunday evenings, I'd find her back in the dorm—pale as death, froggy in the face, and slumped over on her bed.

"I'm so *tired*, Cati," she'd sigh, jabbing herself in the belly with an insulin syringe. What a hot bitch. I fucking loved her!

I started going into Boston with Greta T. and the international student boys from my school: the Saudis, the South Americans. They were kind of nerdy on campus, but on the weekends—wow! I was very impressed watching them pay off the bouncers at Avalon with hundred-dollar bills. Inside, I mimicked the other girls and kicked off my heels to dance barefoot on a banquette. God, was that fun! I only climbed down to take licorice-flavored shots the boys kept pouring. (And pouring. And pouring . . .)

I was all good as we left and piled into a taxi. But then . . .

"*Blerrrrgh*." I yakked out the window. "*BLERRGGGH!*"

"Hey!" the driver yelled.

"*Cati!*" Greta shouted in her German accent. "Stop doing that!"

We finally got to the Beacon Hill building where this rich Qatari junior from our school kept an apartment. The foyer of his place was huge, with glossy white floors.

"*BLAAAARRGG*," I . . . well, not *said*, exactly, right when we walked in. All over the marble! Greta T. marched me to a room with a king-size bed. I capsized on it with my legs splayed open.

"Stay here," Greta T. said. She was *not* impressed.

I woke up to someone rubbing my inner thighs and my stomach up under my tank top. It was a chubby Brazilian junior from my school—let's call him Playboy—and he had his dick out.

"I want to be with you," he murmured. "Please . . . "

"*Noo,*" I groaned.

But he wouldn't go away. He kept touching me and rubbing me.

"Stoppp," I kept saying.

Then I went under again. Then next time I opened my eyes, Playboy was kissing me softly on the forehead like a Disney prince.

"You are too sick," Prince Charming whispered. You think? Then he zipped up.

"Thank you," I mumbled. I meant it, too. I was genuinely grateful that he walked away.

Other weekends, I went to New York City with Alistair. I felt so cool walking around Manhattan with him in his North Face fanny pack and Diesel jeans. I tried cocaine for the first time at his family's Sutton Place penthouse. Alistair loved David Bowie, and "Fame" was playing on the stereo. I went out on the balcony and looked at all the lights. It was all so . . . *stimulating*: the cities, the music, the sex, the . . . stimulants.

My dad would have yanked me out of my fancy boarding school in about two seconds if he'd known how unsupervised I was on weekends. Lawrence Academy relied on the ever-reliable medium of carbon triplicate "sign-out" forms. You'd scribble down a "friend's" name and phone number, then hunt down your faculty advisor on Friday afternoon to sign off on it. (I always nabbed my advisor in the hallway of the schoolhouse in between classes, when she was distracted.) Then, you posted the signed form on your dorm room door, and that was it! You were free to hop into the backseat of a car service sedan with your friends and head into Boston.

The clubs were fun, but the real scene was the hotel parties. "Prep" schools ostensibly prepare young people for college, but they also prepare them for, like . . . Plato's Retreat. Sex clubs! The Playboy Mansion grotto. You know—orgy scenarios. Weird stuff goes down when kids *jam* into little rooms together for days at a time. And that's what the wildest kids at my boarding school did every weekend. (I'm not going to go into details—writing about teen sex is gross—but . . . trust me.)

The Lawrence Academy party hotel was the Buckminster in Kenmore Square, practically on top of Fenway Park. Maybe it still is. It wasn't the Ritz, but the shitty concierge let the dealers up and didn't call the cops on anything. Greta T. and Alistair practically lived there when they weren't at school. It's illegal for minors to rent hotel rooms, so it's also *très* possible that the Buck accepted credit cards without asking for ID. I'm just speculating, of course.

Also legendary was the McDonald's down the block, where we all convened on Sunday mornings looking like the mutants from *The Cremaster Cycle* and nibbled on hash browns to calm our stomachs. Hangovers in high school were *hangovers*, right? I feel like puking just remembering them, actually. Sometimes, on the ride back to Groton, the town car would have to pull over so someone could hurl by the side of the road. Oh, junior year was fun.

So those were the weekends. Back at school, during the week, I had a new friend who wasn't in the party crowd at all. His name was Nicky, and he was in eleventh grade, too. He'd been at Lawrence his freshman year, so everyone knew him already except for me. Nicky was from New Hampshire, and his eyes underneath his red Boston Bruins hat were brown and twinkly. We went to the student center every afternoon when I didn't have soccer practice. The "Stud," as it was called, was built in weird layers like a tree house, so you could hole up and hide out in the nooks into the rafters. Nicky and I spent hours every day up there, crushing up my Ritalin with the end of a Maybelline Great Lash Mascara wand. We'd talk and laugh—Nicky was so funny—and snort my pills and laugh some more. Then the sky would turn pink and lavender and orange, and we would walk to the dining hall for dinner.

"You guys are obsessed with each other," Greta T. teased.

"Nah," I always said. "We're just friends."

But that would change soon enough. There's no intimacy like boarding school intimacy. You do literally everything together: laundry, meals. Nicky's dorm, Spaulding Hall, was only fifty yards away from my dorm, Dr. Green. We'd message back and forth via our school's e-mail system. *Ping. Ping. Ping.* Red flags would pop up next to his name in my inbox all night long.

By Christmas, I'd stopped clubbing with Greta T. and partying at the Buck with Alistair. I just wanted to stay on campus with Nicky. We were having sex, which wasn't the easiest thing to pull off at boarding school. (Besides, teen lust is so intense and conspicuous. Everyone knew what we were up to!) And *safe* sex? That was even more difficult to have—well, without half of Groton hearing about it in line at Cumberland Farms, anyway.

"Can I please get some . . ." *Mumble mumble.*

"What?" the cashier would say.

"Condoms?" I'd whisper. What an operation! Why did they keep them behind the register like that?

Eventually I went on birth control pills. Which I was never very good at remembering to take.

Hmm, I'd think, and swallow two at a time. I was starting to take my Ritalin two or three at a time, too. So was Nicky, who by Valentine's Day was officially my first boyfriend. I was basically sharing my prescription with him, which meant I had to hit up my parents for more and more. They kept it coming, though. Why wouldn't they? Ritalin was helping, clearly. I'd go on to make high honor roll my entire junior year.

"I am so proud of you," my dad said—over and over—when he visited in the spring. He was so happy. I was proud of me, too. It really *was* incredible, wasn't it? I'd turned everything around.

Chapter Four

IT WAS THE SUMMER THAT JFK JR. and Carolyn Bessette-Kennedy's plane went down. God, wasn't that the worst. Anyway, Nicky and I spent six weeks together on a "teen trip" through Europe. Rhiannon, my advisor at Lawrence, was the leader. We traveled in a group, but it might as well have been just Nicky and me. We were crazy for each other—making goo-goo eyes on the Metro, feeling achingly in love in the haunted beauty of the Père Lachaise Cemetery, which overlooked Paris. All that cheesy stuff. We slept in a barn on an organic farm in the south of France and put goat's milk in our coffees; we visited Salvador Dalí's tomb in his museum in Figueres; we frolicked on Portuguese beaches surrounded by red rocks and purple water. It was very romantic.

Then Nicky and I were apart all of August. Agony! When I returned to Groton in September 1999—a week before my seventeenth birthday—I *ran* across the campus until I found my boyfriend. Then I jumped into his arms.

Senior year was going to be the best of my life. I could feel it! My new dorm, Loomis House, was slightly off campus, down by the soccer fields. I was rooming with Canadian Wendy, a friend since sophomore year. She was superathletic, healthy, and popular, and her boyfriend, Beau, was a varsity hockey star. Alistair had graduated and Greta T. was back in Germany, but that was okay, because I was all about my boyfriend, all the time. I was so proud of Nicky! He'd been elected to the student council, which meant he would sometimes lead the whole school in morning assemblies in the auditorium. He was so cute up there on the stage; he always winked at me.

We were full-on Selena and Justin, you know? We talked every night on our dorms' pay phones after everyone else had gone to sleep. When we hung up, I'd go back to my Ritalin and my homework. By the end of fall term I was tied with Marcus, the German genius, for the top GPA in the entire class: a 3.87.

After Thanksgiving, Nicky and I both became very busy with our new class, Directing Seminar. We were two of only three seniors chosen to produce one-act plays. It was a special honor but tons of work: auditions, rehearsals, all that. The showcase was in March. Nicky and I were with our casts two hours a night, four nights a week. So we weren't seeing as much of each other.

In December, Nicky took me to his family's house in the White Mountains and we drank Hawaiian Punch–rum cocktails in front of the fire, and we exchanged gifts. I gave him a DVD box set of Akira Kurosawa films. The next day I went to my parents' house for the long Christmas break.

Back at Lawrence in January, it occurred to me . . . that I hadn't had my period for a while.

"You're on the pill, right?" Wendy said.

"Yeah," I said. I didn't tell her that I was always forgetting to take it, though.

"Then don't worry," Wendy said. But I did. I put on my L.L.Bean boots and sloshed through the snow and slush—it was a vicious winter—to the supermarket downtown. It was embarrassing to hand the e.p.t to the old lady cashier. I stuck the bag into my coat and hustled back to Loomis House. Then I peed on the stick.

I was pregnant.

Thank God I had my amazing boyfriend of fifteen months to get me through it all. Oh, wait, no I didn't.

I can't remember if I realized that Nicky was fucking the hot junior girl he'd cast in his one-act play—who lived *across the hall from me*—before or after I realized that I was pregnant. I don't remember how I found out it was happening; I don't remember Nicky and I "officially" ending our relationship, which was already over, obviously. I think I blocked a lot of this out. All I know for sure is, I melted down faster than a stick of butter in the microwave. I was completely destroyed.

What a horrible, horrible time. I mean, even writing about this period *still* makes me want to take a huge blunt full of PCP to the face—and it's fifteen years later! Nicky stepped right out of a relationship with me and into one with her. Now all eyes were on the three of us. And *I* was the pregnant (though no one knew) Bridget Moynahan to their Tom and Gisele. Remember that scandal? When it was in the papers in 2007, I flashed back to my own triangle at Lawrence in 2000. Mr. Student Council would smile at the new girl from the stage, and kids would turn their heads and look at me. Humiliating.

It went so dark inside of me. And it was dark outside, too, in those miserable after-Christmas months: cold and wet and icy. I felt like I was trapped inside a snow globe with Nicky and the girl. Every time I saw them together—and they were always together—my whole world got shaken up. The Loomis pay phone was right outside my door, and it rang for her every night just like it used to for me. This girl would sit out there murmuring to Nicky until two in the morning. They were falling in love. He brought her roses on Valentine's Day. Can you imagine? It was such a nightmare. It was *beyond* a nightmare, because I couldn't wake up.

And then there was the issue of my "condition."

What I am supposed to do about this pregnancy? I'd e-mail Nicky. *You have to help me.* He always wrote back, and he said he would help, but we never spoke in person.

I had no idea who to call. The Internet wasn't superhelpful back then like it is now. I literally looked up "abortion clinics" in the telephone pages. Once I found some numbers, I didn't know where to call them *from*. I didn't have a cell phone; no one did. Everyone could hear everyone else's business on the Loomis pay phone. My dorm parent, a math teacher, was a known eavesdropper; she was always lurking at the bottom of the stairs. We were only allowed to use it at night anyway, when the clinics would be closed. It was one roadblock after another. Plus, I was a procrastinator.

It took a few weeks, but one day in late February, I skipped out of English and cut back across Main Street to Loomis. The dorm was finally empty: everyone was in class, including the math teacher. I called a number I'd scribbled down and tried to book an appointment.

"How old are you?" the woman asked.

"Seventeen," I said. She told me minors needed parental consent in the state of Massachusetts.

I hung up.

A few weeks passed before I started researching my options again. Eventually, I booked an appointment for a few weeks later in New Hampshire. Nicky promised he would drive me. In the meantime, I was about as stable as a suicide bomber! I had *no* idea how to process the devastation and rage I was feeling all day, every day. And hell hath no fury like a pregnant teenage girl scorned: I was out for blood. Fuck secrecy! My life had already gone down in flames. It was time to take Nicky down with me.

"Guess what?" I stopped the class gossip, Vivian, in the schoolhouse. "Nicky got me pregnant before he dumped me." Her eyes bulged. "And I'm *still* pregnant!"

"Omigod . . ." She didn't know what to say (for once).

"Don't tell anyone," I said. Sure enough, within a week, half the kids in the school were looking at me sideways. Blabbing had been a spectacularly self-destructive move, but I couldn't take it back.

Here's a life lesson for you kids: it's *much* easier to go through something upsetting when you're on drugs. The more intense the drug, the more you forget your problems! It's basic science, really. I numbed my bad feelings with Ritalin (and whatever else I could get my hands on). I was tweaked every night, grinding my teeth at my desk until five in the morning. Wendy started wearing headphones to bed. And a sleep mask.

During the day, I started hanging with another druggy senior—wild, WASPy George, who kept a beat-up Oldsmobile sedan parked outside Spaulding Hall. We snuck off campus in it on a Tuesday (*very* against the rules) and drove to another boarding school, Northfield–Mount Hermon, to buy ecstasy from Shady Leo. Have you heard of him? He was a prep school–circuit teen dealer legend in 2000! I wish *he'd* write a memoir. Anyway, it was snowing hard on the drive back to Groton.

"*AHHHHH!*" we screamed as the car slid across the road—it was somewhere near Athol—and *slammed* into a mailbox. We got out and inspected the damage. The front was crumpled on one side, like a curled lip. A headlight was out.

"Whoops!" George said.

Back at Lawrence, all of the spots were taken except for one directly in front of the dining hall, where faculty parked, too. The smashed-up car sat there sneering conspicuously like Johnny Rotten.

That Friday night at an "AIDS Awareness" dance, we sold all the tablets to freshmen and sophomores, who rolled their faces off like little champions. George and I were fucked up, too; I didn't care who saw.

"You need to be careful," Wendy said, an hour into Sunday study hall. She'd been avoiding our room, spending more and more time with Beau. I wasn't talking much to anyone besides George lately, anyway.

"Huh?" I said. Playing dumb.

Sure enough, on Tuesday night my advisor stopped by after study hall, car keys in hand. Rhiannon was only twenty-six and had long, white-blond hair. She cared about me more than anyone in the school.

"Pack an overnight bag," Rhiannon said. Sleep over at a teacher's house? We had a special relationship, but not that special. But I could tell by the look on Rhiannon's face that it wasn't optional.

Her pretty rental cottage was only five minutes off campus. Rhiannon made me a bed on the sofa and brought me a mug of peppermint tea. She sat down and stared at me for a minute.

Then it began.

"Were you drunk at the AIDS dance?" Rhiannon asked.

"No," I said.

"Were you on drugs at the AIDS dance?"

"What?" I said. "No."

"Were you *selling* drugs at the AIDS dance?"

"Rhiannon!" I said. "No!"

"What happened to George's car?"

"I have no idea!"

Rhiannon studied my face. I took a little slurp from my mug.

"People are saying you're pregnant."

"I know," I said. Carefully. "You know how the rumors are around here."

"If you are, I'll help you. You have to let people help you."

"But I'm not."

"Are you lying?"

"Why would I lie?" I said. It was a moot point anyway, wasn't it? My appointment was coming up. "Rhiannon! I'm *not* pregnant."

Rhiannon didn't answer. She just looked at me. So I just . . . looked at her.

Finally, my teacher gave up and went to bed. I lay awake for hours in the dark, listening to her wind chimes banging around.

A week and change later, Nicky picked me up in his mom's SUV. It was snowing, as always; the drive to Manchester was long and slow. And silent. We weren't speaking. We got to the doctor's office, and I went in the back. Nicky stayed in the waiting room. I was so nervous. The doctor put cold jelly on my belly and gave me a sonogram.

"We can't proceed," he said.

"Pardon?" I was on an examination table in a paper gown.

"You're fourteen weeks pregnant," he said. "We don't perform second-trimester abortions in New Hampshire. It's against the law."

"*What?*" I said.

"I can refer you to a clinic in Massachusetts," the doctor continued. "But you'll need parental consent."

"But I can't!" I started to cry. "I can't get parental consent!"

"I know you're frightened," the doctor said. "But at this point . . ."

"*You don't know my dad*," I bawled. The nurse took my hand. I got dressed and walked back out to the waiting room in a stupor.

Nicky drove me back to school. I wept in the passenger seat the whole ride. We were both in shock. He dropped me off at Loomis House and we never spoke again. We stopped e-mailing each other. I just did not know what to do.

And so I shut down. Winter raged on, but I stopped thinking about my pregnancy. I pretended it all wasn't happening.

Boarders were required to stay on campus on the first weekend in March to study for finals. I was glad. This ensured a fantastic turnout at the one-act plays on Friday and Saturday nights. I was so excited about my production of *Naomi in the Living Room* (by one of the funniest writers of all time, Christopher Durang) that I didn't even care that Nicky's play, starring his new girlfriend, was debuting, too. Rhiannon would be grading from the front row.

I peeked into the black box theater on opening night. The house was packed! Even the varsity hockey team had showed up. I was wearing those ridiculous twenty-three-inch-waist high-waisted Sergio Valente jeans I'd ordered sophomore year. They'd fit me once, but now they felt like they were compressing my insides. To this day, I blame them for what happened next.

I was giving my cast final notes when the cramping began. I went to the girls' bathroom, sat down in a stall, and pulled down my jeans.

I apologize in advance for what I am about to describe.

Imagine a jellyfish as big as an ashtray. Now turn that jellyfish dark bloodred and multiply it by a few hundred. Now imagine pulling down your Sergio Valente jeans and seeing hundreds of ashtray-size bloodred jellyfish *pouring* out of you. That's what happened to me.

"AUUUUUUGHHH!" I started screaming. "AUUUUUGHHH!"

The bloody pieces—the lining of my uterus, I guess—kept gushing from my body and into the water. It was like my insides were falling out. I tried to catch them in my hands, to stop it. There was too much. *Plunk, plunk, plunk, plunk.* It was endless. A deluge!

"AUGGHHHHHH!" I was still screaming. "HELP ME! SOMEONE!" Someone ran in.

"Hello?" a girl called. "Are you okay?"

"NO! GET RHIANNON!" I hollered. I was still sitting in the stall with my pants down. My hands and legs and the toilet seat and the floor were covered with blood. "IT'S CAT! I NEED RHIANNON!"

My advisor burst in a few minutes later.

"Cat?" she shouted.

"I HAVE TO GO TO THE EMERGENCY ROOM!" I sobbed.

"Stay right there!" she said. I stood up and stuffed my jeans with paper towels as she ran for her car keys.

I moaned and cried all the way to the hospital.

By the time my legs were in stirrups, the hemorrhaging had stopped. The ER doctor prodded at my uterus and poked very long Q-tip-like things inside me and pulled out any straggler clots. He put them into a hazmat bin next to him.

I was—again, forgive me—hoping I'd miscarried. But no.

"You're still pregnant," the doctor confirmed. I stared up at the fluorescent lights.

On the ride back to campus, Rhiannon stared straight ahead—as one does while driving, I suppose. But still. It was tense in that car.

"I'm sorry we missed the plays," I finally said.

"It's okay," Rhiannon said.

"I'm sorry I lied," I said. "Please don't tell my parents."

"I don't know what to do."

"Please, Rhiannon." I started crying again. "*Please.*"

"I don't know what to do," Rhiannon repeated.

She dropped me off at my dorm. I carried my bloody Sergio Valentes inside in a plastic bag.

At breakfast, I got a nice surprise: everyone was raving about *Naomi in the Living Room*! That night, I got to see it for myself. It was perfect, beat for beat. My brilliant actors got whoops and whistles as they took their bows. Nicky's play was a dud. Rhiannon gave me an A in Directing Seminar.

What did the pregnant senior-class pillhead get on her Algebra 3 exam? Drool! It was the week after the one-acts. I was sitting with some kids at breakfast the morning of math final day.

"Wanna try something?" the shadiest kid in our school said. His name was Bruce, but people called him "the Iceman." He was only seventeen, but rumor had it that he'd already had a meth-induced heart attack. The Iceman held out a white pill. "It's Super-Ritalin!"

"Really?" I said, and put it in my mouth like the moron that I was then and remain today. Then I swallowed.

It was a sunny morning—almost spring break. I sauntered across the grassy quad (where, increasingly, fewer and fewer people were saying hello to me, but whatever) and into the gymnasium-size hall in the schoolhouse where every senior at the school would be taking their math exam at the same time. Dude, I was *so* prepared for this final. I felt *very* confident. I took a seat and pulled out my pencils and hundred-dollar graphing calculator and all that horrible stuff, which you truly couldn't pay me to think about ever again after I finish typing this sentence.

The papers were handed out, and I got *crack-a-lacking*. Everything was going great until about twenty minutes in, when I suddenly felt . . . underwater.

Huh, I thought.

I couldn't read the page in front of me. The words were swimming. I looked around. Kids were hunched over their desks, but they looked like blobs; the teachers walking around supervising were blurry, too. And that's the last thing I remember.

The next time I opened my eyes, I was in an entirely different building: the infirmary. Jaclyn, one of my actors, was holding my hand like she was the nurse in *A Farewell to Arms*. The *actual* nurse was glaring at us from across the room. I was on a twin bed.

"What happened?" I croaked.

"You passed out in the math exam," Jaclyn whispered. She pressed a Dunkin' Donuts bag into my hands. "I got you a bagel."

"Fuck," I groaned. My head felt like it weighed a thousand pounds.

"You were rolling around on the ground," Jaclyn whispered. "You fell out of your chair."

"I'm gonna get kicked out," I mumbled.

"What did you take?" the nurse asked later.

Good question, I thought.

"Nothing!" But my eyelids were heavy. "I just didn't eat breakfast!" I found out later that Bruce had given me Zyprexa—a powerful antipsychotic. Stupid Iceman!

I didn't get expelled, but I did receive a suspension—of sorts. Lawrence's signature two-week specialized study program, Winterim, was always right after winter term exams. There were loads of options, from scuba diving in Belize to Habitat for Humanity in Peru. Junior year, Nicky and I had stayed on campus together for a filmmaking course. I don't remember what I'd chosen senior year, but it doesn't matter. I was sent home for the two weeks instead.

What did the school tell my parents? What did *I* tell my parents? No idea. But I had two more weeks off for spring break after that.

So in total—and I only understand this in retrospect—Lawrence gave me an entire month to take care of my "situation." Which—still—I did not do.

I was still pregnant when I returned to Groton for spring trimester in early April. If you're confused about the timeline—how far along I was—well, that makes two of us. I don't know, man. It was *so* crazy. I was sick. Truly. Just . . . messed up.

Let's say . . . eighteen weeks?

I started acting out.

"Oh no!" I said, dropping a baby doll on the floor of the library. George and I had found it in the prop closet of the theater department, and I'd smeared stage blood on it. Very Michael Alig at Disco 2000. "My baby!" George and I laughed and laughed. Nobody else did.

My flamboyant friend and I were trouble together. We'd both been accepted into Bard College, a dope school about an hour outside of New York City. After we got our letters, we sat in the library and went on the Bard Accepted Students Message Board together. We messed with other students-to-be and posted provocative replies on their threads.

It was dumb (most social media self-sabotages are). George and I thought it was a big joke, but Bard's Department of Admissions didn't feel that way. They tracked the posts back to Lawrence and reported us to the college counselor.

And that was it. That was what the school finally used to nail us. Between the drug-dealing rumors, my pregnancy and emergency room trip, my math exam blackout, the baby doll dropped on the quad, the crushed Oldsmobile in the parking lot, and now the Bard mess . . . they'd had it with George and me. It wasn't a total shock when Lawrence finally summoned our families. It was a *little* shocking, though—since it was late April, and we were both seniors. Graduation was only six weeks away.

My parents arrived from the airport in a rental car. My dad was stone-faced; my mom looked very nervous. I wasn't allowed to go into the assistant headmaster's office with them, so I sat on a bench in the rotunda. It was very quiet in the schoolhouse on this weekday morning. Everyone else was in class. I stared at the floor, where the school motto was set in marble: *Omnibus lucet.* "The light shines for all."

The door to the assistant headmaster's office opened. Rhiannon was the first to step out. I didn't know she'd been in there. Her eyes met mine. She'd told them everything. I could tell.

Sure enough, my dad emerged looking like a ghost had stepped into his body. His face was white. And my mother was crying. Crying and crying and crying. When her eyes met mine, she started crying harder. When I stood up to comfort her, my mother . . . *recoiled*; I will never forget it. She absolutely did not want me to touch her. I was too toxic.

I don't remember much about those last few hours on campus, only that my mother and I packed up, fast. Over at Spaulding, George and his parents were doing the same thing. I never saw him again.

My parents were quiet in the car to the airport, but I couldn't escape the voices in my head. *You failure. You disaster. You disgusting girl.* The self-loathing was like a radio station between my ears. *Loser. You mess.* Over time, I'd learn to turn the volume down on SHAME FM, but I could never totally shut it off.

As for saying good-bye to Boston, well . . . When the plane took off, I stared out the window as the city got smaller and smaller for the last time. I never could spell "Massachusetts" anyway.

The only thing worse than getting abortions is reading about abortions. Am I wrong? Please skip ahead if you are squeamish. Life-murdering can get *rather* gory, you know.

My mother took me to a clinic in DC soon after we returned. She filled out her parental consent forms while I sat in the waiting room. It was jam-packed with girls and their partners because the doctor was running late. He was driving in from Philadelphia. It was hot outside. I killed time at a thrift store in the shopping center parking lot.

A few hours later, it was my turn. I put my legs into the stirrups. The doctor injected my cervix with a numbing agent, but I was awake the entire time. My mom had declined the anesthesia that puts you under—she just didn't know better. Huge mistake. (*Always* ask to be put to sleep before an abortion—then it's over in the blink of an eye.) It was brutally painful. More than pain, it felt like . . . *torture.* I was splayed out there on this table just . . . *vibrating*—all *guh-guh-guh-guh-guh* from the sheer force of the vacuum machine. Remember the scene in *The Princess Bride* when the mustachioed bandit guy is getting pumped full of water—*is* that what's happening to him?—and his whole body is thrashing and shaking and straining? And it's almost unbearable to watch? That's how I see me in this memory of my life. I also saw what was coming out of me, since there was a tank that was covered by a paper cone with a slit in it, and the paper cone was off-kilter. I saw it all.

Then it was done. I sat in the recovery room with the little cookies they give you. I was crying and crying. *Loud.* I mean, *uncontrollably* crying. I couldn't *believe* what I had just been through. I was in shock. Still shaking. It was like the machine was still in there, shaking me from the inside out. The procedure had been *so* awful. So *violent.* It looked like murder. It *felt* like murder. I'm not saying that in any kind of political way. I'm just telling you how it felt.

My crying was starting to freak out the other girls. A nurse went out and found my mom. She came in and sat down next to me.

"Shh," my mom said, patting me awkwardly on the back like she was trying to burp me. Awkward as fuck. She didn't know what to do. I was still doubled over when we finally walked out to the parking lot. We got in the hot car and just sat there for a few minutes. I guess my mom was waiting for me to calm down, but I was still sobbing all crazy-like right in the passenger seat. Finally, my mom couldn't take it anymore. She got out and made a call on her cell phone. Then she got behind the wheel.

My parents' house was empty when we got there. It was about one o'clock on a weekday. By then, I'd stopped crying. I went right to bed. When I woke up, it was dark out. I could smell the blood. There was a paper bag on the nightstand. I opened it. It was a little orange plastic bottle with just a few pills inside. I read the label: Xanax. The prescribing doctor was my dad.

Chapter Five

I'D THOUGHT THAT THE WHOLE SECOND-TRIMESTER abortion thing had been the cherry on top of the most catastrophic adolescence of all time, but it turns out *that* honor belonged to the letter Bard college sent informing me that I was no longer enrolled as a freshman in the fall. Not only had I been expelled from high school six weeks before graduation, I'd been kicked out of college before I even got there. Oops.

It was *awkward* around the house, to say the least. I kept waiting for my dad to lose it, but he never did. Instead, he didn't speak to me or acknowledge me—and that was even worse.

So anywhere was better than at home. Every morning, I was relieved to take the Metro to Emerson Prep in Dupont Circle. It was barely a school—more like a bunch of classrooms in a town house. The place was sort of a joke. Kids smoked weed on the front steps; no one cared. Emerson offered a pay-per-credit program (it's where I'd ultimately earn my diploma); accordingly, it was full of wealthy derelicts who'd been booted from St. Albans and Georgetown Day.

I fit right in—literally. Four hours into my first day at Emerson, I was squished in the backseat of an Audi at the Connecticut Avenue Burger King drive-through, smoking weed and listening to Big L. Giggling on a lap. You know me. That was lunch. After school, everyone went to the O Street Mansion to drink. Have you ever been? It's one of my favorite places in DC. It's, like, three town houses combined, and full of secret passages and hidden stairwells and walls that open into other rooms— like in a murder mystery movie! And there's a log cabin duplex on top, and all these other themed rooms; every item in the place is for sale, even the toilet paper. Rosa Parks lived there. Anyway, there's a pool out back in the garden, and that's where we partied that first day. I took shots and fell into the pool in the back garden à la Brian Jones (and not in a cool way).

I woke up on a leather sofa in a basement recording studio next to a boy drinking an Amstel Light.

"You were rolling around on the ground!" he told me. I'd heard that one before. "In the bushes!" He'd pulled me out of the pool and put me in the back of his car. And that's the romantic story of how I met my summer boyfriend, Oscar.

I spent the next two months careening around in Oscar's dad's BMW sedan with my eyes closed, empty Corona bottles clinking at my feet. Praying not to die! Everyone on the DC private school party circuit drove drunk. Everyone! Oscar was tight with a top-ranking Politician's Kid. The three of us would cruise around Northwest in his Oldsmobile and park under a streetlight. The Secret Service would park right behind us. Then Oscar and Politician's Kid would sit there for an hour, cracking can after can of beer as they talked. When Politician's Kid started the engine an hour later, the operatives wouldn't swoop in and try to take the keys or anything. (They'd confiscate a disposable camera at a house party, though—lickety-split.)

Yup. Those Sidwell Friends kids were wild, man. Girls with tanned abs and Tiffany charm necklaces were always vomiting into koi ponds and things; Destiny's Child's "Jumpin' Jumpin'" was always playing at the house parties. One night we were smoking weed in a kid's backyard in Northwest and two men in camouflage leapt out from behind trees—with fucking machine guns! They were protecting Elián González, the little Cuban boy who floated into the United States on an inner tube. Remember him? He was in government custody in the house with a backyard adjacent to this kid's. DC stuff.

I was still only seventeen, but my dad didn't care what I did anymore. He couldn't even look at me. Half the time I didn't even sleep at home. That August, Oscar took me to the Hamptons for the first time. We went shark fishing and snorted heroin off old issues of *Robb Report*. The glamorous surroundings worked like drugs: they made me forget how ugly I felt on the inside. Yes, I'd devastated my family. Yes, I'd murdered that baby. Yes, I'd totally fucked up my future. But wasn't it lovely here off Amagansett? Didn't I look fly in my Calvin Klein bikini, smoking Camel Lights? The boys caught a shark and cut it open at the belly. The blood spilled out all over the deck.

With my eighteenth birthday approaching, there was only one thing to do: figure out a way to move to New York City. That's when I started auditioning for acting schools in Manhattan. I got in; the ever-generous dad agreed to pay for it. And I was on my way.

Mimi drove me and my stuff up from DC in her red Honda van to my first-ever place in the city: a room in a boardinghouse—since torn down—on West Forty-First Street. It was one block from Times Square and practically on top of Port Authority bus station. If you require further visuals, Google the paparazzi photos of Jennifer Lopez's bat-faced boy toy Casper Smart emerging from an Eighth Avenue peep show. That was my block!

For eight hundred dollars a month, I had a bunk bed with a desk underneath, three Korean roommates, and a fantastic view of the

Tex-Mex restaurant Chevy's, where tourists devoured delicious mes-quite-grilled tacos before taking in *Mary Poppins* the musical. I sat at that window for hours, looking out at my crazy new world. I'd never felt more at peace in my entire life. Finally, I was home.

It was September 2000. Coldplay's "Yellow" was on the radio; the George Bush–Al Gore presidential race was popping off, and I started acting school. Acting school! Oh, Lord. I thought it would be fun, but it *so* wasn't for me. A typical assignment would be re-creating our morn-ing routines, right? Every day, I'd watch an aspiring actor arrange black wooden boxes to look like his bedroom. He'd "make" the box bed with sheets he'd brought from home. Then he'd lie down and "sleep" for a long time. I am talking like fifteen full minutes.

Finally, the actor would be jerked "awake" by an imaginary alarm clock. Everyone would shift in their seats, like, "All right, time for some action!" But then the actor would hit his imaginary snooze button— and go back to fake-sleep *again*. For ten more minutes! And we'd all just sit there watching this in *silence*.

Well, in almost silence. *Crunch. Crunch.* That would be *moi*, surrep-titiously nibbling on a dose of my *new* medication, Adderall. Generic name: amphetamine salts! (I'd switched from Ritalin. Adderall—some kids called it Gladderall—was more fun.)

Then it would be time for two hours of voice classes, where I learned the phonetic alphabet and studied anatomical diagrams of the tongue.

"Toy boat," I'd stand there saying. "Toy boat toy boat toy boat toy boat toy boat. Minimal animal. Red leather yellow leather. Red leather yellow leather. Unique New York. Unique New York."

Then we'd go to movement class, where we studied the Alexander Technique: walking with purpose, "freezing" in place, flopping down and folding at the waist to "sway like a willow tree in the breeze."

"Relax your neck, Cat," the instructor would say when I lifted my head to peep at the clock.

The acting school kids all hung out together after class at a spot on Park Avenue South called Desmond's Tavern. There was beer on tap, live Jethro Tull cover bands, and a laid-back dive-bar vibe; being there for more than twenty minutes made me suicidal. This was Manhattan, for Chrissakes! I wanted to go to the hot clubs, like I had with Alistair and Greta T.! But I didn't know where to find that scene, and you couldn't just look it up in *Time Out New York*. (Believe me, I tried.)

So I explored my new city alone every night instead. If Ritalin had made me focus, my new shit got me *high*, honey (especially when I took two pills at a time). It was like I was in a video game or something! Suddenly I could travel vast distances—through rain, snow, anything—and never get fatigued. I just kept walking and walking and walking, listening to BT and dodging rats and smoking cigs and walking and *whoops!* Was it three thirty in the morning already? I'd always wind up somewhere weird at the end of these excursions, like on the Bowery in front of a fifteen-foot bronze statue of Confucius. I'd cab it back to West Forty-First Street and take a sleeping pill from the box of samples my mom sent me. Classes didn't start until two o'clock every day, so I could stay conked out until noon. After school, I'd go night walking all over again. And this is how I got to know "Unique New York."

Only a real weirdo would stay living across the street from Port Authority, of course, so in the spring of 2001 I moved thirty blocks downtown to a loft on Broadway, just south of Union Square—right by the famous Strand Book Store. I was renting a room from a professional storyteller—a friend of Mimi's friend. The place was decorated all gypsy-boho with Indian cotton fabrics. It was a real, old-school Manhattan loft: strange, creaky, and cavernous, with eighteen-foot ceilings.

The storyteller had twenty-nine thousand rules, and two cats. I wasn't allowed to have people over; I *was* supposed to let the cats into my bedroom whenever they wanted. And they always wanted! Those cats were *extremely* bossy. And though the loft was huge, I wasn't allowed in most of it. I was only supposed to go in my room, which was built into the middle of the space and had no windows, and the skinny bathroom, where a cockroach the size of a Pepperidge Farm Milano was always perched on the exposed pipe over the shower. It was my first encounter with that particular breed of New Yorker. I'd look up and scream like Janet Leigh in *Psycho* every time I saw him! I was always racing out of there with shampoo suds still in my hair.

My first year of acting school had ended in May, so I was off for a few months, waiting to hear if I'd been accepted into a second year. The storyteller was always away on her . . . *storytelling tours*, I guess, and I was too shy to hang with her cool, super-nice adopted son Ishmael, who had a room down the hall when he was home from Oberlin. He was a DJ, always messing with his turntables. Years later, he'd write the bestseller *A Long Way Gone*, which is about his time as a child soldier in the Sierra Leone armed forces. Yeah, you should probably be reading that memoir instead of this one.

It was an extra-lonely summer. The prescriptions kept arriving in the mail, though—my mom's handwriting was on the envelopes, and my dad's name was on the labels on the little bottles. I took longer and longer walks, and I went to tanning beds and lay there with Wink-Ease on and wondered when I'd ever have another boyfriend. I bought a little television with a built-in VCR and four channels, and I watched ABC 7 Eyewitness News and Conan. I did hundreds of sit-ups on the floor each night. The cats watched from under the bed with their shiny little eyes.

I was flat-out depressed by the Fourth of July. It was a bad, bad day. I desperately wanted to go to FDR Drive and watch the fireworks, but I didn't have anyone to go with; I couldn't go watch them alone, I thought, because people would know I was a loser. I babysat—as I often did—in the West Village all day. I kept checking my phone, hoping someone from acting school would hit me up about a barbecue or something. No one did. Why would they? I never called anyone. My primary relationship was with pills.

When my job ended that evening, I walked home along West Eleventh Street alone. It was drizzling, and everyone was whooping and running through the streets to get to the big show over on the East River. I didn't think I'd ever felt so low. By the time I got back to Broadway and bought a chocolate soft-serve ice cream cone with rainbow sprinkles from the truck parked outside the Strand, I was practically crying. And all because I didn't have friends on the Fourth of July. Being young is so funny, isn't it?

The fireworks started just as I reached the door to my building. *Pop pop pop.* I could still hear them as I climbed the steep stairs to the storyteller's loft. My ice cream was melting all over the place. I slurped the mess from my hand as I unlocked the apartment door. No one was home.

I went into my little bedroom and turned on the TV. *Pop pop.* I switched it off right away. Seeing the fireworks bursting all glittery on the little screen just made me feel worse. I sat on my bed and finished my cone.

Now what?

The silence felt very heavy.

Then I did something I'd never done before. I went into the bathroom, knelt at the toilet, wiggled my fingers around in the back of my throat, and made myself sick. It didn't taste bad at all! I was surprised. The ice cream came up cold and sweet, just like it had gone down. The sprinkles were intact in the bowl.

I stood and washed my hands at the sink.

That was easy, I thought. My eyes were teary in the mirror. I could feel the cockroach watching me.

I turned nineteen on September 10, 2001. The next morning was 9/11, and of course, I was living downtown, just a few blocks below the police barricades at Fourteenth Street (I showed a piece of mail as proof of address to get past every day). It all stays with you for life: the missing posters, the bitter air, the ashes, the chaos. I will spare you fifteen pages of rambling recollections and just say . . . I love you, New York!

Now please forgive me in advance for diving right back into my sleazy story line.

My second year at the acting school started in September 2001. I don't remember much about the first term. But in January, I began a stage makeup course that I really liked. I learned to make fake track marks! You apply some tacky glue—it's almost like rubber cement—into the crease of your arm until it gets sort of blistery looking, and then you pat some red and yellow eye shadow on top if you want them to look all infected and raw and oozy. You can also make faux meth scabs this way. Cold sores. Whatever you want! *Or*, if you want an *ex*-junkie look, you can use purple shadow, and that makes the glue-lumps look like gnarled old scars. I did it all! I also pocketed loads of Ben Nye: I mean, if it's a pretty, natural stain you're after, there's nothing better than a little stage blood dabbed just so on the lips.

I was still unhappy with my social life. I didn't hang out with people much: mainly I just took Adderall and shopped. But then something major happened.

It was spring 2002—near the end of my second and final year at the acting school. Okay, so do you watch *Louie*? You know how in the opening sequence Louis CK eats his pizza slice, and then he goes into that subterranean club? That's the Comedy Cellar, a stand-up club in Greenwich Village, and it's legendary—if you come to New York, you gotta go. In April, I went with three girls from my acting school. We got sloshed on sangria; then, after the show, we flirted with two of the comedians. Back then, Godfrey was best known as "the 7UP guy" (he's also whom Ben Stiller turns into when he goes undercover as a black guy in *Zoolander*) and Ardie Fuqua was just wonderful, affable Ardie (who, sadly, was in the news as I wrote this book because he was in that terrible bus accident with Tracy Morgan—though he's okay now). Both guys had crazy-positive energy and fantastic teeth. I *lovv-vve* them, truly—still!

Anyway. Ardie and Godfrey herded all of the sangria-swilling white girls—aka me and my three friends—into two taxis and told us they were taking us to the club! We got out on Lafayette Street, just around the corner from where Britney Spears allegedly kept an apartment above Tower Records. There was a line outside, but the doorman lifted the velvet rope for Ardie and Godfrey right away. I took one step inside and knew immediately that I'd found what I'd been looking for.

Pangaea! That was the name of the club. I'd go on to be a regular there. It's one of the best clubs I've ever frequented to this day. (If you are young, you *have* to move to New York and go to the clubs while you still have the energy! I have no regrets.) Everyone was always gorgeous, and the place was always packed. There were white squishy couches, masks all over the wall, and there were live drummers banging with the music. Every table, it seemed, had a big ice bucket with a champagne bottle on it, and if you were a teenage girl you could just sit down anywhere—there were *tons* of couches—and immediately be offered a glass or three. And a bump of coke! Men were always giving girls bumps from their little baggies, and the baggies were always lavender and pink and red. And underneath the DJ booth and behind heavy curtains, there was a whole hidden room *just* for—unofficially—doing coke. Chosen ones got to stay on the couches in there for after-hours. And there were always celebrities there—famous male models, famous magicians—hitting on all the bitches.

That first night, I walked into the club and there was P. Diddy, who was still Puff Daddy back then, and he grabbed my arm and wanted me to sit with his table. It was so exciting; I mean, I was nineteen! I didn't join him, though. I just kicked off my sandals and gyrated to "Hot in Herre" on a sofa elsewhere—though I might as well have been dancing on a cloud! *Bliss*, man. I hadn't been that happy in a long time.

I never wanted the night to end, but of course, it did. I walked home at four thirty in the morning, feeling throbby and exhilarated. I *had* to go back—not just to that club, but to that world. But how?

Well. Lucky for me, going to nightclubs is very easy when you are teenage, blond, skinny, friendless, wired on stimulants, and quietly desperate. Anyone can do it! And the lower your self-esteem is, the more you put yourself out there. And eventually you become (vaguely) popular.

Three nights later, I showed up at the Olive Branch—the restaurant above the Cellar—around midnight, doused in Michael by Michael Kors perfume, my cleavage shining like the top of the Chrysler Building with Revlon Skinlights Face Illuminator Powder. It was around midnight. Ardie was at a table with some other comics. I trotted over in my hot-pink stilettos.

"Hey!" I tried to act cool. "Remember me?"

"Hey!" Ardie stood up and gave me a hug. "What are you doing here?"

"Just wanted to say hi," I purred.

"Who are you here with?" Ardie said. "Where are your friends?"

"Oh," I said. "I was *just* with them, but they went home. And I was nearby, so . . ."

Later, I sat downstairs in the Comedy Cellar and watched Ardie do his set. When he was done, he gathered up the trashed white girls from the audience again—I guess Godfrey was out of town—and we piled into his SUV. This time, we went to Lot 61 over by the Hudson River, then to Suite 16 in Chelsea. I hit it off with the manager, Matt Strauss (hi, Matt!), and he and I sat with Nicky Hilton and her MTV VJ boyfriend Brian McFadden. Wow!

I was hooked. I spent hours getting ready every night: shaving my whole body and blow-drying my hair. And putting together outfits! The whole thing was finding the tiniest, shortest skirts. I took dresses to a tailor to be hemmed until I started doing it myself at home—a timeless Adderall-tweaker tradition, unfortunately. I ruined so many dresses, just hacking them way too short with big orange-handled kitchen scissors and my hands shaking. Then I'd slather Body Shop Coconut Body Butter, spritz Banana Boat tanning oil on top of that, strap on my Gucci fanny pack, and hit the streets. I used to get into cabs and *slide* across the backseat; I was so greasy. Absolutely lubricated! But that's how you keep your legs gleaming all night.

I showed up at the Comedy Cellar five or six nights a week like this—dressed for the club. It was a crazy steez, but . . . *I* was crazy. I could *not* stay home. I was at the Cellar so often that I got to know Lisa Lampanelli, Judah Friedlander, Sherrod Small, Colin Quinn, Dave Attell, Tony Rock—all of the comedians who were there every night as well. They were all very nice to me (to my face), even though I was obviously a lonely weirdo. Dave Attell even kissed me once! Yeah, that was strange.

Every night, Ardie took me to a different club after his set: Butter or Veruka or Groovejet or Sway or Spa or Lotus.

After a few months, I started bypassing the Cellar and just going out on my own. I saw the same party people everywhere, every night. Everyone seemed as messy as I was, if not messier. This one guy everyone called Jesus was rumored to live in a unit in Chelsea Mini Storage! They were all nightcrawler vampires who raged until dawn and slept until dusk. This is terrible for the soul, but great for the skin—no sun damage, you know? So everyone looked good.

I particularly hit it off with another smoky-eyed blond girl named Dara, who went out every night even though she was still in high school. She and her spiky-haired boyfriend, Ben, had just been profiled by Nancy Jo Sales in a *Vanity Fair* story called "Ben and Dara Are in Love (And Nothing Else Matters)." They had a crazy-dysfunctional, *yayo*-fueled relationship. They became . . . well, not my *friends* exactly, but something like that.

I still didn't have *real* friends, and I was very ashamed about this. Sometimes I got called out on it.

"Why don't I ever see you *with* anyone?" sneered Ben one night when I plunked down at his table at Flow. "Don't you have any friends? Where are your *friends*?" He was being a jerk, but he had my number.

What do you give the blond teenage pillhead who has everything? Antibiotics! Ardie had always driven me home after our nights together— he was such a good big brother—but once I started going to the clubs without him, I really wound up sleeping around. You know how it is when you're nineteen! Promoters are always taking their dicks out in the backseats of cabs and pulling you on their laps or biting your nipple through your wifebeater or something comparably unspeakable, and you feel very embarrassed that the taxi driver can see and hear but you let it keep happening anyway. Why? It's all just part of being young in New York, I guess. No one was taking me home to *make love* to me, let's put it that way.

One particularly bad night I had sex with a stranger in the bathroom at Flow on Varick. It was a Sunday: "hip-hop night." It went down right at four o'clock, when the club was clearing out; the lights were up. Security guards were banging on the stall door and it was humiliating; but this guy—I didn't even know his name—had a *grip* on me in there, and I was totally naked. He'd told me he was a guitarist in a famous band. I wound up going home with him because . . . well, I guess because he told me to. The first thing I looked for when we got there were instruments. I saw none. Uh-oh.

I had sex with Not-a-Guitarist on the butcher block in his kitchen anyway—that is, I did until I saw an *eyeball* in the crack of the door.

"AHHHH!" I jumped off the counter. The creepy little peeper came into the kitchen with his dick out. He was like . . . a tiny man! Not a dwarf, just . . . small. Anyway, that's not relevant to the story. The point is, he was masturbating furiously! And Not-a-Guitarist was naked, and I was naked, and I don't know if they were trying to double-tag me or what, but I had to go. I looked around. Where were my clothes? Where was my phone?

"You're not leaving." Not-a-Guitarist grabbed my arm. Like, *hard*. I had to *pull* it away and *snatch* my tube minidress and jacket and my shoes from the floor and *flee* this building—sprint down the stairs and everything. My phone was in my jacket pocket, but I'd totally left my gold Baby Phat purse with all my money and makeup and my fake ID! So I didn't have any money; I couldn't take a cab. I walked home on the dark streets without any underwear on.

But those were the bad guys. The good guys were *good*. My favorite was a really grungy cokehead Calvin Klein model named Michael. Gosh, I'm *still* in love with him! He had greasy brown hair that hung in his face and wore glasses and beat-up Marc Jacobs clothes. Oh, and he had just a perfect body. *Perfect*. God, Michael was *so* hot. And no matter how much blow he did back then, he always had this glowy, gold-flushed skin tone, like he went to tanning beds or was part Cherokee or something. And his cheekbones! Ugh. He had the *best* cheekbones— though you could barely see them underneath the aforementioned hair.

I first met this divine creature at Ben's duplex in the Village over a plate of jam! Yes, *jam*. That is Hamptons surfer-slang for cocaine. So Michael and I snorted the jam, and I had no idea he was this big-deal model. He looked like a hobo! The hobo and I left Ben's at that presunrise time when the sky is just starting to change, and we walked around downtown until my stupid *nose* started absolutely *dripping* blood all over the white tank top I'd just borrowed from Dara. So then I went back to the hobo's apartment on Ninth Street "to change" and stayed for four days.

We were thick as thieves after that. I soon realized that Michael the Hobo was actually Male Model Michael, and that he was in the window of every store in town, wearing Calvin Klein. He was *gorgeous*. But he wasn't modeling much anymore. This was because he had a serious drug problem. So did I, but I was only nineteen and really didn't understand that yet. Male Model Michael was twenty-nine, and he did coke in the shower! Yes, I did it with him, but *he* brought it in there.

"Let me really look at you," he'd murmur after we'd both taken six bumps apiece. Then he'd start to scrub my makeup off. My face would be so numb that I couldn't even feel the washcloth! Just like in that song by The Weeknd. Argh, it was *so* sexy. "Let me see how beautiful you are." After we got out, he'd dress me in his clothes and we'd do more lines, and he'd read to me from his favorite book, *The Prince of Tides*, and then we'd do lines and he'd tell me all about how he and his male-model friends used to go down on one another, then we'd have sex again and order more coke and do *more* lines and talk about Bret Easton Ellis, and then we'd order more coke, and then we'd have sex again and then . . . well, you get the idea! He always called me "darlin'." It was a really dreamy relationship.

After our binges Male Model Michael would need days and days of space to isolate and sleep and be depressed. I didn't understand that when I was nineteen, but of course I do now. Addiction: it's rough.

Male Model Michael would go on to sort of lose his mind and have to move out of the city and back in with his parents (who were—incidentally—honest-to-God rocket scientists). It's sad that the drugs took him down. But of course, he might say the same thing about me.

That summer, I went to the club and met the guy who would alter the course of my life, and with whom I am still close to this day. Alex was twenty years old, tall, charismatic, and preppy, with dark hair and icy-blue eyes. He drank Dewar's on the rocks and had grown up on the Upper East Side. His mom still lived on East Ninetieth Street, but Alex was always fighting with her. He only liked his little sister, who went to Chapin and was sort of wise beyond her years about Alex's behavioral problems. It was all very Holden and Phoebe Caulfield.

Alex's *chosen* family were his friends, a crew of New Yorkers who went out five nights a week, wore Ralph Lauren Polo, and listened to Wu-Tang.

There was Josh—whom everyone called the Fat Jew—who rocked gold chains and an Afro and lived in a Riverside Drive triplex; SAME, who'd steal thousand-dollar cashmere sweaters from rich girls' dads' closets just to spray-paint his tag on them; Sebastian, who looked like a hunky Disney villain with his muscles and white-blond curls; Alden, a white rapper who lived with his mom. And loads more!

They were the coolest people I'd ever met, even if they weren't the nicest. I wanted to be in their in crowd so badly that I'd overlook their oft questionable behavior, like when I closed my tab at Bowery Bar and found that three hundred dollars' worth of drinks had been charged to my credit card. Besides, I was falling in love! I stopped seeing Michael; I only wanted Alex. We'd go to Cafeteria after the clubs closed and share fourteen-dollar bowls of tomato soup. His family would be away in Sun Valley or Sag Harbor or somewhere, so we'd cab uptown and curl up in his mom's clean Tempur-Pedic bed with the AC on blast. Half the time, Alex would have a fresh split lip or a black eye from fighting—blame the Dewar's—so I'd lie there watching him toss and turn in his sleep, drunk-babbling and bleeding all over the pillowcases. The sun would rise through the blinds, and I'd feel so happy.

It was hands-down the best summer of my life. Of course, nothing that good lasts. Alex and his friends were moving to San Francisco for a year in September. I knew it was coming, but still, when the day came, I cried for a week. I celebrated my twentieth birthday at Lotus with a gaggle of FIT coke sluts on September 10, but I was so depressed. I'd finally had a crew to go out with, and now everybody was gone.

I was still feeling low as I began my sophomore year (my acting school credits had transferred) at Eugene Lang College on West Eleventh Street. It was a good program and I wanted to care, but no matter how much Adderall I took, I couldn't focus. I thought of how motivated I'd been to make straight As just a few years ago. Had that really been me? Now I stared out the window every class, if I showed up at all. I didn't make friends. I didn't declare a major. I had no idea what I was interested in or what I was ever gonna do with my life besides party.

Chapter Six

HAVE YOU EVER SLEPT FIFTEEN HOURS and woken up looking like a trash can? Well, that was every late afternoon in the fall of 2002. I'd open my eyes in the dark. Nothing is more dismal! I'd moved to East Fifth Street, just around the corner from my favorite bar, Lit, where you could literally drink vodka-grapefruits in a cave. The first-floor railroad apartment that I shared with an alcoholic musician was just as grimy, with dry dog food all over the kitchen floor, but I was so strung out all of the time that I didn't even notice.

"I think I have seasonal affective disorder," I cried to my mom. She ordered me a light box. It looked sort of like a wee microwave, and I'd wake up hungover and stare at it for half an hour.

I was gorging on speed, but it wasn't making me perky anymore. I'd get a manicure on Second Avenue and my hands would be shaking as the lady tried to paint the polish on. Plus, they'd be, like, blue; the blood wasn't circulating right or something. And sometimes my *chest* would feel mad tight. But the worst amphetamine-abuse "side effect" was my short, ratty, uneven hair. I'd cut it myself—just hacked it off with the same orange kitchen scissors I'd used to shred all those dresses. My hair had been down to my elbows; now it was up by my ears, with feathery, too-thin Tonya Harding bangs. Oh, it was criminal what I did to myself! Adderall and scissors do *not* mix. You should only be allowed to have one or the other at home. Never both.

Alex and I were still in love, but San Francisco was so far away. I started seeing Male Model Michael again—that is, as much as anyone *could* see Male Model Michael. He'd by then lost his apartment and was holed up at *the* premier Dewey decimal system–themed hotel in New York City (fine, there is only one): the Library on Madison Avenue. Each room had a theme. Michael's was full of books on alchemy and black magic—Aleister Crowley and all that. The demonic arts. It was fitting, because he opened the door that first night looking like a fucking bat out of hell.

"What did you do to your *hair*?" he greeted me.

Michael wasn't exactly looking photo shoot–fresh himself. He'd lost fifteen pounds and his fingernails were dirty. His hair was *plastered* down to his head, and his skin didn't glow like he was part Cherokee anymore. He was wearing a tank top and I could smell his BO. There were empty wine bottles and room service trays all over the place. He'd clearly stopped letting the maids in. Credit and ID cards from Michael's wallet were on a plate on the coffee table. Lavender drug baggies had been ripped open and licked clean. It was a total nightmare! I moved right in.

I hid out with Michael at the Library for a while, coming and going. Every morning I'd put on the same dingy white velour Juicy Couture sweatsuit, grab complimentary coffee in the lobby, and taxi downtown for class. Then I'd come back. Michael barely ever left the suite. The hotel employees had started banging on the door; his parents were after him. He was maxing out their credit cards because he'd run out of cash, and he owed money to dealers. Things were really closing in on him. Once in a while we'd go to the Poetry Garden on the fourteenth floor and hook up next to a heating lamp, but eventually Michael became too paranoid for sex. It happens.

My own life wasn't any better in the East Village. If I was home, I was bingeing—in bed, and late into the night. After I purged, I'd take Ambien—sometimes this was the only way to make myself stop—and pass out surrounded by Cap'n Crunch boxes and pizza crusts and half-empty packages of Double Stuf Oreos. Garbage would be on the bed, on the sofa, and on the floor.

One night not one, not two, but three mice—a *gang*—pushed through the crack of the French doors into my bedroom, then scattered.

"AAAAAAUGHHHH," I screamed. "AUGGGH!"

Bulimia attracts mice: *fact*. My roommate helped me move my mattress to a loft space meant for storage. I was always banging my head on the ceiling, but at least it was ten feet off the ground. I spent Thanksgiving alone up there that year, hunched over a turkey dinner in a Styrofoam container from the Moonlight Diner on Second Avenue. When I was finished eating, I climbed down the ladder and threw up all of the stuffing and cranberry sauce and potatoes and gravy and pumpkin pie. It was an awful thing to do with holiday food.

Alex came home for Christmas, and we spent a week in bed at the Hudson Hotel, doing coke and ordering room service. He even asked me to marry him—and got down on one knee with a diamond ring! I was thrilled. There was only one thing to do: drop out of college. What?! Getting engaged is very serious. I *had* to move to San Francisco to be with my fiancé.

My dad was furious, of course. Not only did he cut me off financially, he stopped writing my Adderall prescriptions—which meant when I ran out of what I had, I'd be sans stimulants for the first time in five years.

Whatever, I thought. I mean, I was a *teensy* bit worried, but I was in love with Alex and that was better than ADHD medication, right? Besides, right before I left, I found a trash bag full of drugs in Mimi's guest room closet. The prescriptions belonged to her best friend's daughter

Sally, a bipolar hermit who received disability checks from the government. Sally lived across the street from my grandmother in her parents' basement, where she chain-smoked and popped pills all day. I guess her mom had gotten fed up, confiscated them all, and brought them over to Mimi's in the garbage bag for safekeeping.

I'd known poor Sally my whole life. Still, when I found this stash, I robbed her blind. There were at least fifty bottles; about half were narcotics: benzos like Klonopin and Valium, and a few painkillers. That's what I took—the "fun" stuff. I left the mood stabilizers and antidepressants.

A few days later, I was on a plane heading to sunny, gorgeous Northern California! Life was about to be beautiful again. I could tell.

Someday I will write at length about the surreal half-year that I lived with Alex, SAME, the Fat Jew, Alden, and Sebastian in a Mission District minimansion—but we have a lot of life-murdering to get to. So for now, all you need to know is that after my Adderall ran out in February, I spent four months in bed. The crash was death! It felt like I had mono or something. I was *so* beat. I started taking the tranquilizers I'd stolen to get through it, and that made everything worse.

Alex would come home from the clubs and find me facedown on our mattress. He'd drag me out and try to stand me up, but my legs were like jelly, and I'd fall to the floor of our bedroom.

"Cat!" He'd slap me across the face. "CAT!"

In June, the boys were evicted from the house on Guerrero Street (again, stories for another time) and we all flew back to New York. Alex and I found a one-bedroom sublet on Grand Street on the Lower East Side. I still wore my ring, but we never talked about getting married anymore. San Francisco had not been good for us. We got in vicious fights and went to bed angry all the time. One morning he woke me up by splashing a glass of ice water in my face—and not even to raise awareness for ALS or anything! Just to be a dick.

Despite this, I was feeling so much better. The trash bag pills were all gone, I was all set to reenroll at Lang in September, and—most crucially—I was back on Adderall (my dad had relented when I told him I was going back to school). Now I needed a summer job.

Leave it to Alex, who knew everyone, to hook it up. His friend Jessica was the daughter of the French socialite and *Vanity Fair* fashion director Anne McNally. Jessica got us a gig in the fashion closet. It paid eighty dollars a day, and it was easy work: steaming clothes, printing out messenger forms, wheeling the racks down to the messenger center. That sort of thing. It was laid-back—the radio was always on—and Alex and I took long lunches out in Bryant Park. On the way back to the closet, we'd pass the editor in chief, Graydon Carter, with his signature swoopy haircut and beautiful suits in the corridor. So cool!

Vanity Fair was a Condé Nast publication. It was on the twelfth floor of the iconic publishing company's headquarters in midtown Manhattan. I loved being at 4 Times Square. The lobby was cavernous and busy as a beehive, with a Hudson News stand stocked with exotic foreign fashion titles, electronic *whoosh*ing gates, a messenger center, and an army of security operatives. The famous elevators (I'm hardly the first to write about them) were packed with editors from the *New Yorker*, *Vogue*, *Teen Vogue*, *Glamour*, *GQ*, *Details*, *Bon Appetit*, *Allure*, *Condé Nast Traveler*, *Domino*, *Wired*, *Self*, *House & Garden*, and *Architectural Digest*, and I'd take great care to steer the wheels of my unwieldy, garment bag–laden carts away from all these people's sexy toes.

Alex got bored of the fashion closet after a month and stopped coming in with me, but I stayed on all summer. Being at Condé Nast made me feel as electric and neon as all of the billboards and flashing lights outside the floor-to-ceiling windows. It was better than a nightclub! I never wanted to leave.

In September 2003, I reenrolled at Eugene Lang College. The *Vanity Fair* gig was over, but I'd been bitten by the magazine bug. I just *had* to get a job at another one. But how?

Then an opportunity fell in my lap. Alex had a friend named Heather. She showed up to my birthday at Suede on September 10 with a gift bag full of products: Dior bronzer, Too Faced mascara, Clarins eye cream . . .

"I can't accept all this!" I said, gladly accepting all of it.

"It's nothing." Heather shrugged. "I get them free at my new job." She told me she was an assistant at *Nylon*.

"I love *Nylon*!" I said. I really did. Back then, it was *the* street-style Bible—full of photographs of baby-faced, Garbage Pail Kid–glam "It" girls (think Cory Kennedy—a future cover star) lurking by chain-link fences in Studio City vacant lots and coquettishly chewing on locks of their own stringy-on-purpose ombre peach-dyed hair. It was very young, very downtown, and—of course—very appealing to *moi*, age twenty-one.

"Our beauty editor Charlotte needs an intern," Heather said.

"But I don't know anything about beauty," I said.

"You're a girl, aren't you?" Heather said.

A week later I was sitting on a bench at *Nylon* headquarters in Soho, clutching my résumé, waiting for the mysterious Charlotte. The office was a loft on West Broadway above the Patricia Field boutique. It was *all* very hip. Hole's "Celebrity Skin" was playing on the stereo, and instead of desks, there were big wooden butcher blocks. A wrinkly dog was wandering around—I mean, a *really* wrinkly dog. It should be illegal for a dog to be that wrinkly! It was the kind that Patrick Bateman slices open in *American Psycho*. A shar-pei. Another one was . . . *splayed* out on the floor by the Xerox machine. Everyone was stepping over it to get to the bathroom.

"Cat?" someone said. It was Charlotte. She was tall, with light blue eyes and lanky, white-blond hair. We went into the conference room and sat down. Surely I was gawking. When Charlotte crossed her long, bare legs, I glimpsed the bright red soles of her nude patent-leather pumps. I'd only seen shoes like that once before—in the Condé Nast building.

I'd never met a beauty editor before, and I'd expected an ice queen with a perfect blowout, perfect nails, and perfect makeup. But Charlotte's cream eye shadow looked like it'd been smeared on with her fingers, and her hair was in a messy topknot—with a lip liner stuck in the middle to hold it in place! And Charlotte wasn't scary at all. She was bubbly and scattered, and she even talked like my favorite actress, Drew Barrymore. We liked each other right away. I got the internship.

The shar-peis, long since dead, belonged to the spiky-haired editor in chief, Marvin Scott Jarrett, and his wife, Jaclynn, who was also the publisher. She'd sweep in like she owned the place (which she basically did), wearing full-length fur coats. The couple had a loft full of sixties mod furniture a few blocks away, but it was being renovated. In the meantime, they were staying in a suite at the Tribeca Grand. It was Heather's job to walk the dogs from the hotel to the office and back again. One time I saw them dragging her down West Broadway through the rain! The wind had turned her umbrella inside out. Still, I thought Heather had the greatest job ever. Being an assistant to an editor in chief at a fashion magazine meant access. Heather went to the best parties. She had half of downtown New York in her flip phone and a comp card at Bumble and bumble. What more could you want?

Everybody was glamorous, but no one compared to Charlotte. Her parents were British, but she'd grown up on the Upper East Side and gone to Sacred Heart just like Paris Hilton. Now she lived in a loft duplex on Mercer Street. I loved going over there. The fridge was full of Moët & Chandon rosé, and rock-star girlfriend and groupie memoirs (*Faithfull*, *I'm with the Band*, etc.) were stacked everywhere. Her closet overflowed with vintage clothes; she was always draping me in sequined scarves and things. If I liked anything, Charlotte would try to give it to me. She was so generous.

I'd never met anyone like her. Charlotte had a pedigree and a half, but she never talked about it. And I probably shouldn't either. But omigod I have to. It's so good. Her father had been the Rolling Stones' tour manager in the seventies; he'd also booked the plane that crashed and killed Lynyrd Skynyrd. Her stepfather was Elia Kazan, the Academy Award–winning director of *A Streetcar Named Desire*. I found all this out—from other people—years after I met Charlotte. She was classy with a capital *C*! If *I'd* had that family tree, I'd *never* shut up about it. And I'd probably have a reality show.

Charlotte was a mess in the most appealing way possible. She had no legitimate office supplies; instead, her desk was swamped with Bobbi Brown concealer compacts, Tocca roller-ball perfumes, Malin+Goetz peppermint shampoos, Santa Maria Novella baby perfumes for chic Italian toddlers, and L'Occitane almond oils, which my mentor liked to absentmindedly slather all over her lovely neck and arms. Her pencil cups were stuffed with eyeliner pencils and Lancôme Juicy Tubes. A Leaning Tower of Pisa–like stack of press releases teetered behind the computer monitor. Every beauty brand had a team of publicists trying to get their shit into the magazine, so the bags of products never stopped. *Clunk.* A messenger would plop 'em down three, four, five times a day. Charlotte couldn't keep up.

It's a good thing her intern was on amphetamines, right? One morning when I had nothing to do—Char wasn't in yet—I popped two Addys and went to town. I threw away old coffee cups from Café Café on Greene Street and aligned all of the papers and taxi receipts and Labello lip balms and Claus Porto hand soaps and Oliver Peoples sunglasses and random gift certificates to the Culinary Institute.

My "supervisor" finally fluttered into the office in a cloud of Narciso Rodriguez for Her fragrance oil and a silk polka-dot Agnès B. baby doll dress. It was noon, but no one cared. Everybody loved Charlotte.

She was *thrilled* with her new workspace.

"Omigodddd," she gasped. "Babe, this is *amazing*." From then on, she always asked me to "do . . . that *magic* thing you do to my desk." She was sweet as a sugar scrub—easy to please.

Not everyone was so nice.

"CAN YOU NOT *HOVER* OVER MY FUCKING DESK?" roared the fashion director—who sat next to Charlotte—one day. She was even louder than the new Kelly Osbourne single cranking on the office sound system. Everyone turned and stared. Oh, I just wanted to melt down like a Diptyque candle and die! Charlotte still talks about it.

Internships: they are full of awkward moments, and uncomfortable initiation rituals! For example: Charlotte used to leave me lists of products to "call in" for stories. Like:

Biologique Recherche P50
Yves Saint Laurent Touche Éclat
Givenchy Le Prisme Yeux Quatuor—smoky?
Kérastase Bain Satin leave-in
Chantecaille blush in Emotion

Easy enough, right? No. I didn't know how to pronounce *any-thing*—and I didn't use e-mail at *Nylon*, just the phone on Charlotte's desk. So everyone in the office could hear me screw up.

"PR," someone would answer.

"Hi, um, this is Cat from *Nylon*," I'd mumble. "Can I speak to someone from . . . *yevs* . . . *saint lorent*?"

Pause.

"You can talk to me about YSL," the publicist would say.

"I need to call in a . . . *tush-ayee-clat*."

"A what?"

KILL ME, I'd think.

"A . . . *touchy clay*?" I'd say, eyeing the mean fashion editor one butcher block over. The office was dead quiet

"What?" the publicist would say. "I can't understand you."

"I'll spell it," I'd whisper desperately.

"Can you put it in an e-mail?"

"Actually—" I'd start.

Click.

It was brutal. Years later, when I had my own cute beauty interns, I wrote out anything tricky for them on Post-its. (*SHU UEMURA = SHOO-YOO-MORA.*)

My first fashion week, in February 2004, was even worse. Charlotte had asked me to go backstage at Proenza Schouler and ask the models about their must-have beauty products. I'd never heard of this Proenza woman, but I was amped to report to the white tents in Bryant Park. Fun!

Backstage was loud and crowded with publicists on headsets, stylists, photographers, garment racks, and a craft services table loaded with crudités and chicken skewers. Models were slouched in rows of directors' chairs, reading or staring off into the void. They were chic and intimidating with their spaghetti legs and blank eyes.

I approached my first victim, clutching a pen and notepad like an old-timey reporter. She was in street clothes—a destroyed T-shirt and black leather skinny jeans—and getting her hair done by a female stylist.

"Excuse me," I said. "Hi, I'm writing a story for *Nylon.* Would you mind answering some questions for the magazine?"

The model stared at me.

"Okay," she finally said.

"Oh, fantastic," I said. "Uh, okay, so I was wondering . . . what beauty products do you use in your . . . your regular life? Or something you can't live without when you travel?"

"You're in my way," the hairstylist said sharply.

"Sorry." I stepped back. "Like, is there a makeup item you like?" Silence. "Or a hair product, or a skin-care product . . . ?"

The model sighed.

"I like . . . the blue cleanser . . . you know . . . " she said. She had an Eastern European accent. "For taking my makeup off."

"Oh, great!" I babbled, scribbling madly. "*Blue . . . cleanser . . . for . . . taking . . . makeup . . . off.* Got it! Do you remember the brand?"

"No."

"Oh," I said. "Okay." I stood there for a moment. "Was it, like, Kiehl's, or—"

"*Still* in my way!" The stylist got in front of me again.

"Um. Was it like a blue *gel*, or just in a blue *bottle*, or—"

"I don't know."

"Okay," I said. "That's okay!" The model turned toward the mirror. We were clearly done.

Except . . . oh no.

"Uh." I cleared my throat. "I'm so sorry. But could I get your name?"

The stylist shook her head. The model narrowed her eyes.

"*Sashjakjadha Rakdfnfsbuipi,*" the model said.

Fuck.

"One more time?" I squeaked.

The model repeated her name.

"Could you spell that?" I said. "I am sorry. I am so sorry."

The stylist lost it.

"GET OUT OF HERE!" she screamed. Neighboring stylists and models looked up. I skedaddled, all right—right out of the tents.

Pretty bad, don't you think? But my first-ever beauty event was worse. It was a sit-down dinner for the launch of a high fashion house's signature fragrance. Charlotte sent me in her place at the last minute.

"This isn't really an event for interns," the publicist huffed. But she led me to a seat anyway. The dinner was in an industrial loft space in the Flatiron District. The white walls matched the "white notes" (whatever that meant) in the fragrance, as well as the sleek, minimalist white bottle. There were white candles, white napkins, and white orchids at every table. Even the marketing people were white! No, I'm just kidding. (Sort of.)

I sat down shyly in Charlotte's chair and snuck peeks at the place cards on either side of me: *Vogue* and *Elle*. Whoa. Beauty editor equivalents of high rollers! This dinner party was gonna be off the heezy. I couldn't wait.

I was right: it was *so* much fun. No, I am lying. Nobody spoke to me the entire four-course ordeal! Not one word. The hours *dragged* by. So I just kept tossing back (white) wine. How the hell did people get through dinner parties? It was the first time I ever sat alongside industry ballers at a fancy table and tried to will a plate of gnocchi to turn into cocaine—but it certainly wouldn't be my last.

I stayed at *Nylon* a full year. On my twenty-second birthday, on September 10, Jessica and Anne McNally—the *Vanity Fair* fashion director—took me and Alex to the Cartier Mansion on Fifth Avenue. It was a New York Fashion Week party for the "It" boy designer Zac Posen. There was a crazy-long line of people trying to get in, but the publicists practically fell all over themselves to open the velvet rope for our group. Then we waited by the door as Anne hit the red carpet and posed for the throng of paparazzi. She looked *ravishing* with her thick bangs, black jersey dress, and hefty jeweled necklace. Jessica was so lucky.

We went inside the Cartier Mansion. Right away, a waiter in a tuxedo walked by and handed me a glass of champagne off a silver tray. Hooray! I was midswig when Puff Daddy (him again!) *bumped* into me, truly; he's lucky I didn't spill on him. Right behind him was a shrimpy, coked-up-looking movie actor—I guess I won't name him—who sort of *hounded* me all night, even though I was with Alex. He tried to follow me into the bathroom! And he kept grabbing my arm and ordering me to go to Bungalow with him, and making Lothario eyes at me from across the room. Alex saw this, and—because he and I *happened* to get separated that night—he and the Fat Jew still to this day say I slept with the movie star. So I'd like to state once and for all that I did *not* have sex with him!

Anyway. Why am I blathering about these guys? There were *real* celebrities at this party whom I should be telling you about. I was thrilled to find myself smoking Parliament Lights outside with Alex, Jessica, and her friend Bee Shaffer—Anna Wintour's daughter. Young Bee had recently helped her mom launch *Teen Vogue*, the digest-size monthly that everyone in fashion and publishing was gaga for. Bee was so nice—personable and giggly—plus very cute with her shiny brown hair and her head-to-toe blue tie-dyed Zac Posen ensemble and her ciggie. (I just love a teen smoker—don't you?)

We went back inside and joined Jessica's mother, who was deep in conversation with Bee's mother, Anna. Then we were all standing there in a group: Anna Wintour, Anne and Jessica McNally, Bee Shaffer, Alex and me.

"Having a good birthday?" Alex said under his breath. I nodded dumbly. I'd only been talking his ear off about magazines for an entire year; that's why he'd brought me to this party. (Best. Boyfriend. *Ever*.) I couldn't believe I was in the same orbit with these people!

I tried not to stare, but it was hard. The editor in chief of *Vogue* was literally two feet away. I could smell her Chanel No. 5. I snuck peeks at her tennis arms, at her immaculate blowout. She was so perfect. Anne McNally was, too. I felt like a crusty gutter punk standing next to the two of them with my grown-out Adderall haircut, beat-up strappy sandals, and dumb denim Fendi baguette full of Dentyne Ice and broken cigarettes. Anne and Anna were so . . . *together*. I couldn't imagine either of them getting hammered, much less addicted to anything. They were too successful—and creative and beautiful and smart and powerful. I wondered how you became a woman like that.

Chapter Seven

THE FALL OF 2004 WAS THE beginning of an infamously obnoxious era of New York City nightlife—so you just know I *had* to be there. Clubs had started cluttering far West Chelsea, north of all the art galleries. This followed the popularity of Bungalow 8, with its palm trees and striped booths where you'd see Prince sitting all alone like a weirdo. Drunk *America's Next Top Model* contestants were always falling through coffee tables; an MTV star would be rubbing his dick up on you at the bar . . . and you wouldn't know if it was on purpose. *Anyway*, then this huge place Marquee opened around the corner on Tenth Avenue; it had two stories and a fab clear staircase. That's where Alex and I were all of the time.

And after Marquee, *another* zillion clubs popped up. Within a few years, the whole area was nuts! It would be so gridlocked on West Twenty-Eighth Street at three o'clock on a Monday morning that the drunk girls trotting in high heels and miniskirts outside your window would be making better time than your taxi. There would be an Escalade not moving in front of you, and your cabdriver would snarl something and lean on his horn, and the drivers in the taxis behind you would lean on *their* horns, and finally teenage, bright orange Lindsay Lohan—these were the salad days of her reign of terror—would jump out of the SUV and dash into the club. *Then* traffic would finally move. And this was, like, every night.

Alex and I had both moved uptown, but we weren't living together. My new place—an airy sixteenth-floor studio in a high-rise called the Colorado on East Eighty-Sixth Street—was pretty dope. You could see half of the Upper East Side from my windows. And the tops of the trees in Central Park, which was a few blocks away. Alex's apartment was nearby, too—he was on East Seventy-Fifth Street—but we weren't getting along. We suspected each other of cheating when we were apart (I *was* doing him dirty, truth be told), and when we were together, we were constantly up in each other's phones.

Things usually got stormy around five in the morning, after we'd returned from the club.

"EEEEEEYYOOWWWWWNAUUGRHH!" I'd wail, smashing a plate over my boyfriend's head. Then *SMASH! SMASH! SMASH!* I'd throw all his plates to the kitchen floor, one after another.

Other early mornings, I'd come over when he wasn't answering his phone and find him passed out on the sofa after a night out. I'd try to shake him awake, and when he wouldn't come to, I'd just slap him in the face—over and over! *Hard!*

"WAKE UP!" *Slap. Slap.* "*Asshole!*" His friends would just gawk.

Alex was no saint. *His* favorite move was to snatch my flip phone and snap it in half. Omigod, it used to drive me *crazy*. I'd replace it and then a week later, he'd grab *that* phone out of my hand during another brawl and throw it out the window! I'd run out onto East Seventy-Fifth Street half-dressed and howling. I'd be barefoot, sobbing, and digging through the trash when the cops arrived, which they did every other week.

Alex's neighbors hated us. They started petitioning to have him thrown out of the building! Someone even posted a sign in the lobby that was all, "THE TENANT IN 4B BEATS WOMEN."

When we weren't throwing down, our relationship was boring. Alex was selling weed out of his apartment, so the buzzer was constantly ringing; he could never go anywhere. I'd sit with him and his friends while they watched Yankees games or *The Sopranos*, but I couldn't engage with them *or* what was on the screen. Have you ever taken a lot of speed? You literally cannot watch TV! It's very weird. Instead, I'd be all tweaky and in the corner, reading the *New York Post*.

"Ha-ha," I'd say when someone told a funny story—which is different from laughing. The meds were flattening me right out.

That's what happens when you double your doses. Oh yes! Unbeknownst to my boyfriend, our toxic relationship wasn't entirely to blame for my recent behavior—for the detachment, for the paranoia, for the aggression. I was cranked!

I had a new psychiatrist. In New York, doctors put their names on plaques outside their buildings, and I passed Dr. M.'s like sixteen times a day. It was on my block. Eventually, one afternoon, I gave him a ring. A receptionist answered; she sounded about eighty thousand years old. I told her I was looking for a shrink, since mine had "recently retired." (Uh-huh.)

"Do you have insurance?" she asked. I wasn't sure, so I called my mom. I *did* have insurance—through my college. Then I called the doctor's office back. I would be covered for the appointment! The receptionist squeezed me in.

I showed up a week later dressed to impress. I'd never tried to score pills from a stranger before. Would it be hard? Dr. M. was ancient, too.

"I've been taking eighty milligrams of Adderall every day for five years," I told him on my first visit. "And Ambien to sleep." It wasn't technically a lie; I just didn't mention that Dr. Dad was already sending me these medications from out of state.

"Okay," Dr. M. said, writing the scripts.

Then I went to Rite Aid across the street to fill 'em up. I sat and read tabloids until they called my name. The grand total was . . .

"Two dollars," the cashier said. I practically skipped away from the pharmacy counter. As soon as I hit the escalator I popped an Addy like a Mentos. Health insurance was like magic! I couldn't believe I hadn't known about it before.

After a year at *Nylon*, I was ready for another magazine—and I knew just where I wanted to go: *Teen Vogue*. I even had an in: the beauty director, Kara Jesella, had been the beauty editor at *Nylon* before Charlotte, and they were good friends. Plus, Kara's assistant Holly had just graduated from Eugene Lang. Charlotte helped me score an interview, and I got the internship! I'd be there two full days a week: Tuesday and Thursday, from ten to about six. Once again, I'd get school credit—which meant I didn't have to go to *actual* college classes as much. Fantastic.

Teen Vogue! I was psyched but also a teensy bit terrified. It was a *real* fashion title—under the editorial umbrella of Anna Wintour. The digest-size monthly was full of wealthy girls posed on Marimekko-print beanbag chairs in their Park Avenue bedrooms, explaining how they accessorized their Spence uniforms with Chanel barrettes and Delman flats. I was more of an accessorize-your-Juicy-Couture-sweatsuit-with-cigarette-burns kind of slag. What was I going to wear? I stood in my closet, despairing: I had approximately nine thousand pairs of "Thong Song"–era Frankie B. low-rider jeans, five ratty split-seam rabbit fur jackets, and enough miniskirts to dress a THOT army, but nothing for *Teen Vogue*. The vintage rock T-shirts I'd spent a fortune on to fit in at *Nylon* weren't going to fly, either. *Argh.*

Secondhand stores! They're fantastic in New York City, particularly on the Upper East Side. I could find whatever I wanted, especially since I was twenty-two and absurdly skinny (everyone consigns stuff they can't fit into anymore). The secret to finding gems is to take as much prescription speed as humanly possible: this way, you won't get tired as you plow through the racks. I spent days at INA, Tokio 7, and Michael's on Madison Avenue, hunting for the designers I saw in the magazine. In the end, I bought Cacharel blouses with Peter Pan collars, Miu Miu smock dresses, Marc Jacobs Mary Janes, and a Hussein Chalayan skirt for a fraction of what they'd cost new. I thought it was all ugly as fuck, but hey, that's high fashion, right? Blame Miuccia Prada.

Unsexy, disgusting outfits in place, I was finally ready for my first day. Wasn't I? Not really. I was a nervous wreck that morning! I messed up my "minimal" makeup twice. My liquid eyeliner had to be subtle and on *point*, but I just could not get it perfect—and it *had* to be perfect. Perfect perfect perfect! I mean, this was *Teen Vogue*.

When I left the Colorado, it was nine thirty, and I was supposed to be at Condé at ten. *And* it was raining. I hustled to the train as best I could in my new velvet Marc Jacobs pumps and a brown Prada pencil skirt. When I finally got underground, I saw that the entire Eighty-Sixth Street 4/5/6 station at Lexington Avenue was flooded. *Really* flooded. *Mammoth* puddles. I could no more leap over this mess in my tiny, tight skirt than I could have levitated over it à la David Blaine.

WHY?! I screamed to God, not unlike Russell Crowe in Darren Aronofsky's *Noah* (a film I was forced to watch—incidentally—at my most recent rehab).

God-fucking-dammit. I tried to tiptoe through the shallowest bits, and my shoes got soaked through and stained with swampy subway-station water. It was horrible! The situation on the other side of the puddles was even worse. The platform was a mob scene. Which meant that the trains were all screwed up. Everyone was peering into the tunnel, tsk-tsking. The minutes ticked by.

AUUUUUUUUGGGHHH, I stood there screaming inside my head.

When the subway finally arrived, it was nine fifty-five. Everyone *jammed* on it like we were in Tokyo or something. And then the train kept stopping in the tunnel. I hadn't eaten since the afternoon before—amphetamine, honey—and there was hardly *any* oxygen in there. After a few minutes, I was panting like a pervert on a creepy phone call. Then I was seeing . . . black . . . spots . . .

"Are you okay?" the woman pressed up next to me said.

"*No*," I rasped as I collapsed. The train car was so packed that I couldn't even fall! I just crumpled in the knees.

"LET HER SIT!" a man shouted. Someone cleared a seat for me, and I put my head between my knees.

When I finally got to *Teen Vogue*, it was ten forty-five. I was nearly an hour late, with ruined shoes—and practically berserk.

I greeted Holly, the beauty assistant, like I'd just run her dog over with a car.

"I'm *so* sorry," I said. "Omigod. I am so sorry. I'm so sorry. I'm *so* sorry. I'm—"

She cut me off.

"Relax," Holly said. She was born and raised in Brooklyn, and had freckles and long, golden hair. We'd go on to be real-life friends. "It's okay. Things happen." I exhaled. The lesson: always eat breakfast before your first day at your dream job, Adderall girls. And wear shitty flats when you commute.

Teen Vogue was *quiet*. As I've already said, it was an intense environment dictated by the cult of Anna Wintour. Even though *Vogue* was three floors up, her presence loomed. In the beauty department, we didn't even talk among ourselves: everything went through AOL Instant Messenger. Well, almost everything.

"You guys have to do better!" This would be the beauty director, Kara, bitching out Holly and Fiorella—the associate beauty editor. Her voice would carry through the gray-carpeted office. "I don't know what else to tell you!"

Someday I'm *gonna be in a meeting like that*, I'd think dreamily. Fi and Holly would emerge looking sheepish. I never knew what they'd done wrong.

But most of the time, you could hear a mascara drop (literally—they were always rolling off our desks). Kara would instant-message Holly her breakfast order at quarter past ten—fashion magazines start the day at ten, not nine—and Holly would IM *me* at my intern desk, and I'd grab Kara's dining card and zoom down to the fourth floor. Or I guess I couldn't really "zoom" anywhere in my stupid secondhand YSL wedges. It was more like I clip-clopped. *Clip-clop clip-clop clip-clop. That* is the sound of interning!

If I was lucky, there would be someone interesting in the Frank Gehry–designed cafeteria, like Si Newhouse, who owned Condé Nast. He was short and old and *really* cute; he always rocked a gray sweatshirt over a neon-yellow polo. He'd be slowly helping himself to things at the fruit salad bar. I'd grab Kara's smoothie and two turkey sausage links. Then *clip-clop clip-clop clip-clop.* I'd hustle back upstairs and deliver her food. Service with a smile.

"Thanks!" Kara would say.

"Of course," I'd answer. Then I'd go right back to my desk. Holly would have forwarded me ten call-ins. I'd stay busy all day.

It felt great to be back at Condé and around all the exotic birds I'd admired since *Vanity Fair*. I was particularly impressed with Jane Keltner, the beautiful young fashion director, who wore five-inch stiletto black patent leather Louboutins. People said she was going to be an editor in chief someday. And then, of course, there was the *actual* editor in chief, Amy Astley, who was blond and willowy—a former ballerina. She'd been the beauty director of *Vogue* when Anna handpicked her to helm *Teen Vogue*. And Kara was great, too. She was a *real* writer, and an academic feminist. She'd gone to Vassar and had a reputation as a "smart" beauty editor. ("She's, like, *really* smart," Charlotte had told me.) Sometimes I got to sit in on story meetings in Kara's office. She had funny convictions about beauty products. (All beauty directors do—but I didn't know that yet.)

"Eye shadow?" she'd exclaim, when Holly pitched an item. "Nobody wears eye shadow! I don't know one *person* who wears eye shadow!" I was the eye shadow queen in my nightlife drag, of course, but I wasn't about to argue.

But no one, of course, compared to Anna. She was always around. *AW is on the floor!* Holly would IM me warnings. I never knew exactly what to do with this information, except to shut up even more than usual and look alive. Then, sure enough, Anna would stroll by with Amy. She'd look at everyone—including me—with this curious laser stare. She was *not* afraid of making eye contact. A true queen. I practically want to get up from my computer and genuflect on my sheepskin rug just typing her name over and over. What a woman!

Incidentally, my internship coincided with the impending release of *Front Row*, the "scrupulously researched investigative biography" of Anna by Jerry Oppenheimer. (Other Oppenheimer tomes: *House of Hilton: From Conrad to Paris* and *Martha Stewart: Just Desserts*.) It was a huge deal: everyone at *Teen Vogue* was *obsessed* with "the book that has no name"—as Kara called it—even though it hadn't come out yet. When it did, we all dished (over AIM), mostly about the allegations that she'd had a love affair with Bob Marley! Do you die? Swag on, Anna.

I spent the semester doing standard beauty intern stuff: calling in products, e-mailing publicists for press releases. Printing them out. I had my own Condé Nast e-mail address, so I didn't need to worry about mispronouncing things over the telephone anymore. (Not that I would have—by then, I was practically fluent in *beauté*.)

When I wasn't at my desk, I was in the beauty closet. It was small—and dangerous! No, it really was. Things are already *always* clattering down on your head when you're a beauty intern, and the closet situation at *Teen Vogue* was particularly precarious, with wonky, off-kilter shelves. One time a bottle of Thierry Mugler Angel nearly gave me a black eye. The footstool I used to reach everything was a joke—it had *wheels*—I was always flying off it. But who cared? There were heaps of intriguing items to play with. *Teen Vogue* got way better stuff than

Nylon. I hung out in there secretly testing things—with mixed results. Let's just say that there's a reason that the Lancôme "freckle pencil" is no longer on the market today.

Being a good intern was easy. I wrote down instructions, and I always had a pleasant smile frozen on my face. It was like being in an improv workshop at acting school: I just kept saying *yes, yes, yes.* If I said no even once, then game over—or so I imagined. I never said no, so I didn't get a chance to find out!

There was nothing that I wouldn't agree—cheerfully—to do. For example: do you know what a "beauty sale" is? Well, neither did I when Holly first asked me to do one.

"No problem!" I said.

I had no idea what I was in for. Most magazines host beauty sales a few times a year, and everyone is allowed in: receptionists, messengers—even the cashiers from the cafeteria. If you can ever get into one, go! They're the best sample sales in town. The beauty closet essentially gets emptied out and moved to a conference room, and every item costs only a dollar. Then the money is donated to a charity like Dress for Success. Everybody wins!

Well, except the beauty intern in charge of the whole thing. It was *tons* of work. I spent all morning lugging overflowing mail bins—full of T3 blow-dryers, Aveda salt scrubs, John Varvatos cologne, you name it—from the beauty closet to the conference room. I was wearing another dumb pencil skirt and high heels, so every step was a baby step. Ridiculous. I was already exhausted as I spread out products—OPI nail polishes, Too Faced mascaras, Ted Gibson flat irons, the Body Shop foot creams—on every surface of the conference room. Women circled, studying my progress.

"Hey, sweetie." A fashion market editor stuck her head in. "When do you think it's going to start?" Staffers who hadn't given me a nod hello in four months were suddenly sweet as *sizzurp.*

Then I opened the floodgates. Like a zillion people came!

"Fifty-four, fifty-five, fifty-six, fifty-seven . . ." I tallied their bags of

one-dollar beauty products for six hours straight. By early evening, I
wanted to stick a gun in my mouth, but I had a manila envelope stuffed
with cash for Holly. Hopefully she wouldn't notice my trembling hands.
I'd been taking triple Adderall all day. Could you blame me?

Another morning, Holly asked me to go to West Chelsea to pick
up four dozen cupcakes for a staffer's birthday party. Yes, Billy's Bakery
could have easily messengered the order to 4 Times Square. Yes, Holly
could have given me cab fare or sent me in a town car. But I'm glad she
didn't. The whole point of having interns is to haze them and make
them fucking *earn* their future careers! High five, Holly. She didn't even
offer me a MetroCard.

It was November. I took the subway in four-inch heels, the only
shoes I had at work that day. It was frigid and blustery over on Tenth
Avenue, by the Hudson River. My legs were bare. The wind was blowing my hair all around and making it stick to my Dior Addict lip gloss.
Clip-clop, clip-clop. Always with the clip-clopping! I was like a show
pony.

The dude at Billy's came out with the order. The cupcakes were
in big, oblong boxes. I could barely carry them. And they were *heavy*.
These stupid bakeries just *load* on the frosting! *Clip-clop, clip-clop.* I was
staggering down Tenth Avenue with these plastic bags and huge boxes
of cupcakes. I didn't have gloves on, and my knuckles were chapped,
and my hands hurt from carrying the bags. I was zigzagging on the
sidewalk; I couldn't walk a straight line in the wind. It was just miserable—like, Leonardo DiCaprio–filming–*The Revenant* miserable. I was
very privileged, and *very* cold.

When I got back to the office I set the cupcakes in the art department, along with plates, napkins, and quarts of milk from the kitchen.
Then I sat and shivered at my desk. Holly sent out a mass e-mail, and
people from all over the office got up to go to the party.

I stayed at my desk for twenty minutes until Holly returned.

"Why are you sitting here?" she asked.

"Uh," I said. "I . . . Were interns invited?" Holly laughed at me

---

"Get a cupcake!" she said.

I went to the party. No one seemed to mind that I was there. A fashion editor even smiled at me. I selected a vanilla-vanilla and ate it standing up next to the art director's office. It was the best cupcake I ever tasted.

Alex and I broke up for good in December. I tried to feel better the same old ways: by dancing on banquettes at promoters' tables and fucking mad dudes. But it wasn't fun. Every night I'd crammed into taxis after the clubs with Alex, SAME, Alden, and Fat Jew and hit the after parties. Now I cabbed home drunk and *dolo*. I was lonely and getting lonelier.

At least I had a new hobby: doctor shopping. There were so many psychiatrists in my new neighborhood that I just *had* to try them all.

"Can I try Dexedrine?" I'd ask my new shrink. Dr. A. was an old white dude, just like Dr. M. (I was still seeing him, too). "Can I try Lunesta?" The answer was always yes. My secret? Charm! Plus, I'd grown up lying to a psychiatrist. Oh, and doctors like cash.

Back in midtown, it was my first holiday season at Condé. Everyone at *Teen Vogue* was in a jovial mood, opening the loot that arrived from PR firms and fashion houses. I helped Holly pile Kara's gifts in her office—CDG wallets, Dior bags, Fendi planners—and oohed and aahed over the less expensive stuff that arrived for Holly, like Tory Burch flats. I hadn't handled so many bottles of Dom Pérignon and Moët & Chandon since my coked-out summer at Pangaea! The guys in the messenger center were up to their husky necks; they came by nine times a day. Over time, the S.W.A.G. (Sealed With A Gift) thing became normal to me—you get numb to it—but back then, the excess was very intoxicating. It made me want to be a magazine editor even more.

My remaining time at *Teen Vogue* whizzed by. It was festive and very busy. Late one afternoon, I sat on the floor outside the editor in chief's office, helping her assistant gift-wrap bottles of champagne. It was tranquil there on my knees, with fluffy snow blanketing Times Square outside the windows on my left, and Amy Astley working quietly at her white desk in her white-carpeted office on my right. I could have stayed there Scotch-taping for years! Or at least until my Adderall ran out.

"Thanks so much for helping," amazing Amy said when she left at half past five.

"My pleasure." *My pleasure?!* I was so lame. But whatever. A Condé editor in chief had spoken to me!

That was the end of my time at *Teen Vogue*. I'd worked hard.

"Where do you want to work next?" Holly asked.

I'd been thinking about it.

"*Glamour!*"

Holly e-mailed the beauty assistant. She replied immediately: they *were* looking for someone to work in the beauty closet.

Two days later, I met with the beauty assistant. She e-mailed later that afternoon to invite me to start at *Glamour*. I'd landed another internship. Three in a row! I couldn't believe it. I'd start in the New Year.

Until then, I had a few weeks off. I was getting into some real pill-head shit, like twisting time-release capsules open to make them work faster. I'd pour the tiny, bitter sprinkles into my mouth and they'd get stuck in between my teeth. It was my first Christmas without Alex and his friends in years. But that was okay. The more amphetamine I took, the more *fun* being by myself was, actually. Speed was like magic! Lonely magic.

Chapter Eight

GLAMOUR. G-L-A-M-O-U-R! WHAT MORE COULD I WANT? The iconic women's magazine took up the entire sixteenth floor of 4 Times Square. It felt very different from *Teen Vogue* up there: instead of high-strung fashionistas in Lanvin, *Glamour* was staffed by very nice editors and assistants with shiny hair, headbands, and wedding bands. The editor in chief, Cindi Leive, wore turtlenecks under her jumpers, and everyone was very kind. No "Nuclear Wintour"—to borrow a phrase from the British press—frost anywhere.

Working there—even as a ten-dollars-an-hour "beauty freelancer," my new title—was a good look. So while *Vogue* got the most attention, it was *Glamour* that *Adweek* called Condé's "biggest cash cow." According to condenast.com, one in eight American women "engage" with *Glamour*, and the print audience is 12.2 million readers. What does this mean? Money! The higher a mag's circulation is, the more it can charge their advertisers. That's why those subscription cards are always falling into your damn lap at the nail salon.

At least that's how I *think* it all works (I'm a real know-it-all for a dope fiend with no job). What I do know for sure is that every issue was full of expensive ads for skin care, hair products, and perfumes. They ran alongside the editorial content in the beauty section, which was considered the best in the business. Felicia Milewicz ran that shit. She was born in Austria and raised in Poland, and had started her career as a lowly fashion assistant in the early seventies. Now she was considered the most powerful beauty director in publishing. When I arrived in 2005, she'd been killing it at Condé for over thirty-five years.

She was an industry legend! And I knew this because everyone kept telling me so.

"She's the Coco Chanel of beauty editors," Mary, her second in command, liked to tell me.

What did this actually mean? No idea. But Felicia sure looked the part. She rocked black tuxedo jackets with white Chanel camellias in the lapels, immaculate blouses buttoned up to the collars, eyeglasses, and red lipstick, always ("Mrs. Lauder" had personally advised her to start wearing it years ago, and she had ever since). Her signature red hair was maintained by the colorist Gad Cohen, and she wore it bobbed above her shoulders. She wore Guerlain Vol de Nuit *parfum*, and she had a wonderful, heavy accent.

She was an icon. And I could not pronounce her last name.

ME-LAY-VICH, I wrote on fifty thousand Post-it notes. It didn't help: I always panicked when I was put on the spot. This was unfortunate because I often had to sit in Felicia's assistant's chair—right outside the boss's office—and answer the phone.

"Felicia"—pause—"*Me-a-leeel-a-weave-itz*'s office," I'd mumble. It was a thousand times more painful than *Nylon*! And forget relaying messages from the fashion director Xanthipi Joannides. She's probably still waiting for Felicia to call her back.

Felicia was the last of the old-school beauty directors. I never saw her put a pen to a proof—those are oversize pages that circulate between editors—though surely she did. She oversaw the *concepts*, darling. The *vision*.

"*Peenks*," Felicia would declare grandly, waving her manicured hand in the air. "*Eet's* all about beautiful *peenks* this month." She'd be holding court at her desk in a department meeting, while everyone else—all five of us—squished on to her love seat. It was my responsibility to open the dozens of bags that arrived for Felicia every day and place the products—*neatly*—on that very midget sofa. She'd keep what interested her (not much—maybe a By Terry Baume de Rose here and there) and dump the rest into plastic bins outside of her office. I would haul that stuff into the beauty closet and file it away.

My other big Felicia-related job was getting her a piece of seven-grain toast with peanut butter and a small coffee with a "*leetle beet* of *meelk*" from the cafeteria every morning. With so much beauty director breakfast-fetching experience under my belt, you'd think I'd be awesome at this, but no.

"Cat," Felicia would call out thirty seconds after I left the toast and coffee on her desk.

I'd double back.

"Yes, Felicia?" Pleasant as a picnic basket. I knew what was coming.

"*Eet's* not hot enough," she'd say, apologetically.

"I'll get you another!" Sometimes I got her a third.

The coffee thing drove me fucking bananas for months. How could I make it hotter? I didn't want to put *the* Felicia Milewicz's cup in the *Glamour* kitchenette microwave; it was gross. I decided it would be okay to zap just the "*leetle beet*" of milk to a boil in there, then pour it in separately. It worked! Felicia was happy with her coffee. I was elated. I've said it before: interning is strange heaven.

Felicia did the hiring, and it was obvious she had a type: good girls. *Glamour's* two full-time writers, Stephanie and Tram, were pretty, supersmart, and mature. Even though they were only in their late twenties, they were both married. They spoke in quiet voices. They drank tea and pulled pashminas from their desks when they got cold. Felicia's assistant, Alix, was only twenty-six, and she was engaged. They'd all gone to *really* good colleges: Penn, Georgetown. (Incidentally, I was by this time a senior at Sleeping Pill College of Tanning Bed University— no, at Eugene Lang—and on track to receive a degree in nonfiction writing the following year.)

Slaggy prescription crackheads like *moi* were surely a *Glamour* "DON'T." I never, ever revealed my "wild side" at the office. Instead, I did my best to fit in: I started wearing red lipstick like Felicia's; I attempted tidy ballerina buns. I dressed in tangerine, polka-dot Marc by Marc knee-length skirts and Diane von Furstenberg cardigans. I even used to put Scotch tape in *X*s over my nipples in the morning so they wouldn't show if they got hard. (Try it! Especially for job interviews.) Still, I felt like a back-door teen mom in church around the women of *Glamour*. I mean, no one even swore!

Or maybe Mary did. The executive senior beauty editor was Felicia's right-hand woman; they'd been a dynamic duo since *Mademoiselle*. It was she who executed Felicia's fashionably vague ideas and made sure they turned into stories with gorgeous photographs and placement for all the latest advertiser-brand launches. Mary was different from anyone I'd worked with at Condé. She didn't wear makeup and she didn't color her hair. She wore sneakers for her rush-hour Metro-North commutes back and forth from upstate New York, where she lived with her husband and two young kids. Mary was *go-go-go* all of the time. She went to like thirty beauty events a day! Truly a force of nature. The only time I ever saw her relax was when I spotted her puffing a ciggie out on West Forty-Third Street by the town car lineup. I'd never seen a beauty editor smoke before. It was nice to know someone at *Glamour* had a vice.

Mary could be intense—it was all about the deadline, the deadline, the deadline—but her anxiety kept the trains running on time. Besides, by then I could handle anything. Mary would *burst* into the closet with a no-name foam roller she wanted to shoot for Hair Guide and I'd track down the manufacturer in Florida and get someone on the phone to confirm credit information in fifteen minutes flat. Or if an eyeliner I'd called in that morning for a how-to story hadn't arrived and Mary was bugging, I'd go down to the messenger center and personally rummage through the bags instead of waiting for them to come up. And if it still wasn't *there*, I'd run back up to *Glamour*, grab another product from the closet, bolt to Sephora in Times Square, and exchange it for the product we needed. Then I'd hurtle back up to sixteen and *careen* into Mary's office.

"Here we go!" I'd say.

"Thank God!" Mary would exclaim. "Digital studio!" And I'd *fly* back out to the elevators. Only when I'd returned—with confirmation that the eyeliner would *absolutely* be photographed that evening, so the art department would *positively* have the image for the layout tomorrow morning—could Mary relax. She'd pop her head into the closet, where I'd be fanning myself with a press release, waiting for my heart rate to go down.

"Always remember," she'd say. "This is just beauty. We're not doing open-heart surgery!"

"Right," I'd answer. Then we'd both laugh sort of nervously.

I had more Adderall than ever, so I took more than ever. My addiction was progressing, as addictions do. Stimulants made monotonous jobs bearable—and Mary *always* had a monotonous project for me. Have you heard of "the Glammies"—the magazine's beauty awards? Over eighty thousand readers snail-mailed their handwritten paper ballots in 2005. Crates full of them piled up in the conference room. And guess who sat in there with a spiral notebook tallying the results—ballot by ballot—two years in a row?

Best Drugstore Mascara: Maybelline Great Lash. Check. *Best Department Store Mascara: Lancôme Defincils*. Check. *Best*

Department Store Fragrance: Britney Spears Curious. Check.
Adderall. Check!

Mary dug my "amphetamine work ethic," if you will. She started asking me to come in additional days. Mary's "special projects" were the worst—*she* knew they were the worst; everybody did—but I never said no. In fact, I cut college classes to come in and do them. I just wanted to be in the building as much as possible. To me, Condé was the happiest place on earth! Plus, *Glamour* paid ten dollars an hour. And I had doctors to see. When the beauty closet was renovated, I packed every cuticle cream and lip liner into dozens of crates, dragged them out, and then moved everything back in, and unpacked and reorganized it all a week later. Mary's "new" closet looked exactly the same, just three feet wider. I also did beauty sales—huge ones. I donned a pink, long-sleeved *Glamour* logo T-shirt to take coats at a Fashion Week event at the Royalton Hotel. I never said no.

Sometimes I got a little bonus. It was on a "special project" of this kind that I first scored opiates—the doctor-shopping Holy Grail. *Glamour* sent me undercover on "consultations" with plastic surgeons and had me essentially try to bait them into telling me what was "wrong" with my looks and what I needed to have done. Or something like that. It wasn't the greatest conceit for a story; I wasn't writing it or anything. I was just the guinea pig.

"So, why are you here?" Dr. X would ask.

"Well," I said. "I want something . . . *improved* . . . but I don't know what."

It was harder to get a bite than you'd think. These were Park Avenue doctors—they didn't need my money! I booked a nose job (which I later canceled, swear to God) with one doctor and took home a folder of papers. A script for generic Vicodin was paper-clipped to the inside.

"You're going to want to fill that so you'll have them ready at home after the operation," the office manager said. I strolled out and went straight to Rite Aid.

A week later, at another appointment for the same *Glamour* story, I booked the same procedure.

"Oh," I told the doctor. "I've had a bad reaction to Vicodin in the past, so if it's all the same to you . . ." And his office manager sent me home with a prescription for Percocet. I filled that one at Duane Reade. For weeks, I was always a little bit extra-high on the job, though of course, no one knew. I kept the orange bottles in the zipper pocket of my mom's Chloé Silverado bag—hidden away. A secret.

When I wasn't doctor shopping, I was grocery shopping—at four thirty in the morning! I'd return from a night at the Coral Room or Home or wherever, change out of my party outfit into something terry cloth, and hit the twenty-four-hour Food Emporium on Second Avenue. I'd be the only customer in the store, and the night employees would give me the eye as I walked up and down the aisles. The supermarket would be eerily silent—well, except for the smooth jazz playing over the sound system. But smooth jazz really creeps me out! And the lighting was always sort of green. I'd load a whole cart: Scooby-Doo fruit snacks, Nestlé chocolate milk, Pepperidge Farm Sugar cookies, Jif Creamy Peanut Butter, Smuckers Sugar Free Apricot Preserves, whole wheat bread. Throw in a carton of skim milk—that would make the PB&J come up easier. And if I was buying milk, I thought, I might as well buy a box of Cap'n Crunch or Lucky Charms. Or Cookie Crisp. Or all three.

BLLLLARRGGH. Shlosh. Those are the sounds of me vomiting. (Onomatopoeia! You can send my Pulitzer to my agent.)

I went through crazy phases. Like carrot cake. God, the carrot cake. Never has anyone eaten more fucking carrot cake than I did when I was twenty-three! The best was from a twenty-four-hour spot called Hot and Crusty on Lexington Avenue by the subway station. I was there so often that I eventually got embarrassed and started scoring it from other places (Starbucks, the supermarket bakery—anywhere I could find carrot cake). In rehab I'd learned that alcoholics switched up liquor stores to throw people off the trail of their addiction, so I gave it a shot. Which was a joke. Bulimics are very conspicuous! I mean, people are always telling me my face looks swollen on Instagram.

I binged during the day, too. Sometimes it was the first thing I did when I got up. Once I'd been to Food Emporium, Hot and Crusty, the Rite Aid junk food aisle, and the corner deli—my circuit—I'd hustle the two blocks home with my bags full and my heart pounding. Just *so* excited to binge. I couldn't *wait*. And God forbid the streets be busy! Whenever people got in my way, or if the light at the crosswalk turned red and I was stuck at the curb for a minute—I'd feel just *murderous*. Same with when I was on a crowded elevator in my building with my grocery bags. *Ping*. Every time it stopped at a floor before sixteen I'd feel exponentially more homicidal.

Then, finally—I'd be home. I usually ate with the blinds closed— my Upper East Side Central Park view shut out—and the lights low, if they were on at all. The TV would be on but I wouldn't see it or hear it, and sometimes my shirt would be off, so I wouldn't get food all over it. I would go in on a hoagie like I was the monster ripping the head off that little man in the Goya "Black Paintings"—the murals he did on the walls of his house before he died.

Then I'd go into my bathroom—the vomitorium, if you will—kneel at the toilet, strip my tank top off if I still had it on, pull my long, blond hair back into a ponytail, and glug tap water from an old Poland Springs bottle I kept in there. Water helped. Then I'd throw it all up.

Some days, I'd resolve to stop and would dump all the food in the house down the trash chute in the hall. But the next day, I'd wake up feeling depressed and go buy it all again. I was allowed to use my parents' credit card for groceries, which enabled me for sure. Bulimia is expensive—a real rich-bitch disease, quite frankly. All that waste! It's so wrong; I knew it was. But that never stopped me. Bingeing straight-up anesthetized me, and I was hooked. I mean, you could've shanked me so long as I had a box of Entenmann's chocolate frosted donuts in my lap. That's how numb I got.

I'd been at *Glamour* for over a year when I got to go on my first press trip for the magazine. It was with Ralph Lauren fragrances, which was owned by the L'Oréal Group (who also owned Lancôme, Shu Uemura, Kiehl's, and more). They were flying beauty editors via private jet to Memphis for a day to tour Sun Studios, the "birthplace of rock 'n' roll"—where Johnny Cash recorded back in the day—and Elvis's home, Graceland. And this was to celebrate the launch of a perfume called Ralph Rocks. Get it? No one on staff at *Glamour* could go—but Ralph was such a big advertiser, *someone* had to. That's when Felicia and Mary called on me.

"Are you sure you can handle it?" Mary called me into her office to give me the spiel.

"I'm sure!" I said. I was *so* down. I'd never been on a private plane before. And this one would be full of the crème de la crème of beauty editors—the people I wanted to know and impress most in the world!

On the big day, a town car picked me up at my building on East Eighty-Sixth Street. I felt so special climbing into the backseat! It took me to Teterboro Airport in New Jersey—and dropped me off on the tarmac. Wow!

I felt very shy as I boarded. A few editors were seated already.

"Hi," I said to a publicist. "I'm Cat . . . from *Glamour*." I found a cushy, creamy leather seat to sort of . . . hide in. I watched cars arrive one by one on the tarmac.

Last to board was Eva Chen, the new beauty director at *Teen Vogue* (Kara had left to write a book). Everyone said young Eva was being groomed by Anna Wintour herself to be a Condé editor in chief someday.

"I'm so sorry I'm late!" she exclaimed.

"No problem!" the publicists cooed.

I gawked from my little corner of the plane. Eva was wearing a tiny navy minidress over black opaque tights—she had long Edie Sedgwick legs—and a perfect little fur jacket. I wondered who made it. Probably J. Mendel.

We took off for Memphis. The day went well! I was shy at first, but it was fun seeing Elvis's mansion, and I joked and chatted with the group as we took our tour and had lunch. I even talked to the vice president of Lancôme the whole flight back. The Ralph Lauren publicist thanked me warmly as she put me in a car home from Teterboro late that night. Playing editor for a day was like being Cinderella: the clock struck midnight, and it was over.

Someday, I thought as the car approached the Upper East Side, *I'm gonna be a beauty editor for real.* I couldn't *wait* to be like Eva Chen. It was all going to happen for me; my dreams were going to come true. I mean, I'd been working so hard! I was sure of it.

When I graduated college that spring, I was officially on the job hunt. I liked *Glamour* and was freelancing there four days a week, but they weren't about to put me on staff or promote me. It was time to move on.

Easier said than done! I wanted a staff beauty assistant job—a good one. But they didn't open up often. My top ten choices were (in no particular order) *Teen Vogue, W, Elle, Harper's Bazaar, Lucky, Glamour, Jane, InStyle, Cosmopolitan*, and *Allure. Vogue* was never on my list because I wasn't delusional. You had to be *really* together to work there! And I hated getting blowouts.

I interviewed and interviewed. And then I interviewed some more. I did informational interviews with Human Resources at Hearst Corporation, Condé Nast, and Hachette Filipacchi. I interviewed for nonbeauty gigs, like assisting Anne Slowey at *Elle* and Marvin and Jaclynn at *Nylon*. I interviewed for beauty assistant jobs at titles I didn't even like, like *Shop, Etc.* It was Hearst's low-rent knockoff of *Lucky*, the game-changing "magazine about shopping" that Condé Nast had launched to great fanfare in December 2000. *Shop, Etc.* offered me the position, but I turned it down. The magazine folded a few months later anyway.

My worst experience was at one of my top-ten titles. After our first interview, the beauty director asked me to write up a list of pitches for feature stories. I slaved over this fucking list! It was good, too: long, detailed, and creative. When I was done, I dropped everything off with reception at the magazine, along with a thank-you note. I was excited. I knew my test was strong.

I waited and waited, but I never heard from the beauty director again. No call, no e-mail—nothing! My follow-up messages went unreturned. Radio silence. I was crushed.

Less than a year later, I opened the magazine and saw a story I'd pitched. It was uncanny: the idea had been unique, and the specifics I'd laid out were all in there. The only thing missing was my byline. It was rotten business—all of it. I'd name the beauty director here, but the past is the past, *dah*-lings.

Then my dream job opened! *Teen Vogue* was hiring a new beauty assistant. The lucky girl would be working directly for the impossibly glamorous Eva Chen. Condé HR called to tell me I was on the short list and to schedule my interview. *Whoa.*

I took my "emergencies only" Discover card to Bloomingdale's and bought two outfits: a $780 pleated Marni skirt (I wiggled the tags off the plastic chad, then fussed them back on again to return it) and a black, structured dress from DKNY with a chic silhouette and pockets. I got a neutral manicure. I got a blowout. I woke up the morning of the interview and did nude makeup. I arrived early. This job was *mine.*

Eva met me at reception.

"I have the same skirt," she told me. "I love Marni. Don't you?"

"Totally," I said. It was a sign!

The interview was great. Four days later, I was in the editor in chief's office for round two. Now it was down to me and another girl.

"Who are your favorite designers?" Amy Astley asked, just like Holly told me she would.

"Rodarte, Dries, Miu Miu, Rick Owens, Marc Jacobs . . ." I didn't miss a beat.

I called my mom the second I left the Condé Nast building.

"This is it," I said. "This is it! I can feel it!"

"Oh, Caitlin!" She was as excited as I was. "Don't jinx it!"

On Monday, I got the call. This was it! The first day of the rest of my—

"I'm so sorry . . ." the HR woman, Kirsten, began. I fell to my knees on the floor of my studio. They'd chosen the other girl. I didn't mean to cry on the phone with the HR operative, but I couldn't help it. She told me that I was at the top of her list for other beauty assistant openings. Still, I was shattered.

Later that month, I got a handwritten letter in the mail from Eva. It was long, covering both sides of her *Teen Vogue* stationery. She thanked me for interviewing and told me she just knew I'd find an amazing job soon—and that I was so passionate and smart that I clearly had a big future in the industry. I read that note about twenty times a day for a year! I have never forgotten her generosity. That Eva Chen is a *class* act.

Months passed. I was getting desperate. I'd been at *Glamour* for over a year and a half. But at least I was in the building every day. If I left Condé Nast, I feared, I might never get back in. So I stayed at *Glamour*, on autopilot, waiting for another "dream job" to open.

Every magazine I've ever worked for has had a "giveaway table": a designated space in the office where editors deposited things like bedazzled Betsey Johnson thongs from Fashion Week gift bags (I still have one and let me assure you—wearing it is *always* a mistake) and nail polishes that are too fug to bother filing in the beauty closet. One day I was walking past *Glamour*'s giveaway table and spotted a galley— that's an advance copy—of a book called *Free Gift with Purchase: My Improbable Career in Magazines and Makeup*. It was by the beauty director of *Lucky*: Jean Godfrey-June.

I started reading it on the train home that night, and whoa! Jean Godfrey-June was so weird! And self-deprecating, and funny. Her writing was so *glamorous*. Like, the way she used *words* was glamorous. And I ate up her anecdotes about wearing a bonnet during an unhappy phase of her Northern California childhood, her strange encounters with JFK Jr. at Hachette Filipacchi, the terrifying French editors at *Elle*, the time Tom Ford gave her bedroom eyes at the Bryant Park Hotel, and supermodels who couldn't answer easy questions about their own skincare lines. By the time I finished the book, I was obsessed—*obsessed*— with Jean Godfrey-June.

"How was the Sephora lunch?" I'd ask Mary as she bustled in with a bag. "Was Jean Godfrey-June there?"

"Uh-huh . . ."

"Did she say anything funny?"

"I didn't sit with her," Mary would say. Then: "She's just a person, Cat!"

"I know," I'd answer dreamily.

I read *Free Gift with Purchase* over and over. I highlighted it, I dog-eared it. I kept it in my handbag at all times. I e-mailed Jean herself— we both had Condé Nast e-mail addresses, after all—telling her how much I loved it. She wrote back thanking me right away! I almost fell out of my chair.

I'd still never seen her in person, though. I was dying to!

JEAN, I would think, looking around in the elevator every morning.

Would *this* be the morning I finally spotted her in the verbena-scented flesh? *GODFREY. JUNE!*

Do you believe in the Secret? *I* do. I had never thought more positively about anyone in my life than I did about Jean Godfrey-June and her book and her column in *Lucky*, and then, in August—a month before my twenty-fourth birthday—Condé Human Resources called. The beauty assistant job at *Lucky* was open. Did I want to apply? Was auto-erotic asphyxiation sexy? *Of course!*

One week later, I was being escorted to Jean's office on the sixth floor of the Condé Nast building to interview with the woman herself.

"Hello," Jean greeted me. She looked just like I'd imagined, with long, wavy brown hair (Sally "founder of the thousand-dollar haircut" Hershberger had made Jean throw away her blow-dryer, she'd explained in *Free Gift*). She had a sun-kissed glow that I knew came from frequent applications of Lancôme Flash Bronzer for legs. Her desk was obscene with incredible beauty products, as well as art books, four floral arrangements, about nineteen lip balms, a Chanel boomerang, and—curiously—a rolling pin–size syringe full of chocolate pudding.

"Hi," I said. *Breathe.*

The interview went well. Jean remembered my e-mail about *Free Gift with Purchase*, and she seemed impressed with my résumé. Both Felicia and Charlotte (who had once been her assistant) had sent recommendations. Then she sent me away with a mock-up page of *Lucky*. The photos of the products were in the layout, but there was "dummy text" (TKTKKTKTKTX OXLXOIJDSXOTJTOEDSMA OAFXTTL, $tktk, sephora.com) for heds (headlines), deks (subheadlines), and captions. I'd be filling in the blanks for my edit test.

It wouldn't be too hard. The secret to nailing an edit test is familiarity with the publication for which you're "auditioning." I brought that page right home, took an Adderall, and went to town. JGJ *was Lucky* beauty, and I'd read her book so many times that her irreverent tone wasn't hard to mimic. I also knew Jean's rules; they were right there in *Free Gift with Purchase.* For example, she hated "locks" and "tresses"— goofy synonyms for "hair" that other magazines, obsessed with not repeating a word on any given page, used interchangeably. In Jean-world, you were allowed to use the word "hair" twice on one page. So I did.

Jean was also a playful writer, so I wanted to show her that I, too, could play. For a hair-mask item, I wrote something like, "This appealingly hefty brown tub looks like it's just been fetched from a palm tree by a mischievous monkey—and the goopy, ultra-emollient deep conditioner inside smells fantastic and coconut-y, too." The sentence structure and adding a "-y" to "coconut" was lifted directly from other *Lucky* stories: I had a stack of back issues in front of me. You've got to really pay attention! I took the "mischievous monkey" thing in and out forty times before deciding to keep it.

Then I sent in my test. A week went by, and I didn't hear a thing.

I was walking home from the subway with headphones on, listening to—swear to God—"Lucky" by Britney Spears when the familiar number lit up my phone. It was the same Condé HR rep who'd called with bad news from *Teen Vogue.* But this time, she sounded happy! It was official: I was the new beauty assistant at *Lucky* magazine.

Chapter Nine

I LOVED EVERYTHING ABOUT MY NEW JOB. I loved taking the elevator to the sixth floor and walking past the three-foot-high, bright red *Lucky* behind the two heavy glass doors that only opened with my *very* special and exclusive pass. *Beep*. Then *swish*—I *remember* that *swish*—I'd be in, turning left, and heading down a long, gray-carpeted corridor, past the fashion closet filled with racks of clothes by obscure designers that I could borrow whenever I wanted. Then I'd hang right, past the edit conference room and the big beauty closet—which was full of the usual plastic bins and products, plus floor-to-ceiling windows overlooking Times Square—and the mail room, which was stocked with heavy note cards and envelopes: *Lucky* stationery.

The business cards that eventually arrived for me were even more exciting:

Cat Marnell
Beauty Assistant

They were white and red, like Valentines. I sent a bunch to Mimi right away!

And then I was in the beauty department! It was L-shaped: three cubicles for the assistant, associate beauty editor, and senior beauty editor, respectively, and then Jean's glass-encased office was to the left. The beauty interns sat at a desk in the closet. That's right—*I* had interns! Cute ones, too. It was the best feeling. I was in charge of hiring them, and I mentored them closely. (I'm still tight with a few of them to this day.)

I loved my desk, which was messy with Davines NouNou deep conditioners and MAC Cosmetics black eye shadows and Clean perfumes and press releases in chic Viktor & Rolf folders and little Kid Robot toys and dangly St. Mark's Place earrings I was always taking out midafternoon when my lobes started feeling all throbby. The floor was piled up with black NARS bags and white Olay bags and brown-and-gold Gucci bags and white Fresh bags and hot-pink Alison Brod PR bags and bags and bags and bags and bags full of lipsticks, eye shadows, and perfumes. Did I mention that there were bags?

I loved my ugly black phone, which lit up when people called my very own CNP "(212) 286" extension—which I also loved—or to speak to JGJ. I was on that thing so much that I broke out in "phacne"—phone acne—underneath my chin, but I didn't care.

"Jean Godfrey-June's office," I chirped like a Disney bird about ninety times a day. "This is Cat."

I arrived every morning at nine forty-five. Beauty directors have approximately four thousand appointments per week, so I started each day working on Jean's planner. I was very meticulous, as an assistant must be. And I used mechanical pencil:

Estée Lauder lunch at the London Hotel 1 PM
Burt's Bees deskside 3 PM

Jean would call around ten to check in, usually from the backseat of the town car that picked her up every morning. She lived in Nyack, a crunchy-glam town in upstate New York.

"How's it going?" she'd ask.

"Good!" I'd say. We'd chitchat about what proofs were on her desk—Jean edited and signed off on every page in the magazine, not just beauty—and about the celebrity fragrance launch she'd attended the night before and did Gwen Stefani have good skin up close or what? Then the call would cut out; her reception was always terrible. I never called back—she'd be in soon enough. Besides, then JGJ could go back to listening to Howard Stern (whom she loved so much that once, when a Barbara Bui fragrance came into the office, she giggled like mad for a week because it sounded—vaguely—like "Baba Booey").

After I'd spoken to the Notorious JGJ, I'd go into her office to make sure it was in *absolutely* tiptop shape. I'd line up all the tinted lip balms in front of her keyboard in a tight, tidy pyramid, like bowling pins. Then I had to make sure the computer was up and running. Jean loathed her computer, and so did I. I never shut it down at night like I was *supposed* to—those Condé Nast "Green Initiatives"—though housekeeping sometimes did. Then I'd arrive in the morning and panic, because I couldn't figure out how to turn it back on! (Those Mac desktops have that *sneaky* flat button on the back of them, you know. My interns had to come in and find it for me. I always was looking for the "tower" under the desk like it was 1998 instead of 2008.) Jean also detested her Treo phone, did not fully understand that the tech support department was based in India, and blamed almost everything that happened, technology-wise, on Mercury being in retrograde. I was just as bad: I didn't file her expense reports for my first seven months because I didn't understand the computer program! We made quite a team.

Like many top Nasties at that time, JGJ was all about print and knew nothing about the Internet.

"Don't worry," she said darkly, when beauty was asked to start contributing to the new luckymag.com. "This"—the online craze—"will all be over in a year. Remember, you work for me, not them." Indeed. When someone from luckymag.com would come over and innocently request a quick beauty write-up here and there, I would smile and nod. Then I would call my boss at home and immediately report them. I was loyal as fuck. One must be.

Anyway. Next I'd sweep the petals from her desk. Jean received so many $150 "thank you for putting my product in your magazine" bouquets that she liked to rearrange them for sport. I'd carry a vase in and she would reach to take it from my hands before I could even put it down on her desk. Then she'd weed out what she didn't like (calla lilies, driftwood) and send the rejects sailing through the air and into a trash can across the room. *Plunk*. Without looking! *Plunk*. She was like a Harlem Globetrotter—but instead of whistling, JGJ hummed. (It was her thing—I could hear it from a mile away, like a special assistant sixth sense.) Then I'd arrange gifts on Jean's love seat. Beauty companies were always sending her iPod shuffles, Jimmy Choos, Versace cookies with a handwritten note from Donatella herself ("See you Saturday!" in gold ink), Lalique rings in tiny jewelry boxes, parcels of rainbow macaroons like something out of the *Marie Antoinette* movie—you name it.

But the best gift in her office was in a long, skinny-as-a-snake orange box on top of her sofa. It was an Hermès riding crop—a whip! I was *enchanted* by it.

"*Ooooh*," I said the first time, I opened the box.

Not only was it the most glamorous thing I'd ever held in my two hands, it represented everything I loved about my career. When a high-strung, *thoroughbred* Condé Nasty like Jean (who could be *scary*, believe me)—or Anna or *any* of them—was cracking her Hermès whip, it was an *honor* to jump. It was an honor to ask, "How high?!" And if the whip got so close it hurt, well, go in the closet, slather some sixty-nine-dollar Organic Pharmacy Rose Balm on your open wounds, and then get right back to work, you whiny baby! That's what publishing was—is—all about. And this was, in my opinion, what Andrea—the fictional millennial narrator of *The Devil Wears Prada*—didn't understand.

Jean Godfrey-June had a hypoallergenic cat named Fydor—after Mr. Dostoyevsky—that cost over two thousand dollars, and I knew this scintillating information and more because I was in charge of reading my boss's e-mail. I'd be doing just that every morning when the editor in chief, Kim France—or KF, as everyone called her—would pop her head in.

"Marnell," she'd greet me. Kim called us by our last names like we were players on her football team. *Lucky* had been her idea; she'd pitched the "magazine about shopping" concept to James Truman—Condé's dashing ex–editorial director—at a party. KF was laid-back and accessible, always roaming the corridors. I never heard her coming—well, except for when she wore this one purple, gypsy-looking dress that was covered in chimes. Otherwise, she was always catching me spinning in circles on Jean's desk chair or something comparably embarrassing. "Where's JGJ?"

"She'll be here in fifteen!" I'd say.

When the interns arrived, I'd send one down to the Starbucks on Forty-Third Street to get Jean's *very* special coffee: a *grande* misto made with organic milk.

"They'll tell you they don't have organic milk," I told my interns. "But they do! Really make them go downstairs and get it!"

Then my new coworkers would arrive. Cristina was the senior beauty editor. She was about twenty-eight and from Northern California, like Jean. Cristina was the nicest person I'd ever met. She was creative and weird—she took botany classes for fun—and always called me "dude." Dawn, the associate beauty editor, was pretty and preppy and so together. She ran on the West Side Highway every morning before work and never missed a deadline. She'd sit at her desk with a pair of nail scissors, trimming her split ends one by one. I mean, my whole *head* was basically a split end, you know? The *Lucky* beauty department was a motley crew! Fine, it was four white women. My point is, we all got along.

Dawn, Cristina, and I would be joking around and poking around in our bags from the messenger center when the intern returned with Jean's misto. I'd take it from her, remove the lid—JGJ did *not* tolerate lids ("It's just one more thing I have to do," she'd told me)—and place it on the boss's desk. And then . . .

Ten minutes later, there she was! Of all the things I loved about my new job, I loved Jean the most. She'd wander in wearing a swishy YSL leopard-print chiffon skirt, a tiny Prada cardigan, and sensible two-and-a-half-inch-heel Loubs, her cornflower-blue Hermès satchel slung over her self-tanned shoulder. Dawn, Cristina, and I would gather in her office with our coffees. Jean would tell us what it had been like eating quail eggs the previous afternoon with Salma Hayek at LMVH Tower—or whatever kooky thing she'd done—and pat on her favorite Stella McCartney organic face oil. Jean just *lived* to be dewy—and she thought everyone else did, too. Like *Teen Vogue*'s Kara "nobody wears eye shadow" Jesella, my new boss had deep, inflexible beauty-director convictions that no one dared contest.

"*No one* uses pressed powder!" Jean would sweep the whole lot of them off the desk into a shopping bag. The ultimate antidewifying product rarely made it onto the pages of *Lucky*. "*No one* wants *matte* skin. *Everyone* wants to be dewy! Youthful! Dewy dewy dewy!"

Other edicts included:

- Your whole life you really only need one razor.
- Manicures are unnecessary.
- No perfume bottles shaped like curvy women (think J.Lo Glow)
- Crème de la Mer is the best thing to give someone being treated for breast cancer.
- Deodorant *gives* you breast cancer.

- Combine any two lipstick shades and you will get a flattering lipstick shade (FACT: JGJ did not herself wear lipstick).
- When writing, never refer to your own body parts—toes, stomach, bikini area—or prisoners will use the imagery you've created for their masturbatory fantasies, and you will get letters from them.

JGJ lived in a Stanford White house with an honest-to-God monkey pen out back. She liked Joan Didion and *World of Interiors* and Liberty prints and Rice Krispies Treats and the Mohonk Mountain House and Weleda Skin Food moisturizer; she took classes alongside celebrities like Russell Simmons—she *loved* Russell Simmons—at Jivamukti Yoga in Union Square twice a week; she hoarded tissue paper and ribbons; Jean was constantly being flown first class to Europe by beauty companies; when in Paris as a guest of Chanel *beauté*, Sofia Coppola's nanny Lala cared for JGJ's kids while she toured Coco's apartment at 31 rue Cambon (Jean had once deboned a chicken with Sofia Coppola, incidentally). When in Los Angeles, Jean stayed at the Chateau Marmont on Sunset Boulevard, and she sent the general manager, Philip Pavel, boxes of thank-you beauty products for her special rate.

Jean's best friend in the building was Hilton Als, the *New Yorker* theater critic (and now the author of the wonderful *White Girls*) and friend of Kim and Thurston (and Juergen Teller . . . and Matthew Barney and Björk). I loved answering Jean's phone and hearing his velvety speaking voice. He visited our floor often. Sometimes I could beg some juicy gossip out of him about someone in his famous, artsy clique. Other JGJ BFFs included a *House & Garden* columnist, who'd swagger in wearing a white fur coat like P. Diddy and reeking of marijuana, and at least one actress who was distraught when Heath Ledger died because—I believe—she'd fucked him.

What else? Oh, I could write this whole *book* about Jean Godfrey-June! I also loved how she talked.

"*Qu'est-ce que c'est?*" she'd ask, anytime a product caught her eye that actually interested her.

"Gnarly," she'd say, making a face, when presented once, twice, fifteen times a week with some sort of "chocolicious" edible foaming shimmery foot butter, or a body splash that smelled like a dead stripper in an orange grove.

Jean was a huge fan of the Ricki Lake home-birthing documentary, as well as a sucker for exotic packaging and—as I said—silly wordplay.

"Escense Chembur!" she chuckled, reading the label of a new eau de parfum I'd placed on her desk for consideration. "Chembur! Chemburr! It sounds like a . . . a ruddy-cheeked English schoolboy!" Chembur—a $220 fragrance by Byredo you can get at Barney's, FYI—made it in the issue, because it delighted JGJ so.

And JGJ was a terrific editor. She would call us into her office individually, and we'd sit down with her. She'd explain the changes she'd made, line by line.

"You don't even want to suggest something negative," she'd explain. "So I cut 'Washing your face with oil sounds counterintuitive.' Just say 'This bestselling oil cleanser is incredible.' "

I learned *so* much. JGJ truly made me—for better or for worse—not only the writer but the person I am today. I utterly worshipped her.

After Jean left around five o'clock, I was free to do whatever I wanted. As an assistant, I didn't get invited to the good events yet, but there were plenty of minor product launches and parties—which were okay in a drink-champagne-with-other-assistants-on-the-terrace-at-Bendel's sort of way. You always walked away with the new perfume, a buzz, and a pair of Agent Provocateur crotchless stockings in the gift bag. Or sometimes I'd *have* to attend something hosted by advertisers when the editors didn't want to go—like an (atrocious) Jennifer Lopez concert and meet-and-greet with Coty fragrances, say. But nothing compared to the Conair cruise (not to be confused with Connor Cruise,

Scientologist DJ and son of Tom) around the island of Manhattan, which got stuck in a thunderstorm. Beauty assistants, publicists, marketing VIPs: we were all out on this fucking boat on the Hudson River for *hours* together. The water was so rough that the shrimp platters and crudités slid off the tables! When we finally stumbled off the boat, clutching our shopping bags of new curling irons and blow-dryers, it was nearly midnight.

I was hounded by publicists wanting me to try their clients' beauty services. Everything was free. Comped! I didn't even pay my own tips—I put them in my expense reports! "Salon gratuity: $100." I got my eyebrows tinted and waxed every month by Maral Balian—she's incredible; she'll change your face, *and* she also does *the* Diandra Douglas, ex-wife of Michael—at the Warren-Tricomi Salon, which was past the Eloise portrait and up the stairs in the Plaza Hotel. And I got my bikini area lasered gratis at Completely Bare. The Flatiron District spa had white leather sofas and bowls of lavender M&M's and chatty young aestheticians who put goggles on you and then . . . *shaved* you, you know, before gooing up your nether regions with ice-cold jelly and *zap-zap-zapping* your hair off.

What else? I got highlights from Sharon Dorram—a big, *big*-deal colorist—at John Frieda uptown, where four people worked on me at once.

"Foil," Sharon—who was hugely pregnant—said to her coven of assistants every minute or so. Otherwise, the salon was dead quiet. I felt like I was getting brain surgery! "Foil."

But the biggest treat by far was getting to go to Dr. Frederic Brandt—Madonna's dermatologist, and JGJ's, too. His offices were in east midtown over by the river, and decorated with photos of nearly nude men. The first time I went, I saw a famous editor in chief with white numbing cream all over her face! She was teetering down the hallway looking lost and clutching a Birkin bag. Dr. Brandt was almost Warholian looking—kind of bizarro and awesome, with platinum-blond hair—and very kind. He was a Botox maestro who'd invented a special bent-needle technique, but he only ever gave me laser treatments. (Like everyone in my industry, I was shocked and saddened by the news that Dr. Brandt had hung himself in his Palm Beach home on April 5, 2015.)

I didn't take advantage of these after-work perks nearly as much as I could have, though. I took a *lot* of Adderall throughout the day; by the time everyone else left for their evening workouts at Equinox or dinner at Café Cluny with their boyfriends, I was weird and speedy—flying high—and I wanted to stay put and fuck around. There was so much to do! I even became friendly with the crew who cleaned at night; I gave them perfume and colognes and body wash. I'd stay at the office until ten or eleven—and sometimes well past midnight—amped up, researching beauty products online, organizing Jean's office. Oh, and scavenging through the trash. *Lucky* shared the sixth floor with Condé Nast International, so there was always a Dumpster over there full of treasure. I'd root through it for *French Vogue*—then edited by Carine Roitfeld, and full of killer Terry Richardson fashion shoots—and *Vogue Italia*, which regularly featured fifty or sixty pages of unbelievable photographs by Steven Meisel. I'd use the excellent *Lucky* color copiers to reproduce my favorite images for collaging.

I never wanted to go home. Whenever I wasn't at *Lucky*, the badness came back. I would be *très* gloomy—Eeyore-esque—trudging to my building from the train. And I was probably the only twenty-four-year-old on the planet who dreaded weekends. I didn't go to clubs anymore; I binge-ate and vomited pizza and muffins on Friday nights. Sometimes I took Adderall at two in the morning just to make my bulimia stop, but then I couldn't sleep. I'd crash at two o'clock Saturday afternoon and then wake up around ten at night, go out and buy food, and do it all again. (Is reading this stuff getting repetitive? Welcome to addiction.)

I was always relieved when Monday came. *Beep.* I went through the gates in the Condé lobby in a Vera Wang slip and a fresh layer of Kiehl's Sun-Free Self-Tanning Formula from head to toe.

Insomnia? Bulimia? Drug problem? Me? I hoped the look said. *But I have such a healthy glow!*

I was self-soothing with food on weekends because I was—can you guess?—lonely. I had my dream job, but I'd worked so hard to get there and had isolated myself on pills for so long that I still didn't have any friends. Alex and I hadn't spoken in months. No one from his world—my old one—called me. And I had no romantic or sex life at all. I daydreamed about having a boyfriend like all the other Condé assistants, but that was a joke. How could I sleep next to a man every night when I couldn't even sleep by myself?

Instead, my steady dates—and no matter how drained I was, I *always* kept them—were with psychiatrists. I was seeing a new guy named Dr. C. He had an office on Park Avenue in the 70s with arched French doors, beautiful crown moldings, and a waiting room full of Sotheby's catalogs. I'd found him by cold-calling every uptown shrink in my new job's health insurance directory. Dr. C. was first to call back. After a few appointments, I realized he was my favorite doctor I'd ever been to—which is different, mind you, than being the *best* doctor I'd ever been to. He was *very* liberal with his prescriptions. His handwriting was so shaky that pharmacists sometimes couldn't even make it out—that's how old he was—but he basically just jotted down what I told him to on his pad.

"Thirty milligrams of generic Adderall four times a day," I'd say.

"Thirty . . . milligrams . . ." Dr. C. would repeat. "Adderall . . . generic . . . four times . . ." I could barely even take all the speed I got from him! But somehow I managed.

Work made me feel okay about myself—better than okay, sometimes. Jean and I would tear through the products in her office, and I'd think of unusual ways to frame them.

"How about 'The Smell of Tan'?" I'd suggest titling an item pairing Jo Malone Vitamin E Scrub and Mario Badescu Summer Shine Body Lotion.

"Love it," Jean would say.

"It's a 'Moonbeam Cream'!" I'd declare of a wet n wild illuminator in another. "It makes your skin luminous like when you take a romantic night walk!"

"You're so *good* at this," Jean would say. I'd grin at her. We were very in sync—and I'd only been her assistant a few months.

I was lousy at one thing, though: hitting deadlines. And when you work at a magazine, you *can't* be bad at hitting deadlines. It slows down everyone else. There was an entire department—production—to remind me of this. These people paced the corridors with their clipboards, nudging us along. It made me nervous.

Concentrate, I'd think after one of them popped by to check on something I was working on. Then I'd take another dose of ADHD medication.

The main beauty section of *Lucky* was called Beauty Spy. These were eight or nine pages of smaller items (about two hundred words each) that ran "front of the book" in every issue. Once a month, we'd kick the interns out of the beauty closet and gather around the large countertop where we'd been accumulating new products all month. Cristina would show JGJ "a wee owl, made of soap"; Dawn would show her black-brown eye shadow and a black-gold nail polish and declare that "off-black" was *officially* trending; I'd present a trio of fluorescent lip balms named after iconic New York City nightclubs. JGJ would roll her eyes at half our dumb-ass pitches but throw them into bags to be shot anyway, and then I'd lug everything back to my desk, type up the list, alert the production department, and take the bags up to the digital photo studio on the eighth floor.

Then it was writing time. Cristina would divide the items—the little stories—between me, Dawn, and herself. The idea was to get Beauty Spy to Jean for her edits before the corresponding images came back from the digital studio a few days later. This way, the text and the photos could be laid out together by the art department right away. The pressure was on! Which meant I would start shutting down.

My poor coworkers. We always handed in Beauty Spy as one big document, so when my work was late, their work was late. Dawn would finish first on deadline day; Cristina would be next. I was always last—that is, if I finished at all.

"Marnell," Cristina would come over and say. I'd be at my computer fussing over five sentences on a lip balm like I was drafting the Constitution. "Dude. Can I take an item or two off your hands? I don't mind. We just have to get this in on time."

"I got this," I'd swear. "I'm almost done!" When she left the cubicle, I'd sneak another Adderall.

Jean edited Beauty Spy by hand, on paper, in the car back to Nyack or on the way in the next morning, and half the time she'd leave for the day without anything to work on. The entire magazine's production would be slowed down. And it would be all my fault.

"I'm so sorry," I'd say every month. Then I'd *still* not finish until late the next day.

Dawn and Cristina never ratted me out, though, so Jean never knew I was her weakest link. Instead, she praised me. Jean valued good writing above all else, and she thought *I* was talented. She told me all of the time!

One morning, Jean came in and told me that she'd seen Felicia at a luncheon.

"Thank you so much for passing Cat along!" JGJ had said to Felicia. "I'm so thrilled to have her. She's such a good writer!"

"Cat can *write*?" Felicia had supposedly answered.

Hearing that anecdote skyrocketed me straight to cloud nine. Of course, JGJ didn't know that I full-on *Zero Dark Thirty*–tortured myself and everyone around me to procure the work that pleased her so—and I wasn't about to tell her.

Seeing *my* words in *Lucky* ruled. Every time a new issue hit my desk, I'd page through it, slap Post-its on the items I'd written, and send it to my Mimi along with some Estée Lauder lipsticks or something. There were no bylines in the Beauty Spy section, though. And I was *dying* for a byline! I'd only get one if Jean decided I could handle a larger writing assignment on top of my regular duties. Assistants didn't usually get this privilege in the first year, though. I know, I know: millennial bloggers are all, *huh?* But the print world *was* hierarchical and particular like that in my day. I don't know if it still is.

Finally, my moment arrived! I was assigned a one-page story called "Secret Ingredient: Goat's Milk." My byline would run at the end of the text. I had to call in ten products that had goat's milk in them, write a caption for each, and draft a simple paragraph about the curative properties of this unusual "secret ingredient." No prob.

Flash-forward to the day it was due. I'd labored over the story all week. I'd cut and pasted information about goat's milk into a Word document; I'd played with paraphrasing every day. But all I had to show for my effort were sentence fragments. This was supposed to be the story that proved to Jean and my coworkers that I could take on *more* juicy assignments. I had to get it together.

I was taking double Adderall—so why couldn't I concentrate? Everything I put down was gibberish. I had an online thesaurus open; I was arranging and rearranging the few half sentences I had. But then it all stopped making sense. So I erased it all.

By three o'clock, I'd rewritten the short paragraph—sort of. I was so cranked that you could have called me an old-timey car and sold me to Jay Leno. Clammy, too.

Cristina came over to my desk.

"You okay, Marnell?" she said—very quietly. JGJ was right there in her office.

"Fine," I rasped.

"Do you want me to help?" she said. "It's no trouble."

"I got it."

Five o'clock came, horribly and too soon. Everyone was trying to help me. Jean had even been answering her own phone.

My boss approached, holding her jacket and her Hermès handbag.

FUCK! I screamed inside.

"Err, do you . . . have 'Secret Ingredient'?" She was very nice about it.

"No," I said, and handed her a car reservation number on a Post-it. "I'm so . . ." I couldn't say "I'm sorry," because JGJ hated "I'm sorry." "I'm still working." As soon as she was out of sight, I put my head in my hands. I'd blown it again. But at least I had bought some time.

By seven, the office was clearing out, and I was "hyperfocused" and lockjawed.

"Dude." Cristina stopped on *her* way out. She looked worried. "Take a break."

"I'm fine . . ." I'd just taken another thirty-milligram Adderall. I was sure I could get the story done that evening.

Instead, the . . . *disorientation* got worse and worse. Hours passed: I was surprised every time I checked the clock. At ten o'clock, I was the only person on the sixth floor, and I was sitting in the dark. The lights had flickered off to save power as they always did at night. Usually I jumped around in the hallway to activate the motion sensors—this would light up the beauty department for a while—but that night I stayed locked into my chair. The housekeeping staff came by, and they vacuumed and emptied the trash cans around me. I didn't greet them like I usually did.

It was eleven o'clock. My underarms were wet, and my forehead was greasy. I was still fussing, obsessing. Rewriting, editing. Then it was midnight. Then it was one, then two. At three o'clock, the jumble on the screen was more incoherent than ever. I realized I was going to be there the entire night.

I took another Adderall. I probably took an Adderall every hour. At dawn, my eyes and face hurt; my hands were blue; I was shaking. I was very, very high and wearing the same clothes I'd worn the day before.

At nine thirty, when everyone started trickling in, I grabbed a floaty Phillip Lim dress I had in a shopping bag under my desk and changed in the beauty closet. My hair got caught in the zipper as I pulled it over my head. That's when I started weeping.

By the time Jean arrived ten minutes later—our editor in chief at her side—I was back in my chair. Now I was full-on *bawling*. Loud!

"Are you all right?!" Jean asked.

"*I'm just finishing 'Secret Ingredient.'* " KF and JGJ looked confused—concerned, too—but they let me be.

I'd never cried at the office before, but now I couldn't stop. The tears and snot dripped on the keyboard as I continued "working" on this story. Wretched, guttural *sobs* kept bursting out of my body. *SOB.* The fashion girls across the way had long since stopped talking among each other. *SOB!* I was weirding everybody out. *SOB!*

Finally Jean could take no more. She pulled me to her office and slid the door shut.

"What is *wrong*?" she said.

"I cah—cah—cah—cahhn—cahn-*can't do it*," I said. "The *go—go—goat's milk story*!"

"*That's* why you're upset?" Jean said. "Just bring me what you have!"

"I cah—cah—cah—"

"Print out what you have," JGJ repeated. "Go wash your face first."

I went to the ladies' room with some Mustela Facial Cleansing Cloths and GO SMiLE mouthwash from the beauty closet. My mouth tasted awful. I looked like a monster in the mirror.

Idiot. I hated myself. *Fucking retard.*

I almost lost it all over again when I printed out my two single-spaced pages of unintelligible nonsense, but I took a breath and brought them into Jean's office anyway. She was waiting.

"I . . . I—" I started.

"Let me see," Jean said, holding her hand out for the papers. I gave them to her.

"I did the product captions," I sniffled. "But I'm stuck on the paragraph."

"Great," Jean said. She went in with one of her blue pens right away. I settled in across from her and watched.

I'd been working on "Secret Ingredient: Goat's Milk" for over twenty-four straight hours. Do you want to know how long JGJ worked on it?

Two minutes.

She figured out the entire story in two minutes.

"Here," she said, and handed the papers to me.

I took the papers and looked at them. She'd completed my sentences and pieced everything together. This is the paragraph I'd lost my mind writing:

Secret Ingredient: GOAT'S MILK

Milk—or more accurately, the proteins, minerals, and lactic acids it's made of—has been used as a gentle exfoliant (and a powerful moisturizer) since Cleopatra's famous baths. And goat's milk does the stuff from cows one better: it contains lots more nutrients, and its smaller proteins absorb more quickly into skin. Soothing for both psoriasis and eczema, it hydrates and subtly glorifies all skin types.

—Cat Marnell

That's it. That's all I had to fucking do!

Drugs: they are wild.

"Secret Ingredient: Goat's Milk" was bad—the lowest point of my career so far. Little did I know, though: the lows were about to get *much* lower. And all because of a mouse.

Chapter Ten

OH, GOD. THE MOUSE. THE MOUSE! *The* Mouse. I am so scared typing those words. What if I summon him—like the Slender Man?! But I have to keep going.

Rodents. I hate them! I hate their filthy, hairless tails. I hate the squeaks you hear before you see them—motherfuckers are *loud*—I hate the rustling in the trash bags piled in the street. I can't even *Google* "mouse"! I do not go into Petco.

In New York, the rats are foot-longs—like Subway sandwiches! You see them absolutely everywhere at night. Some blocks are worse than others. I know that shit so well I could draw you a map. I've leapt off the sidewalk and into oncoming *traffic* to avoid rats, and if the dope doesn't get me, I will probably die that way. Anything would be better than what happened three years ago. I was walking home at dusk and *stepped* on one—right on the back. *Crunch.* It screamed; I screamed (there will be loads of *screaming* in this chapter). I was wearing Topshop ballet flats that were so thin, they barely counted as shoes—and I could *feel* the bend of that creature's spine! (I *think* rats have spines. Again—not Googling it.) When I got home, I called everyone in my BlackBerry in absolute hysterics! My friend SHAUN RFC told me to soak my foot in hot water diluted with bleach. He called it the East Harlem pedicure.

New York, New York, the city of dreams. No, it is vile! Out on the streets, rats run this town à la Rihanna and Jay-Z; the mice here are far more insidious. They invade your apartment, and so they invade your life. You're up late cracker-jacked on ADHD medication and *zing*—out of the corner of your eye you see a black flash dart under your refrigerator. Then your entire world turns upside down for three years. At least, that is what happened to me.

I'd been at *Lucky* nearly a year when I decided to ditch the Upper East Side and move downtown. Away from Alex and my bulimia circuit and my Dr. Feelgoods. I wanted to be in the East Village, my favorite Manhattan neighborhood. The second apartment I saw was an alcove studio at 112 First Avenue between Fifth and Sixth Streets. I liked that it was near St. Mark's Place, the former punk rock mecca, and Tompkins Square Park, which filled up with cute teen runaways in the summer. The creaky, dark, small building was above a strange Polish restaurant and a porny video shop; there was also a McDonald's and a combination Dunkin' Donuts/Baskin Robbins on the block. The setup *screamed* "mice." But of course I screamed "impulse control problems."

"I'll take it!" I exclaimed. It reminded me of a treehouse. I loved the weird shelves built into corners and the wood-paneled walls. There were three closets, which was crazy for four hundred square feet. And I liked that the treetops were right outside my windows. It was special to have a green view in downtown New York! The branches danced right up the glass. It reminded me of my dorm room junior year at boarding school.

I moved in over Labor Day weekend. It was a walk-up; my new

place was on the fifth floor. The blue-carpeted stairwell reeked of . . . what *was* that, exactly—the sticky sweetness mixed with the garbage smell? The broker had said that the trash room was in the basement. Okay.

I settled in and got straight to work tacking up my favorite Madonna by Steven Klein for *W* tear sheets, Sonic Youth *Dirty* LPs, and Thomas Ruff *Nudes* I'd torn from Christie's contemporary auction catalogs I bought at the Strand. I created the same cocoon I always did.

So why did I feel uneasy? My new place felt . . . *different* at night. *BANG! BANG! BANG!* The leafy tree branches I loved during the day weren't so whimsical when it was dark outside—when they were rapping at my windows like some sort of demented sex predator! Jesus.

But it was something else. I sensed I wasn't alone. I have the least appealing superpower ever: rodent intuition. I feel them before I see them. And as the weather grew colder, and the apartment grew darker—I knew. I just *knew*. I think I could hear them in the walls. It was only a matter of time.

I felt so creeped out up there that I kept inviting a girl I knew from acting school, Beth, to crash on the nights she did bottle service at a club nearby. That way, she wouldn't have to drive back to her family's place in Jersey at five in the morning. And I wouldn't have to be alone. Beth half moved in for a while, but after one trip downstairs to do laundry, she refused to ever go down there with me again. I didn't blame her. The basement was terrifying: full of trash cans and shadows. Plus, there was a sort of . . . *mechanical arm* that beat the side of the furnace every thirty seconds—like something the one-armed drummer from Def Leppard might use to beat a snare! *Thump thump thump.* And what were those . . . large *pellet* things on the floor? I couldn't be down there for more than a minute before I raced upstairs. I started throwing my garbage away on the street.

I cornered the superintendent, Ricky, which was a complete waste of time. He was, like, twenty years old, with three kids under five at home—and he had two other buildings, and he was a first-time super. He was always misplacing his big key ring and running around looking overwhelmed. He didn't have a poker face, either.

"There aren't any . . . *rats* in this basement, right?" I asked him one day. "That thing that hits the furnace isn't for scaring them, right?"

Ricky winced.

"Nah," he said.

"How about mice?" I asked. "Has anyone ever had a mouse in my apartment?"

Ricky grimaced again. I was doomed.

What could I do? I'd just moved in; I'd paid a broker. I couldn't move again. All I *could* do, I decided, was never—*ever*—bring food into the apartment. No snacks, no groceries. I at that point did not own a single plate and weighed approximately fourteen pounds, so I was fine. I even stopped bingeing! My fear of mice was more powerful than my eating disorder. Hooray.

They tell you not to bring your "devices" into a spa treatment, and now I knew why. Over Thanksgiving weekend in 2007, I was "facedown, ass up"—like the 2 Live Crew song—on a massage table at JGJ's favorite spa on earth, Ten Thousand Waves in Santa Fe, when I got the text.

Girl, it read. *I have really bad news.* Beth had broken the only rule and brought pizza into the apartment. She'd left the Lil Frankie's box on the floor. *Then I picked up your yoga mat*—Stella McCartney for Adidas, if you were wondering—*and a mouse ran out*.

I ended my first-ever massage right then and there. Ten Thousand Waves was ruined! I didn't even go into the famous outdoor hot tubs with all the naked hippies.

I thought of nothing else until I arrived back in New York. Beth had fled for Jersey, but she met me in front of the building so I wouldn't have to go in alone. We climbed the stairs, opened the door, and . . . oh, I couldn't believe what we found! If you, too, are *musophobic*, brace yourself. No—*anesthetize* yourself. Slap on a Fentanyl patch! I sure wish I had one.

Ready? Okay.

Every single surface was covered with . . . with *mouse droppings*. I can't even believe I am writing these words in my book; I am so grossed out. Mouse shit! Little black pellets. They were on my bed. They were on my pillows. They were in my bathroom, on the bath mat, on my bathroom scale, on the tiles. They were on every windowsill. They were on the sofa. They were on the floor in all three closets.

"*AUGHH!*" I clutched Beth. Beth clutched me! "*AUUGH!*"

Ugh, I am going to puke all over my MacBook Air just remembering all this! And not even on purpose, to lose weight.

Mouse shit was on my *i-D* magazines. They were on my *Dazed & Confused* and *Self Service* magazines. I had bulletin boards propped up against the wall, and there was mouse shit along the top edges of *those*. Excrement was on the bookshelves, the kitchen counters, and the cable box. The coffee table!

I'd never seen anything like it. I was sure an *army* of mice had invaded my apartment! The exterminator who came that evening didn't think so.

"Nah," he told us. "It was probably just one. Looks like he was trying to find his way out of here."

The exterminator found holes all over the apartment—but then he wouldn't cover them up! He said he was going to put out traps and leave poison everywhere, but that was it.

"Please fill the holes, sir," I begged. I was curled up in a ball on a windowsill.

"She's *really* phobic," Beth said.

"You have to let it eat the poison first," the exterminator said. "Then it gets thirsty and goes to look for—"

"FILL THEM!" I screamed. "YOU DON'T UNDERSTAND!" I got my way. I usually do.

Beth slept over that night, but she couldn't stay forever. The next day at work, I was weepy and demented: all I could talk about was the Mouse, the Mouse, the Mouse.

It was the Christmas season at Condé Nast once more, but I wasn't exactly in the holiday spirit.

"*You need to hire another person and get in there NOW!*" I sat in my cubicle and screamed—at management, at exterminators, at my mother, at the incompetent Ricky. I ignored the gift bags pouring in. "*This one isn't working! No, the poison isn't working. NOTHING is working!*"

The halls at 112 First Avenue, Apt. 5B, were decked with boughs of arsenic! Or whatever they use to exterminate these days. There were hunks of turquoise poison in all of my closets; Ricky poured bright orange powder poison *piles* in all the corners—like anthills. There were traps: snap traps, glue traps, an electronic trap that I'd read about on Martha Stewart's website. Oh, and mouse turds. I found fresh ones every time I looked after work. Also: greasy smudges along the bottom of the wall—the exterminator had taught me to look for those.

"Get a cat!" Jean kept telling me. But I was strung out like a strand of Christmas lights 24/7. I couldn't have a pet. Wouldn't that have been wrong? Beth brought her parents' *chunky* calico in from Jersey instead. Lucy had just one ear, and a bad attitude. Absolutely *permanent* stink eye. And she was no mouser. Beth took Lucy home after a few days, and I was all alone.

If deadlines sent me into meltdown mode, the Mouse sent me into a downward spiral. I went *right* off the rails. I was convinced that I saw him constantly, darting behind a bookshelf or something. Who knows what was real and what wasn't?

"AAAAUUUUGGGGGGHHHH!" I screamed every ten minutes, jumping practically to the ceiling. I was like Spider-Man! (Fine, not really.)

I came to sense that the Mouse was *always* there. Either I'd sealed him in, like the exterminator warned me, or—as I came to suspect later—he'd *nudged* his way out from underneath my kitchen sink and the cupboard door had closed behind him, so he could never get back home ever again. Either way, the Mouse was as trapped in my shitty, Adderall-shambolic life as I was.

I *hated* being at the apartment. When I was, I had a Dustbuster minivacuum at my side at all times. Every time I thought I heard or saw the Mouse, I switched it on and let it roar while I pounded my feet on the floor. I'd be wearing knee-high Fryes: my mouse-stompin' boots. And I turned my bed into a fort! I bought four big box fans at Kmart and arranged them on the floor around my bed, facing outward. They were *loud*—it sounded like an airplane taking off—but I hoped the din and wind would keep the Mouse away. But still, I couldn't sleep. I was too afraid. I came home from work and found new mouse . . . *evidence* every day—sometimes on the bed.

"Get a cat!" Jean said again.

I had another idea.

"I need sedatives," I told Dr. C.

"Why don't you try watching *Ratatouille*?" he suggested.

"The cartoon?" I was trying not to scream. "The kids' movie?!"

"My grandson and I loved it!" Dr. C. chuckled.

"*Please*," I begged. "*Tranquilizers!*"

Dr. C. prescribed Seroquel, an antipsychotic, and Xanax bars—those are two milligrams each. I took so many of the latter that I might as well have put them in a Pez dispenser. Combining the two medications knocked me out like a punch to the head and kept me blacked out for hours with my boots on, all the lights burning, and the Dustbuster tucked under my arm. But suddenly getting up in the morning was *so* hard. My bed felt like a wad of gum.

I don't want to go to work, I'd think as my alarms went off . . . and off . . . and off. I could barely lift my head or open my eyes. *I just want to sleep.* Addiction versus ambition: it starts small.

Sometimes I couldn't conk out no matter how many downers I took, so I'd just stay awake taking three Adderall at a time, vigilant, like a soldier in Vietnam on Dexedrine looking for Charlie. Things would get weird fast: I started wearing one of those flashlight headbands, and crawling around. Since the stupid exterminators couldn't figure out where this mouse was coming in, *I* would! I stuffed steel wool into the tiniest, skinniest crevices. Everyone said mice had flexible spines, right? If I could slide a butter knife into an opening, it had to be sealed. Years later, I heard a story on *TMZ Live* about Lamar Odom (another life-murderer) doing this sort of thing—during a crack binge!

I was just possessed. But nothing worked. One such night, I was on hands and knees, cleaning my closet floor. I got up to wring out the rag in the bathroom sink, and when I got back, there was fresh mouse shit right there—on the wet patch I'd *just* wiped down!

I think we all know what happened next.

"AUUUUUUUUUUUUUUUUGHHHHH!" I grabbed my purse and hurtled out of the apartment, down five flights of stairs and out onto First Avenue in knee-high stompin' boots and crusty white Proactiv sulfur acne mask spots dotting my face, but I didn't care. I was mental. I flagged a cab and dove into the backseat, but I didn't know what to tell the driver. My sister—who had moved to New York to work in PR and totally had her life together, unlike me—was out of town. Who could I call? I scrolled through my phone. I had psychiatrists; I had coke dealers; I had fuck boys. Why didn't I have any friends?

There was only one place to go.

"Forty-Second and Broadway," I said.

Jean's office was just as I'd left it. It was three in the morning. I took the gifts off the love seat and placed them on the ground. Then I tried to get comfortable. Times Square was flashing outside, so I pulled a Pucci beach towel over my head. Then—finally—the downers in my system put me under.

A cleaning lady came in at eight fifteen. I jerked awake.

"Sorry," she said, and quickly shut the door. *Omigod.* I'd been so blotto that I hadn't even set an alarm! I changed into fresh clothes and applied makeup in the beauty closet. Then I began my day.

I never told anyone that I'd slept in Jean's office. It was too dark, too weird. Embarrassing.

It was the worst winter of my life—even worse than the cheating-Nicky-pregnancy winter (and that was saying something). In January, I moved out for a month to sublet a West Village bachelor pad—an "extermination vacation," if you will. But my nerves were so shot I might as well have been at home.

"*NO!*" I shrieked every time this dude's old-timey heater piped up. "AHHH!" Then I'd bolt down to Washington Street in tears just like I did at home.

On February 1, I returned to First Avenue. The mouse was still there, but not for long. On Valentine's Day, I was fussing with a heavy wooden drawer a previous tenant had built—poorly—into the bottom of a closet. The stupid thing was always going off the tracks. I gave up and dropped the drawer on the floor. Then I sat down in the tub for a bath.

I was midshampoo when I heard it.

EEEEEEE-EEEE-EEEE-EEEE! This was *earsplitting*—and coming from the closet. High-pitched, distressed cries! *EEE! EEE! EEEEE!*

"AHHHHH!" I joined him. "AHHHHHH!"

After a few minutes, the noises stopped.

I called Ricky, who ran over to confirm what I suspected: the Mouse had been hiding in the closet—and I'd crushed him with the drawer and killed him! I couldn't believe it. The Mouse was dead; Ricky removed the body. The nightmare was over. Wasn't it?

Spring came—and a special anniversary. It had been ten years since my dad left that first bottle of Ritalin on my desk in boarding school. I'd been on prescription stimulants for exactly a decade. How were things going?

"AUUUGGHHHHHH!" This would be me reacting to a garbage bag *shifting* and settling, as they sometimes do. That would be all I needed to run out the door without a bra on or my purse and go to Lit Lounge on Second Avenue. I'd sit at the bar watching girls dancing to "Bizarre Love Triangle," and Erik Foss, the owner, would give me free vodka-grapefruits until I was juiced enough to return home.

Were there still mice in my apartment? No. But by this time, I was so heavily drug dependent, traumatized, and bonkers that it didn't matter. The imaginary ones had infested my mind.

I was still high and paranoid, staying up all night looking for things. And the more I looked for things, the more . . . *creatures* I saw. Like translucent spiders—imagine a Lucite daddy longlegs—creeping across the shag of my bath mat. They were so strange looking that they didn't even frighten me. They couldn't be real.

I reached out and touched them. The spiders vanished.

Everything was coming alive. Another night I stared at a fur coat until it twitched.

You haven't slept for two days, I kept telling myself. My Kmart floor fans roared like the subway.

But then it twitched again!

"DIE!" I screamed, and flung a book or a shoe at it. "*AAAUUUGH!*" Then I flew downstairs and walked the East Village until sunrise, listening to the Stones on my headphones.

The less I slept, the more emotionally and psychologically disorganized I became. But no matter how muddled I was, my doctor-shopping game was always on point. I had two prescribing psychiatrists; their scripts had to go to different pharmacies. There were two big ones in Times Square: Duane Reade on Broadway, and the new Walgreens right across the street. I also had two interns: Jenna and Ramona. We called them the Twinterns. Perfect! Jenna was my Walgreens girl. Ramona's beat was Duane Reade.

"What would happen if *I* took these to Walgreens?" Ramona asked once.

"I'd go to jail," I said darkly. Her eyes widened.

"Really?"

"No!" I said. "I'm not doing anything illegal! You just gotta protect ya neck, you know?" The Twinterns nodded. They were learning so much.

One day I took off my baseball cap in front of them. Yes, I was wearing baseball caps to Condé Nast. I'm telling you, I was fucking tired!

"Whoa," Ramona said. "You have dreadlocks!"

Did I? I reached up and touched my hair. Oh, wow.

I hadn't brushed it in . . . well . . . *hmm.*

"Just . . . how could you have let it get like this, Caitlin?" my sister asked.

We were at her apartment on East Twenty-Third Street.

"Stress," I whimpered. Right.

Emily didn't recognize that I had major drug problems yet—even as I sat weeping on her Crate and Barrel sofa, a severely underweight pillhead mess with zombie affect and dirty feet, my hair tangled up in knots of emotional disease and serious self-neglect. No one in my family did. No one in my *life* did.

I, of course, understood what had happened to my hair. Tranquilizers! And the antipsychotics and sleeping pills I mixed with them. Oh, and amphetamines.

I was hooked on it all—and in much, much deeper than I ever had been before. The horrible winter with the mouse had made my drug problem much worse. I was *exhausted* all of the time, particularly in the mornings. I moved through my getting-ready-for-work routine like I was underwater. I was too tired to stand in the shower and wash and condition my long, highlighted-blond hair. Half the time I got light-headed and saw black spots and had to turn the hot-water faucet off and sit down.

So for months—since the mouse winter—I'd been washing my hair sitting down in the bathtub. I had a lot of hair and I didn't rinse very well; I'd pour cups of water over myself, or, more often, just dip my head back in the water, baptism style, to get the suds out. Then I'd wrap a dirty towel around my head, slather on depuffing face treatments—when you get $145 Sisley Eye Contour Masks for free, you might as well use them—and slap on self-tan like a vampire who wanted to walk among the living undetected. Which, of course, I basically was doing.

But I didn't comb my hair out after I washed it. I was too tired. And forget blow-drying! That's exhausting work when you *aren't* a drug addict. I'd just twist it up into a bun, throw on a Helmut Lang dress, and take a thirteen-dollar cab to Times Square. (I was too *tired* to take the subway.) Fast-forward a few months and there I was, in the beauty closet with the interns. Feeling my new dreadlocks.

I should have started taking care of my hair better right away, but I didn't. I let the dreadlocks turn into dense knots. A few weeks later, they were the size of fists.

"Try the Philip B. detangler," Cristina said.

"How about the L'Oréal Paris spray for little kids?" Dawn suggested.

"Call them in," Jean instructed me. But I never did. I was too—can you guess?—tired.

Weeks went by. The snarls got worse—and my job performance along with them. Jean never asked me outright what was wrong with me, and I never told her. But more and more, I was putting my boss in the uncomfortable position of having to be concerned about her as-sistant, instead of vice versa. I came in strung out every morning and spread my poison around. Everybody got a taste. I talked—and talked and talked and talked—about my problems.

"Can rats climb up the sides of buildings?" I'd interrupt a Hair Guide discussion. Lately I'd been watching *something* move back and forth and up and down—like a video game—on the screens outside my fifth-floor windows. I was sure they were rats. I cannot tell you how terrified I was of this. Every time my brain latched onto the possibility, I couldn't stop seeing it.

"I'm not sure," Jean would say flatly.

"I don't think so, dude," Cristina would say. Dawn would look at her nail beds.

Then it would be time for everyone to try to help me with the knots.

"Go see [so-and-so] at [this-or-that salon] today," Jean would say for the fiftieth time. "Call PR and get an appointment." I'd nod, but I was too embarrassed to call a publicist and explain the situation, much less walk into Frédéric Fekkai with a nest on my head. Also, I was too tired.

More time passed. My hair got worse, but instead of stressing about it now, I ignored it the way I ignored everything that I didn't want to deal with. I wore the knots twisted into one *big* knot on the top of my head, and I stopped asking for advice about them. Problem solved!

"How's your hair?" Jean asked one day. I guess she thought it was better.

"Oh," I said. "Fantastic!" Haha! I took my hair down from the megabun, and it sort of flopped onto my neck in three thick sections. It had been all the way to my elbows; now it barely grazed my shoulders.

"Oh, no!" Jean cried.

"You know what?" I said. "I just decided, it's just *hair*."

"Oh, *no!*"

"It's okay," I said.

"Did you try the Philip B.?" she said. "Or the L'Oréal?"

"No . . ."

"None of them?" Jean said. She was incredulous.

"No," I whimpered. "I didn't try any of them. I didn't call in anything."

"But why not?!" Jean cried out.

"I don't know."

"Cat," she said. "You *must* do something about your hair. Do you understand? You *must* make that appointment."

"'Kay."

"I'm not going to tell you again!" Jean said. She looked extremely angry (and also: extremely dewy).

I went to Butterfly Studio in the Flatiron District later that week. We'd just featured the owner of the salon, Kattia, in *Lucky*, so I knew they'd be kind to me. It was late evening. An assistant brought me a flute of champagne while the stylist felt around in the knots with her fingers. I could tell by the look on her face that it wasn't good.

"I've been growing my hair out for six years," I said. "I can't cut it!"

"How did this happen?" the stylist asked.

"I haven't been taking very good care of myself," I whispered.

Kattia came over and conferred quietly with the stylist. Then she squeezed my shoulder and locked eyes with me in the mirror.

"They're going to have to cut them out," she said.

"I know," I said numbly. I felt so ashamed—and like everyone in the salon was looking at me.

God, I was beat.

"Give me one sec," I said. I took my handbag into the bathroom and fished out an Adderall. I looked at myself in the mirror. *Ugly.* I was sort of tipsy. *Idiot. Stupid girl.*

I went back out and sat down. The stylist went to work. Soon enough, tears were rolling down my smock. Old Waterworks Marnell. You know me.

"Are you okay?" the stylist said.

"I just didn't sleep last night," I sniffled. God, I hated myself. I *hated* myself. I counted the bundles as they hit the floor. *One. Two. Three. Four.*

Chapter Eleven

BY EARLY SUMMER, I WAS THE sickest I'd ever been in my life. I was so desperate to feel better that I did the unthinkable: called my family, told the truth, and begged for help.

I must have been extra exhausted and really deep into the darkness. I don't remember the first part of the conversation that I had with my mom, just that I was crying really hard on the phone and I just . . . told her.

"I think I'm addicted to Adderall," I sobbed. "I think I have a serious problem."

There was silence on the other end.

"Let me get Dad."

I sat there weeping in the mouse apartment surrounded by chaos, not knowing what the hell was about to happen.

"Cait?" my dad said, picking up the phone.

"*Hi—h-hi—h-hi, Dad,*" I hiccuped.

"Tell your dad what you just told me," my mom said.

"I'm—I'm—" I was crying so hard I could barely talk. "*I think I'm addicted to Adderall.*"

"WHAT?!" my dad roared. "WHAT?!"

"I'm addicted to it, Dad!" I screamed. "I'm addicted to Adderall!"

"But that's impossible!" he sputtered. Oh, Dad. He knows better now (as do a lot of doctors). "Adderall isn't addictive!"

What?!

"Yes it *is*, Dad," I cried. "I'm sure it is! I take like ten pills a day! I have a serious problem!"

He was livid.

"Well, that's it, *Cato*," he snarled. As in Cato Potato. "You're not getting any more from *me*!"

"I don't *want* it anymore!" I sobbed. "I'm just trying to tell you the truth!"

My dad hung up.

"Mom," I whimpered.

"We'll figure this out," she said. "Maybe you should go back on Ritalin. Hmm."

What did you just DO?! My addiction screamed. *You fool!*

Sure enough, my dad never wrote me a prescription again. But my mother did come up to New York the next week to take me to an ADHD specialist (and also do a little shopping).

Dr. Julia Jones did *not* take insurance. Swag! Her practice, Manhattan Neuropsychiatric, PC, was on Forty-Eighth Street in midtown—a mere six-minute power walk from Condé Nast. She was in her late thirties, with great legs and board certifications in psychiatry and neurology. I wouldn't be able to pull the wool over her eyes. But that was okay. Maybe she could actually help me feel better.

She charged three hundred dollars per forty-five-minute appointment. My mom came along to meet her.

"I've heard such wonderful things about you, Julia," my mom said.

"Her name is Dr. Jones!" I said.

"Oh, sorry," my mom said. "Dr. Jones. My husband and I are also mental health professionals, so . . ." I rolled my eyes. "I'm sitting in today because, well, I don't really trust Caitlin. My husband and I are paying for this, and it's a lot of money to spend if she's not going to be telling you the truth."

Dr. Jones looked at me.

"It's fine," I said.

"So," my mom began. "Let me give you the situation from a mom's perspective. Caitlin has had ADHD her whole life. My husband and I had her tested at NIH to make sure. She's textbook. Chaotic . . . irresponsible . . ." My eyes glazed over. "We sent her to a wonderful boarding school . . . put her on Ritalin . . . signed her up for neurofeedback . . . She didn't like it . . ." They'd tried to attach wires to my head! "It's crisis to crisis . . ." Dr. Jones scribbled notes. "*Blah blah blah blah blah blah blah. Blah blah blah blah blah blah blah . . .*" I tuned out. I'd heard this stuff a million times. "And then there was . . . the abortion."

"The *pregnancy*," I snapped.

"She got kicked out of her boarding school six weeks before graduation and they told us she was pregnant and on drugs," my mom continued. "When we got home to DC, we found out she was at almost five months."

"Mmm," Dr. Jones said.

"We've tried everything . . ." my mom went on. "Her ADHD is out of control. There's always another disaster around the corner."

"Caitlin—" Dr. Jones started.

"It was just *so* awful." My mom was still going. "I took her to the clinic. It was horrible. Just *horrible*. And then Caitlin moved to New York. We paid for her life here. She and her father have barely spoken since. They haven't had a relationship for years."

"*Mmm*," Dr. Jones said, scribbling notes.

"I *can't* talk to him," I said. "He's—"

"Caitlin's dad just *adored* her when she was little," my mom interrupted.

I stared at a potted plant.

"I just want to help Caitlin," my mom said. "With her ADHD medication. She called recently and said she was having . . . some pretty major . . . issues with her Adderall." My mom sat back. "So that's why we're here. To find something else."

Dr. J. scribbled more notes. Now I was looking up at the ceiling.

"Caitlin?" Dr. Jones said. "Do you have anything to add?"

I thought about this.

"Young female bodies are *built* to get pregnant, you know," I said coolly. I was still gazing up at the ceiling. "And it's been that way since the dawn of time."

We all sat there for a moment.

"Why don't Caitlin and I have some one-on-one time?" Dr. Jones suggested.

My mom didn't look too pleased.

"I just want to make sure we get her on the right medication," she said. "For her ADHD."

"Got it." Dr. Jones nodded.

My mom left the room. Dr. Jones watched the door close. Then she turned back to me.

"So," Dr. J. said. "What's *really* going on?"

"I'm not a failure!" I said. "I work at Condé Nast."

"Okay," Dr. J. said.

"And my problem isn't ADHD," I added. "It's drugs."

"Explain," Dr. Jones said.

I'd never told the truth to a psychiatrist before. Once I started, I couldn't stop! I told her about the doctor shopping, the bulimia. I told her about my crazy apartment and the nightclubs and the cocaine and the ecstasy and the sleeping pills and the champagne. I told her that I thought I didn't love my family, about how I thought no one in my family really loved each other. I told her about the Adderall, the Adderall

XR, the Dexedrine, the Provigil, the Vyvanse, the Valium. The Ambien, the boxes of Lunesta and Sonata I'd been swiping from my dad's office since I was a teenager . . . I told her everything!

"Mmm-hmm," she said, scribbling notes and listening to all this.

"And then I left my *Xanax bottle*," I said, "at the Genius Bar, you know, and the Apple Store called me and were all, 'We have your prescription bottle,' but I never got it back, so I couldn't sleep for like two weeks, plus my friend Marco bought this *crack rock* and I *hated* it because it made me so *cranky* but I kept smoking it anyway and then at work I was so *tired* that I was all—"

BUZZZZZ. Dr. Jones's next appointment arrived.

"We have to stop," she said.

"Wow!" I said. "I feel ten pounds lighter!"

"You need to go to rehab," Dr. Jones said.

"Excuse me?" I said.

"*Rehab*," she repeated. "Cat. You are in *serious* trouble."

I was?!

"I can't go to rehab!" I said. "I have a job!"

"Okay, well," Dr. J. said. "You have to come see me twice a week. And you can't see anyone else. The 'old guys.' "

"I can't promise you that," I said. "But I will be honest about when I see them and what I get from them."

She considered this.

"Fine—for now," she said. "So . . . deal?"

"Deal!" I said. I mean, I wasn't paying for it.

Dr. Jones *tried* to help me. For a while, she truly did. I stopped seeing other doctors for about five weeks straight. She prescribed me a cute pink mood stabilizer called Lamictal, which sounded like a dinosaur and could give you a deadly rash. She weaned me off Seroquel and Xanax bars with adorable quarter-milligram Klonopin wafers that tasted like strawberries. They came in bubble-gum-pink boxes and popped out of foil like Alka-Seltzer. My new friend Marco and I would pass a sheet like kids sharing candy.

"Your new psychiatrist is the best!" Marco would say. (More on him later.)

"Right?" I drooled.

Dr. Jones also finally agreed to prescribe ADHD medication—she knew I'd get the pills elsewhere if she didn't. But she wrote up a special contract where I had to promise that I wouldn't use other stimulant drugs—cocaine, Adderall, crack, whatever—or, again, see other doctors. I signed, and she prescribed me a week's worth of Concerta, a once-a-day, navy-colored . . . *pellet*.

"I don't think this is going to work," I said. It was the drug equivalent of portion control, and I was a binge eater.

"Just try it," Dr. Jones said.

Concerta was wack—Ritalin-ish; amateur hour. It wasn't long before I was uptown scoring Gladerall—breaking my agreement. I didn't tell Dr. Jones.

By the first week of August, I was a mess. It didn't take long for me to violate the cocaine clause as well—at a party in a suite at the Union Square W Hotel. I left with a white rapper and hooked up with him in his Chelsea recording studio, where a plaque fell off the wall and split my face open between my eyebrows. My face bled all day at work and the wound wouldn't stop.

"Maybe you should go home," my intern told me. I was hiding in the beauty closet, trying to fix it.

"It's fine," I said. No one asked too many questions. Everyone at *Lucky* was focused on getting the November issue shipped before they took their summer breaks. (As a rule, Condé Nasties generally don't work in August.)

I walked home along Broadway that evening. *You MUST stay in and sleep*, I told myself. I was *so* tired; plus, I had a special appointment with Dr. Jones in the morning. She was all excited to give me some expensive neurological test. My parents had agreed to pay for it.

That night, I slipped under the covers with a dog-eared copy of Jonathan Franzen's *The Corrections* and was asleep by eleven. Just kidding! Charlotte and I went to the Box on Chrystie Street and watched a surly drag queen light her dick on fire. We were still drunk at dawn, so Charlotte took me on a tour of "Bob Dylan's Greenwich Village." At eight o'clock, I went home and dipped into a bath; changed into a navy chiffon Theory slip, my leopard-print Louis Vuitton–Stephen Sprouse scarf, and strappy black Givenchy platforms; applied NARS Cruella to my lips and dabbed a little Laura Mercier Secret Concealer on my crusty forehead wound; hit Dunkin' for an extralarge iced coffee with half-and-half and no sugar, please; and took a taxi to midtown for my appointment.

I thought I looked pretty good, but apparently not. Dr. Jones's hand flew to her mouth the second I walked into her office.

"What?" I said.

"You *have* to go to rehab!" Dr. Jones cried out. Do psychiatrists "cry out"? Am I remembering this correctly? She looked very afraid. "I can't treat you anymore until you do!"

"Okay," I said. I never took the test.

Dr. Jones said she'd make arrangements at Silver Hill Hospital in Connecticut, and that she'd call my mother. I had to tell my boss. It was ten o'clock in the morning. I stumbled down Sixth Avenue in a daze.

Am I really about to do this? I thought in the Condé elevator. There would be no going back.

Jean was in her office.

"I have to talk to you," I said straightaway—so I wouldn't lose my nerve.

"Okay . . ." Jean looked up. "Come on in." I shut the door behind me.

Over the next forty minutes, I told my boss . . . well, not *everything*. But I told her a lot. I cried a lot, too.

"I care about this job so much," I sobbed. "I love working for you. It's the most important thing in my life." I meant every word. "I didn't mean for this to happen. Please, please, please know that."

"Your job will be here when you get back," Jean said firmly. She was so supportive, so kind. "Look at me. Do *not* worry about that." So loving. "Take as *much* time as you need." I was so relieved. "I admire you so much for telling me the truth and taking this step to get well." She'd deal with Human Resources, she told me, and I'd be placed on paid disability leave.

I cabbed home. I'd scheduled car service to Connecticut, but just after dark, my dad called. He'd hopped in his car and driven up from DC. And now he was downstairs in front of my building. *Surprise!*

I looked around. Stella Artois bottles cluttered the windowsills, pill bottles were lined up like toy soldiers on the kitchen counter, full ashtrays were by the bed. What could I do? Nothing. So I buzzed him up and listened as he ascended the vile carpeted stairs. Then my father stepped into the apartment he was paying for and saw my life.

"Hi, Dad," I said.

He didn't even say hello back. I was in big trouble. I watched him take everything in. It was not good.

"*Goddammit,*" he finally said.

"Dad, I haven't been well . . ." Then I just shut up.

He walked over to my bookshelves, where I had my collection of "drug rep" stuff he'd given me over the years—an Adderall XR stapler, a Prozac basketball, a Zyprexa brain puzzle, a pill-shaped Ambien XR squeeze toy.

("You really like this crap?" he used to ask me, amused. "Yes!" I'd tell him. "Bring home more!")

"*GODDAMMIT!*" He knocked it all to the floor.

That night, my dad slept on the sofa while I messed around in the bathroom until two o'clock, packing makeup and applying Clarins Delicious Self Tanning Cream. I took a Lunesta; my dad woke me up at six. I trudged to the bathroom. My tan looked fantastic! I was ready for rehab.

My dad and I zoomed up the . . . I don't really know *what* that road is from New York City to Connecticut, but it is extremely good looking as roads go. Zillions of trees. The drive was an hour or so. New Canaan was as gorgeous as a movie set. *Stepford Wives*! The houses were storybook classic, with converted barns and vegetable gardens and gazebos and raspberry bushes. Summer squash and guesthouses. You get the idea.

We were mad early for my ten o'clock admissions appointment, so we cruised around the ritzy little town. There was a Ralph Lauren Rugby store and a J.Crew. Then we had breakfast at a little diner. Well, *I* had breakfast. Pancakes! My dad looked really skinny; he had just quit carbs, and his hair was white and he was wearing khaki pants. Slacks. He didn't eat; he just stared at me. I dove right in when the food arrived. It tasted *so* good; I hadn't taken any Adderall that morning, and I was starving. When was the last time I had a fucking pancake?

"Cait," my dad kept . . . *growling*, almost. "This is it."

"I know, Dad," I said.

"This is the end." He was like a wolf! "It stops now."

"I *know*, Dad," I said. God, he was grim! Was this real maple syrup?!

I cleaned my plate. Then we drove to Silver Hill Hospital. It was almost as pretty as my prep school: sprawling and green, with gardeners on tractors everywhere. There was a red clay tennis court and a chapel and a big grassy hill. The main building looked like something Taylor Swift would buy to impress the Kennedys: huge as a cruise ship, and white with black shutters. Very moneyed New England.

We drove over a bridge and I spotted a Tudor house that I knew I'd seen before. But where?

"That's the house from *Edie*!" I shrieked, launching myself halfway out the car window like my parents' pet boxer at the dog park. "Edie Sedgwick stayed there!" I'd only read her biography two hundred times. My dad gave me a death stare; I guess I wasn't supposed to be excited. I'd forgotten that the Warhol star had been one of my *new* rehab's most famous patients! Her brother, Minty, had even hung himself at Silver Hill. I believe he used his own pants.

My dad and I got out of the car. Gosh, the air smelled divine—like pinecones! And like fresh-cut grass. Silver Hill should really make a candle; it would be a bestseller. Anyway, my dad and I sat in the admissions office. There were lots of wonderful snacks in the waiting room, like delicious buttery shortbread cookies, and I ate them and ate them. I was ravenous, as I said. Besides, I just love shortbread, don't you? My dad ate absolutely zero snacks, even though we were waiting like two hours. And the two hours felt like ten hours, because I knew he just hated me.

"Ms. Marnell?" Finally! Intake took another hour. We went over my drug history, medications I was on, *yadda yadda yadda*.

"Where do you work?" the lady asked.

"Condé Nast Publications," I said proudly. "Magazine publishing." She smiled.

"Of course," she said. "We have people here from Condé all the time." Say what?!

Then intake was over, and a cute man came and took my suitcase. I was looking around, anticipating what new adventures were to come, waiting— *Ack!* Suddenly I was wrapped in a tight *bear* hug.

"This is it, Cait," my dad was saying. Oh, Jesus.

"I know, Dad," I mumbled into his button-down, trying to pull away just a smidgen.

But he just squeezed me tighter—like he was part boa constrictor or something!

"This is it."

"Got it." My face was all smooshed into his chest. Then my dad *kissed* me—on the head!

"You are loved," he whispered. Which I knew.

My dad drove off. I couldn't wait to get down to the Edie mansion and unpack my rehab outfits, but instead, an orderly took me to a dark room in a tiny, unglamorous little house. There were two twin beds and plastic curtains. The rehab operative closed them and asked me to strip naked and do the old "squat and cough." I will spare you the details, but I had not *boofed* anything—so it went fine.

Then she went through my luggage. Talk about a beauty edit! This lady was more ruthless than Jean Godfrey-June! Giorgio Armani bronzer? Out! I could shatter the mirror and shank someone right in the spleen. Clinique Clarifying Lotion? Out! A desperado like me could pour that shit over ice and make toner cocktails. Everything containing alcohol had to go.

The only place I was allowed to go besides my room was the fenced-in outdoor area behind K House, which was packed with newly admitted clients. Some of them were pacing around the perimeter of the fence like weirdos, but most of the addicts and alcoholics were chatting cheerfully, like they were at a barbecue instead of a private hospital. And *everyone* was smoking. I stepped into the ring.

"For drunks, all you need is Librium," a woman wearing a turtleneck (it was August) was saying, waving her skinny cig in the air. Her name was Pam. I got cornered right away by a chick named Robin. She told me she was from Norwalk and was just doing five days at Silver Hill—a detox.

"I'm in New York all the time," she told me. "Lemme get your connects."

"Connects?" I said.

"Yeah," Robin pushed. "Your connects."

"I don't have any connects," I lied.

"Yeah, right," Robin said. "You're doing twenty-eight days? Transitional living?" I nodded. "You must be rich."

"Not really," I said. "I'm a magazine assistant."

"Who's paying the twenty-eight grand, then?"

"Excuse me?" I said. Twenty-eight thousand dollars?! Was Dr. Jones out of her mind, putting me at this place? That was more than I made in a year! No wonder my dad was so pissed off.

I stayed in K House two more days, being monitored for alcohol and benzodiazepine withdrawal. I was in the basement watching a dude on methadone nod off in front of *Talladega Nights: The Ballad of Ricky Bobby* when someone called my name. It was time to go to the lower campus for a month of thousand-dollar-a-day rehab.

Many important authors have written about Silver Hill, and since I am decidedly not one of them, I'll make this snappy, *papi*.

So. I was *very* fortunate to get to go to Silver Hill and be in the Transitional Living program. So many sick addicts can't afford treatment centers, much less luxury rehabs. I was out-of-this-world privileged. I was on-Pluto privileged.

That being said, I've had tanning-bed experiences that were more transformative. Don't get me wrong; the program was fantastic. *I* was the problem—my state of mind. Before I arrived, I'd thought rehab was, like . . . I don't even know. A place where a party girl could recharge her batteries. You know—before she could return all refreshed and healthy feelings to her regularly scheduled party-girl life!

But no. At Silver Hill, "party girls" were just addicts—"people in the grip of a continuing and progressive illness whose ends are always the same: jails, institutions, and death." That was from Narcotics Anonymous; someone read it out loud the first night. Then: "This is a program of complete abstinence from all drugs." *Excusez-moi?* "There is only one requirement for membership, the desire to stop using."

Well. I did *not* meet that requirement. Even after all the pain and chaos of the last few years, I wasn't ready to quit drugs and drinking for good! Not at all.

So I checked out early—in my head, at least. Physically, I stayed a month, and I had a great time. Rehab was like boarding school, except I didn't get to take my Ritalin and I took drug tests instead of math exams. Silver Hill really did remind me of Lawrence Academy: I lived in a two-story house with a dozen other females, there was a big kitchen where someone was always making popcorn, and the bedrooms were pretty and cozy. We shared two pay phones; when someone called asking whether so-and-so was there, we had to be all, "I can't confirm that person is here, but I can take a message."

About half of my housemates were in their early twenties, in residential treatment for the first time. My favorite was Rosy, who was from a particularly infamous branch of an iconic American family. I mention this not because it is germane, but because I have *Vanity Fair* for brains and I am very shallow. Anyway, Rosy was a hard-core Adderall aficionado—fine, *addict*—just like your favorite narrator, me. She'd been caught stealing prescription pads from her psychiatrist and had a car-accident scar on her cheek from when a tree branch had popped right through the skin. Hard-core. (Sort of.)

The other key demographic in Barrett House were wealthy older women—Republicans (they were always talking politics) from Connecticut who called themselves "drunks," never "alcoholics." Turtleneck Pam from K House was in this group. (She was very elegant but let herself grow a white beard; it really freaked me out.) Pam had more DUIs than Paris Hilton and Nicole Richie combined. They all did!

The two groups had beef, particularly over the living room television we shared. It was the summer of 2008 and the Beijing Olympics, and my crew obviously wanted to see Michael Phelps, you know? It was supposed to be his year! But the drunks *had* to control the remote—just like they had to control everything and everyone else in their lives. (I'm joking, I'm joking; alcoholics in their sixties are lovely.) They only wanted to watch reruns of *Law & Order*. Guess who won?

"*Quong-quong!*" I heard that fucking *Law & Order* gong about thirty times a day. As for Phelps, a few years later, *he'd* be in rehab, too. I read it on TMZ as I was writing this book! Who would have guessed?

We only watched television on the weekends. Monday through Friday, I carried a three-ring binder full of recovery worksheets from classroom to classroom. I listed my triggers (*carrot cake, deadlines, weight gain, mice, insomnia*), studied relapse prevention, and learned dialectical behavioral therapy (DBT) skills, which I liked because you could apply them to life, not just recovery. My favorite was "Teflon mind," where you imagine your brain being like nonstick cookware: negative thoughts just slide *right* off.

Just like in real classrooms, however, I got bored and squirmy fast. Thank God for rehab romance. Do you know what that is? A rehab romance is a relationship that you have with someone you'd never date or even encounter in real life, but whom you meet in a treatment center when you are both newly sober and horny. You sit together at every meal and make bedroom eyes at each other instead of paying attention in Alcoholics Anonymous meetings. And the rehab staff notices and bans you from hanging out, so you sneak all over the place, and then it's even *more* narcotic—the thrill of the forbidden and all that—and you think you're in love, and you plan your sober, loved-up life together outside of the treatment program. It never actually works out—but boy, does it pass the time!

My rehab boyfriend, Brian—a dual-diagnosis bipolar-alcoholic by way of Long Island—and I would go to the gym, hold each other's feet down, and pretend to count "reps" as we talked filthy-dirty to each other. We'd make intense, sexual eye contact in the Silver Hill library as we rubbed our legs together under the table in the computer room. I did kiss him once—in the pine grove behind the gym—and it lasted half a second. We would've been kicked out if we got caught—and you know me. I just *live* for getting kicked out of things.

I always wanted to look sexy for Brian during Saturday screenings of *My Name Is Bill W.*, but the dress code was strict.

"Cat," I was constantly being told. "Change your shirt."

No tank tops allowed. *That's* how sex-crazed addicts get in treatment. There was a swimming pool, but it was closed; we were only allowed to wear bathing suits on the secluded lawns behind our dorms. The girls would oil up and lie out like lazy cats, puffing on Marlboro Lights from the drugstore and picking apart our thousand-dollar-a-day program. Over at Scavetta, the boys were doing the same. You'll find them at every nice rehab, in fact: spoiled, shit-talking adult children on chaise longues, smoking cigarettes that they charged to their parents. Sorry, but it's true.

I had minimal contact with the outside world apart from crazy-looking letters from my new friend Marco. Seriously, they looked like they'd been ripped from the serial killer's notebooks in the movie *Se7en*, which of course ends with Gwyneth Paltrow's head in a box. They were written in tiny, illegible script on both sides of graph paper; sometimes he'd draw a rabbit getting stabbed through the neck or something. Marco's signature was always four times the size of anything else on the page. (You must be *very* curious about him by now.)

My only visitor at Silver Hill was Charlotte, in a vintage, chauffeured black Mercedes, no less. She looked fabulous in her baby duck–yellow tube top, bell-bottom jeans, wedge heels, and huge sunglasses—like she'd just had sex with Jimmy Page! I showed her the Edie house—Scavetta, where my Brian lived—and the building that Mariah Carey allegedly rented all for herself after she went on MTV's *TRL* and pushed that ice cream cart around without any pants on.

I didn't hear from my parents.

"It's so strange that your mom won't return my calls," my counselor said.

"Shocking," I sneered. Always the victim, you know. It turned out that my parents were out West on one of those bizarre "we're-ending-our-marriage" vacations you always read about celebrities like Jennifer Garner and Ben Affleck taking in *People* magazine. My dad called when they were back.

"Do you have any questions you want to ask me?" he said. "About me and Mom?"

"No," I huffed. I was in *rehab. God.* Did it always have to be about *them*?

I only spoke to my mother once the whole month—and no, not to ask her if she was okay. To berate her! It was late August—I'd been in treatment three weeks—and the lease on the mouse apartment was up September first. My mom was in charge of packing up my crazy life and putting it into storage.

"Mom, I know every *single* magazine in my apartment!" I freaked out over the phone. "Do not throw out *any* of them! I will never speak to you again!" I should have been grateful, but instead I just felt out of control.

The person I heard from the most was Jean Godfrey-June. She and the girls in *Lucky* beauty sent care packages of every tabloid from Hudson News—plus bags of treats and Blow Pops. Coconut and vanilla-scented beauty products, too.

And there were letters from Jean. I took the first one into the backyard and sat under a tree and opened it. It was on baby-blue stationery, with Jean's familiar scribbly handwriting in blue felt-tip editing pen.

The page I have in front of me now begins—midletter—in a typical JGJ way:

> *And Hilton saw Jay Z & Beyoncé get out of an Escalade in front of Nobu.*

. . . which made me laugh. And then:

> *I miss you TERRIBLY—everyone does—& I'm so proud of what you're doing. It takes guts & strength, which I know you to have in spades, but it's still amazing. I will repeat the only advice which has ever really resonated with me re: pain—emotional as well as physical—which is:*
>> *It's not always going to feel the way it feels today.*
> *It's just true & key to remember. It certainly helped during childbirth!*
> *You are so full of imagination & brilliance & humor, & those*

things will shine out even brighter as you take care of yourself.
Think of how you will RULE!!

I cried and cried—I can see that I did! The ink on the page is all smudgy from my tears. No one had ever said such nice things to me. I knew I would keep this letter close to my bed for the rest of my life.

Connecticut in late summer is reliably just *beyond*; accordingly, the weeks I spent there in 2008 passed in a jiffy. The friends, the rehab romance, the clean air, the clean body—it all did wonders! By the end of the month, I was happy, fit, and properly socialized. Again, I'd had a lot of fun—which isn't against the rules. It's good for addicts to realize they can have a great time without drugs, you know?

Then it was early September 2008, a week before my twenty-sixth birthday. The month was over, and it was time to go home. The women in my dorm gathered in the living room for a special ceremony and said good-bye one by one.

"You came here because you lost your marbles," Rosy recited. Someone handed me two of them. "And now we are giving them back to you . . ." I still have those marbles in a lab beaker on my desk, incidentally.

It was a lovely ceremony, and I went through the motions . . . but look. I think it's really hard to get sober in your twenties! We've all heard about people who have to lose everything—their homes, their jobs, their husbands or wives, their teeth—to finally get clean and start over. Maybe I'd lost my house keys a few times (I really had to stop letting cokeheads pass them around at parties), but that was it. I was only twenty-five! I still had my job at *Lucky*; my family's support; my health . . . I hadn't lost anything. Not yet.

Chapter Twelve

I RETURNED TO WORK ON SEPTEMBER 9, 2008. The next afternoon, Dawn, Cristina, and I sat in Jean's office eating banana cake from Billy's. It was my twenty-sixth birthday. Jean gave me a two-hundred-dollar John Derian Company gift certificate and a handwritten note on her favorite D.L. & Co. skull stationery. She told me that she was so proud of me for being brave and getting help, and that I was so valuable to her and to the magazine. I had the best boss ever. That hadn't changed.

But two things were *très* different at 4 Times Square. Number one: there was a new delicacy in the cafeteria! Flatbread—an oversize cracker piled with chicken cubes and asparagus spears—was very low-carb, not least of all because it was almost impossible to eat. The toppings *always* fell off. It was impractical, ridiculous—*and* a sensation! Jean was just mental for it; all the Nasties were. On Thursdays, aka Flatbread Day, I sent interns to stand in the line, which was always out the cafeteria door.

The other big thing was . . . an *economic crisis*, of sorts, in publishing and perhaps the world at large. For some reason the magazine industry was getting it the worst. Ad sales were plummeting! At least I think that's what was happening. I actually do not have much insight into what the hell was going on, quite frankly. The economy isn't my thing (though I have been profiled in the *Wall Street Journal*). So forgive me if I'm not writing the circumstances of this messy time quite right.

All I can tell you for sure is what it was like in the thick of it. In the fall of 2008, we gathered over and over again in the sixth-floor conference room for ultrasomber staff meetings. KF and our managing editor, Regan, always had bad news. CEO Chuck Townsend and Mr. Newhouse were ordering cuts, cuts, and more cuts. Budgets for expenses and meals and freelancers were to be absolutely *reduced*. I wasn't supposed to take a town car home, no matter how late I worked (I did anyway). We weren't even allowed to expense flatbread anymore! Shit was getting real.

Magazines kept shutting down. *Men's Vogue*—folded! *Portfolio*—kaput. *Vogue Living*? Bye, bitch! Even *Teen Vogue* was rumored to be on the chopping block. Hearst Corporation had just shuttered *CosmoGirl!* Nothing was performing well.

Dark days. Every morning there was something in the papers.

"IT'S NASTY OVER AT CONDÉ," a typical *New York Post* headline from that October read. Then:

> The ax fell yesterday at Condé Nast. When the counting is done, it is expected that more than 100 people will be out of work in a one-day bloodbath that is unprecedented in the history of the company.

"You're not going anywhere," Jean told me privately.

Phew.

So my career was secure after rehab. My home life? Not so much. Everything from the shambolic mouse apartment was in a storage unit on the West Side. Whenever I thought about going over there, I felt terrible dread.

In the meantime, I had Empire State Building views from my sister's sofa in her immaculate Gramercy Park apartment. It was like an issue of *Real Simple* in there! So nice. I borrowed outfits from Em's color-coded closet and bathed in her squeaky-clean tub. I was sober and enrolled in an outpatient program. I dutifully attended groups and one-on-one therapy at Realization Center in Union Square.

"I'm going to need the names of these psychiatrists uptown," my counselor would say.

"Give me a few days," I always answered.

Then I'd go pee into a cup—or at least try to. Stupid drug tests! I've been taking them for nearly a decade now and I *still* get pee on my hands. I'd really like to invent some sort of contraption for female addicts and take it to *Shark Tank.*

"What would even happen if I tested positive for something?" I asked my counselor one day.

"Nothing," she said. "We'd just talk to you about it."

Hmm.

Being clean had felt really great in Connecticut. But back in Manhattan, not being on stimulants just felt . . . wrong. My energy didn't match the city's energy anymore. I felt very fuzzy around the edges, and just . . . weird and lazy. And I was always hungry! *So* hungry. I'd gained fifteen pounds since I'd stopped taking Adderall.

"I'll have a plain bagel untoasted with sun-dried tomato cream cheese . . ." I ordered Pick a Bagel at least once a day. "A large fresh-squeezed orange juice . . ."

Blerrg! Then I'd barf it up in my poor sister's toilet while she watched *Gossip Girl* in the living room. It's *very* bad bulimia manners to yak in other people's cribs. But I was desperate to feel like I was in control.

I missed speed. I felt very out of it. One day I forgot I was running a bath and the tub overflowed. The water spread out into Emily's foyer and closet. It wasn't the kind of flood you mopped up with towels. Her super brought up a special "wet vacuum."

"I'm so sorry," I told Emily over the din.

"It's okay." But it wasn't. The parquet tiles popped up as they dried out. Then her floor had little peaks, like a mountain range.

Hurricane Cat had to go. I looked on Craigslist and found a room for rent. It was on the lower level of a three-bedroom, two-bathroom duplex in the West Village, a picturesque neighborhood famous for its tree-lined cobblestone streets and gay bars. The old me never would have considered living there. It was *very* different from my beloved East Village. Where were the teen runaways? The only cuties nodding off on Christopher Street were French bulldog puppies in the pet-store windows. Was there even a methadone clinic? People lined up for cupcakes at Magnolia Bakery instead.

It wasn't exactly my scene. But I was Healthy Cat now—or at least I was pretending to be. I hit up Dave, who was moving out of the West Village duplex. He invited me over for an "interview."

"Do you party?" Dave asked. "Because that's the one thing that you can't really do here . . . drugs." He lowered his voice. "I mean, *I* like a little coke now and then, but Becky doesn't approve of that stuff at all."

"I don't do drugs," I said. We were standing in the empty bedroom. It was huge and shaped like a pentagon. Craig and Becky—the other roommates—lived on the second floor. They worked in finance and were never home, Dave said. It showed. There were black leather sofas in the living room but no television; the kitchen looked untouched. The terrace was covered in pigeon mess, and the issues of *Forbes* magazine stacked on the toilet tank were two years old.

"I'll take it!" I said. Whatever.

Moving day was October first. It was time to face the music—that is, my life.

My new building, 29 Seventh Avenue South, was in a strange industrial pocket of downtown near the Holland Tunnel. When you crossed Houston Street, Seventh Avenue turned into Varick—a scary-at-night strip of West Soho lined with warehouses and the odd nightclub. It was also home to the storage-unit facility where my mom had put my things.

Oh, God. Manhattan Mini Storage! I am getting the shivers just thinking about it! When I see it in my mind's eye, I hear a wolf howl, and a bat flies across a green moon. And there's all this creepy horror music. It was only a few blocks from my new apartment. The first night I went, I arrived at nine o'clock, an hour before closing. You entered through the garage. I hadn't taken one step in the place before a *monster* rat crossed my path. It scurried over to the loading dock, where the moving trucks were parked. I wanted to leave right then and there, but instead I got my key card from the front desk.

The fourth floor was completely silent. It looked like a haunted, abandoned psych ward or something—white on white, aisle after aisle of doors! There were barely any lights on. The only lights flickered along with me as I walked—motion detectors. (Or a poltergeist. Who knows?) Finally, I found my unit. The door was huge. And I really, *really* did not want to open it.

Maybe it won't be that bad, I thought. Right.

I took a deep breath and unlocked the door. *Creaaakkk.* And there it was: the mouse apartment. Crammed up to the ceiling in trash bags and boxes.

I can't handle this, I thought immediately.

. . . *without Adderall.* My addiction finished the thought for me.

But it was just a thought. *Teflon mind. Nothing sticks.* I closed my eyes and let it pass by me like a cloud in the sky, just like I learned at Silver Hill. Then I shook my head for a second. Then I got to work.

Needless to say, the reality of my prerehab life in the mouse apartment was *way* scarier than any storage facility could ever be. I went through bin after bin of junk: glass stems, an orange Hermès box full of drug baggies. My mom hadn't even thrown out all of the empty pill bottles I'd been hoarding in the crisper drawers of my refrigerator. There were shredded T-shirts and stained dresses. Had I not noticed how dirty my clothes were? Had I worn them in this condition to work? Everything reeked of stale cigarette smoke and the fragrance diffusers I'd used to cover up the dead-things-in-the-wall smell.

To my mom's credit, every magazine was there—crates and crates of them. And all of my papers! I'd begged my mother to save those, too. There were papers, papers, and more papers. I'd been *such* a tweaker—like a hamster. My entire apartment had been wallpapered. It had looked so shamefully crazy toward the end that I hadn't let *anyone* up.

Well, except for Marco.

I suppose it's time to introduce you to him, isn't it?

One morning in late spring—this was postmouse, prerehab—I was in Tompkins Square Park chewing Bubble Yum and lugging around dirty shopping bags full of Gavin McInnes–era *Vice* magazines I'd bought off Craigslist.

"Cat?"

I turned. The kid who'd said my name was tall and great-looking, with spiky white-blond hair. He was wearing a shredded T-shirt spotted with what looked like bloodstains.

"Marco!" I said.

I hadn't seen him since I lived on the Upper East Side. We weren't close friends or anything: back then, we'd merely had a mutually beneficial "business" relationship of sorts.

Can you spot me 15 Addys until I see my shrink on Monday? I'd text him once every few months or so.

Come through, he'd write back. Marco was an Adderall habitué, too; he was also deep into benzos. Neither of us took our medications as prescribed, and our respective supplies always got too low, too soon—though usually not at the same time. Marco and I would have each other's back.

I'd swing by. Marco lived across the park with his girlfriend, Sylvia, who was lanky, pale, and half-dead looking. He had studied sculpture. He was an RISD dropout, and talented, and he now worked in every medium. Sometimes he showed me his crazy sketches of girls with sharp weapons in their asses and ball gags in their mouths. We'd talk a little and he'd spot me the fifteen pills to get through the week. As soon as I got my next script, I'd pay him back. Then when Marco was inevitably short himself a week or two later, I'd spot *him* until *his* next doctor's appointment. We never screwed each other over. Pillhead honor code.

We'd continued this arrangement for years. Then I'd moved downtown and forgotten that Marco existed—and here he was, in Tompkins Square Park. He and Sylvia had broken up, he told me.

"Some shit went down." He shrugged. "Where are you living these days?"

"Around the corner," I said. "But I don't bring anyone up there. It's too crazy."

"Oh, come on," Marco said.

Fuck it, I thought. I was lonely.

I took him home and up to the fifth floor.

"Don't say I didn't warn you," I said.

We stepped inside. The whole place was wallpapered. Probably half of the clothing I owned was on the floor. *Artforum*, and vintage *Hustler* and *Lui* magazines spilled out of the oven. Art books were all over the bed. There were nightclub matchbooks and coke bags everywhere, and Make Up For Ever glitter pots and La Prairie sunscreen and on and on. Plastic rosaries were dangling in all the doorways to keep mice away. False eyelashes that I'd pulled off and tossed aside danced in the corner (I still kept the mouse fans on—just in case) like spiders. The seashells I used as ashtrays overflowed with lipstick-stained Marlboro Ultra Lights butts.

Marco's jaw dropped.

"This is amazing!"

"What?!" I said.

"You're so creative!" Marco marveled as he walked around, taking it all in. "Cat! I had no idea!"

"No I'm not." I laughed. "I'm just messy." And yet . . . through Marco's eyes, I saw all of the things I hated about myself differently for the first time. We stayed up all night, talking and talking. It was as easy to be with him as it was to be alone. Maybe it was all the prescription speed we were both on, but it was also what happens when you find a true friend.

At dawn, he showed me how his "breakup" had made it into the newspapers: he had broken into Sylvia's building.

"Hilarious!" I said.

We started hanging out all the time. He lived near me, deep in the Lower East Side, where the subways didn't run. It was a foul block, but perfect for Marco. He shared a terrifying lair with five or six other people. The kitchen and bathroom were exceedingly unclean, and his bedroom was cramped and crazy: full of meticulously organized collections of glassine heroin bags (we both kept them for the stamps), pills, sketchbooks, filthy designer clothes, and an expensive Apple laptop computer on which he obsessively chronicled his life. We'd sit in there stoned on morphine pills that Marco's Section 8 friends had stolen from their grandmas. Marco didn't have a heroin connect right then, he told me, but he was working on one.

"Amazing," I said. I'd always loved the dope game. I'd give him my parents' money to go out and buy us crack.

Marco never had a cent, and his fingernails were black. I never felt tired when I was with him, no matter how little we'd slept. He was the only other person I'd ever met who would stay up multiple nights in a row collaging his walls, then pass out in a bed piled with paper scraps and garbage. I did it every weekend! And now I had someone to do it with.

After a day of working in Times Square and riding the elevator with Lauren Santo Domingo–types or God knows who, I would come home to my apartment, where he was doing my drugs, looking through all my drawers, waiting for me.

"You have the greatest stuff!" he'd tell me.

"Thanks!" I'd say, then join him on the floor. "What are you looking at?" We'd drink warm Veuve Clicquot that a lovely Herbal Essences PR rep had sent and look through my Richard Kern and Juergen Teller books. I'd give him Smashbox eyeliner to put on like Keith Richards. Then Marco would take pictures of himself. He rarely took any of me. But what did I need photos of myself for?

I started rediscovering the city with my new buddy. We took walks through downtown all night long, passing a bottle of red Gatorade spiked with Ketel One back and forth. Marco would scribble his signature on walls with a drippy Krink marker and look at his reflection in all the windows. Sometimes we bought pink rubber balls from the deli—the kind kids played handball with—and we'd bounce those as we walked and walked and talked and talked and walked . . .

"At Sally Hershberger Downtown there's a Bert Stern Marilyn with the X, you see, that she did herself with a marker, and she was so drunk in the photos that Bert Stern thought he could have sex with her . . . and there's a Warhol Edie," I would tell him. *Bounce, bounce, bounce.* "From a screen test. And there's the Jane Fonda mug shot, and she's got this perfect mullet and she's holding up her fist . . ."

Oh, Marco and I taught each other so much! He told me you could buy syringes as easy as 1-2-3 just by asking for them all la-di-da at the pharmacy counter. I told him about my favorite drugstores that were twenty-four-hour. He showed me how to smoke weed out of a glass stem by stuffing it with steel wool as a filter, and he taught me about Pete Doherty (I will always be indebted to him for this) and Babyshambles and the Libertines, and he played me Guns N' Roses *Live at the Ritz.*

Marco told me stories, too. He starred in all of them.

"One time I went in there . . ." he said, pointing at the restaurant Lucky Strike. "And went up to the bar and *demanded* a Pellegrino." He cackled. "And they just *gave* it to me!" He was arrogant and flamboyant with his punky haircut he'd given himself, and his shredded jeans. He was exceptionally tall, like an NBA player.

One night when we were strolling through Chelsea, he stopped in his tracks.

"I can't walk here," he said. "It's Sylvia's block."

"Okay . . ." I said. She had a restraining order against him. I didn't think anything of it.

Marco was always doing funny stuff. One day at four in the morning, he sort of grabbed my chin and said, "Open your mouth." I did, like a baby bird. "Swallow."

It was an ecstasy pill—not Adderall!

"Marco!" I should have thrown it up. Instead, I laughed. I started rolling just as the sun was rising. I went to work, grinding my teeth in the cab. I was supposed to film a beauty tutorial video for luckymag.com that day called *LUCKY How-To: Mastering the Face-Framing Braid.* I sat cross-legged on the floor and tried to practice for the video, but . . . I couldn't do it. I couldn't French braid my hair. I was too high.

"Dude!" Cristina said when I told her. Charlotte—who was now a freelancer at *Lucky*—sat for the video shoot instead.

Oh. I was so happy to have a friend! I talked about Marco all the time. I showed Jean a picture on my desktop computer.

"Isn't he good-looking?" I said.

"Hmm." Marco was leering in the photo. His chest was bare.

"This is his shirt!" I was wearing a striped polo. "Dior Homme Hedi Slimane!"

"You need to be careful," Jean said.

"I really love you, Cat," Marco said one night. He was watching me apply my new favorite lipstick—YSL Rouge Volupté no. 17—in a compact. "I'm serious."

"I love you, too!" I said. Then I gave him an oversize Swarovski black-crystal snake ring that looked like it was slithering up his finger. The first time I got a nosebleed in front of him he took my face in his hands and sucked the blood out of my nostrils. I shrieked and struggled and tried to pull away.

"We're really family now," he said when he'd finished. I laughed for three days. It would be almost two years before I understood what I was really dealing with. *That* was Marco.

And now it was October, and Marco was calling all of the time, wanting to catch up and check out my new place. I hadn't seen him since before I left for rehab.

"You can't come over yet," I told him on the phone. "I'm still getting to know my roommates." He was too wild. Also, I didn't need him leading me into temptation. I was Cat 2.0, remember? Well, sort of.

"I'll have a margarita," I told the waiter at a packed Mexican restaurant on Jane Street. I was at dinner with my new roommate, Becky, who was blond, cute, and from Chicago. We talked about guys and about our jobs; I told her nothing about my past. I felt so healthy sitting there eating an enchilada with a girlfriend! So when Becky ordered a drink, I didn't hesitate to order one, too. *This is how* normal *people live*, I thought, swirling my straw in the glass. Then I took my first sip of alcohol in over two months, and it didn't feel like a "relapse" at all.

By ten o'clock, I was sloshed after just a few drinks. Shitfaced! That was unusual for me. It was probably because my tolerance was low after rehab, but back then, I blamed this on being pill free. When I took Adderall, I figured—as I stumbled home—I could down vodka all night and still be bright-eyed at four in the morning when the clubs closed! But without it, I was a messy drunk. That wasn't going to do.

On the evening of October sixth, my magazine celebrated the publication of *The Lucky Guide to Mastering Any Style* at the Bowery Hotel. Like many of my coworkers, I was even *in* the book (not by choice), wearing a French ingenue–meets–rock 'n' roll getup: a boatneck striped top and Daryl K rubber leggings. Yes, *rubber* leggings.

My book party outfit was much better. I borrowed a violet silk slip dress from the fashion closet. The editorial assistants had been allowed to duck out of work early and go downtown together, before the bosses. When we arrived at the hotel, the fete had barely started. There was an open bar. Two of them! I went to the one in the back, where no one would be able to see me before I saw them, and started drinking.

By eight o'clock, the party was bumping. I saw everyone arrive: JGJ walked in with Kim and Andrea Linett, *Lucky*'s creative director (it was she who had styled me in the rubber pants). Charlotte was there, since she'd written the book. Charlotte's *mom* was there. I'd never met her. Gee, didn't they look—

"MISS!" Suddenly someone was upon me—*whipping* my back and head! "YOU'RE ON FIRE! YOU'RE ON FIRE!"

"WHAT?" I shrieked, twisting to see. "AAAAUGH!"

My hair *was* on fire! And a bartender was *beating* me with a dishrag. Then, just as fast, it was out. Oh my *God*.

I looked around wildly. Jean Godfrey-June and Kim France hadn't seen. They were all on the other side of the room! *No* one had seen, actually. I'd been behind a potted tree.

"Ugh," girls were saying now. "It smells like burnt hair!"

"Are you all right?" The bartender caught my elbow.

"Yes." I nodded—but then I stumbled a bit.

Oh boy. It was time to go home. I walked right out of the party without saying good-bye to anyone, hailed a taxi, and slid into the backseat.

"Seventh Avenue South and Bedford," I told the driver. Then I put my head in my hands. How drunk must I have been, to lean my hair back into an . . . an *open flame*—and then to not notice until a bartender started slapping me with a towel?

We were heading across town on West Third Street.

This never would have happened if you were still on speed, a flea in my ear whispered.

The cab pulled up to my building.

"You know what?" I said. "Can you take me a little further down? Varick and Vandam. The Manhattan Mini Storage."

It was past nine. The facility closed at ten. I went up to my floor and opened my storage unit.

I had been careful to only pull out a few boxes at a time on previous visits. But tonight I went in hard; I filled the hallway. The man downstairs kept making "last call" announcements over the intercom, but I didn't care. At five minutes to ten, I found what I was looking for: a Marc Jacobs silver sleeping bag, rolled up and stuffed into a silver pouch. And inside that, stuffed down at the bottom: one bottle of amphetamine salts, thirty milligrams, almost full to the top, and one bottle of Adderall XR—time-release speed. I'd stashed them before I left for rehab—while my father was asleep on the couch.

I extracted a pink Addy, put the blessed thing on my tongue like I was taking Communion, and chewed it up like it was baby aspirin. It was bitter, but to me, it was better than a Laudrée macaron. I closed my eyes and sat against the wall. I felt my heart beating harder.

Ahhhhh.

Now *that's* what a relapse was supposed to feel like.

That night, back at 29 Seventh Avenue South, I organized my entire room. I put garment racks together; I hung up all of my clothes and color-coded them. When the sun came up I went out and got a coffee, which was very delicious for exactly three sips. Then I forgot about it on a windowsill. It was collage o'clock! I started taping things on my walls: Coco Rocha touching the flame of the candle in French *Vogue*, by Terry Richardson. Kate Moss with a boa constrictor by Juergen Teller, British *Vogue*. Sasha Pivovarova eating a Popsicle by Steven Meisel, *Vogue Italia* . . .

"You're up early!" Becky said when she came downstairs and found me buzzing in the kitchen, looking for scissors. She left for work at seven thirty every day.

"Right?!" I said.

I put my projects aside at eight thirty and I went into *Lucky* early for once. It felt great! I organized my desk. Then I went into Jean's office and organized *her* desk. I looked out the window at Times Square and it was bright and crazy: the crossroads of the world. How lucky was I? I loved New York. I loved my job; I loved working. I fucking *loved* Condé Nast. And I loved being high.

Chapter Thirteen

NOW THAT I WAS OUT OF that bizarre . . . *sobriety fog*, I could see everything *much* more clearly! I stood in Times Square after work that night in a Velvet by Graham & Spencer cashmere minidress and Chloé motorcycle boots, puffing a ciggie, my thoughts on a loop like the electric ticker-tape headlines and Dow Jones average updates on the buildings all around me. I'd been a real moron—popping speed day and night, for days on end. Of *course* I'd turned into a self-destructive swamp thing. I'd done it all wrong! If I was going to be back on Adderall—which I was, technically, already—I needed discipline, structure, and limits! That is, a plan for *controlled* use.

I went to Walgreens and picked out a brand-new pill organizer. The plastic grid was as big as a serving platter, with a square for each day of the month. Perfect! Now I needed some ground rules. I listed them on a *Lucky* notepad the whole subway ride home. *NO ADDERALL AFTER DARK.* And I was *not* allowed to stay up all night anymore.

NO DOWNERS!! No Xanax, no Klonopin, no Ambien, no Lunesta, no painkillers. I would let my ADHD medication taper off at the end of the day, and then I would go to sleep naturally. *IN BED AT 1 AM ON WEEKNIGHTS. LIGHTS OUT AT 2!*

I sat on my bed at home, counting pills and dividing them into the squares. I was still having a million thoughts a minute. I would take a time-release thirty-milligram Adderall every day, in the morning, and then I would take a twenty-milligram regular Adderall in the afternoon around three o'clock, and that was *it*. No more. I kept scribbling down "rules" as they came to me: *NO HARD DRUGS.* Ooh, wasn't it fun counting these pills and organizing them in their cubes and opening and closing the plastic doors? They were like little pink pill-people living in storage units. *La la la.* No, drugs were not going to rule *my* fucking life anymore. This was a *new* era! *I* was in control now. *I* made the rules; *I* was in charge of how I felt! *I* determined what happened to—

"Knock knock!"

"AUGH!" I screamed, and nearly fell off the bed. "Come in."

"Sorry, did I scare you?" Becky opened the door. I pulled a blanket over the pill organizer.

"Not at all." My heart was pounding.

"Do you want to get sushi?" Becky asked. "Whoa. Cool collage!"

"Thanks," I said. My neck and my shoulders were so stiff! I'd been frozen in the same position for over an hour. "Oh, you know what? I already ate."

"Okay!" my roommate said. "Next time."

When she closed the door, I went right back to strategizing. *ONLY TWO DRINKS ON WEEKNIGHTS.* And I had to drink *with* people like Becky, never alone . . .

I lay down at one o'clock, just like I was supposed to. I was feeling very confident. I really had it figured out! But there was a problem with my new plan: now that I was back on uppers—and not downers—I couldn't sleep. I got up and walked to the deli across the street for Tylenol PM. An hour later, I went back for NyQuil. I gagged down half the bottle.

Nothing worked. I was awake when my alarm went off at eight thirty. I dragged through the day. That night, I couldn't sleep again.

"I just don't understand," I whined in our Beauty Spy meeting after a third awful night.

If you've ever experienced insomnia—and I'm sure you have—then you know that there is nothing as brutal. You truly suffer, and it feels unbearable. The people around you suffer, too, because not sleeping makes your personality blow. I felt *very* sorry for myself. Still, I was determined to stay off tranquilizers and sleeping pills. I hadn't visited a shrink since I got back from rehab. Instead, I took horrible over-the-counter tablets that melted on your tongue. They were cherry-flavored and gave me a headache. I stared at the ceiling until I felt suicidal.

"How's it going?" JGJ greeted me every morning.

"Not good," I'd whimper.

Jean—who thought I was sober—felt sorry for me, too. She recommended the This Works Deep Sleep Bath Soak. Cristina suggested melatonin. Dawn didn't give me any suggestions. She was distracted because she was getting married on November first. Jean, Cristina, and I were all attending the wedding.

That evening after Jean left, I called my mom and complained to *her*.

"I have a sound machine that makes thunderstorm noises," my mother told me. "Or why don't you take half a Xanax? That always works for me!"

"I just got out of rehab for pills, *Mom*!" I screeched. "Are you serious? *God!*" I hung up on her.

It was six o'clock. Dawn was putting on her trench coat in the next cubicle. "Heading home?"

"Last dress fitting." Dawn smiled.

"So exciting!" As soon as she was gone, I snuck an Addy out of my pants pocket and chomped it in half.

"Please help me sleep," I'd beg God at night. "Please let me sleep. Please help me." "*Please.*" But God wasn't feeling me. So I kept raiding my pill organizer like a little kid jumping ahead to get the chocolates out of an Advent calendar. I *had* to. Amphetamine messed with my internal clock, sure, but it also totally helped me push through the fatigue. What was I supposed to do—just drink coffee? Get real.

As for the "no hard drugs" rule, well, it was only a matter of time before I reconnected with Marco. I cabbed to the Lower East Side on a Saturday night. He was waiting outside his place smoking a Red. We hugged.

"Let's go for a walk," he said.

"I can't do anything too crazy tonight," I warned him, like I always did.

"Don't worry," Marco said. Then he took me to the worst fucking building in downtown Manhattan. It was a project on Avenue D. The lighting in the lobby was straight-up green. A security guard was slumped on his desk. It didn't look like he was taking a nap, either. It looked like he'd just slurped down a propofol milk shake.

"Come on," Marco said. He pulled me into the elevator—and there was a puddle of piss on the floor!

"Are you serious?" I said, covering my nose. The smell didn't bother Marco. He grinned at me like a jack-o'-lantern.

Marco knocked on the door to an apartment on the tenth floor. Someone opened it. The first thing I saw was the Japanese porno on the television.

"*AH!*" A teenage-looking girl was getting fucked by a bunch of teenage-looking Japanese boys. "*AH! AH! AH! AH!*"

Then I saw who was "watching": four grown-ass men piled on one tiny sofa, limp and flopped over each other in a heap—like a litter of sleeping puppies! No, like a litter of *dead* puppies. What were the people in this building *on*?

"I'll be right back," Marco said, and left the apartment.

I sat there waiting for twenty-five minutes.

ZZZZZZZ, one of the dudes snored. At least that meant he was alive.

Finally Marco came back, his eyes looking bright, like a little bat in the night.

"C'mon," he said.

"Where did you go?!" I exploded when we were in the elevator. "You can't just leave a girl in a place like that!"

Marco looked genuinely surprised. I'd never raised my voice to him before.

"I wouldn't have left just any girl," he said. "But you're different. You're so tough." That shut me up.

We went back to Marco's house, where we listened to *Shotter's Nation* and caught up over a few grams of coke. I told him about Dawn's wedding.

"Can I come?" Marco said.

"Can you imagine?" I laughed.

We stayed up until four in the afternoon. By the time I got back to the West Village on Sunday night, I was ready to drop. Still, I couldn't sleep.

My insomnia continued through October. One weeknight I was up late, in bed with an orange, a can of seltzer, and a box of Benadryl. I'd taken the over-the-counter antihistamine every night at Silver Hill to sleep, so I'd bought it when I spotted it at the deli that night.

I took two of the little pills. Then I peeled my orange and read Perez Hilton on my laptop, waiting for the medicine to kick in and make me drowsy, but nothing was happening. Shock-a-roo. I took another Benadryl.

It was raining outside. *Bat-a-tat-tat*. The drops bouncing off the air conditioner unit outside my window kept startling me.

My room was a mess. Earlier that night I'd gone to my storage unit and dragged home a plastic Container Store trunk full of clothes. I'd taken off the lid and pulled a few things out, but then I'd gotten tired. So that stuff was everywhere. My nine thousand pairs of strappy black work heels were piled under the garment racks I'd put together. There were beat-up Jimmy Choos, Fendi velvet sling-backs, and mesh Louis Vuitton pumps I'd bought on sale in a rare (fine, I have them all of the time) Carrie Bradshaw moment.

Something kept drawing my attention to those shoes.

Bat-a-tat-tat. I jumped a little. I finished the orange, set the bag of peels on the ground, and reached to switch off the lamp. *Just* as the room went black, I saw the flash of movement under the garment rack.

I sat frozen in the dark.

No.

Then I switched the light back on and looked right where I knew I did not want to look. And I saw it: a big mouse, with black eyes, staring at me from the shoe pile.

"AHHHHHHH!" I jumped out from under my covers so I was standing on my pillows. "*AUUUUUUUGGHHHH!*"

This couldn't be happening again. *This couldn't be happening again.*

Oh, but it was.

The mouse darted into my closet.

"HELP!" I shrieked. "AHHHHH! SOMEONE! HELP!" No one came. Craig and Becky were asleep on a different floor. The mouse streaked out of the closet and past the bed—and another one followed right behind. "AUUUGGGHHHHHH!"

How many were there? How was this even possible?

Then I spotted something moving at the bottom of the clear plastic crate I'd brought home from storage. Was I hallucinating? I had to be. I focused my eyes. Something *was* wriggling around in my clothes. I could hear it now, squeaking. I *wasn't* hallucinating. My memory flashed to the big rat I'd seen scuttling through the horrible Manhattan Mini Storage garage. Suddenly, I put it all together: there had been mice living in my stuff in my storage unit, and I had brought them home with me.

"AUGGGGGGGHHHHHH!"

I leapt from the bed, ran out of the room, *slammed* the door behind me, fled past the bathroom into the dark living room, and climbed up on the black leather sofa. Where else could I go? What was I going to do? I stared at the crack of light under my bedroom door.

But then—I swear to *God*—I saw the creatures' forms silhouetted in that crack of light. *Gathering* there.

"NOOOOOO!" I screamed.

And *then*—swear to God *again*—the mice *squeezed under the door and bolted into the living room.*

"AUUUUGGHH!"

There were four of them! Can you fucking imagine?! They were dark, and they weren't small. Jesus. Were they rats? One dashed behind the refrigerator. I vaulted off the sofa, hightailed it to the bathroom, and got up on the ledge of the tub with a rolled-up *Forbes* magazine in one hand. I clung to the shower rod with the other. My bare feet gripped the tub, and I was sobbing, bracing myself for another invasion.

I saw the shadow before I saw the actual mouse. It was creeping toward me . . . slowly . . .

Mice don't creep, I thought for a second. Did they? But the shadow *was* there—sneaking closer . . . *closer* . . .

"AUUUUUGHHH!" I threw the magazine at the shadow and jumped from the tub and ran back into the living room and up on the sofa. I scanned the area. Nothing was moving. Where did they go? Mice will do that—just disappear.

I stood there in the dark on the sofa—weeping, trying to breathe—for twenty minutes or so.

Then something came over me. Was it bravery, or was I just drugged and crazy? Who knows? Either way, I decided to go into that storage bin. If there was a mouse trapped in there, I wanted to confront it head on.

I went back to my bedroom door and *flung* it open. Then I stormed over and went HAM on that bin. I pulled out a pair of Alice and Olivia black leather jeggings and shook them out. Nothing! I pulled out my Keith Richards T-shirt and shook it. Nothing. I pulled out my Lucien Pellat-Finet pot leaf sweater and shook it. Nothing! I was crying, howling, retching—just in the absolute *height* of psychological agony—as I did this. And so it went with item after item.

Finally I got to the bottom. There was one thing left: a pair of white shredded J Brand jeans. Sure enough, something—a lump—was moving in the pants leg. I wasn't crazy. It was real.

I grabbed my YSL suede wedge and started beating the lump. It was like that carnival game: Whac-A-Mole. *Wham! Wham! Wham! Wham!* "AUUUUUGHHH!" *Wham! Wham! Wham! Wham!* "AAUUGG-HHHH!"

Finally the lump stopped moving. Blood spread out all over the fabric in a big red stain. I flipped the storage crate upside down again to cover the gore. Then I stumbled out into the living room and collapsed. I'd killed another mouse. I couldn't believe it.

I woke up to whispers at the top of the stairs.

"Is she sleeping?" someone was saying. It was still dark outside, and in the living room. It was early. I was sprawled out on the couch like a freak in tiny American Apparel terry-cloth shorts and a filthy old polo shirt.

It all came rushing back.

I pulled myself up as Craig and his girlfriend, who also worked in finance, came down the stairs. I told them everything.

"That's so crazy!" Craig said. "We've never had mice before!"

"It's my fault." I shook my head. "I attract them wherever I go!"

"We'll call an exterminator," Craig assured me. Then they left, and I went back to sleep. When I opened my eyes again it was sunny in the apartment, and I was alone.

Time for work. I was covering Dawn's events while she put in extra time at the office before she took off for her honeymoon, and that morning I was supposed to swing by a personal care brand's preview in Nolita. I ran into my bedroom to grab my purse and a dress and *ran* back out. I didn't look at where I killed the mouse.

I took an Addy to calm my nerves and cabbed over to Elizabeth Street. The event was in a white minimalist space. There was a DJ spinning Flo Rida—at ten in the morning—plus the usual floral arrangements and tables of new body butters and fragrances.

I can't handle this, I thought.

"Smoothie?" a waiter chirped. The DJ put on "Single Ladies (Put a Ring on It)." I shook my head no.

"Cat!" A publicist greeted me with a clipboard. "Welcome!"

"Sorry I'm late," I croaked. I was hoarse—and woozy. "Where's the restroom?" She pointed.

The bathroom was peaceful and industrial-chic, with a white candle burning. I sat down and peed, and put my head in my hands. I never wanted to get up.

But I had to. I stood up and was pulling up my tights when I noticed a bug on the wall. It had no spots, it was distinctly round, and it was the exact same shade as the paint.

It was a white ladybug. And it was crawling up the wall in the bathroom at this beauty event.

What.

I reached out and pushed it like a button.

It disappeared under my finger. And that's when I snapped.

"*Bwahhh!*" I *burst* out of that fucking bathroom!

The nice publicist with the clipboard came rushing over.

"Cat!" she said.

"I saw a bug . . ." I wept. "It wasn't there . . . I was up all night . . . I killed a rat . . ." I was crying, crying. People stared. "I have to go. I can't be here! I have to go."

"Okay," she said. "It's okay. It's okay." She held my quaking shoulders and led me outside. Then she put me in a taxi. (I have no idea who this kind publicist was to this day—but bless her, wherever she is.)

I was a wreck at the office.

"I killed a mouse in my new apartment last night!" Dawn and Cristina exchanged glances. We were supposed to be meeting about the next issue. "I brought them into my house from my storage unit!"

"Oh, no!" Jean exclaimed. "Again? I can't believe it!"

"Me neither," I sniffled.

"I'm so sorry, dude," Cristina said. Dawn didn't say anything.

I couldn't go home, so I stayed at my sister's for two nights. On Friday afternoon, we headed to 29 Seventh Avenue South together. I didn't want to go into my room.

"I'm so scared," I blathered the whole subway ride. "I'm so scared I'm so scared I'm so scared."

My sister practically had to drag me off the elevator and through the living room at 29 Seventh Avenue South and into my bedroom. The instant I saw the murder scene—the YSL wedge, the bin, the jeans underneath—I was up on the bed, screeching like a gibbon. "I CAN'T! I CAN'T!"

Emily was afraid, too, but she went right over and lifted the bin, picked up the jeans, and shook them out . . .

"There's nothing here!" she said.

"WHAT?!" I stopped monkey jumping.

"There's nothing here," my sister repeated.

I clambered off the bed and looked. There was no blood. No mouse. I should have been relieved—but instead, my knees buckled. What the *fuck* was going on?

"How can that be?" I said. "I killed it. I saw the blood spread."

"I don't think so," Emily said.

"But I did," I said. "I saw it. I saw the blood spread. I *know* I saw it."

"Stop saying that," my sister said.

"I saw the blood spread. *I saw the blood spread,*" I replied. "I SAW THE BLOOD SPREAD!"

"Caitlin!" My sister grabbed my shoulders. "Stop it!"

"I SAW THE BLOOD SPREAD!" I howled. "*I SAW THE BLOOD SPREAD! I SAW THE BLOOD—*"

"Knock knock!"

"AUUUGHH!" My sister and I both jumped a foot in the air.

"Sorry!" Becky stepped into the room. "Did I scare you?"

"It's okay," I said. "Becky, this is my sister Emily."

"I'm helping with the . . . the mice," Emily explained.

"I was telling Cat it's weird," Becky replied. "Because we've never had mice before . . ." As they chatted, I skulked around looking for clues. *Hmm.* No little black pellets . . . No greasy trails around the perimeter either . . .

That's when I saw the Benadryl box on the bed. I picked it up.

"How many of those did you take?" Emily said.

"Three?" But almost all of the pills were popped out of the little sheet. My sister rolled her eyes.

I crashed at Emily's again and stayed up late on her MacBook, reading all about Benadryl. Diphenhydramine hallucinations are terrifying, vivid, and different than other "trips"—several websites claimed—because you aren't aware that what you're "seeing" isn't real.

That made me feel better, but not much. The next day at work I used the beauty closet phone to book a psychiatrist appointment. I needed to be back on sleeping pills and benzos. Prescription-drug dependency sucked, but insomnia was even worse. Being clean just wasn't worth it.

Then it was Halloween—a Friday. The city was nuts. I walked over to see Marco. He was waiting outside his apartment on Madison Street, wearing a black suit with a skinny black tie.

"I can't do anything too crazy," I said as I hugged him. "I have to go to my coworker's wedding tomorrow."

"Cool," he said. "Look what I got!" He opened his palm and showed me a rock. It was bigger than Dawn's engagement ring. Jeez!

We went to Chez Marco. My friend put on David Bowie's *Scary Monsters (and Super Creeps)* as he fixed up a stem.

"I shouldn't be doing this," I kept saying as we passed it. "My boss is going to be at that wedding tomorrow."

"Jean Godfrey-June?"

"The one and only," I said, exhaling the freebase smoke.

"I want to meet her," Marco said. "Do you think she'd like me?"

"Nope," I said.

"I still think you should bring me as your date," Marco said.

"Not gonna happen."

"Why not?"

"You wouldn't fit in at all!" I said.

"What do you mean?" Marco was indignant. "This is a Dior suit!"

"It's very nice," I said. "But no."

At eleven in the morning, we split a pill of real ecstasy that Marco had in his pencil case.

"Let's go look at art," I said as it started to kick in.

We went to the New Museum on Bowery and walked through the Elizabeth Peyton paintings. They were okay. I liked the Sid Vicious portrait best. Afterward, we shuffled around in the gift shop. I pocketed a button that read: I ♥ TERROR.

"Dope," Marco said, pinning it on my jacket when we got outside.

I nodded. I wasn't talking so good.

I decided I wanted something new to wear to the wedding, so we went to Tokio 7, the secondhand designer resale boutique on East Seventh Street. I piled things at the register without trying them on: a gold and silver Missoni tube dress, a Joie brown rabbit fur jacket, a Dior button-down for Marco. The total was $379.99. I threw a pair of Tom Ford sunnies on top of it all: $479.99. The shop was . . . *vibrating*. I could barely hand over my credit card. The cashier took it from my hand.

"*Shankssh*." Marco took the bag with one hand and my elbow with the other.

"Thanks," he said to the clerk. Other customers were staring. "Let's go."

I lurched out of the store. It was sunny in the East Village.

"*Idunrillyno what time thish wedding shhtartshhh*," I said. "*I sshhink I should take a nap and ammyhoush*."

"I'm coming with you," Marco said. He was still holding my elbow.

"Don't do *anyshhing* crazy," I said. I'd never let him up into the West Village place before. "My *roommateshharrr* home."

No one was at the duplex. Marco and I rested on my bed. By the time it was dark outside, I sobered up considerably.

"I gotta get ready," I said. "I gotta go."

"Let me come with you," Marco said. "Cat. Seriously."

"But I RSVP'd as a single . . ." I shook my head.

"It's a wedding!" Marco said. "It's a *party*. Everyone is going to be there with a date!"

"I'll text Dawn," I said—and did. (In retrospect, I imagine this message was a bit . . . messy.)

An hour passed. I sent another message to my coworker. Still—no answer.

"I guess you can come." I shrugged.

The New York City Fire Museum was just a few blocks from my apartment. Marco and I hustled down Varick. We were a little late. Then we hung a right on Spring Street. I spotted Dawn's friend Leigh standing outside a building down the block. She was wearing a bridesmaid dress.

"That must be it," I said, and picked up the pace. We had both sobered up; I was feeling pretty good and wearing my new glittery Missoni tunic over black tights. Marco looked dreamy in his black three-piece—

"I DON'T THINK SO!" Leigh was yelling in our direction. She was waving her arms around. "YOU'RE NOT COMING IN HERE."

"Is she talking to you?" Marco said under his breath.

"No way," I said.

Marco and I turned around.

There was no one behind us.

We were almost at the Fire Museum. Leigh was still hollering. Then she was *charging*—toward *us*!

"I DON'T THINK SO, CAT MARNELL!" Marco and I stopped in our tracks. "GET AWAY!"

"Excuse me?" I said. I had met this chick before, but what?

"YOU'RE NOT COMING IN HERE," Leigh yelled. I was very confused. What was happening? Was she talking to Marco?

"But . . . he's wearing a Dior suit," I said.

"GET OUT OF HERE!" Leigh's face was bright red. "GET AWAY FROM HERE. YOU'RE NOT WELCOME."

"What are you talking about?!" I said. Of *course* I was welcome. I knew everything *about* this wedding. I'd sat next to the bride for two years. "I texted Dawn—"

"I KNOW YOU DID!" She was *screaming*—right there on Spring Street! "I READ YOUR TEXT! YOU THINK THAT'S WHAT SHE WANTS TO DEAL WITH ON THE MOST SPECIAL DAY OF HER LIFE?"

"I—I—" I stammered.

"WHILE SHE'S GETTING READY FOR HER *WEDDING*?" Leigh raged on. "HOW *DARE* YOU!"

"I'm calling Dawn!" My hands were trembling as I fumbled in my purse and pulled out my BlackBerry.

"OH NO, YOU'RE NOT!" Leigh *lunged* for it. Like she was going to take it from me and smash it on the ground!

"What the fuck is your problem?" I cried out as I dodged her.

That *really* got her going.

"*MY* PROBLEM?" she roared. "*YOU'RE* THE ONE WITH THE FUCKING *PROBLEM*. YOU MAKE YOUR PROBLEM EVERYONE ELSE'S PROBLEM. I KNOW ALL ABOUT IT! I KNOW ALL ABOUT

YOU, CAT MARNELL. EVERYBODY GIVES YOU A PASS." They did? "DAWN *HAS* TO PUT UP WITH IT, BUT GUESS WHAT? I DON'T. AND I DON'T GIVE A *FUCK* ABOUT YOU! AND I'M NOT LETTING YOU RUIN THE MOST IMPORTANT DAY OF MY BEST FRIEND'S LIFE. NOW GO HOME."

My jaw was on the sidewalk. Marco's was, too.

What could I do? What could I say?

"Let's go," Marco murmured.

He grabbed my hand. We turned around and strode quickly back up Spring Street toward Varick. I was shaking.

"THAT'S RIGHT! GO ON NOW," Leigh bellowed at our backs. "*GO HOME, CAT MARNELL! AND DON'T COME BACK!*"

I was in such shock that I couldn't even talk. I felt like I'd just been Tased! What the *hell* had just happened?

"I thought you were close with your coworkers," Marco finally said.

"I am." I started to cry. "We're all friends." Weren't we?

"Fuck those people, Cat." Marco put his arm around me. "At least you have me. Come on. Let's go do some drugs."

"Okay," I sniffled.

It was only a few minutes' walk back to my apartment. Inside, I texted Jean and told her Dawn's friend wouldn't let me into the wedding.

What? Why? she wrote back.

I stared at my phone. Then I just never responded.

I was upset for a while, but my friend had me smiling soon enough.

"To think that all happened . . . because you wanted to bring *me* to a wedding," Marco snickered.

"Right?" I giggled, passing him the glass stem.

"Shows how much that bitch knows," he said. "I mean, this a *Dior* suit."

Chapter Fourteen

ON MONDAY I WAS BACK AT the office, but Dawn wasn't. She was on her honeymoon. Jean, Cristina, and I had our usual morning meeting. I told them about the confrontation with Dawn's "crazy friend," but I kept it brief and vague.

"So weird," Jean said. Then we moved on to brainstorming about the March issue.

I *really* needed to get back on track at work—which wouldn't be that hard to do. After two years, I could assist JGJ in my sleep—or, for that matter, on no sleep. All I had to do was show up, which I always did. My boss wasn't around half the time, but when she was, I put my best face forward. Simple enough.

But there was no saving face back at 29 Seventh Avenue South, where my mission to pass for "drug-free" and "normal" had gone over like the *Challenger*. I hadn't seen Craig or his girlfriend again since the mice night. Then one evening I came home from work and there they were, sitting in the kitchen with Becky. I had to say something.

"I'm so sorry about that crazy morning," I said. "Did I weird you out? I'm just *so* scared of mice."

"Huh?" Craig said.

"Last week," I said. "When I was out here on the sofa. I was all upset telling you guys about the mice in my room . . ."

Craig's girlfriend was looking at me like I'd just spoken in tongues.

"I was in Chicago last week," Craig said. "I just got back today." He pointed at a suitcase by the stairs. "See?"

What?

"I wasn't over here," his girlfriend said. "Because Craig was out of town."

"That was me you were talking to that morning, Cat," Becky said gently. "Remember?"

I stared at her.

"Oh, right," I shook my head and chuckled. "Sorry."

If it wasn't awkward living with these people before, it was now. I started looking for a new apartment.

Speaking of awkward. It was mid-November, and Dawn was due back from her honeymoon. I got to work first that day; I always did. Then Dawn arrived. We greeted each other. I fussed with the stuff on my desk, stacking makeup palettes, killing time. She took off her coat. Then I sort of cleared my throat—and just came out with it.

"Dawn?" I said. She turned. I looked her straight in the eye. "I'm sorry about what went down at your wedding. I didn't mean to cause you any stress."

"No worries, Marnell." Cool as a cucumber. Dawn always was.

Exactly one week later, the entire editorial staff was summoned to an afternoon staff meeting. Do you remember the Condé Nast "bloodbath" I told you about? Every magazine was required to make staff cuts. Now it was *Lucky*'s turn to bring down the ax. Very *Hunger Games*. Kim was emotional as she named the people who were losing their jobs. I knew I was safe, but it turns out that my newly married coworker wasn't. I looked around: Dawn wasn't in the conference room. They'd already told her. Geez.

And just like that, I was promoted. I was a beauty editor at Condé Nast.

A girl named Simone took my place as Jean's assistant. Back in August, a temp agency had sent her to sit in my cubicle and answer Jean's phones while I was in rehab at Silver Hill. Everyone at *Lucky* had flipped for willowy, smart, chic Simone and her A.P.C. smock dresses. And now she was on staff.

I trained her like a Navy SEAL.

"If she goes to Dr. Brandt, it will *always* be on an afternoon, at the end of the day, and the traffic is terrible over there so you *cannot* let the driver leave . . . Sally Hansen is not a real person; that is something I learned the hard way . . ." Simone scribbled everything down. "She needs new appointment book pages for the New Year, but she likes to go to the Hermès store herself and buy those . . . Don't put cellulite products in her office; she thinks they are *fraudulent* . . . If she's not flying first class, she likes to sit by the bulkhead. You can call the airline twenty-four hours before the flight . . ."

With JGJ taken care of, I had more time than ever for my favorite extracurricular: doctor shopping! I'd started seeing Marco's psychiatrist, Dr. X. On my first visit, I walked in with two hundred dollars cash and out with so many paper prescriptions that I could literally spread them and fucking fan myself. No wonder that kid was such a crackhead! I filled everything at the twenty-four-hour Walgreens in Union Square, where I'd been reading the same romance novel from the rack of paperbacks by the pharmacy counter for over a year. (It was about a woman who had attention deficit disorder—*and* was looking for love! Amazing, right? I swear on my life. No one ever bought it, or even messed with my bookmark, which—fun fact—was a Juicy Fruit wrapper.)

But you know what they say: mo' prescriptions, mo' problems. My dad had picked me up from rehab in September and driven me back to Manhattan just to give me a stern warning. Our conversation had gone something like this:

"It's time to cut the crap, Cait."

"I know."

"If you fail to remain sober, the rent checks stop. I'm out."

"That's . . . fine. I'm . . . that's totally fine."

"This is it. Or I'm out."

"I *know*, Dad."

"Or I'm out. This is it, or I'm out."

"I hear you."

"The crap stops now, Cait. Or I'm out."

"I got it. I really do." *Omigod get me out of this car.*

Was I crazy-spoiled and nauseatingly privileged? Duh. But I "hated my dad" (most ungrateful and entitled adult children do) back then, and I *was* only making twenty-six thousand a year at *Lucky,* and I wanted that rent money. So now I was pretending to be in recovery whenever I spoke with my parents. Whatever, I'd been lying to them all my life.

But lying to my big sister was another thing. I felt so guilty. Emily was proud of me for getting clean. We'd been spending a lot of time together lately, talking about our parents' divorce. I didn't care at all that they were splitting, but Emily was really upset. She'd been ultrasensitive to family stuff ever since Cross Creek Manor.

In mid-November, she asked me if I wanted to have Thanksgiving together in New York, just the two of us. I said yes.

"Are you sure?" she asked. "We don't have to. Just tell me now."

"I want to!" I was at work with the phone tucked under my chin, applying Givenchy Mister Light concealer to my magnificent under-eye circles. "I'll be there!" She made a reservation at a restaurant in Soho called Zoe for six o'clock on Thanksgiving.

On the Tuesday before the holiday, Emily checked to make sure we were still on.

Yes! I wrote back. I was texting from Dr. X.'s waiting room on East Seventy-Second Street, flopped in a chair. I was wiped out. I stayed up all night opening Vyvanse capsules and pouring the fine powdered speed onto my tongue anyway—and went into *Lucky* for a half day on Wednesday on no sleep.

That evening, Marco texted me.

I found a heroin dealer! Oh, Lord. I'd already popped a few lay-me-downs, so I ignored him. Then I set my alarm and passed out on my bed.

When I woke up it was dark outside. My BlackBerry had frozen. (They were *always* doing that, right? The worst.)

It was eight o'clock on Thanksgiving.

"NO!" I screamed.

I restarted the phone and all of the messages flooded in. My sister had sat at the restaurant, crying and crying. Then she finally had gone home. I found all this out from my mother—because Emily wasn't talking to me. I'd called my sister over and over and left a dozen messages. No response.

"How could you *do* that, Caitlin?" my mom said. She sounded disgusted—and my mom never sounded like she cared about anything. This was really bad. I felt sick.

I was sitting on the floor in the dark with my head in my hands when Marco called. He wasn't with his family, either.

"I'm sorry, Cat," he said, after I tearfully recounted what I'd done. "At least you and I can hang out."

"Do you want to get dinner?" I sniffed. "I'll pay."

We had turkey and pumpkin pie at 7A, and then walked through Tompkins Square Park. It was practically empty—well, but for the scuttly night-rats. I held Marco's arm.

"What are we going to do now?" I asked, though I knew the answer. I was already looking for an ATM.

We squirreled away in Marco's apartment and snorted tiny piles of off-white heroin all night. His roommates were away. I sat on the bed in a nest of clothes and sketchbooks with my eyelids at half-mast. The smack was nice.

"Thank God I have you," I murmured at one point, reaching out in slow motion. Marco took my hand and kissed it.

"I love you, Cat," he said.

"I love *you*," I said. Then I nodded off again.

After the Thanksgiving fiasco, my dad had guessed that I was back on drugs. He never sent me a check again. But it was cool. As associate beauty editor, my new salary was forty-six thousand. Now I could pay my own rent, and that felt really good. I mean, the timing of my promotion had been sort of perfect.

I'd been killer at managing Jean's professional life, but now that I was an editor with lots of freedom and work obligations outside of 4 Times Square, how would I manage my own? If you've been reading this book, I think you know the answer, but back then I was in serious denial. Sure, I had problems . . . but this was what I'd worked so hard for, right? The trips! The glamour! The perks! Surely I wouldn't fuck everything up *now*.

I was about to find out. My first press trip was right in the beginning of the Christmas season, and it was a doozy. Procter & Gamble—"the largest advertiser in the world," per WWD—owned the beauty licenses for Gucci and Dolce & Gabbana, and they were flying editors to Rome and then Milan to fete launches from both brands. Eva Chen was going. The beauty director of *Vogue*, Sarah Brown, was, too. So was *Elle*'s beauty director, Emily Dougherty. And so on.

Representing *Lucky*: one Cat Marnell.

I'd be out of the office a full week.

"Are you excited?" Simone asked.

"Yes!" I said. It was Monday, and I was leaving on Friday. I'd already gone to Tokio 7 and blown two hundred dollars on a velvet Gucci baby-doll dress with floaty chiffon sleeves to wear to the Gucci party.

I spent the next few nights dressing up in the mirror, my suitcase open on the floor.

On Thursday morning, I was at my desk reading TMZ and eating a high-protein Condé cafeteria breakfast even though I *hardly* had an appetite. My Addy was kicking in, you know, and—

"Dude!" Cristina cried. She'd just arrived. "What are you *doing* here?! Why aren't you at the airport?"

I swallowed my bite of turkey sausage and sort of blinked at her a few times.

"Huh?" I said.

"You're supposed to be flying to Rome today!"

"*What?*" I said. "I am?!"

"Yes!"

I thought about this.

"But today . . ." I said, "is Thursday!"

"Yes!" Cristina said. "Today is Thursday! Your flight is today!"

"Really?!" I said.

"YES!" Cristina said. And this is what it is like working with a pill-head.

I raced home. Sure enough, a black Lincoln Town Car was waiting outside of 29 Seventh Avenue South. I tapped frantically on the window.

"I'll be down in fifteen!" I shouted. Yeah, right.

Upstairs, I completely fell apart. I couldn't find matching shoes; I couldn't put outfits together. Worst of all, I couldn't find my Xanax or my Ambien. I shook out the sheets; I dug through the piles. Finally, I left without them. Have you ever heard the thing about pillheads—that if you really want to see their addictions, just take their pills away? Yeah, this was gonna be bad.

JFK was an inferno of holiday travelers, and once I got there I had no idea where to go or what to do. I didn't even know what airline I was flying. I sat down on my suitcase and took out my BlackBerry, but I couldn't access my Condé e-mail from it. I called Cristina repeatedly, but she wasn't answering. I was going to miss my flight. I was going to be in such deep trouble. *I can't do this. I can't handle this.* I couldn't go to Italy. It was all too much.

Finally I got Cristina. By then, Jean was in the office.

"Dude," she whispered—protecting me, as usual. The senior beauty editor was the associate's immediate supervisor, so I reported to Cristina now, not to Jean. I'd only just been promoted and I'd already exploited her kindness and put her in a fucked-up position like seven different times. "Calm down. You can do this."

Cristina had gone over to my computer and found my itinerary. When JGJ stepped away, she called me back and told me to *run* to the Delta first-class counter.

"You're not going to make it," the agent told me. No surprise there.

But now what? I wove back into the throngs and sat on my suitcase again. I took my third Adderall of the day. Whatever was next, I wanted to be high for it.

"Dude," Cristina said when I broke the news. "Okay. I'm calling PR."

Twenty minutes later, I had another flight—Air Italia, coach. Of course I made that one. The plane was nuts—even worse than the airport—with demented babies, canoodling teens, and a garrulous Italian pilot babbling on the intercom. I didn't sleep the whole nine hours; when we landed, I was *un disastro*. Thank God for town cars. I practically fell into mine.

I felt better when I got to the Hotel Eden, though. It sat atop a hill, and the view from my suite was just glorious. I had time before the Gucci party, so I decided to go for a stroll. I'd never been to Rome. It's a *rather* walkable city—especially if one is on Vyvanse—and so I had a nice time navigating the winding streets in the rain. Plus, there was great shopping—rosaries everywhere! I had to bring a few back to Marco. I stopped at a Bancomat machine by the Fontana di Trevi to take out some cash. *Tra la la.* It was lovely to be in Europe; I hadn't been there since high school, and gee, look at those pigeons—

INSUFFICIENT FUNDS, YOU SPOILED IDIOT DRUG AD-DICT FUCKING RETARD LOSER BRAT, the Bancomat screamed at me. GO THROW YOURSELF IN THE RIVER.

No, no, *no.*

I checked my balance: negative eighteen hundred dollars.

"FUCK!" I shrieked at the pigeons. How was this possible? My head spun like a slot machine, remembering the shopping spree before Dawn's wedding, cash I'd laid out for Dr. X., cash I'd given Marco to buy drugs—and, of course, my sixteen-hundred-dollar rent check. So much for self-sufficiency.

I was going to be traveling for a week. What was I going to do? I couldn't call my parents. Those days were over.

There was only one person I could think of.

"Darlin'?" Mimi accepted the collect call. She was living in Charlot-tesville, near the University of Virginia. "Caty? Is it really you?" I hadn't spoken to her in over a year.

"Mimi!" I wailed into a pay-phone receiver. "Mimi, I need your help. I'm all the way over in *Europe*, I am all alone and I have *no* money! I am negative two thousand dollars in the bank!" I started crying. "I'm at a pay phone in the middle of Rome. *All by myself!*" Liar. "I don't know what to do. I DON'T KNOW WHAT TO DO!"

"I'll go to the bank right now!" Mimi said.

"Thank you," I wept. "I love you so much." Asshole.

Mimi really did *rush* right out: she wired me three thousand dollars within the hour. I'd frightened my eighty-one-year-old grandmother to—well, not *quite* to death. But surely a little closer to it.

Gucci headquarters was in a gargantuan sixteenth-century palazzo just across the river Tiber from the fabulous Castel Sant'Angelo. If that sentence sounds like it was lifted directly from the Internet, well—bingo. I barely remember anything about this party. That's how out to lunch I was. At one point I felt so wobbly that I had to lean against a big pillar! I also remember an awkward chat with Gucci's foxy blond creative director, Frida Giannini; she didn't seem to particularly speak English and at that point I barely did either.

Next up was a sit-down dinner. The editors at my table were from the best magazines from all over the world. A healthier me would have been on cloud nine, but I just wanted to crawl into one of the chic bottles of bubbly Italian mineral water on the table and drown.

The American editors returned to the Hotel Eden and said our good nights. When we got to the hotel I was so drunk that I thought maybe I'd actually sleep—especially since I hadn't on the flight from New York—but instead I just lay awake feeling agitated, clammy, and anxious. I'd left my sleeping pills and Xanax behind, remember? So now I had "rebound insomnia," which was ninety thousand times worse than the insomnia I had in the first place. I couldn't have dozed off for a million dollars. I took baths and did deep-breathing exercises in bed. Nothing worked.

By three in the morning, I was *freaking* out—*screaming* inside. I wasn't used to being so uncomfortable and helpless. In New York, I would have been at the twenty-four-hour Rite Aid, buying Cinnamon Toast Crunch, Pop-Tarts, and Powerade.

Then I did something that I absolutely should not have done: picked up the phone and ordered binge foods—*expensive* binge foods—from room service. This wasn't specifically forbidden or anything, but . . . you just don't do that on a press trip. Especially on a press trip with a major advertiser! I was representing Jean and *Lucky*, Procter & Gamble were paying for the room, and the publicists would see the bill when we checked out. I'd already missed my first-class flight; ordering a bunch of room service was just . . . a bad look. I *knew* all this. But I ordered pizza, tiramisu, and a pastry basket anyway. I was hoping to spike my blood sugar and then come crashing down and into sleep—an old "trick" of mine.

Yeah, right. After I binged and purged, I picked up the phone *again*—I was in a half-hypnotized state, truly—and ordered room service *again*: a cheese and charcuterie plate, a basket of bread, another tiramisu. Another order came up on another rolling tray. I threw all that up, too. By then it was six in the morning and all of the alcohol had worn off. I took two Vyvanse and started packing up my stuff. We were all going to the airport together and flying to Milan. At nine, I met the other editors in the lobby. The publicists were at the front desk, checking out. I wanted to disappear. But no one looked at me funny; no one said anything. At least, not to my face.

The Hotel Principe di Savoia was magnificent, but I blew that Popsicle stand the second we checked in and hit the streets. It was hailing in Milan. While the other beauty editors had afternoon tea, I slogged through the icy-cold rain, looking for lit-up green crosses. There were—I knew—*farmacia*s everywhere: elegant little shops you had to be buzzed into, not big drugstores like in the States. It didn't take long to find one. I stood and rang the doorbell outside. I was wearing leather Goldsign jeans, Nike Dunk Lows, and a soaking-wet white fox fur coat. It was *freezing*. Why weren't they letting me in?

BZZZZZ. Finally! I burst inside. I looked for something like Tylenol PM or NyQuil, but didn't see it. I went to the counter. There were two people working in the pharmacy.

"I need medicine for sleep, *medicina*," I said. "Please."

The *farmacistas* stared at me.

"For sleep, for sleep." I made a pillow with my hands like a little Hallmark Store angel. "Please. Sleeping pills. Tranquilizers."

"*Americano*?" the woman said rather . . . *snidely*.

"*Si*," I said. I mean, what did *that* have to do with anything?

The male pharmacist gave me the ol' Italian stink eye, but the woman came down from behind the counter. She led me to a wall of herbal sleep supplements. Everything was in cute packaging, like beauty products.

"*Thees*," she said. "*Melatonia*."

"Oh, um, *grazie*," I said. Yeah, that wasn't gonna cut it.

"Okay?" the pharmacist said.

I pointed behind the counter.

"Do you have Valium?" I said. Wasn't Valium over the counter in some parts of the world? Maybe not. "Or cough syrup?" Then, as an afterthought, I fake-coughed: *Cough*.

"No," she said coldly.

Fine. Stupid Europe! I grabbed every incarnation of shitty *melatonia* in the joint—tablets, gel caps, powders in capsules—and brought it all up to the register. God knows how much I paid. It didn't matter. I knew none of it was gonna work.

The next night, at the Dolce & Gabbana party, I got a smooch on both cheeks from either Dolce or Gabbana—I do not know which one, but he was very tan and smelled predictably fantastic. It was another glittering cocktail reception. I sipped white wine. There was more to drink at the sit-down dinner, which felt more like a wedding reception. It was a huge party—so many guests! The dining room was decadent and dazzling—no overhead lighting, just ten thousand candles, and exotic flowers spilled on every table. This time I actually knew someone at mine: Eva Chen—*the* Eva Chen—was seated next to me.

I actually had something to talk to her about. Charlotte had attended Eva's wedding over the summer and had shown me the photos when she visited me at Silver Hill.

"Congratulations on getting married!" I said. I was a little toasted. "Charlotte showed me the pictures over the summer . . ."

"Oh, she did?" Eva said. She was still the beauty director at *Teen Vogue*. I'd never forgotten how kind she was when I interviewed there. Which may explain—along with my usual excuse, sleep deprivation—what happened next.

"Yes," I said. "When—when—" *Don't.* "When she visited me . . . *in rehab!*"

Then I started blubbering—right there at the table, into my glam risotto.

"Cat," Eva said, putting her fork down. She reached out and touched my shaking arm. "Are you okay?"

"It's a g-g-g-ood thing you d-d-didn't h-h-hire me," I wept. "I'm a d-d-drug addict." I told her everything: about forgetting my downers at home, the room service I'd ordered, how Jean didn't know I'd relapsed, and how I'd stepped into Dawn's job.

"It's okay." Eva Chen patted my back. She probably couldn't even understand what I was saying, I was crying so hard. At least it was so fashionably dark in that dining room that no one was watching us. "Shhh."

As the first course arrived, I went into the bathroom and cleaned the eyeliner from my cheeks. I was such a freak show. Thank God Eva was so nice.

I *gorged* on melatonin that night. I probably took thirty herbal pills. They did nothing except make me feel sick. I lay in the dark in my suite at the Principe di Savoia, waiting for sleep. I would have swallowed arsenic if someone had promised that it would put me under for at least a few hours—that's how bad prolonged insomnia feels. But eventually I gave up: on sleeping, on self-control, on my career, on myself. I gave up on all of it. I just fucking gave up.

This time I got prosecco—a whole bottle—plus pastries, cheese plates, pizza, and tiramisu. The bill would be . . . God, I don't know. A hundred and fifty euros? Two hundred? I couldn't stop. I knew that I should quit my job when I got back to New York. And I was so fucked up that I didn't care. I was wearing a purple silk slip and I kept taking it off to vomit in the marble bathroom. When I'd emptied my stomach of the first giant room service order, I called and ordered it *again*. It was so sick.

The bathroom was the size of a New York studio apartment. At some point—I guess I'd gotten really drunk—I finally passed out in there. When I opened my eyes again, I was on the marble floor by the toilet in my underwear. I knew I'd slept for a few hours. *Thank you, God.*

I got up and put on a robe. Then I went to the window in the bedroom and peeked out the heavy hotel room curtains. Was it light out? Not yet. The sky was dark purple. Then it slowly turned into light gray. I sat there watching for a long time. I heard the Italian birds wake up.

I'm never going to be okay, I thought.

The trip had been such a disaster, but at least it was almost over. I was a wreck. I was wearing a baseball cap; my face was crazy swollen. We took cars to the airport. Then the editors waited together in the first class terminal. I felt so uncomfortable sitting there that I got up and went to the gift shop and bought a bunch of toiletries. Then I returned to the group and . . . talked about them.

"Italy has the prettiest cotton balls!" I said shakily. "They look like cotton candy!"

A few women smiled—but just a few. I wanted to disappear.

Finally, it was time to board. I was the last person in our group to get on the plane. The cushy, gray leather seats in the first-class cabin were arranged in pairs—and the only vacant single was next to the beauty director of *Vogue*.

NOOOOOO! I began praying *immediately. PLEASE PLEASE*

*PLEASE PLEASE DO NOT SIT ME NEXT TO THE BEAUTY DIREC-
TOR OF VOGUE FOR NINE HOURS WHEN I HAVEN'T SLEPT IN
A WEEK AND I HAVE BEEN UP ALL NIGHT THROWING UP AND
CAN BARELY SEE STRAIGHT, PLEASE PLEASE PLEASE—*

When I opened my eyes, someone else was sitting there. *Whew.*
God is real. I'm telling you.

I hadn't seen my actual seat because a lady had stashed her cranky
Italian baby there, and I wound up sitting next to that very bambino the
whole flight home. I couldn't have been happier if it was Pete Doherty
himself.

We took off. I curled up under a blanket and took *melatonia* after
melatonia. The herbal pills bothered my stomach and kept . . . *rising* in
my throat, making my chest burn, and I would feel like there were bub-
bles stuck in my chest, like I needed to burp. It was uncomfortable and
vile. Hours passed, and I didn't doze off once. I never even got *drowsy.*
About six hours in, I watched *The Dark Knight Rises* for the first time—or
tried to, anyway. I couldn't understand anything anyone was saying—the
airline headphones sucked, even in first class. Eventually I just turned
off the sound. Then I sat quietly in the dark cabin. It was so surreal to be
crossing the Atlantic Ocean with the top beauty editors in my industry
snoozing all around me. I was really living my dream life. Wasn't I? I sup-
pressed another *melatonia* belch. Heath Ledger was on the little glowing
screen in front of me in his nurse's uniform, smoky eyes, and smeared
lipstick, smirking as he set off bombs and burned the hospital down.

I found my pills somewhere obvious right when I got home—isn't that
always the way?—and was out cold all weekend. When I returned to
4 Times Square on Monday, the beauty department was neck-deep in
Christmas swag: Marc Jacobs bags from Revlon, YSL wallets from YSL,
jewelry from Shiseido. I opened gifts all morning.

JGJ swished in at the usual time and was happy to see me. I could
tell that she didn't even know I'd missed my original flight.

"How was it?" she asked.

My stomach twisted. All morning I'd imagined going into her office, pulling the door shut, and coming clean—about the trip, about my relapse. About everything. I'd imagined what would happen after that: Jean would have to tell not just Kim and Regan but the ad side—our publisher, our sales team—what I'd done. She'd have to call Procter & Gamble and personally apologize for her employee's ghastly behavior. And she'd have to fire me or—if I was *incredibly* lucky—put me on disability again.

I couldn't do it.

"Good," I said. "It was great! I met Frida Giannini . . ."

The morning passed uneventfully. Simone didn't need my help with anything; she'd really gotten into her assistant groove while I was gone. That was good news. JGJ seemed comfortable, too. I opened my mail, listening to the two of them laughing and talking in Jean's office.

At noon I sidled up to my boss's door. She was typing away, her back toward me.

"I'm going to the cafeteria," I said. "Do you want me to grab your lunch?"

JGJ twisted around and looked at me sort of curiously.

"Er, no," Jean said. "Simone will get it."

She resumed her work. I returned to my desk to open drawers and rummage around for my dining pass. I looked at the back of my boss's chair. We were sitting just ten feet apart, but suddenly she felt far away.

On Christmas Eve, I gave Marco his presents: a handheld Flip video camera—the "It" gadget at the time, gifted to me by a beauty company—and a box of Giotto be-bè crayons that I bought in Rome.

"Dope!" Marco said. He got right to work in his sketchbook.

I ♥ CAT, he showed me later. The big Italian-crayon-red heart was beautiful, like a smashed lipstick.

We snorted skag and watched Marco's looping *Eyes Wide Shut*

DVD for a week straight. Literally—a week. I couldn't even take a sip of water without running to the filthy toilet. But of course on heroin throwing up feels good.

On New Year's Eve, I was standing at the mirror in Marco's grimy bathroom, doing my makeup, applying MAC Fluidline to my heavy, heavy eyelids . . .

Tap. I jerked awake. I'd fallen forward and hit my forehead on the mirror on the medicine cabinet above the sink! I shook my head.

I closed my eyes again . . .

Tap. I jerked awake again! Fuck, man. I'd keeled forward into the mirror *again.*

Tap.

Someone banged on the bathroom door.

"Cat?"

"I'm good," I whispered. I fell asleep again. *Tap.*

And it went on like this for . . . well, I couldn't tell you.

Finally I snapped out of it. I floated through the garbage-filled kitchen and found Marco on a futon. *Eyes Wide Shut* had just started again.

"Hey," I mumbled.

"Don't you think one of the charms of marriage is that it makes deception a necessity for both parties?" Sandor was waltzing Nicole Kidman around the glittery gold ballroom.

"What the fuck were you doing in there?" Marco slurred.

"Is it as bad as that?" Sandor said.

"I dunno . . ." I sat down next to Marco and leaned on his shoulder.

"As good as that," Nicole Kidman said.

"Happy New Year, Cat." Marco shook me. When I opened my eyes, I saw that it was midnight. The DVD had started again and we were watching the same scene, from the same movie.

Chapter Fifteen

THAT WINTER WAS DOPEY, ITCHY, SLUSHY, and dark. During the week, I zombie-wrote eye cream captions; feigned interest in deep-dish side parts backstage at Fashion Week; received complimentary lash extensions in the basement at Barneys; and hit 1 OAK nightclub at three in the afternoon to chat with 50 Cent about his new cologne, Power by 50 Cent—as well as his debut novel, *The Ski Mask Way.* ("HARD LIFE. HARD LUCK. HARD DRUGS. HARD DEALS." Indeed!)

After work, Marco would pick me up in his father's old Fiat, which was white and full of garbage. He'd be wearing a sheepskin denim jacket. Marco knew every pothole on the FDR Drive. We'd race up there along the East River, then *career* across town to Washington Heights.

"Slow DOWN!" I'd scream, but he never did. He'd be blasting Pulp (we loved "Common People"). Then we'd buy a special kind of weed called *pudé*, which made us giggle like little kids. We'd park next to the Hudson River and smoke in the car.

Marco had lost his room on Madison Street; he couldn't keep up with the five-hundred-dollar-a-month rent (I don't know how he ever did). He'd relocated to the Bronx, where his dad owned a few buildings. His dad, who spoke in a heavy Romanian accent, was elderly and always sick. I think he'd been close to death a few times. Marco hardly ever talked about it.

When I visited on weekends, I heard Marco's dad's hacking cough in the other room. He was always trying to feed us. I remember his kind face in the messy little kitchen as he unfolded wax paper. The family only ate beautiful thinly sliced meats from the butcher: prosciutto and things.

"Butchers have the softest hands because they work with fat," Marco told me. This was the European elegance he inherited. He always taught me special things like that.

Underneath the apartment buildings was a phenomenal maze of tunnels and cement rooms: a spooky underworld for vampires like Marco and me. It was built as a two-hundred-thousand-square-foot nuclear fallout shelter during World War Two. The signs were still up from back then. The black corridors seemed endless. His father had filled them with discarded furniture, and Marco had dragged it around and set up hidden rooms everywhere. That's where he'd paint me. I'd take off my minidress and tights and Hanky Panky thong and arrange myself on a throwaway sofa. Eventually I'd nod off with an orange juice in my hand. Marco usually removed it before I dropped it. He worked on canvas, in oils. Lots of blues and blacks: corpse colors. I could stay still for him for hours when I was on the skag.

One modeling session I woke up to a *flash* and the mechanical crunch-and-hum of an old-school Polaroid camera. Marco had snapped a photo of me with my legs spread.

"Funny," I mumbled, closing them. Then I went back under.

"My eyes are rolling back in my head!" I said, inspecting his painting the next day.

"That's how you looked." He liked women to look dead.

On Sunday night, Marco would drive me back to Manhattan and on Monday morning I'd be at my desk, staring at my computer monitor, feeling very very dead indeed.

That spring, I found a new place to live, and a new roommate. You may know Nev Schulman as the star of *Catfish* (as well as MTV's spin-off series *Catfish: The TV Show*). The documentary, which was directed by Nev's hot older brother Rel (who was moving out of the apartment) and his partner Henry Joost, explored how people pose with fake identities on the Internet to lure unsuspecting rubes into relationships. When I met these guys, they'd just finished filming; Nev wasn't all famous yet. I'd come across his looking-for-a-roommate ad on Craigslist. I e-mailed him and I'd said that I was a Condé Nast editor and that I would be a great roommate and could we meet?

"I am VERY healthy and normal!" I wrote. Nev took the bait. *Catfish*.

I moved into Rel's old room in March of 2009. The clean, stylish two-bedroom on East Sixth Street was full of art books and vintage Eames chairs. The Schulman boys had great taste. My room had its own entrance from the fifth-floor stairwell and two large windows. I was particularly excited to be living in Alphabet City, a magical pocket of the East Village full of secret gardens and stuttering dustheads.

Marco came to inspect.

"This is good." He nodded. He especially liked the private entrance. He was studying the lock on that door when one of Nev's two cats wandered in and . . . *mewed*, as they do. *Mew*.

Marco's gaze snapped up. He *lunged* at the cat—like he wanted to stomp on its head with his boot! The cat jumped a foot in the air.

"Marco!" I said as it scampered away.

"I fucking hate cats," he grumbled.

He didn't like *any* animals, as far as I could tell. I'd also once stopped Marco from kicking a drug dealer's dog in the projects. And this was one of the . . . many *weird* things I'd started to notice about my sweet soul mate, about my dreamy best friend.

But I was too busy at work to dwell on Marco's quirks. Online was now a "thing" at Condé, and even the all-powerful Jean—who championed separation of print and web with all the conviction of Thomas Jefferson—couldn't get us out of blogging for the new (i.e., no longer just a place to subscribe to the magazine) luckymag.com. I, too, was Team Print all day, but to my surprise, I actually enjoyed drafting my once-a-week blog post. I could play around. It was more fun than writing boring, phony-sounding fragrance captions for the magazine.

"I know black eyeliners better than the busboys at the Sea Org snack bar do. . ." I opened one post. I referenced Pete Doherty, Britney Spears's meltdown, Sharon Stone—all of the weird stuff I was into. I was no Richard Pryor or anything, but humor in beauty writing was definitely a little edgy at that time—particularly in the world of women's magazines. Sometimes I snickered to myself while I was writing.

My wacky beauty blogs were a hit. Well, not with readers (no one was reading luckymag.com, let's be real), but Jean praised my work for the site every week.

"I know when I hear you laughing at your desk that it's going to be good." Jean would smile when I turned in my posts (which she edited by hand before they went online—old-school). And you know I'd just beam. Kim was into my blogs, too! Our editor in chief came over, laughing, to tell me how much she'd liked something I'd written. It felt so good.

I guess she really meant it, because in June, Kim chose me—*me*, out of everyone on staff—to cover music festivals for luckymag.com.

All summer long! These special assignments had nothing to do with beauty, but JGJ wasn't about to tell Kim no. Simone and Cristina would pick up extra work while I was away.

What a time! I traveled all over—to the New Orleans Jazz Fest, Lollapalooza in Chicago, Bonnaroo in Tennessee—scouting "real" girl style and interviewing rock stars. I hung in catered press tents with writers from *Rolling Stone* and *Spin*. I saw MGMT, Jay Z, Nine Inch Nails, and Jane's Addiction. I also saw a *lot* of fucking gladiator sandals. Every day a photographer and I would prowl the fields for hours, hunting for chic concertgoers.

"I SEE ONE!" I'd squeal over the music. "CATCH UP WITH ME!" Then I would *sprint* across the grassy plain and pounce. Half of my victims were 'shrooming so hard that they could barely sign their model release forms. Even the "talent" I met was out to the ball game.

"Can you tell that I'm rolling my face off?" an up-and-coming pop singer (now a big star) asked at Lollapalooza. Glitter was literally leaking out of her nose. Had she been snorting it? (Swag.)

My special project ended in August. All in all, it had been a success. Kim and other high-ranking *Lucky* operatives were very pleased with my performance. Which meant Jean was very pleased with me.

Marco got a girlfriend. Carly drank whiskey from a flask and weighed seventy-five pounds. She was perfect for Marco.

Their romance meant I saw my friend less and less, but that was okay. Lately he'd been acting sort of . . . obnoxious.

For example: one Tuesday, Marco had stopped by to bum a few sexy Dexys. Or was it to borrow cash? Marco never seemed to have either those days. That wasn't the annoying part: I was happy to spot him. It was just that . . . he never said thank you. For anything, ever. Had it always been that way? I couldn't remember.

"You're such a good girl, Cat," Marco said—instead of "thanks"— after I gave him what he wanted. He was drinking a beer and had his dirty boots propped up on my bed. (I'd also noticed how lazy and enti-tled my friend had been acting lately—like he was a king in my home.) "I always tell Carly she's wrong about you."

"What?" I said.

"She thinks you're jealous." Marco shrugged.

"Huh?" I said. I caught his eye in the reflection. "Of you guys?"

"Are you?" Marco said.

"No!" I said. "Why would I be jealous? She's just insecure." Then: "Don't tell her I said that."

"I won't." Marco smirked. Then he stood up. "Gotta go."

"You just got here!" This was the second time this week he'd . . . whatever. It wasn't a big deal. "Throw this out for me?" I held up a small plastic deli bag knotted at the top.

Marco looked at the bag like it was full of rotten meat and maggots instead of Diet Sunkist cans and Popsicle sticks.

"No." Marco shook his head.

"I beg your pardon?" I said.

"My hands are full," Marco whined. He was carrying a Jean Paul Gaultier gym bag (which he'd been lugging around ever since he lost his apartment and had become "transient")—but only with one hand. The other was free.

"Just take out the trash, please," I said—sharply.

Marco stared hatefully at the plastic bag.

"Fine," he finally said, snatching it from my hand. He slammed my door shut behind him. The next morning, I couldn't find my Dexedrine bottle.

A few nights later, Marco returned.

BUZZZZZZZZZZZ. BUZZZZZZZZZZ. BUZZZZZZZZZZZZZZZZZ-ZZZZZZZ. BUZZZZZZ. BUZZZZZ. I jumped up and ran through the living room to the intercom. Nev came out of his room half-asleep.

"I'm so sorry," I said. He was standing in his boxers. His girlfriend was sitting up in bed; his two black-and-white cats were weaving around his ankles.

"Can you tell your friends not to buzz this late?" he mumbled.

"Of course," I said. "I'm so sorry."

Marco sauntered into the apartment in his leather jeans. The cats ran from him.

"Marco!" I said. "Apologize to Nev!" But Marco didn't even look at him. He stormed into my room and slammed the door. I followed and found him lighting up a Marlboro Red.

"Hey!" I said, yanking him over to the windows and opening one. "What's the matter with you?"

Marco had scratches on his face. He put his gym bag on the floor and unpacked his stuff: a copy of Oscar Wilde's *The Picture of Dorian Gray*—and Carly's passport.

"I stole that bitch's passport," he said unnecessarily. Then he stared at it, curled his lip.

"That's fucked up," I said.

"Fuck that cunt," he growled. "Next time she falls asleep around me, I'm gonna cut off all of her hair!"

"Marco!" I recoiled. "Don't even *joke* about doing that to a woman! That's the sickest thing I've ever heard!"

Suddenly Marco was sugary sweet.

"Just kidding," he said. "I'd never do that." Still, I shuddered. Love really *was* a battlefield, wasn't it? That's why I preferred Vyvanse to boyfriends.

I sat on the sofa with my best friend until sunrise, chewing gum to keep my eyes open. He was hopped up, hogging my computer, talking about himself.

"And then," Marco said. "I walked up to the bar at Lucky Strike—"

"And you demanded a Pellegrino and they just gave it to you," I finished. Lately he'd been telling me the same stories—ones in which he was fearsome, audacious, and glamorous—over and over.

"Isn't this great?" Marco turned my laptop around to show me a black-and-white photo. It was of him, of course.

"Nice," I yawned. Marco had thousands of self-portraits banked in his Gmail. He was always e-mailing them to me and to Carly and his mother.

Giving him a Flip cam had been a bad idea. Now Marco always wanted me to film him—and sometimes it got weird when I did.

"MEN WANT MY PENIS!" he'd shrieked to the streets a few weeks ago. We'd taken ecstasy and he'd handed me the camera. "MEN WANT MY PENIS! *MEN WANT MY PENIS!*" He'd pulled out his bouncy ball. *Bounce bounce bounce.*

A few weeks later, he showed me the stickers he'd had professionally printed from a photo of his body in silhouette—with a *huge* erection. He slapped these things all over downtown (there's still one on a stop sign on Broome Street in Soho). I tried to appreciate his "art," but I was a little . . . perturbed. What did it all mean? Sometimes I felt like my friend was a puzzle I had to figure out.

Tonight was definitely one of those times—but I was too tired to think too hard about it. I had a beauty event in Connecticut in a few hours. I begged Marco to keep it down, gave him a kiss, popped a pill, and returned to bed.

I woke up an hour later to rapid-fire camera sounds.

Click-click-click-click-click-click. I sat up on my elbows. My room was light blue and purple: the sun was just starting to rise outside. *Click-click-click-click-click-click.*

Marco was hanging out the window as he shot himself with a thirty-five-millimeter camera. *Click-click-click-click.* He had on my Chanel aviators and my leopard-print fur Adrienne Landau vest. YSL Rouge Volupté no. 17 lipstick was smeared all over his mouth. He was vamping like Buffalo Bill ("Would you fuck me? I'd fuck me") in *The Silence of the Lambs*—and this was long before selfies were a thing.

"Are you serious," I mumbled. It was such a surreal tableau that I wasn't sure I wasn't hallucinating.

If Marco noticed me stirring, he didn't let on. Bitch's natural lighting was too good. *Click. Click. Click. Click. Click. Click click click click.* I passed back out.

When I opened my eyes again, it was morning. Marco was next to me, on top of the covers with his boots still on. I left him and let him sleep. I spent the day in Ridgefield at the opening of a beauty boutique in a flagship CVS store. I made small talk with Kristin Davis of *Sex and the City*—and applauded dutifully at the VIPs' speeches.

I didn't go back to the office that afternoon. Instead, I came home early with Marco's favorite sandwich from Sunny & Annie's—the Mona Lisa—and a green juice for me. But when I opened my bedroom door, Marco wasn't there. Oh well. I scanned the room for the cute note he usually left me: nothing.

Actually, there *was* something. I'd left the room messy, but now it looked . . . different-messy, like someone had been rummaging through things. My drawers, my closet, the papers on my desk all seemed to have been disturbed.

I walked around the room and took in the odd energy I was feeling—was I imagining things?—and wondered what my best friend could possibly have been looking for.

The next time Marco visited Nev's apartment, he brought a wee octogenarian. The old man wore a ratty cardigan and appeared to be hunched over his own rib cage.

"This is my friend Lester Garbage Head," Marco said, ushering him into the apartment. Nev and his girlfriend were in the kitchen cooking tortellini, perhaps.

"Nice to meet—" Nev started.

Marco grabbed Lester and darted into my bedroom, *slamming* the door in my roommate's face.

"Nev, I'm so sorry," I apologized, and ran into my room after them.

"Marco!" I said. "I'm not going to tell you again. That's my roommate! You can't be so *rude*! Say hi to Nev!"

Marco made a big fuss of rolling his eyes. Then he popped open the door and stuck his greasy, handsome head out. "Hi, *Nev*."

Then he *slammed* the door shut again.

"You're the worst," I said. But I had him over every day, so I don't know what that made me.

"Nice crib," Methuselah said. Upon closer inspection, I saw that Lester was probably only about twenty years old. What was Marco doing with him?

"Lester's gonna teach us to fix," Marco announced. Ah. He'd found a junkie—a *real* one—to tutor him.

The junkie was taking a kit out of his backpack: a bag of syringes, a belt . . .

"I don't know," I said. I'd never shot dope before. Also, it was, like, a random Wednesday evening.

"Need a spoon," Lester Garbage Head said.

"I'll get it—" I said, but he was already out in the kitchen. I followed.

"Got a spoon?" he asked Nev, who was stirring a pot.

"Yes," my roommate said. "Why?"

"Magic trick," Lester Garbage Head said.

Nev shot me a look.

"He's really talented." I swallowed.

Nev looked suspicious, but slowly reached into his perfect silverware drawer anyway.

"Here," he said, extending the spoon to Lester Garbage Head.

"Thanks." Lester snatched it.

"Heh-heh." I smiled at my roommate. Then I scurried after Lester and shut my bedroom door.

As I said, I didn't want to mainline heroin on a work night, but I decided that a little cocaine would be okay. I had some in the house, so I just let Lester Garbage Head shoot me up with that. (I know what you're thinking, and yes, I always used clean needles. I am HIV free! The ER doctor told me so the last time I overdosed.) I thought it would be awesome, but I didn't like the feeling at all. It was extremely wild and overwhelming to have a stimulant flooding my body like that. Too much. I felt like a pinball was ricocheting around inside me for like twenty hours. (Injecting gives you hep C. Don't even think about it, teens.)

That night after he left, I didn't see Marco again for weeks. I tried not to take it personally, but it hurt my feelings. He was spending *so* much time with Carly. And he was my only close friend! My text-message alert would chime, I'd pick up my phone, expecting it to be my bestie, but it was always Lester Garbage Head. I'd let him come over. I'd watch him shoot up and he'd ask me out. I always declined—the dates, not the dope—but it was nice to have a dude paying attention to me, even if he was a baghead. A guy hadn't had a crush on me since . . . God, I didn't even know.

I was mad lonely. So one afternoon, I hung out with Marco's "other" best friend, Trevor—who was gay—after work. We watched *Ab Fab* and smoked weed.

I missed Marco. When he did finally come around to my house again, I mentioned that I'd hung out with Trevor without him—and Marco *lost* it.

"Fuck that faggot!" Marco ranted. "He's obsessed with my dick!" The penis thing again. "That faggot wants to suck my dick!" He was pacing in my room.

"Don't say those things!" I said. I was so confused. Marco loved Trevor! They'd grown up together; he was over there all the time.

"What did you guys say about me?" He was all paranoid. "*What did you talk about?*"

"*AB FAB!*" I said. "The TV show!"

"*That's it?*" Marco didn't believe me. "WHAT ELSE?"

"Um . . ." I couldn't even remember; we'd gotten so stoned. "Cicciolina!" I cried. "David Lynch! *Twin Peaks!*"

Marco glared at me.

"You're not allowed to hang out with him again without me there!" Marco barked. "He's not your friend!"

"Fine, I won't," I said. "I won't!"

"You promise?" I nodded. "You *swear*?"

"Yes!"

And just like that, Marco stopped pacing the room and, like . . . *mutated*—into something soft and doe-eyed. He plopped down on the sofa and started rubbing up on me like one of the cats he hated. "I really love you."

What the *hell* was going on? Whatever; I was just happy he'd calmed down. I gave that weirdo eighty dollars to go out and score us crack, just like old times. Marco hit the streets. I messed around in my shelves, organizing my art books. Then I lay on my bed. An hour passed, then two. My friend's phone went straight to voice mail. I felt angrier and angrier. Marco never came back.

It was around this time that I was escorted out of Cirque du Soleil by my elbows at the instruction—I believed—of the Vice President of Marketing for a major advertiser beauty brand. Remember? (I sure do.)

A few weeks after that fiasco, I was at my desk at *Lucky*, working *very* hard at trying on the latest Poppy King lipsticks. It was an afternoon like any other. Simone had been up and down all day, escorting beauty VIPs to Jean's office with their bags of new products. I listened in on these "desksides" all day whether I wanted to or not, since I sat so close to Jean. She always left the door open.

At around four, Simone brought back . . . the Vice President of Marketing.

We locked eyes right away.

"Hey," I forced out. The Vice President of Marketing nodded. Barely.

That's when I noticed that the Vice President of Marketing didn't have any gift bags with her—nor her usual gaggle of publicists.

"Good to see you . . ." Jean air-kissed her visitor.

"Can I close this?" The Vice President of Marketing gestured to the glass office door. Then she slid it shut.

"Is the Vice President of Marketing here for a deskside?" I asked Simone.

"I think it's just . . . a meeting," she said. Oh, bloody hell.

Twenty minutes later, the door slid open again. I looked right at the Vice President of Marketing as she exited my boss's office. She did not look back at me.

"Simone will walk you out," Jean said. The vice president continued to stare straight ahead as she followed Simone back to reception.

I picked up a press release and pretended to be engrossed.

Three . . . two . . .

"Cat?"

Yep.

I went into JGJ's office.

"What's up?" I said.

Jean looked at me.

"That meeting . . ." Jean said slowly, "was about *you*."

"Oh," I said.

"Were you . . . wasted at Cirque du Soleil?" She sounded like she was still processing what she'd been told. "And at the Mayflower?"

"No!" I assured her. "Jean, let me explain . . ." And you can imagine how it went from there. All I could do was spin, spin, spin: "That woman has it out for me, Jean! You know I'm not disrespectful!" Deny, deny, deny: "I was late for dinner at the Mayflower because I wanted to skip the cocktail hour!" Lie, lie, lie: "She *thought* I was drunk at Cirque du Soleil because I tripped on my way to the ladies' room!" Accuse, accuse, accuse: "She had me thrown out in front of everyone, Jean! It was *insane*! *She's* unprofessional! Not me!"

"Mmm . . ." Jean said.

I looked her straight in the eye.

"It wasn't drugs or alcohol, Jean," I said. "I wouldn't lie to you about that. Not after everything you've done for me."

She looked at me hard for what felt like ten hours.

"Okay," my boss finally said. "I believe you."

"*Thank*—" I exhaled.

"I'm *choosing* to believe you," JGJ cut me off. "But you must do better. Do you understand? You *must* do better."

"Yes." I was nodding like a bobblehead doll. "Yes. Yes. Yes, I will. Thank you. I'm so sorry—"

"Don't apologize," Jean said sharply. "Just do better." Then she swiveled her chair around to face her computer. Meeting adjourned.

I went back to my cubicle. Simone and Cristina had heard the whole thing. I sat down in my rolling chair. My boss's back was to me as she continued typing.

I'm sorry, I thought.

Gay guys always have better drugs. For this reason, Marco and I drove to New Jersey on a Friday evening to spend the weekend with Trevor and his party-boy friends at his family's house. Our host popped Molly in our mouths before we were even out of the car! Forty minutes later, we were deeper into the matrix than Keanu Reeves, and we stayed there all night.

That's when . . . *it* happened.

Ugh.

Look, I'd *never* felt sexually attracted to Marco, okay? We'd slept in bed together like children our entire friendship. I'd posed naked for him twenty times; we'd done MDMA just the two of us a *hundred* times. But we were *not* like that.

And yet somehow, on this night, we went to a bedroom and got together. *Together*-together. I truly have no idea who initiated what, though I do have a theory on why I went along with it: I wanted to feel

close to my friend, who'd been so distant lately. I'd been feeling insecure, and Marco knew it.

And then somehow that dynamic—that energy between us—turned
into strange, cold sex. Marco's icy-blue eyes were blank and glazed as he
boned me. In the middle of it, my mind flashed to his sketchbooks full
of girls getting fucked up their asses with torture devices. I was relieved
when the sex was over. I knew it would never happen again.

We woke up together in the morning, then got in the Fiat to return
to the city. Something was wrong. With Marco. He was hardly speaking
at all, and when he did, his affect was very flat. He almost sounded like
a robot. I made jokes to lighten the mood, but Marco wouldn't laugh. It
was disconcerting and uncomfortable.

We drove along in mostly silence. I looked out the window at the
highway streaking by. My brain felt fried. I had work the next day.

"Is everything okay?" I finally said.

Marco didn't say anything. He had fully shut down. We got back to
New York, and after that, things were never the same.

Chapter Sixteen

PEOPLE DON'T JUST CHANGE OVERNIGHT, DO THEY? But Marco did: from a sweet boy into a fearsome predator, a bully, a thief. I've spent weeks writing and rewriting the following scenes, trying to make them make sense. The fact is . . . *nothing* about this period made any sense. If at any time you get confused, well—good. Because that's what it was like living through it. Except a zillion times worse.

Back to Marco. Bitch started buzzing at all hours of the night, every night: Big Bad Wolf steez. *BZZZZZZZZ. BZZZZZZZZZZZZZ. BZZZZZZZZ. BZZZZZZZ. BZZZZZZZZZZZZZ.* The only way to stop it was to let him in. I was usually awake to hop up and push the button, but one night Nev got there first. The intercom was right outside his bedroom door and Marco knew it.

I stumbled out in my Xanax haze.

"I'm so sorry!" I said. "Marco is homeless right now and—"

"I DON'T CARE!" Nev hollered. He stomped back into his bedroom and slammed the door.

Enter Marco. He lurched in like a broken machine, hauling his stupid Gaultier gym bag. He was wearing a bunch of the rosaries I'd bought in Rome.

"You can't keep doing this!" I hissed, closing my bedroom door behind us. "You know you're supposed to call my phone if you want to hang out!"

"Let's do some drugs," he said.

"No!" I shook my head. "I have to work tomorrow."

"C'mon," Marco said. "Gimme forty dollars."

"No!" I was a little annoyed with him.

Marco stood there for a second. Then he walked over to my desk, *went into my handbag*, and just *took* the money he wanted—and then he left! "Are you *serious*?" I yelled as the door slammed behind him. Was he literally on crack? It was quite possible.

He called me the next day at *Lucky* like nothing had happened.

"You better not pull a stunt like that again," I said. I assumed he had been wasted. People do crazy things when they're drunk.

But three days later . . .

"Why are you doing this?" I asked, trying to stay calm when Marco grabbed my money and my Adderall and Valium bottles and stuffed them in his pockets. "You know you're just going to have to bring all of that back."

He didn't answer. He just disappeared again.

BZZZZZZZZZZZZZZZZZZZZZZZZZZZZZZZZZ.

It was before dawn in Alphabet City, three days later, and Marco was downstairs. I ran to the intercom. Then I set out some lemonades and Rice Krispies Treats from Sunny & Annie's, sat Marco down on the sofa, and went *in*.

"Honey," I began. "Why would you steal from me when I've always *given* everything to you?" That's what really confused me. I'd always spoiled him! With drugs, with cash, with glamorous gifts: Dior Homme candles, the cashmere Condé Nast corporate Christmas scarf. Anything he admired, I handed over! "I'm on your side. I'm on your team! We're on the *same* team. I'll give you anything you want! I always have!"

He repeated back: "We're on the same team. You'll give me anything I want. You always have."

"Yes!" I squeezed his hand. "Just please be my friend again! Stop this. Just stop!" I thought he needed love. "I love you so much."

Marco said nothing. He didn't even seem to be hearing me. He seemed kind of . . . groggy.

Then, suddenly, he came alive—and shoved me in the chest! I sort of tipped over onto the ground.

"Marco!" I should have been angry, but I was more confused than anything. Why was he *acting* this way?

Then he stood up, pulled a can from his jacket pocket, and spray-painted "GROUPIE" across my bedroom wall—in hot pink!

"HEY!" I shouted. I scrambled to my feet, ran over, and tried to pull the paint can from his hand. Marco pushed me away; I kept coming back. Then he shoved me to the bed, grabbed me by the neck, and tightened his grip—choking me for a second.

Is this really happening? I screamed inside, but it was over so fast I wasn't even sure.

Then:

"WHORE!" he shouted.

He spat in my face.

Well. There was no second-guessing *that*.

This time, Marco snatched my Adderall bottle off the mantel—oh, I didn't *think* so—and . . . my house keys?! I chased him down the stairs. But he was too quick for me.

"It's like . . . it's like . . . Dr. Jekyll and Mr. Hyde," I babbled to JGJ,

Cristina, and Simone the next day. I was hopped up on adrenaline and no sleep. "He's acting, like, *crazy*, and I don't know how to help him . . ."

Jean looked scared.

"He's going to kill you!" she said.

"Oh . . ." I thought that was a bit much. "No, I don't . . . I mean, Marco would never *kill* anyone." Jean shook her head. She told me to cut my friend out of my life. Instead, I left her office and called Marco over and over from my work phone. He wasn't answering, so I left weepy voice mails.

"What can I do to help you? I don't care about the money you stole. I just want my keys back. And I want to make you feel better," I pleaded into the receiver. "I love you. You're my best friend. Let me help you." I thought he wasn't well. Later I found out that he made these voice mails available for purchase on iTunes for ninety-nine cents each. I don't even know what to tell you guys about that.

Over the next two days, I buzzed Nev at all hours to get in, disrupting his sleep and his life. On the third day, I came home from work and Marco was standing on my stoop.

He handed me my keys.

"Thanks!" I was trying to be positive.

"You're welcome," he said—with no irony whatsoever. "Can I come up?"

The East Village was getting dark. I knew that Marco didn't have his apartment anymore.

"If I let you up today, I'm not giving you any more chances," I said shakily. "And I want my bottle of Adderall back. And all of the pills you took out of it!" I didn't mention the eighty dollars he stole. "And you have to apologize for what you did."

"Why?" Marco said.

"What?" I said.

"*Why?*" he repeated.

"Why do you have to apologize?" I snapped. "Oh, I don't know,

Marco. Because you called me a whore and spat in my face? Because you stole my keys and my drugs and my money?"

Marco stared across the street at the synagogue. I stood there with my hands on my hips.

Things with Marco got worse and worse throughout the summer. They never got better. I started to go crazy. I mean, I was already close to crazy from all those years of sleep deprivation and narcotics. But the Dr. Marco/Mr. Hyde thing *really* made me crazy. It was worse than having a mouse!

BZZZZZZZZZZZZZZZ. The buzzer would ring over and over. *BZZZZZZZZ. BZZZZZZZZZZZZZ. BZZZZZZZZ. BZZZZZZZ. BZZZZZZZZZZZZZ.* I'd bury my head in my hands. I knew it was Marco. I knew I couldn't let him up. But I needed my keys—or whatever of mine he had—back.

BZZZZZZZZZZZZZ. BZZZZZZZZZZZZ. BZZZZZZZZZZZZZ. Finally I wouldn't be able to take it anymore. When I'd run out, Nev would already be at the intercom.

"I'm sorry," I'd say. "Marco is—"

"I DON'T FUCKING CARE!" Nev would scream. Then I'd run down the five flights of stairs to East Sixth Street. The buzzer would still be reverberating through the building: *BZZZZZZZZZZZZZZZZZZZZZ.*

"What the FUCK, Marco?" I'd burst out onto the street barefoot in my ratty silk slip. "You woke up Nev AGAIN! I have work tomorrow—"

"Let's hang," Marco would interrupt me.

"*No!*" I always said. "I can't let you up in my house anymore. You steal from me. It's so crazy. I just can't."

But I was lonely. I was pathetic. I was weak. I was a loser. Most drug addicts are.

I'd sit on the steps next to the trash cans and put my head in my hands. I refused to accept that Marco was this . . . *scary monster.* This superfreak. Marco would sit next to me, and I'd spend forty minutes trying to get through to him—to reason with him like he was a rational person.

"You *have* to stop robbing me. This shit is so stupid," I'd beg. "Just come back. Where did you go? This isn't who you are." Then I'd start to cry. "You're a sweet boy. I *know* you." Didn't I? "Act like yourself again." *Sniffle.* "I'm not giving you any more chances." But I always gave him more chances.

I started stashing my pills, purse, money—anything of value—in my closet for safekeeping. Just so he could come up and do drugs with me. Sometimes he stayed for two, three days, being his old charming, funny self before everything escalated into theft, shoving, shouting, and drama. He'd be sweet from Friday to Sunday—happily setting up his Flip camera to film himself—but after a few days without sleeping, his already disorganized personality would come undone. I'd wake up from a weekend of doing dope and catch him rummaging through my drawers. He'd stuff things into a bag right in front of me—a vintage punk T-shirt, my Louis Vuitton Robert Wilson Vernis bag. Fur vests. Sometimes he'd bring things back; sometimes he'd sell them. Sometimes I don't know where they went. And he loved taking my house keys. (When he controlled them—I figured out much later—he controlled me.)

I kept vowing to myself that I would never, ever hang out with him again. But I'd always have to see him one more time—to get back my debit card, or my work ID, or my house keys. Then, if he had drugs—and he always had drugs these days—I would let him up. Then everything would go to hell again. It was a twisted game. I got up in the morning for work and dabbed on my Colette Black Musk and twisted my hair up into messy buns and walked to the subway to work like I always did, but my stomach would be turning the whole time: I could think of nothing else but Marco, Marco, Marco.

I might have kept Marco in my life forever, but in the end, he forced my hand. On the last night I ever let him up to Nov'o, we got into an argument. *I* remember him spraying a syringe full of blood all over me and my dress. For the record, Marco insists that I watched him do this to "a guy on the terrace of the Bowery Hotel" that night—but I *know* that he did it to me. It was in Nev's apartment—in my room! Either way, he was in fine form. And when we started to brawl, Marco grabbed me by the shoulders and fucking *threw* me into my desk so hard that my lamp and glass laboratory beakers full of Sharpies and Silver Hill marbles were knocked over.

I slid down to the floor and burst into tears.

"GO-OO AWAY!" I howled. Marco headed for my walk-in closet.

"STOP!" I scrambled upright as he started rummaging through my clothes, pulling things from shelves. "STOP!" I tried to drag him away from the closet.

Then he spit in my face *again*—a real loogie this time—*spun* me around and shoved me into my closet, face-first! The clothes on the hangers caught my fall. I collapsed to the messy floor and covered my head. Marco pulled my white Balenciaga handbag from the high shelf—*how did he know?*—and slammed the door shut. Then I heard him *dragging* my three-drawer Ikea dresser—it was right next to the closet—to block the door. He wanted me trapped inside. I didn't want to come out, anyway. I lay there under my clothes, catching my breath. Wiping the spit off my face with an old A Bathing Ape hoodie.

A few minutes later, my private door into the stairwell opened and closed. *Thump-a-thump-a-thump.* He was gone.

I pushed the door open against the dresser. It wasn't too hard to get out. It was getting light outside my bedroom windows. I couldn't call the cops on a friend—it wasn't in my drug-addict DNA—but I wanted to call someone. Then I realized that Marco had my phone. It was in the bag he'd stolen—along with my keys, my pills, my cash, and my credit cards. My passport. My Condé ID. My life.

"I HATE YOU!" I screamed.

Then . . . a phone rang.

I whirled around. Marco's iPhone was on my dresser! I picked it up and stared at my own name on his caller ID. I knew he was coming back. I didn't have much time. I ran to lock the door—useless, since he had my keys—and secured the sliding chain-latch above it. Then I went to the living room and did the same on that door. I called Marco's mother. It was around six o'clock. She was sleeping.

"G—," I said. I was hysterical. "It's Cat! He stole my phone. Can you call him on it?" I gave her my number. "Can you get my things from him? Or I *have* to call the police! He went crazy! He pushed me into my desk, robbed me, he—"

"Slow down!" she snapped. She was used to these wakeup calls from Marco's friends. "Goddamn that kid. I'm coming into the city. Where do you live?"

"East Sixth between—" I stopped midaddress. Someone was coming up the stairs. Then that someone was unlocking my private door. I ran to an alcove near my closet, where Marco wouldn't be able to see me.

The door burst open—well, three inches open. The only thing between us was the chain.

"Cat," he growled through the opening. "I know you're in there."

"Hello?" Marco's mom was saying. I hit the button to hang up on her and switched the ringer off.

"Open the door, Cat . . ." I was still frozen in the hidden corner. "I just need my phone."

There was a long silence. Then . . .

BANG! Marco threw his body into the door. *BANG.* Over and over. *BANG. BANG.* He was trying to break the chain. How strong were those things? *BANG. BANG.* Pretty strong, I guess, because Marco gave up after a few minutes.

Then he started messing with the chain-latch. He reached through the crack and around the door to find the hardware. I watched in horror as his long monster fingers fiddled, fiddled, fiddled . . .

He can't *unlatch it from the outside*, I thought.

But after a few minutes, that's exactly what Marco did. I couldn't believe it. Then he *burst* into the room.

"*RAWWWWWWR!*" He went right for me!

"GET AWAY!" I moaned and cowered. "HELP! HELP!" I threw his phone across the room to the bed. "TAKE IT! THERE IT IS!" Marco scooped it up. Then he turned back to me. Oh God. Oh God. I didn't know what to do, so I just opened my mouth: "AHHHHHHHHHH! AHHHHHHHH! AHHHHHHHHHHHH!" It worked. Marco dashed out—but not through my private entrance to the stairwell like he usually did. This time, he ran through my bedroom door—*into* Nev's pristine apartment. Oh, no.

Sure enough . . .

SMASH! CRASH! There was a clamor in the living room. *BANG! SMASH!* Or was he in the bathroom? I was too afraid to open the door and look. Then I heard him run for the front door. *SLAM!* He was out of the house.

Thank you, God, I thought. But Marco wasn't done yet.

CRASH! What could he possibly be shattering in the stairs? *CRASH.* Glass was tinkling and falling. *Thump-a-thump-a-thump. CRASH.*

I walked out into the kitchen. One of Nev's cats was on top of the fridge. The other had scaled a bookshelf. The dish rack was upside down; pots and knives scattered across the hardwood floor. And my poor roommate was standing in the middle of it all in only his boxer-briefs.

"*WHAT IS GOING ON?*" He was freaking. "WHAT THE *FUCK IS GOING ON?*" But I couldn't speak. The sounds of Marco's destruction were still echoing in the stairwell. *Thump-thump-thump-thump-thump-thump.* He was stopping at every floor. *CRASH. Thump-thump-thump-thump-thump-thump. CRASH.* "WHAT IS HAPPENING?" The smashing finally ceased. I raced to my bedroom window and watched Marco run off down East Sixth Street.

Nev was standing in the doorway of the bathroom, agog. What now? I didn't want to join him, but I did.

"Omigod!" I covered my mouth with my hand. Marco had spray-painted a green streak across the mirror, cracked it, strewn beauty products everywhere, and *lit a tea candle* as a shrine to his chaos. That *flamboyant* piece of—

"WHAT THE FUCK IS GOING ON?" Now Nev was screaming again. "WHAT THE FUCK?"

I felt out-of-body. I floated out of the apartment and into the stairwell. I'd forgotten there were fancy deco mirrors on every landing in the building. Emphasis on *were*. The one on the fifth floor, just outside our apartment, was smashed. Bloody shards glittered across the tiles.

I followed a trail of blood down the stairs. The fourth-floor mirror was destroyed, too. More blood—smears on the walls now—and more glass. It got messier and messier.

I smelled the spray paint on the third floor before I saw it:

Marco's signature—in forest green, again—on the wall of this lovely old building. It was three feet high and eight feet long.

"No," I whispered. I ran past it and down another flight of steps. He'd "signed" the second floor as well. I followed Marco's bloody Converse footprints all the way to the lobby. The tile floor was bloody; the building door was bloody; the peekaboo window that looked out onto the street was bloody. Marco's signature was spray-painted across the mailboxes.

"No!" I kept saying. "*No.*"

What the fuck was I going to do? There was nothing I *could* do. But I was sure I couldn't go back upstairs and face Nev. I had to get out of there. It was about seven by then, so it was light out. I walked to Tompkins Square Park and sat by the dog run for hours. One thing was clear: my relationship with Marco was over. I was finally done.

That August was quiet. And although Marco never returned to Nev's for an encore, his mom brought me my Balenciaga. My phone, my keys, my ID, and my credit cards had survived, but the pills and cash were gone forever. I was relieved, but also lonely. And while I could finally put my ringer back on, my phone was silent. I was depleted—physically, emotionally, psychologically—and had very little energy regardless of how much speed I took. Jean told me to take a vacation—half of Condé was away, and work was slow—but I didn't have anywhere to go.

Then Lester Garbage Head called from Arizona. His father had just died and Lester was cleaning out the house. Did I want to join him? Not really, but I did anyway.

He picked me up from the Phoenix airport. He put my suitcase in the back of his truck. I slid into the front seat and watched as he shot up, right there beside me—into veins on the underside of his forearm.

"*Guuh*," he sort of . . . gasped, and made a terrible, twisted face as the needle went in. My pussy got *so* wet. No, I am completely joking. It was the most unattractive thing I'd ever seen in my life! Junkies are the worst.

Then—in this airport parking lot—the kid rolled up his *other* sleeve and injected his *other* arm: "*Guhh*."

He slumped over the steering wheel for a second. People were walking by with rolling suitcases. It was two in the afternoon.

We sat there in the hot car.

"Uh," I finally said. "Are you—are you okay to drive?"

"Yeah," he mumbled. After a few minutes, he lit an American Spirit and put the key in the ignition. The ride to the house in the desert was an hour long.

I spent the next three days in the car with Lester Garbage Head as he cruised around Phoenix scoring heroin. He was *always* high. It was worse than driving with drunk DC kids, but I didn't have a license. At night, we chilled at the house. On the third night, we watched *Revolutionary Road* in his dad's study. My host couldn't stay awake for more than one scene. I was popping Vicodin on his dad's La-Z-Boy recliner, occasionally clawing at my face or my stomach. Painkillers made me so itchy!

At some point, the Garbage Head stirred on the sofa, then looked over at me with his half-lidded eyes.

"Why did you come out here if you're not going . . . to have sex with me . . ." he grumbled.

It was so pathetic that I couldn't even be insulted. I just didn't say anything. I waited for him to nod off.

Blood was spreading across the back of Kate Winslet's skirt in the movie, so I switched that shit off. Then I went outside to check on some Slayer T-shirts I'd bought that afternoon at the Salvation Army. I'd soaked them in sugar water and hung them by some lanterns, hoping moths would eat them and make them look distressed. Adderall makes you do weird stuff like that. It wasn't working.

I wandered into the backyard, which was really just . . . the desert. I stared out at the sand and the cacti and the moon. *Scratch scratch scratch.* Fucking opiates! This was the worst summer vacation ever. I wondered where Alex and SAME and all of my old friends were. Probably the Hamptons.

Lester Garbage Head dropped me off at the airport the next day. I scratched my arms the whole flight home to New York.

Things weren't any better in the city. Nev wanted me out *stat*. I found a studio with loft ceilings and bleached bamboo floors at 252 East Second Street, just four blocks away. But I couldn't get it together to pack up and fully move out.

Instead, two weeks after I returned from Phoenix, I jumped at a chance to get out of town again—this time to Vegas with Holly, who'd moved on from *Teen Vogue* to Charlotte's seat at *Nylon*. The two of us had been invited to present at a ceremony known colloquially in the industry as "the Oscars of Hair." The audience was full of beauty bigwigs; other presenters included *Extra*'s Nancy O'Dell. I'd skipped the champagne at our table, but I still stumbled over my lines as I read from the teleprompter.

Then I flew back to New York. I was waiting for my suitcase back at LaGuardia when I got an e-mail from Nev with an ominous subject line: "*YOU ARE NOT THE VICTIM.*" Oh, boy.

I opened the e-mail, which was . . . epic. A missive! *Way* too long to reprint here. Nev was furious that I hadn't moved out yet. He called me destructive, selfish, messy, and inconsiderate—of him, his girlfriend, his home, his life: "You wonder why people are always mad at you . . . THIS IS WHY!!!!" Then: "It didn't help that I found one of my MANY missing spoons in your drug box covered with crack." Oops.

I sat by baggage claim, reading this over and over. I had no idea how to respond.

"It wasn't crack," I finally wrote back. "It was heroin!" Otherwise—I had to admit it—Nev had some salient points.

Could things get any worse? You bet. Later that week, Jean called me into her office. She was livid.

"Were you drunk onstage at [the Oscars of Hair]?" Jean said incredulously.

"No! I didn't touch alcohol in Vegas!" And I was actually telling the truth this time. "Who on earth told you that?" I never found out. Not that it mattered. This time my boss definitely didn't believe me.

On September 10, 2009, I turned twenty-seven.

"Are you doing anything special tonight?" Simone asked. We were having the usual Billy's Bakery banana cake in JGJ's office. I was wearing a gold lamé Marc by Marc Jacobs shift dress and had my hair in braids wrapping around my head.

"I'm not sure yet . . ." The despair crept up all day.

After work, I took the train downtown. Somewhere between Herald Square and Union Square, I just started crying—right there in the orange plastic seat. In my stupid shiny party dress.

It was still summer weather. I got off and walked through the East Village until I reached a church on East Thirteenth Street. Inside, starting any minute, was a women-only Narcotics Anonymous meeting. I'd looked it up on the Internet.

I opened the door to the basement and stepped inside. It was dark in there. The Chairwoman had long brown hair, tattoos, and sexy-nerd glasses and looked about thirty years old. Since the group was small, she said, we'd go around the circle and share in order; I could pass if I wanted to.

I counted: I would be seventh. I wasn't sure I could make it that long. I sat and tried to listen, but the tears came again, and no matter what I did I couldn't make them stop. I was shaking in my seat. We were still going around the room, but people were turning to look at me.

Finally it was my turn. I *inhaled*, *exhaled*, and tried to regain my composure.

"My name is Cat," I said—with considerable difficulty. "And I'm an addict."

"Hi, Cat," the group said.

"And I'm here because . . . because . . ." The room was silent. "Today is my *birthday* . . ." Uh-oh. I was about to lose it completely. ". . . AND I DON'T HAVE ANY FRIENDS OR ANYWHERE ELSE TO GO." *Bwaahhhh.*

It all came pouring out.

"I'M SO FUCKED UP. I'M LIVING SO MANY LIES . . . I WALK AROUND GOING TO FASHION SHOWS ACTING LIKE I HAVE THIS GLAMOROUS LIFE AND ALL OF THESE FRIENDS BUT I DON'T . . . IT'S ALL A LIE."

I was *bawling*. I wiped away tears with the back of my hand. Someone handed me a tissue box. Every time I had a new thought I doubled over again.

"THE GUY I THOUGHT WAS MY BEST FRIEND ATTACKED ME AND ROBBED ME . . . I WORK AT CONDÉ NAST . . . I'M A BEAUTY EDITOR . . . IT'S THE ONLY THING I LIKE ABOUT MY-SELF. IT'S ALL I HAVE . . . THEY—*LUCKY*—H-H-H-HELPED ME GO TO REHAB . . . NOW I LIE TO MY BOSS ALL OF THE TIME AND

TELL HER THAT I'M IN NA WHEN I'M NOT . . . SHE DOESN'T
EVEN ASK, I JUST *OFFER* THE LIE. IT'S SO *FUCKED* UP."

Sob.

"WHEN I WAS YOUNGER, I GOT KICKED OUT OF SCHOOL
AND MOVED TO NEW YORK . . . I WAS SEVENTEEN . . . I JUST
WANTED TO BE HERE. AND BE IN THE 'IN CROWD' . . . WHAT-
EVER THAT MEANS . . . YOU KNOW?" A few women nodded. "IT'S
NEW YORK . . . DOWNTOWN . . ."

Sob.

"I DIDN'T FEEL GOOD ABOUT MYSELF WHEN I WAS LIT-
TLE . . . OR IN HIGH SCHOOL . . . SO I MOVED HERE AND TRIED
TO BE COOL . . . TO FEEL . . . *B-B-BETTER*, I GUESS . . ."

Sob.

"MY WHOLE TWENTIES I WAS LIKE . . . LIKE A GROUPIE
FOR ALL OF THESE DOWNTOWN GUYS . . . I WAS—I *AM*—BU-
LIMIC AND OBSESSED WITH MY LOOKS . . . I THOUGHT THAT
MY BODY WAS ALL I HAD TO MAKE PEOPLE LIKE ME . . . I WAS
ALWAYS GOING TO CLUBS ALONE . . . PATHETIC . . . GOING
HOME WITH GUYS AND LETTING THEM CHOKE ME AND
COME ON MY *F-F-FACE* . . . I WAS ALWAYS DOING COKE. AND
I FELT JUST WORTHLESS AFTER A WHILE . . . I DIDN'T KNOW
WHO I WAS."

Sob.

"BUT THEN I STARTED WORKING IN MAGAZINES AND IT
GAVE ME HOPE . . . LIKE I DIDN'T HAVE TO BE TRASH ANY-
MORE . . . I WORKED SO HARD . . . I THOUGHT I WAS GOING
TO HAVE THIS AMAZING CAREER . . . BUT NOW I'VE TOTALLY
SCREWED IT UP BECAUSE I'M ALWAYS ON DRUGS. I'M SO
TIRED ALL OF THE TIME."

Sob.

"I STAY UP ALL NIGHT TEARING MYSELF APART WITH
TWEEZERS . . . I HAVE A HORRIBLE INFECTION. I TAKE LIKE

FIFTEEN PILLS A DAY . . . IF I GO OFF THEM I CAN'T MOVE . . . I'M SO SICK. I'M *SO* SICK. I AM *SO SICK*. I CAN'T BELIEVE HOW BAD IT'S GOTTEN. I AM SO *FUCKING* SICK. I DON'T LET MY-SELF THINK ABOUT IT." *Sob.* "AND I CAN'T *TELL* ANYONE."

Sob.

"BUT I ALSO THINK, 'CAT, EVEN IF YOU DID GO OFF THE PILLS, NONE OF THIS WOULD BE DIFFERENT. YOU'D STILL BE A LOSER AND A MESS. YOU'D STILL—YOU'D STILL—YOU'D STILL HAVE NO *F-F-FRIENDS*. YOU'D STILL NOT HAVE A BOY-FRIEND.' I'M TOO SICK FOR ANYONE TO LOVE ME. I KNOW THAT. I'M NOT STUPID. *I* DON'T *L-L-LOVE* ME!"

Sob.

"I KEEP WAITING FOR IT TO GET B-B-BETTER. BUT IT DOESN'T GET BETTER. *I KEEP WAITING FOR IT TO GET BETTER*, BUT IT JUST GETS WORSE AND WORSE. I GET LONELIER AND LONELIER. I GET MORE AND MORE TIRED. I NEVER SLEEP. I CAN'T SLEEP . . . I DON'T KNOW."

Sob.

"I DON'T KNOW WHAT TO DO. I GET ON MY KNEES ALL THE TIME AND ASK GOD TO HELP ME. BUT I DON'T THINK HE'S LISTENING. HE DOESN'T HELP ME. I HAVE JUST GIVEN UP. I WANT TO DIE. BECAUSE THE OLDER I GET THE WORSE IT GETS. IT JUST GETS WORSE AND WORSE. I'M TWENTY-SEVEN TODAY—"

Just then a man stepped into the basement from the street. Every-one except me whipped around in their seats. It was a man with a brief-case.

"*WOMEN'S MEETING!*" the women roared.

"*Er*," the man said, backing up. "Sorry . . ."

I took a few deep breaths to regain my composure. The women glared at the man until he left. When the door closed behind him, everyone turned back to me. I'd calmed down.

"Okay," I sniffled. "As I was saying . . . um . . ." *Sniff.* "I just . . . I don't want to be twenty-seven today." *Sniff.* "It's not about age. I don't want to be *anything*. I just wish I was dead!" *Sniff.* "Thanks for letting me"—*sniff*—"share."

Everyone sat quietly for a moment. I stared at the ground. Then the next person began.

By the end of the meeting, I just wanted to get out of there. Had I really come out of my face like that? I tried the ol' Irish good-bye, but the women weren't having it. They swarmed, giving me their phone numbers on scraps of paper and asking me for mine.

"I'll text you first thing tomorrow," the Chairwoman said. "Text back."

"I will," I lied. Thank God I'd never see these people again.

I slept like a clubbed baby seal that night. The next morning, my Black-Berry was lit up with messages from the NA chairwoman and a few other women, but I didn't write back. I was too embarrassed. Besides, I felt so much better now that I'd gotten some rest. And it was Fashion Week! I had the Charlotte Ronson show that morning. I dabbed on some NARS Heat Wave lipstick and pulled an Isabel Marant Étoile floaty dress over my head. I was a Condé Nast editor, goddammit. How bad could my life really be?

I took the F train up to Bryant Park, hit the tents, plunked down into my not-swaggy-at-all assigned seat, and immediately scanned the crowd. That's when I saw her: CHRISSIE MILLER.

I'll give you a chance to stop swooning.

Okay.

Who was Chrissie Miller? Only the coolest girl in all of down-town, motherfuckers! At least I'd thought so ever since I profiled her in *Lucky*. Where to start? Chrissie's clothing line, Sophomore, had made the PAGE SIX SIX SIX T-shirt famously worn by Britney Spears in 2003; Chrissie's mom was Susan Miller, the A-lister astrologist;

Chrissie's *boyfriend* was the artist Leo Fitzpatrick, who'd played Teli in *Kids*; Chrissie's *friends* were the model Jessica Stam and *Sopranos* actress Drea de Matteo. Chrissie had long blond bangs and wore vintage seventies clothes and DJ'd at Lit. She was just *so cool.* Her whole *scene* was so cool. I saw her on *Purple Diary* all of the time, but hardly ever in person.

And there she was—in the front row! Duh, she was BFF with Charlotte Ronson, too. I *had* to say hello. The show was going to start any minute, but I clomped down the bleachers in my Sergio Rossis and crossed the runway anyway.

To say I approached her *obsequiously* would be an understatement. I mean, Kimye have approached Anna Wintour with less sycophancy.

Chrissie looked up from her phone.

"Oh, hey!" she said. "How's it going, Cat?"

"Good," I lied. Then, lamely: "I'm reporting on this show for the magazine."

"Oh, nice," Chrissie said. "You should meet my friend—she works in magazines, too." She nudged her neighbor, who was talking to someone in the second row. "Lesley! This is the girl who wrote that story about me in *Lucky*."

Lesley turned to face me. She had long brown hair, tattoos, was wearing cool glasses and—wait. *What?*

It was the Chairwoman from the Narcotics Anonymous meeting.

I felt like someone had hit me in the head with a frying pan.

"H-h-hi . . ." I stammered.

Lesley looked stunned, too.

"*Hi*," she said.

We stared at each other.

Chrissie Miller glanced at me and then at Lesley.

"Do you two . . . already know each other?" she asked.

"Uh," I started. "Not—"

"Yup." Lesley smiled. "We hung out last night. Hey, Cat."

"Hey." I tried to smile back.

"I've been texting you all morning," Lesley said. "How was the rest of your birthday?"

"Pretty good," I croaked.

"I didn't know you were friends with *my* friends, Cat," Chrissie Miller said. Suddenly the queen of downtown was looking at me *very* approvingly.

"Oh . . ." I didn't know what to say to that one. "Well, I'm . . . uh . . ."

"Text me later, okay?" Lesley rescued me—with a wink.

"'Kay." I nodded. The lights flickered. "Er, I'm gonna go sit down."

"Good to see you!" Chrissie said. "Bye, Cat!"

"Bye, Cat," Lesley/Chairwoman echoed. I could feel her eyes on me as I climbed the bleachers again.

The lights went down just as I settled back in. Then the music started: Charlotte's DJ sister Sam opened with "Dominos" by the Big Pink. Then the models came out, but I couldn't focus on the clothes. I *knew* something nuts had happened. It would be years before I learned about *synchronicity*—Jung's theory of "meaningful coincidence"—in a "Higher Power" workshop in (yet another) rehab. But when I did, I thought back to this profoundly crazy moment at Fashion Week, and everything made sense. Back then, though, I was very confused—trying to make sense of everything. All I knew was: God was trying to show me He was there. Remember when I told all those women in the NA meeting that I got on my knees and begged God to help me? Well, I guess someone had been listening to me after all.

Chapter Seventeen

THE SECOND HALF OF SEPTEMBER WAS flat and gray. I never returned to NA. Instead, in the evenings, I lay on the charcoal midcentury modern sofa I'd bought from Nev, staring at the ceiling. Even though my new apartment was chaotic with half-unpacked boxes, it felt very empty. So did I.

I needed drugs—hard ones. I hit up SAME and those guys, whom I'd partied with on and off over the years. They were doing coke at a penthouse in Union Square, and I dropped by. I flirted with their friend, a DJ from Los Angeles. I'd never met him before. He walked me home to Avenue C at dawn. Then he told me he needed a place to stay.

"Well . . ." I said. He was sort of charming.

It had been a long time since I'd brought a guy up. My apartment was a disaster. So was my body.

"What's that?" he said when he got my Topshop tights off. I'd forgotten the raw pink mess—healing now—on one side of my bikini line.

A few weeks ago, I'd gone into a hyperfocused state during a speed binge and done it to myself with tweezers.

I wasn't sure what to say.

"Self-mutilation," I finally mumbled.

The DJ from LA shrugged and did his thing anyway—which turned out to be demeaning, marathon "coke sex" that challenged both my dignity and my gag reflex. Still, I gave him my number before I left for work, and we hooked up a few more times. Then he flew back to LA, and I was alone again.

October was even more flat, and darker. I went to dinner at Gemma with girls from the magazine. They talked about Pamela Love. I felt like a space alien. I stared grimly at a pile of arugula. It was the most boring salad in the world.

On the walk home on the Bowery, I listened to "Confessions on a Dance Floor" and tried to resist the . . . ennui that felt like it was about to overcome me like a cloud of poisonous gas. *It's not always going to feel like it does today*, I told myself. I absolutely could *not* give up. I *was* going to get through this strange, joyless, barren patch. I *was* going to meet new friends. My ambition would return, too. The "lightning flash" moment with Lesley had been God's way of telling me: *believe*. I pulled on a Marlboro Ultra Light. I mean, I just had to be patient.

I repeated this stuff in my head over the next several weeks. And guess what? All that positive thinking *really* made a difference. Slowly— day by day—I started to feel better: more social, more creative, more at ease around other people. Healthier. I refocused on my career. I even went out on a few dates.

Just kidding! I caved and called Marco.

He walked into my new apartment on a Friday night like he owned the place.

"This is great," Marco said, nodding. It had been two months since I'd stood at Nev's window and watched Marco fleeing East Sixth Street.

Now he was looking around. There wasn't much for him to see. My passport was underneath my mattress. My beloved Louis Vuitton–Stephen Sprouse scarf was inside a kitchen cupboard. I'd secured the closet with a bicycle chain lock. Smaller items—jewelry, pill bottles—were in pillowcases or at the bottom of my hamper. The keys to everything were on a neon-yellow lanyard around my neck. The place felt sufficiently Marco-proof.

Now I could relax and get high with my horrible BFF. We sat cross-legged on the floor by my coffee table. But Marco was no Lester Garbage Head, let's put it that way. He kept *jabbing* my arm. The plunger would pull back empty instead of drawing blood.

"OW!" I screeched.

"You have impenetrable veins!" Marco insisted. He was high already.

"No, you are just *horrible* at this," I said. "I'll just *snort* it—"

"I'm gonna try it in your neck," Marco said. He pushed my hair away.

"AUGH!" I yelled. "NO!"

"LET ME SHOOT YOU UP IN THE NECK!" Marco said. I smacked the needle out of his hand.

"Get away from me, you *freak*!" But I was laughing. We were blissed out for two days.

We were up until four in the morning on Sunday. Marco was still sleeping as I glued myself together—as Andy Warhol would say—on Monday morning. I sat on the messy bed and took his hand.

"You look so pretty," he said, opening his eyes. His hair was soft and fine like a baby's. The sun was streaming in. I gave him a tiny smooch.

"Look, you can stay and sleep if you want," I said. "But I'm only giving you one chance. Do you understand?" Marco nodded. "This is a test." I rubbed the lipstick trace from his head with my thumb. "Do *not* fuck around."

"I'll be good. I swear," he said. "I'm just so glad that we're friends again."

I looked at him.

"Me too," I said.

When I returned at seven, Marco was waiting with neat piles of pills on a mirror. Nothing seemed out of place or missing. I was very pleased. I sat down to do some drugs.

Three days later, I was in the same hole as before.

"AUUUUGHH," I shrieked. It was five in the morning, and I'd stepped backward and fallen off a drug dealer's stoop in the West Village. *Wham.* I hit the ground on West Tenth Street. I was wearing dirty white Sass & Bide jeans. "OW!"

"What happened?" Marco laughed, emerging from the town house. He picked me up and helped me toward Sixth Avenue. I'd just bought us two hundred dollars' worth of cocaine, and he was on his very best behavior. I leaned up against my best friend, walking at an angle.

"*Oww-www,*" I moaned. "Let's take a cab." We hailed one.

"Second and C!" Marco said to the driver. I was snuggled into his armpit in the backseat. Now we were heading east on Eighth Street. I smelled like Mustela vanilla, Kiehl's Coriander lotion, and marijuana. As per usual, Marco didn't smell like anything. He was scrolling through his phone.

"You can still get phenobarbital in Mexico," he murmured. "I think we should go."

It was just getting light out when we got to 252 East Second Street. There were peachy streaks in the gray sky.

"Keys, keys . . ." I murmured, patting my pockets. I was wearing an ancient Juicy Couture pea coat with a raccoon fur collar.

"Around your neck," Marco said helpfully.

"Ahhh . . ." I took the lanyard off slowly and unlocked the door.

We took the elevator to the third floor. My apartment looked like a crime scene. I fixed a Ketel One–and–SunnyD in a laboratory beaker while Marco polished off the smack.

"Jean won't let me get lip injections," I babbled. Now I was fussing with a vintage Cramps T-shirt that I'd cut into scraps on too much Vyvanse—trying to safety-pin it back together. "But *I* want them!" Marco smiled sleepily. "I wouldn't get big ones—just a little . . . sexy-baby look, you know." I'd been blathering for five hours straight. "I don't even think I *could* have big lip injection-y . . . lip injection-y . . ." What *was* I talking about? "Lip injection-y . . ."

"*Bleerrgrgggg*," Marco . . . well, not *said*, exactly.

"*OW!*" I screamed as I jabbed myself in the middle finger.

"*Guh*," Marco said. Ooh, I was so *happy* to be hanging with him again. Then he nodded off and face-planted into the coffee table. *Thud.* His forehead was on the keyboard of my laptop! The screen was jumping around.

"YO!" I snapped. "WAKE UP AND DO THIS FUCKING COKE YOU MADE ME BUY!" I'd been dipping into it plenty myself. "Here!" I marched over, took the keys from around my neck, and scooped a huge bump from the bag. I shoved it under Marco's left nostril.

"*Ughh*," Marco gurgled.

"*Sniff!*" I barked like a drill sergeant. (I often get a bit *militant* on yay sometimes, I must admit.) My hand was unsteady. Marco kept snorting air. "*Sniff! Focus! Sniff!*" Finally Marco hit the target. I scooped another huge bump. "AGAIN!"

After a few minutes, Marco felt better. He even stood up.

"Let's smoke the coke," he said.

"No," I said. "I don't have the lung capacity for that."

"Tinfoil . . ." Marco murmured. He staggered to his feet.

"*No*, dude," I said, slurping finger blood. "It's a waste. You're going to burn through it all in five minutes." But Marco wasn't listening. "*I* paid for it!" He was hoisting himself to stand on the counter, heading for the hard-to-reach cabinet over the fridge. It didn't have a lock on it. I'd stashed some drug-related stuff up there—pipes, tinfoil. But wait. How did *he* know that?

Paranoia latched onto my brain like a giant squid. I started to shake.

"I SAID I DON'T HAVE THE LUNG CAPACITY FOR THAT!" I said as he climbed down from the counter.

"Relax," Marco said.

"Why—" I could barely talk. "Why do you always know where everything in my apartment is?" I put my hands in my hair. I wanted to pull my entire face off. "You need to get out of here. YOU NEED TO GET OUT OF HERE."

"What?" Marco said. "Why?" He was acting innocent, but I could see him hardening. The tinfoil was still in his hand. He had climbed down from the counter and was standing by the fridge. "You're being crazy—"

"AM I?" I screamed. Was I? Marco was shapeshifting in front of me. I couldn't see him straight. I couldn't see where he really was. I reached out. Then I snatched my hand away. "AM I?"

"Yes!" Marco said.

"You've been going through my stuff while I'm at work. *I told you not to do that*," I said. "YOU NEED TO GET OUT OF HERE. I WANT YOU *OUT*. YOU STEAL FROM ME. YOU STOLE EVERYTHING FROM ME. YOU RUINED EVERYTHING." My thoughts were spinning like a carnival ride. "I CAN'T FORGIVE YOU. I THOUGHT I COULD BUT I—"

"Stop *screaming*," Marco muttered. He was getting up to go.

"JUST LEAVE AND LEAVE ME ALONE!" I started crying. "I HATE YOU. I FUCKING HATE YOU. I CAN'T DO THIS AGAIN. IT'S OVER. PLEASE JUST GO."

"Whatever, bitch," Marco snarled. "You need rehab."

"*You think I don't know that?*" I sobbed. Marco was getting his things together, putting them into his stupid Gaultier gym bag. "*I know that. I know!*"

Now he was putting on his coat. I backed into the kitchen, fumbled in one of my drawers for a knife—I was *very* coked up, as I said—and braced myself for an attack. But Marco didn't pull a single stunt. He just stumbled out of my apartment.

The door slammed behind him. I rushed to lock it.

That was easy, I thought.

Ping. I heard the elevator door open. A minute later I peeked out into the hall. Marco was gone.

An hour later, I was sitting on the floor listening to "Cradle of Love" on my headphones and toasting a marshmallow with a BIC lighter.

"Ow!" I hissed, dropping the flaming treat onto my lap. I was still cranked. My fingertips were burned black, and my arm splotchy with yellow bruises from Marco's amateur-hour injections. "ACK!" I beat the marshmallow with the heel of my palm.

When it was time to get ready for work, I threw on a Tuleh blazer and grabbed my Bottega. Sexy Dexys? Check. MetroCard? Check. Now, where were my keys? When had I last used my— Wait.

Suddenly it felt like Chris Brown was doing backflips in my stomach.

I reached up to my neck.

They weren't there.

No.

I shook out the bed. I felt up my jacket pockets. I pulled my sofa apart. I dumped out my purse. Finally I had to give up. I left my apartment unlocked.

It was a bright, sunny morning—my least favorite kind. I bought an iced coffee at Little Veselka and wobbled down into the train station at 9:46 a.m. The Thursday production meeting that started in fourteen minutes was by far *the* most important responsibility of my otherwise easy-breezy job—and I was gonna be late. Again.

Sure enough, I sidled into the conference room at 10:06. The accessories editor was on deck.

"Sup," Ray Siegel—then a *Lucky* assistant, now an editor at *CR Fashion Book*—mouthed.

Ray passed me a piece of paper: the production sheet. Ooh, I just *hated* that thing! It was double-sided, with two *very* confusing charts. Everyone else seemed to understand it, but I could never decipher a thing. Not that I could even focus on trying today. I kept thinking about my keys, my keys, my—

"Beauty?" the managing editor, Regan, said.

Ray kicked my dirty ballet flat with her beautiful Burberry wedge.

"Uh," I said.

Everyone looked at me.

"Beauty?"

"January opener is 'Strong Brows,' " I said slowly.

"We know," Regan said coolly. "That page shipped three weeks ago."

"We're on to February opener," the assistant managing editor, Faye, said.

"Oh," I said. I looked at the production sheet. It was supposed to have all the answers! But where? "So the new opener is"—*think think think*—" 'Bronzer combined with Blush'!" What had we called it? " 'Brosh'!"

" 'Blonzer,' " Faye corrected me.

"Blonzer." I nodded. "Right." I didn't understand this meeting! Why did I have to tell these people things they already knew?

"Okay," said Faye. "So what's the status?"

"The blonzers . . . are being shot by the photo studio?" I guessed.

"Has it been written? Has Kim approved a photo? Is there a layout?" asked Regan.

I stared at the sheet again.

"I'll have to get back to you," I mumbled.

I squirmed through seven more beauty pages like that.

"Thanks, Cat," Regan said when it was all over. She gave me a steely once-over: taking in my busted face, my dull skin, my under-eye bags.

"Yup." I smiled.

When the meeting was dismissed and the room started buzzing again, Ray turned to me.

"Well," she said. "That was incredibly brutal and uncomfortable."

I chuckled at the absurdity of my failure for a second and then pulled Retrosuperfuture sunnies down over my eyes. Ray laughed, too.

"I'm dead," I said. "What's new?"

"Well," Ray said. "If you were anyone but you, I'd be scared for your job right now."

"I *am* scared," I said. "Come with me to my desk for a minute. I need you to keep making me feel better."

"What are you doing later?" Ray followed me to the beauty department. She watched me slog through the chaos in my cubicle to get to my desk chair. "God, how does your cubicle get so insanely messy? Where are your interns? Oh, and do you know a good Japanese restaurant in the East Village near where you allegedly live? And why won't you ever let me come over to your apartment?"

"Too many questions!" I dialed the four-digit extension to the beauty closet but nobody answered. Where *were* my interns? Someone needed to get me coffee and help me clean my desk. "I barely slept last night! And I don't go to restaurants."

Just then my editor in chief came by.

"Marnell," Kim said right away. "What happened to your knees?"

I took off my sunglasses. I was wearing my white Sass & Bides and the bloodstains from where I'd fallen off the stoop were . . . *seeping* through them.

"Oh." I tried to think of something. I was too tired. "I fell off a stoop." Everyone was looking at me.

"And . . . ?" Ray said.

"It was a freak thing!" I started waving my hands around in the air until I noticed one of *them* was bleeding, too, at the knuckles, and I put them down. "I was on Waverly Place, I was standing there drinking an iced coffee and talking to some, uh, people and I took a step to the side, and I just fell off the whole stoop." I looked down at my knees. "And, well, I guess I got my pants all bloodied up."

"And then you decided to wear those very same pants today." Ray smirked.

"Look." I scowled. "I fell and then I was tired, so I didn't look at my pants." KF furrowed her brow. "And I think I'm just really dehydrated." I gulped from an old Poland Spring bottle. "I don't know what else to say." My voice cracked. Suddenly I felt hysterical. "I FELL OFF A STOOP. I FELL OFF A STOOP."

"What is *wrong* with you?" Ray whispered after Kim had moved on.

"I don't know," I said, burying my head in my hands. "I'm gonna get fired."

"Nah," Ray said. "They'll never fire you." I wasn't so sure.

"How high was the stoop?"

"I don't know, Ray," I said. "It was a stoop! Five steps high."

Ray let it drop.

"Do you want to work out at Chiquinox with me later?" Ray asked. (That's Condé-speak for Equinox gym, where I once downward-dogged with Bruce Willis.)

"Um, sure," I said. "What time?"

"Let's just go after work," Ray said. "I—"

My office phone started ringing. Marco's number was on the caller ID. I snatched up the receiver.

"*Snake!*" I answered. "*Fuck* you. I'm meeting you on the street and you're giving me back my keys, and after that I never want to see you again."

"I'm coming over later," he said.

"Oh no, you're not. You are *not* coming over there, Marco," I hissed. "You're not going anywhere *near* my fucking house again." Ray gave me a little wave. I mouthed "good-bye." "There are *consequences* to things! Don't you get it?" No answer. "You are *not* coming over. I will call the cops. Do *not*—"

"I'll be there at six," he said curtly.

And he hung up.

"GET OUT OF MY LIFE!" I screeched so loud that they could

probably hear it in the art department. Jean Godfrey-June definitely heard it: she'd just arrived, and I hadn't noticed.

"Everything okay?" she said as she sat down at her desk.

"Yup!" I lied. Then we both turned to our computers.

It was a horrible day. I trudged home after work and then sat on the sidewalk outside 252 East Second Street, waiting for someone to let me into the building. A dude in bicycle shorts trotted up with a golden retriever on a leash.

"You can't sit there," he said. Like I was a crackhead or something!

"I live here!" I snipped. The golden wagged its tail at me. Stupid dog!

I followed them in and went upstairs. As soon as I opened the door to 3H, I started screaming.

My apartment was cleaned out. The scarves and handbags were off the hooks—gone. My drawer of Ray-Bans and Chanel aviators and Dior rings—gifts from beauty companies—empty. The closet was unlocked. That key had been on my key chain. Armloads of clothes had been taken—the hangers, too. Every drawer and cupboard in the kitchen was open, rifled through.

I raged for approximately seven minutes. Then I pulled it together to call Marco. I needed to stay calm and figure out as much information as I could.

He picked up. I was surprised. (Later, I'd figure out that he liked hearing me suffer.) It was loud where Marco was. *Thump-a thump-a.* He was driving. That *jerk* had gone and picked up his dad's car just so he could rob me!

I thought fast.

"Hey! I just wanted to say sorry for losing it earlier," I chirped. Marco didn't say anything. "I'm still at the office. Where are you?"

There was a pause.

"I'm on the FDR," he said. I knew he was only allowed to borrow the Fiat for a few hours at a time. He was definitely going back to his dad's with all of my stuff. I needed to give Marco time to get home and—hopefully—unload everything.

"Oh," I said. My voice quavered. "Well, I'm going over to my sister's. Hit me up when you're back downtown." Then I hung up.

I went up on the roof and paced in circles.

An hour later, I called again.

"Hey, *MOTHERFUCKER!*" I exploded when he answered. "I'M OUTSIDE THE PRECINCT. I JUST FILED THE POLICE REPORT. I GAVE THEM YOUR DAD'S ADDRESS." I repeated the address. "I HOPE IT WAS WORTH IT."

"Yeah right." He sounded nervous.

"Don't say I didn't warn you," I said.

He hung up. I hurled my BlackBerry into my closet and slumped against the wall.

Our friend Marco *thought* he was very sneaky; the truth was, his life was so small and predictable that he was easy to track. Ever since he'd lost the apartment on Madison Street, he was always at one of four places: his dad's basement complex, my house, Carly's studio, or Trevor's on East Twenty-Third Street. He terrorized us all equally; and when one of us kicked him out, he would rob us of something, sell it, and buy drugs and maneuver his way into another one of our apartments with them as a peace offering. (Of course, I didn't learn this until later, when Trevor and I finally compared notes. No wonder he freaked out that time when he learned Trevor and I had hung out!)

By pretending to have called the police, I'd hoped that I'd scared Marco out of the Bronx and back down in Manhattan—into "hiding" at Carly's or Trevor's. By my calculations, he hadn't slept yet. So he was about to crash—hard—somewhere. And that's when I would pounce.

I went to bed that night, and then woke up in the morning and went to Condé. I texted Trevor around lunchtime.

Have you seen Marco? Mad casual.

He's been passed out on my bed for twelve hours, Trevor wrote. Bingo.

Don't ask me how I convinced my estranged sister to leave work early, rent a Zipcar and drive to the Bronx late on a Friday evening. We pulled up to his building at around six o'clock. I banged on the kitchen door of the apartment. Marco's dad opened it in his undershirt.

I smiled like I wanted to give him a Mary Kay makeover.

I cooed, "Hi!"

"Hello . . ." he said in his Romanian accent.

"I'm *so* sorry to bother you, but my sister Emily"—she was standing behind me— "and I need to get my things from Marco's . . . *rooms*. He was storing some stuff during my move, and we only have the car for another hour." Marco's dad looked confused, but he let us in. He even helped me unlatch the door in the kitchen floor that led into Marco's lair.

"What *is* this place?" Emily said, taking in the cinder-block walls, the hundreds of Post-its. She'd never met Marco.

I didn't answer. I was too busy not *believing* my eyes. Marco hadn't invited me over in months—since he'd gotten serious with Carly—and now I understood why. Marco's "quarters" were fucking *full* of my things. *My* "Methadone" nameplate necklace (I'd ordered it special) hung on a peg. *My* Paul McCarthy and Terence Koh books were open on his desk. Even *my* tear sheets were pinned to his walls! This wasn't stuff he'd taken recently, I realized. They were items I hadn't seen in a long time—things I hadn't even noticed were missing! Some of them dated back to the mouse apartment. My best friend had been stealing from me this whole time.

"RARRRRRRR," I roared, and just . . . *attacked*. I grabbed a shopping bag from the corner.

"I'm going to wait in the car," Emily said, backing away.

I tore that bunker *apart*. The clothes he'd taken from me the day before weren't anywhere—so I took things of *his*. *His* dope bag "stamp" collection. *His* binders full of special tear sheets. Then I went upstairs and into the little room where Marco slept and ransacked the dresser drawers. *His* favorite sheep skin jean jacket. *His* favorite Black Flag T-shirt. I filled two bags and two laundry baskets; I was out of control. Marco's dad watched television while I marauded.

I didn't say good-bye when I was through; I just ran. I threw all of my stuff in the trunk and climbed into the passenger seat of the Zipcar.

"*Drive!*" I shouted, like we were in an action movie. The adrenaline rush was flat-out *narcotic*, I had to admit. No wonder Marco committed so many crimes! My sister dutifully peeled away.

I was practically foaming at the mouth the entire drive back to Manhattan.

"It wasn't everything," I jabbered. "He still has my best stuff—he has my Prada fringe bag, he has my Balenciaga, Emily. He has Mom's sheared mink coat!"

"Calm down!" Emily kept saying. "Caitlin! It's just stuff! Who cares?" She looked freaked out. Raindrops started splattering on the windshield.

I still didn't have keys, so when we reached my building, Emily and I sat in the car, waiting for someone to come home. I jumped out and accosted a neighbor—who let me in (if only because she was afraid to say no). I propped the door open with a rolled-up *Wall Street Journal* and darted back and forth through the rain, unloading my haul. When I'd dragged the last laundry basket to the lobby, I turned to run out and thank my sister—but the Zipcar was already halfway down the block.

I got everything into the elevator and upstairs into my place. Then I went into the bathroom. My eyes were wild in the mirror. There was mascara on my forehead and my hair was wet. I swallowed three Adderall at once. They got stuck in my throat, so I leaned down and drank from the faucet. I wasn't done yet.

Twenty minutes later, I was in the backseat of a cab heading to East Twenty-Third Street. It was still raining.

"Five F, please," I said to the doorman. "Cat." He gave me a funny look, but he made the call—then he nodded. I went up to the fifth floor and down the hall. Then I opened Trevor's unlocked door.

"Hey!" Trevor greeted me. He was sitting on his black leather sofa, rolling a joint on his Stanley Kubrick coffee table book. Marco was passed out with his boots on, lying on his back on the bed across the room. There was a giant black duffel bag—honestly, it was as big as me—right there in the foyer by my feet.

"Is this Marco's?" I said.

"Yeah," Trevor said. "Why?"

Well. You know what I did! I scooped that bitch up by the straps and *heaved* it over my shoulders.

"Hey!" Trevor yelled. "What are you doing?" I didn't answer—I just sprinted right the hell out of there and all the way to the elevator. It took a minute to arrive—the longest minute ever.

Trevor came running down the hall in his pajama bottoms and a dirty wifebeater.

"You can't do that!" he was yelling. "You're stealing from *my* apartment—"

"GET THE FUCK AWAY FROM ME, TREVOR!" I screamed. "THIS DOESN'T INVOLVE YOU!" The elevator pinged open. I dragged the huge duffel bag into the elevator like a leopard pulling a carcass into a cave.

"STOP!" Trevor was bugging. "I'LL CALL THE—" Lucky for him, the doors closed before he could get to me. I was ready to claw out his eyes! My heart was going a million miles a minute. (Sorry to keep using that same clichéd expression—but this *is* an amphetamine memoir.)

It was pouring outside. I hustled to the curb and hailed a cab on Third Avenue. I hauled my cargo into the backseat and smooshed in along with it.

"DRIVE!" I screamed—for the second time that evening—as I slammed the door shut. "ANYWHERE! A MAN IS AFTER ME!" The driver stepped on the gas.

Trevor was calling my cell over and over. I ignored him and unzipped the bag. The first thing I saw was the Lanvin tote that Jean had given me. Marco knew it was my prized possession. That soulless piece of *shit*.

I dug deeper. There was my Robert Wilson for Louis Vuitton neon-green-and-orange Vernis tote bag. There was my mom's Fendi chinchilla baguette.

I looked up and saw that we were on one of my favorite blocks in Soho.

"This is good, sir!" I told the driver. He pulled over. I paid and tossed my stuff out onto the sidewalk. Then I sat in a doorway with everything, out of the rain, and got to work. There were plastic grocery bags in Marco's duffel, and I filled them with my things—and anything of *his* that I wanted. Screw him, right?

When I was through, the duffel was only half-full. I put it on my back and trudged up the street until I came to the back entrance of the Crosby Hotel, which has a big ledge and a sunken wall of shrubs and what I thought was a hidden Dumpster (it's actually a handicapped elevator shaft).

Only then did I finally answer one of Marco's calls.

"Cat!" he cried. "Thank God!" He was panicking. *Nothing* mattered to Marco more than his stuff. "Where are you? I'm not mad—"

"FUCK YOU!" I shrieked. "HOW DOES IT FEEL, YOU FUCKING BITCH?! HOW DOES IT FEEL?!"

"Where are you?" Marco was begging me. "Please. What are you doing with my stuff?"

"I'M ON THE WEST SIDE HIGHWAY!" I screamed. "I JUST THREW YOUR STUFF INTO THE HUDSON RIVER!"

"*What?*" Marco said. "No—"

I hung up. Marco kept calling me. I didn't answer. I just continued walking up Lafayette Street in the rain. The streets were empty. I gazed up at all of the nice, brightly lit apartments full of normal people cooking pork tenderloin or whatever normal people cook. Then I sat down on a stoop to light a cigarette. My hands were shaking so badly I couldn't strike a match. And I just lost it. I started crying hysterically. What the *hell* was I doing? I couldn't believe what I'd done over the past twenty-four hours. Was this really my life? I was as bad as Marco.

He was *still* calling. I picked up.

"YOUR STUFF IS IN THE GARBAGE BEHIND THE CROSBY HOTEL!" I yelled—but my heart wasn't in it anymore. "THAT'S THE LAST NICE THING I'M *EVER* DOING FOR YOU." I hung up on him once again. Then I looked at the sky for a long time.

It was Friday night. I went home, had my locks changed, and went to sleep. On Monday, I called in sick to work. On Tuesday, I called in sick. On Wednesday, I was in such bad shape at work that the magazine contacted my family. Later that day, my dad drove four hours up from DC to talk me into going away for treatment again. On Thursday, I promised Jean that I was checking into a hospital. I was put on disability leave from Condé Nast. But I just went to bed at home instead. On Friday, Jean e-mailed me and called me, telling me that if I didn't check in somewhere, she would have to fire me. On Friday evening, I got out of bed, gathered a bunch of beauty products into a plastic bag, and took a taxi to the mental hospital.

Chapter Eighteen

I ARRIVED AT PAYNE WHITNEY PSYCHIATRIC Clinic at New York-Presbyterian Hospital/Weill Cornell Medical Center looking like I'd just walked in from sucking dick on Skid Row in black Minnetonkas, a shredded Misfits T-shirt, and neon-pink streaks in my ratty hair courtesy of a temporary color product (that all you blondes out there *must* try) called Streekers.

"Put on one of these," the nurse said, handing over a paper jumpsuit. She put my street clothes in the same kind of brown shopping bag they used in the *Lucky* fashion closet. She even confiscated my bra! (It was chilly on the unit, too.) Then I was released into the pen.

Payne Whitney! The spacious, coed psych ward was on the sixth floor of the hospital. The women's bedrooms were on one side, and the men's were across the way. In between were sofas, chairs, coffee tables, and magazine racks—and, of course, the nurse's station. The south side of the wing had floor-to-ceiling windows overlooking the Fifty-Ninth Street Bridge. You could see the Pepsi sign in Long Island City, and Silvercup Studios, where they filmed *Sex and the City* and *30 Rock*. I particularly dug watching the Roosevelt Island tram go back and forth over the river like a theme park ride.

"Blondie." A little group of Latino guys heckled me the first day. I crossed my arms over my chest. Those dudes were just annoying, but the tall guy on the sofa gave me *real* predator vibes. He kept making eye contact with me—and his eyes were *crazy*—and looking me up and down. In the words of Cher Horowitz: "Ugh, as if!"

I couldn't sleep the first night without my pills, but for once my rebound insomnia was a blessing. I was lying in the dark wide awake at one in the morning when a large man slipped silently into my room with a white blanket wrapped around his head like a turban. I thought I was hallucinating again, but no. It was the scary guy—I'll call him the Predator—right there in my hospital room. And he'd come for me when he thought I would be sleeping!

"AHHHH!" I jumped out of bed and dashed past the Predator and into the common area. "HELP!" The night nurse came running. She hadn't seen the Predator cross the dark corridor.

The Predator was confined to his room after that. A staffer guarded his door 24/7. Still, I was so shook that I never slept with the lights off in my room again. Stupid men! Why were they all so horny?

A few days later, I got a roommate. She had a thick Bronx accent, thicker old-school Coke-bottle glasses, and an anxiety disorder that made her tremble like a tuning fork. She liked that I kept the lights on; she was too nervous to sleep, anyway. I'd wake up at three in the morning and she'd be sawing at apples with a plastic knife on a paper-towel cutting board.

"Did I wake you?" she'd say.

"It's okay," I'd mumble.

We shared a bathroom with a strange, weak shower that only ran for fifteen seconds at a time. You had to press a button over and over to keep the water going. (I don't even know why. So you couldn't . . . drown?!)

"Sorry to bother you," my roommate said on the fourth day. I was combing out my wet hair with one of those black plastic combs that grandpas use. "But did you just use something with chlorine in there?"

"Excuse me?" I said.

"Chlorine," she repeated. "I just can't stand the smell of chlorine!"

"Uh," I said. "I washed my hair with shampoo." (Davines NouNou, FYI.)

"I guess your shampoo smells like chlorine," my roommate said.

"Yes." I nodded. "I guess so."

The showers were so weak that the pink hardly washed out of my hair like it was supposed to. One day I was eating lunch when I noticed a nurse staring at me. She beckoned me over.

"Ms. Marnell," she said. "Have you been dipping your hair in your fruit juice?"

This was a serious question.

"Oh no!" I said. "It's a beauty product! Called Streekers!" She was not feeling me. "I'm a beauty editor. At a fashion magazine."

"Mmm-hmm," the nurse said.

"There's always a beauty moment," Jean Godfrey-June used to say. And it's really true—even in the mental hospital.

The best part of the day was . . . breakfast! It was brought up on a cart from the hospital cafeteria and handed out on trays.

"Marnell," an orderly would say, and I'd leap up like I was a contestant on *The Price Is Right*. I can still smell the fresh-baked hot bagels that came wrapped in foil. *Mmm*. I'd rip off pieces and dip them into a little plastic tub of Philadelphia cream cheese and just savor every bite. It was the best food I'd ever tasted (even though it wasn't) because I was suddenly off my appetite suppressants.

We ate in a little room with windows overlooking the East River.

"*Newwww YYYYYOOOOORKKKKK . . .*" The radio—Z100 or something—was always on the boom box in there. That Jay Z/Alicia Keys song had just come out. It played every hour.

I'd sit and watch the boats out of the dining room window for a while. Then I had ten hours to kill before bedtime. There wasn't much to do. I hadn't brought a book, but I found one of my faves, Bret Easton Ellis's *Glamorama*, in the tiny library. I still have that copy today, stamped "PROPERTY OF PAYNE WHITNEY." And there was this enormous black poodle that got walked around sometimes. It was extremely glamorous and fluffy and we all got to pet it: animal therapy. I've never truly connected with a poodle, though. Like . . . on an *emotional* level. Have you?

I also watched the television mounted on the wall. It was all Animal Planet, all the time. I sat through hours and hours of big cats!

"Solo cheetahs often live lives of solitary desperation . . ."

The people watching was way better. Almost every day, a patient named Anne would interrupt our TV time when she lost it and got taken to seclusion.

"This isn't *your* hospital!" Anne—who was eight months pregnant—would screech at a nurse. "You don't own it! You're hired help!" Orderlies would surround her. "*You* need seclusion! Not me!"

"Warthogs, too, are ferocious, and hardly ever on the menu . . ." the Animal Planet narrator droned on.

A week into my stay, I made a friend. Her name was Veronica, and she had wrist-to-elbow self-mutilation scars: "punk jewelry," as someone called them in a book I read once. Veronica looked twelve, but she was sixteen—and a mother! Her cute baby son was at home with her grandma in the Bronx. We'd drag a sofa to the wall of windows overlooking the East River. I told her about Marco and working in magazines, and she told me what it was like being a teen mom and also her thoughts on MTV's *Teen Mom*.

Veronica had been on the unit for months, so she was used to the pervy guys.

"Get away, freak!" she'd snap every time one neared us. This cracked me up. Everything was suddenly *very* entertaining now that I had a girlfriend. Plus, she loaned me a sports bra.

There was one dude whom we never sent away. His name was Donald. He was from Newark and addicted to smoking paint chips.

"The doctors here keep asking me if I'm gonna go out and smoke paint chips again," he told us. "I keep tellin' 'em, 'Nah.' 'Cause they don't make that shit like they used to!"

Donald was always following Veronica and me around, trying to impress us with his stories.

"I ate cat food once," he announced one evening. We were sitting by the south-facing wall of windows with our legs propped up, watching the traffic jam on the FDR Drive.

"Out of a can?" Veronica asked.

"No, not out of a can!" Donald said indignantly. "From a box!"

"*Why?*" Veronica said.

"It's cheap!" Donald said. "It's $2.99 and you can get it from the corner store!"

"It's cat food!" I said.

"It's not like I eat it all of the time." He was getting defensive. "Maybe once every six years or something."

"You're insane," Veronica said.

"I tried dog food once, too," Donald said. "But that stuff is salty. No wonder they're barking all the time. They have high blood pressure!"

"What are you *talking* about?" Veronica said. I couldn't stop laughing. Then the three of us sat peacefully for a minute, watching the city get dark and electric. It was almost dinnertime.

"It's not expensive being a cat," Donald said thoughtfully.

It was *pretty* cozy on that nice psych ward. I started getting up at six, before breakfast, just to pad down to the south windows and catch the sunrise. A cart came around every morning with new disposable underpants (stretchy mesh boy-shorts—so good), socks with rubbery antiskid traction pads, which I always wore inside out, and a two-piece teal paper jumpsuit for me, always.

"You're a flight risk." My psychiatrist, Dr. M., would shake her head every time I asked for my street clothes. Most patients got them back after three days. "Your room is right by the door, and you're a good talker. I see how you try to charm people." *Moi?*

I was allowed to go back to bed right after breakfast if I wanted to, and to read and nap all day. I caught up on so much sleep; it wasn't like rehab, where I'd been expected to act like an accountable adult. Now if I sat down for an activity and it was boring, I could just wander off like a weirdo and no one would say anything.

Yup! I decided that I could happily play *Girl, Interrupted* and stay a month or three. I'd claimed to be suicidal (and declined to mention my drug abuse) to get admitted. As far as everyone knew, I *still* was. Right?

Wrong.

"Do you want to die, Ms. Marnell?" Dr. M. greeted me one morning. Her usual posse was right on her heels. (Taylor Swift–like, Dr. M. often rolled with a squad—but of medical students, not Hadid sisters.)

"Uh," I said. I was on my bed reading *Ebony's* "Black Cool" issue— the one with President Obama looking fierce in shades on the cover. "No?"

"I have your drug test results."

"Oh?" I said. "Really?" *Fuck.* I'd forgotten about the urine sample I'd given in the ER.

"You're positive for opiates, amphetamine, cocaine, and benzodiaz-epines." She double-checked the chart. "And marijuana."

"Hmm," I said.

"That's quite a cocktail," Dr. M. said. "Why didn't you tell me that you're an addict?"

"I'm not," I said. "I'm depressed."

"I'm going to keep observing you," Dr. M. said. "But I am diagnosing you with polysubstance addiction, and I want you to know that it is my intention to place you in a rehab facility as soon as possible."

"I'm not going to rehab," I said with a smile.

"That's not up to you," Dr. M. said. Then she exited, her squad at her heels.

A few days later, she was back.

"I've been watching you," Dr. M. said. "You're not suicidal. You're not even depressed." I *had* been pretty chipper lately. Must have been all those naps.

"Okay . . ." I said.

"It's time to get you out of here," Dr. M. said.

"You're discharging me?" I said.

"To an inpatient rehab," she said. "And I'm recommending that you stay at least thirty days."

Well. I did not like *that*. Not when I'd just sworn up and down to Jean and Kim France that I was absolutely drug free.

"Not gonna happen," I said.

"It's not up to you," Dr. M. said.

"You don't understand," I protested. "I have to get back to work!"

"I'm not going to discharge you unless it's into rehab," my doctor said.

I thought fast.

"I *might* consider going to outpatient," I said.

"I'm only discharging you to inpatient."

"This isn't negotiable at all?" I said.

"Nope," Dr. M. said.

Face-off, I thought.

"Well, I guess I'll be here forever then," I said brattily. Dr. M. ignored this and turned brusquely on her heel—her signature exit—and was on her way.

Then it was Halloween, and there was a party. The psych ward social director propped a boom box up to the microphone in the nurse's station.

"Ghostbusters," "Monster Mash," and—less explicably—the *Mortal Kombat* theme played on repeat over the intercom system. Everyone scarfed down chocolate cupcakes with orange icing, and minibags of Doritos and candy corn from brown paper sacks with jack-o'-lantern faces cut out of them.

The next evening—on November first—an orderly came into my room and told me I had a visitor. Really?

I walked out into the common space, but then I stopped in my tracks. It was Marco.

"What are you doing here?!" I said. "How did you know I was in here?"

"I wanted to see you." He smirked.

The nurse at the door looked at me, and then at him. Marco and I were staring hard at each other.

"Everything all right?" she said.

"It's fine." I wasn't happy to see him. "Can he come into the cafeteria with me? I haven't eaten."

"Bring your tray out here," the nurse said.

I retrieved my meal. Then Marco and I sat down in the visiting area.

He smiled at me.

I smiled back.

I was very glad to be safe in that hospital.

"So," I said. I poked a straw into my bucket of apple juice.

"That was a pretty epic stunt you pulled," Marco said. He was still smiling. "Stealing my stuff and throwing it away on the street like that."

"Well," I said. Still smiling. "I learned from the very best."

"You know," Marco said, with the same smile. "You still have . . . some of my things."

"Do I?" I pulled the foil back from my dinner: pot roast and potatoes. It was too hot to eat. I fanned the rising steam with my hand.

"You do." Marco smiled.

I pretended to think about this.

"I don't think so, darling," I said. "I think I donated them to the Salvation Army."

Marco could take no more.

"Oh, come on, Cat!" he said. "This isn't funny! I know you went to my dad's house! Give back my stuff!"

"After what you've sold out from under me?" I laughed. "Dream on."

Marco sulked for a minute. Then he eyed my meal.

"Lemme get some of that," he said, reaching for my fork.

"Don't even think about it!" I smacked his hand.

"But I'm starving!" Marco whined.

"Like I'm not?" I said. "God, you are greedy. Get something on the outside! They won't give me another one."

Marco pulled out a cell phone and started taking psych-ward selfies.

"You can't do that in here!" I said.

"No one's watching," Marco said. *Click. Click. Click.*

"Marnell . . ." A nurse paged me over the intercom.

"Gimme a sec," I said, and went to take my meds. When I came back, Marco had eaten all of my dinner.

I kept refusing to go to rehab. Dr. M. was very annoyed with me. So on day ten . . . she brought in the big guns.

"Your parents are coming today," she said on her usual after-breakfast rounds. "I looked up your dad."

"WHAT?" I sat up.

"I'm hoping they'll talk some sense into you," Dr. M. said.

"Sense!" I sputtered. "*Sense?!*" I tried to think fast. "But . . . I don't give you permission to involve them!" Was that a thing? "I'm an adult—"

"Then start acting like one." *Touché.* "They'll be here at five."

She clicked away. Conversation over.

"*Noo,*" I moaned. I fell back on my pillow. My roommate clucked sympathetically. She was organizing her sleeves of crackers.

Seven hours later, there they were: Dr. Dad and my mother, standing at the entrance and looking extremely serious. They didn't see me. So I *slithered* on over there across the hospital linoleum, in my inside-out hospital socks.

"Hello," I . . . *simpered*.

They turned around. My dad's expression got even darker when he took in my paper jumpsuit.

"Cato," he said stiffly.

"Hi, Mom," I said.

"Hi," she whispered. Melodramatic. It wasn't like I had leukemia! I mean, we'd all been on psych wards before.

Dr. M. came over with my social worker, Giraffe Slacks (she loved an animal print).

"Dr. Marnell," my dad introduced himself.

"Dr. M.," my psychiatrist introduced *her*self.

"I'm an LCSW as well," my mom told Giraffe Slacks. I was about to throw up. It was like a convention!

We went into the arts-and-crafts room to powwow.

"I've been observing Caitlin," the doctor said. "She was admitted for depression, insomnia. But she isn't depressed. She's a drug addict."

My dad sat there stony-faced. My mom's eyes looked glassy.

"I'm not going to rehab," I said. "I have to go back to the magazine. I have a job!"

"CAIT . . ." my dad growled.

"What?" I played dumb.

"*Cait*," my dad repeated.

"What?" I said. "What?!"

"But . . . I really . . ." my mom said. "I think the problem is her ADHD . . . That's why she's always had all of these . . . behavioral problems." She shook her head.

"Behavioral problems?" I said.

My mom looked nervous.

"Yes," she said, "I think . . . it's fair to say . . . behavioral problems."

"I don't have behavioral problems!" I said. "What behavioral problems?"

"Let her speak," Dr. M. said.

"What does that even mean?" I whined.

"Cait . . ." my dad warned. I sat back and folded my arms over my chest.

"Go on, Mrs. Marnell," the doctor said.

My mom looked at the doctor and then back at me.

"Caitlin," my mom said slowly and quietly, like I was some sort of . . . well, like I was some sort of mental patient. "You had a second-trimester abortion when you were seventeen years old."

"*Well.*" I pushed my chair back and stood up. "THAT'S IT FOR ME."

"*Sit down*, Cait," my dad commanded. I sat.

"She was so horrible," my mom was saying. "It was so—"

"THAT WAS LITERALLY TEN YEARS AGO!" I screeched. "WHY ARE YOU STILL TALKING ABOUT THAT?"

"*Watch it, Cait*," my dad growled. But I wasn't done berating my mother.

"I am so *sick* of you bringing that up all of the time, *Mom*!" I wanted to get the hell out of there. "I'm not this . . . *failure!*" I stood up. "I'm not! There's a whole side of me you don't see!"

"Okay, let's—" my doctor said.

"I'm an editor at Condé Nast!" I babbled on bitterly. "That might not mean anything to you, but I worked years and years to get where I am! I have people at work who tell me I'm talented and who promote me and tell me I'm a great writer and that I have"—my voice caught—"a—a big future!" Tears sprung to my eyes, but I didn't want my parents or Dr. M. to see. I *did* have a big future, didn't I?

"Ms. Marnell—" Dr. M. said.

"And *you*." I whirled around to face her. "You bring them in here and it *embarrasses* me. I may be in the hospital but this is *my* business! I'm an adult! My parents have nothing to do with my life! I'm twenty-seven years old!"

"We're just trying to get you the help you need," Dr. M. said.

"I just want to go back to work!" I groaned. "I've told you that—"

"Ms. Marnell—"

"*You* brought them here, so *you* talk to them," I snapped at Dr. M. "I'm not talking about my mental health with my parents!" I stood up from the table.

"CAIT," my dad said sharply. "SIT!"

I sat.

Fuck these people! I thought.

I stood up.

"SIT!" my dad yelled again.

"NO!" I screamed. "I'M NOT A DOG!" Now I really *was* acting like a mental patient. I *stormed* out, stomped across the unit to my room, *slammed* my door shut, and flung myself on my bed.

"How'd it go?" my roommate asked.

"Ugh!" I said. "I *hate* psychiatrists!"

Dr. M. came in half an hour later.

"Your parents are leaving," she said.

"So?" I scowled.

Dr. M. narrowed her eyes.

I got up slowly. Dr. M. turned and went back out onto the ward. I lurched out to the main room and there they were.

"Bye," I said.

"That's a wonderful doctor you have," my dad said. He seemed in better spirits. "What a pro! She's *really* smart. What a pistol!" Of course those two would hit it off.

I was back to my room when a crazy impulse just . . . *gripped* me. I did a one-eighty and returned to the common area. My dad was actually laughing about something with Dr. M.

"Hey, Dad?" I interrupted.

He turned around.

"Yes?" he said pleasantly.

"Go fuck yourself!" I squawked.

His face fell.

I ran back into my room with my heart pounding. *Omigod omigod omigod.* I'd never spoken to him like that in my entire life! I thought it would feel good, but it actually didn't at all.

I don't remember exactly how long I was in "the bin," as JGJ called it. I do know, however, that by the time I agreed to go inpatient my eyebrows were so *very* far from on fleek that I practically broke down all over again every time I looked in the mirror. So let's say . . . at least two weeks.

Giraffe Slacks gave me a list of facilities covered by my insurance. Silver Hill wasn't on it. In fact, nothing in Connecticut was—or New York.

"New Jersey or Delaware," Giraffe Slacks said. I mean, Rihanna or Beyoncé? How would I choose?

In the end, I went with Dirty Jerz', since it was closer. Dr. M. and I bickered to the end. I was *still* a flight risk, she said, and she wouldn't discharge me unless I paid for a private ambulance to the rehab. Who did Dr. M. think I was—Jennifer Lopez? That shit is expensive! Finally I handed over my Chase Visa for a regular old car service. Dr. M. personally walked me downstairs and outside. I had my brown paper bag "luggage" and was wearing my tattered T-shirt and Minnetonka boots again. The look was very "Eskimo at the methadone clinic."

"She's *not* to get out before you reach the destination," Dr. M. reminded the driver as I got into the backseat. He nodded.

And we were off. The sedan wound through midtown, through Times Square, and out the tunnel. Then we were in the part of Jersey that looks like the opening credits of *The Sopranos*. I rolled my windows down. Fresh air! Well, sort of.

I was in a pretty *chatty* mood now that I was out of that hospital and all stable and sober, and it wasn't too hard to sweet-talk my driver into stopping at a gas station. I hopped out and bought Juicy Fruit and Ultra Lights. Then I gave my driver a ciggie and we both lit up in the car.

"And then," I said, ashing out the window. "I realized that Marco was *slicing* pages one at a time out of my special Damien Hirst book *with a razor blade* every time I was in the bathroom—"

"We're here," the driver said.

We were in front of a squat brown building in Westfield, New Jersey: Spirit House. Oh dear.

It is very bad form for a privileged addict like me to talk smack (pun intended!) about an affordable treatment center—at a hundred dollars a day, that's what Spirit House was—but I'm going to do it anyway. *That's* how much this place sucked. So what if it was inexpensive? They couldn't keep people there! At least one person got up and bailed or went "AMA"—against medical advice—every day. The rest of us fantasized about it.

"I have to get out of this *fucking* room!" a kid would stand up in the middle of the NA meeting and cry. Then he'd leave. Forever!

Let me tell you about my first few hours at this place. I had an admissions appointment, but no one seemed to care, especially me. There was a flat-screen television in reception. I sat watching the E! network and reapplying hot-pink Tarte tinted lip balm for approximately ninety minutes.

"Is Jon Gosselin spending Thanksgiving with Kate and the kids?" Giuliana teased. "Or will he dine with new love Hailey Glassman?" Needless to say, I was mesmerized (and Team Hailey all the way).

Finally, I went through intake, then was sent upstairs for a medical exam. The entire rehab—living quarters, detox unit, admissions, treatment rooms, therapists' offices, and so on—was in the same building. There was one small elevator for everyone in the place. I took it to the fourth floor and sat by the nurse's station, waiting for my physical. There weren't any other clients—rehab-speak for "patients"—around.

Or were there?

"AUUUUGHHHHH," a man screamed from one of the rooms. Jesus! I practically fell off the bench. *Crush.* "NO! *NO!*" It sounded like the movie *Hostel* in there—like someone was *hacksawing* this dude's arm off. But none of the nurses batted an eye. It went on and on. "AUUGH!" *Crash! Clang!* "NO! PLEASE!"

"Ms. Marnell?" A nurse led me right past the *Hostel* room and into a small office.

"What's . . . going on in there?" I said as she did that *squeezy* thing to my upper arm—the blood pressure test.

"*Hmm?*"

"AUUUUGHHHH!"

"Him!" I said.

"Oh, that's Mister Reggie," she said. "He's having a rough detox."

"Heroin?"

"Xanax," she said.

"*KILL ME. TAKE ME GODDDDDD. OH, FUCK. OHHH!*"

"That's it?" The nurse nodded. Wow.

"Now, Mister Reggie!" a woman was yelling. "Stop banging around!"

"*NOOOO!*" *Crash!* "*AUUUUGH. OHHHH.*"

"Let's get you downstairs with the other kids," the nurse said. On the way out we passed Mister Reggie's room again. The door was open now. He looked like Christian Bale! Well, Christian Bale with ebola. Mister Reggie was mewling and quivering, bare-assed in a hospital gown, bent over the windowsill. A cleaning guy wearing a surgical mask was on his knees wiping up something that I'm not sure how to spell and refuse to Google.

All I can say is: *damn*, son. Coming off benzos was no joke. The detox unit at Silver Hill had been completely separate—far away from the tennis court and the Mariah Carey dorm, and up the hill and hidden in the trees. Now I knew why.

I heard the mayhem in the basement before I saw it. Then the nurse opened the door. Bedlam! The boys were roughhousing: shouting, and throwing fistfuls of Monopoly money in the air. They were shrimpy with gelled hair and hoodies. The girls were the tannest drug addicts I'd ever seen, with long hair, Victoria's Secret PINK sweatpants, and smoky eyes. Everyone looked nineteen years old. That Jay Z/Alicia Keys "NEWWWW YORRRRRK" song was blaring from a shitty boom box just like at Payne Whitney, but since we were underground (and in Westfield, New Jersey), the reception was awful; it was half static. A staffer sat on a folding chair amid the mayhem, messing with her phone.

This was the Spirit House basement. It smelled like Jean Paul Gaultier cologne, Dolce & Gabbana Light Blue perfume, and stale cigarette smoke. There were fluorescent lights, linoleum floors, a wall of board games, twelve-step posters, and two tiny windows near the ceiling, so you could see people's feet when they walked by on the sidewalk outside.

The nurse left me there.

"*Dinner!*" a lunch-lady type hollered. There was a mad scramble as a wall opened to reveal a cafeteria-style kitchen.

Some hyper boys jumped to the front of the line.

"GIRLS FIRST!" the Juicy Couture clan screamed. The boys pouted but retreated. I queued up with the chicks. By the time I emerged with my French bread pizza, the furniture in the once riotous group room had been totally rearranged. Now the place was set up like a dining hall. (The basement served as meeting room, rec room, cafeteria—everything!)

The girls in velour waved me over, so I sat with them. I told them I was twenty-seven years old, a beauty editor at *Lucky*, and lived in downtown New—

"Twenty-seven?" they all gasped.

"You *don't* look twenty-seven," one of them assured me.

"Not at *all*."

"Uh," I said. "Thanks."

The blond ringleader told me she was a former Miss New Jersey. (I've since investigated—and indeed, she was.)

"But then I got into oxy," she said. "Gabby's into oxy, too."

"Everyone here is," Gabby said. She was a sexy brunette with dead eyes. The other girls at the table nodded.

"I also love weed," Miss New Jersey said. "But only vaporizing it, you know?" She shivered. "Smoking it is just so bad for the skin! I—" Just then a fight broke out between two boys at the table next to us. We all jumped up.

"Jesus Christ!" Gabby squealed.

"STOP IT, BOYS!" Miss New Jersey screamed. One of the little guys threw his tray. Salad splattered everywhere. "YOU ARE SO IM-MATURE!"

A staffer interceded. We returned to our dinners.

"So annoying." Gabby shook her head.

"Are they always like that?" I said. The girls nodded.

"Everyone's stir-crazy because we're in this room"—Miss New Jer-sey waved her manicured hand—"twelve hours a day."

"*Twelve* hours?" I said.

"It sucks here," Gabby said.

"You'll see," Miss New Jersey confirmed.

After dinner everyone crammed into the elevator for a ten-min-ute trip to Bergen Avenue, where I stood in the dark drizzle and took deep breaths of secondhand menthol. Then it was back to the basement for Alcoholics Anonymous and more "rec" time. At nine o'clock, we squished into the elevator again—this time up to residential. The floor was coed. All the rooms had connecting bathrooms and two twin beds each.

"I guess you're my roommate," sexy Gabby said. She had a monster tattoo of a thorny rosebush with a knife stuck through it—or some-thing—spread across her lower back. She went in the bathroom. I was unpacking—reluctantly—when someone knocked on the door. A boy from group popped his head in.

"Where's Gabby?" he whispered. Guys weren't allowed in girls' rooms, of course. Just then my roommate stepped out of the bathroom with only a towel on.

"Hey," she said to him. They stared at each other. Then, to me: "Can you look me out?"

"Uh—" The bathroom door slammed shut before I got a chance to answer. I heard the shower turn on. And then . . .

"Ahh!" Gabby moaned. "Ahh!"

"UUH," the boy grunted. "UHH."

"Ahh! Ahhh!"

Ew. I lay on my bed and stared at the ceiling. There was no way I was going to stay here thirty days.

Miss New Jersey wasn't lying. It *did* suck at Spirit House. We *were* in that basement from nine in the morning to nine at night every day.

"*NEWWXGGKWW YORXXKGHK . . .*" Someone switched on Z100 every rec break. "*NEW YOWRXGHHXRK—NEW YOGG-HXRK—NEW YOXGHXRK!*" Alicia Keys was always garbled. By the end of day three, I wanted to climb into the boom box and strangle her.

I *tried* to focus on treating my addiction. I *tried* to think of poor Mister Reggie and all the sick and suffering addicts of the world. I *tried* to be grateful to be there. I *tried* to stick it out. We all did! But we weren't in a "program." We were in a holding pen.

On the fifth day, Miss New Jersey made a big announcement.

"I'm gonna go AMA tomorrow," she said. The tracksuit gang put down their forks.

"No!" said the redhead.

"You're gonna go right back to using," the dirty-blonde protested.

"You'll break your father's heart," Gabby said. They looked at me.

"Huh?" I said. I'd been thinking about *Lucky*.

"Cat's the oldest one here," Miss New Jersey said. "Why don't we let her decide? Cat, should I go AMA tomorrow?"

"If you go, I'll go," I said. "Let's do it!"

"*No!*" Gabby snapped at me. "Are you crazy?" Arguably. "[Miss New Jersey], don't listen to her. Don't you *dare* go. Don't even think about it!"

Miss New Jersey exhaled.

"All right," she said. "One more day." Crisis averted. We all resumed eating our beef lasagna.

On the seventh day, I was so desperate to get out of that basement that I faked a stomachache during morning group and went up to my room to lie down. Someone sent Gabby to get me—just in time for another fun lunch with the girls.

"I'm definitely going AMA tomorrow," Miss New Jersey said again.

"That's your addiction talking!" Gabby said.

"You're just gonna relapse!" the redhead said.

"You'll break your dad's heart," I said. Everyone ignored me. I slurped my fruit punch.

On the eighth day I went to get drug tested on the fourth floor and saw Mister Reggie's room was empty.

"What happened to him?" I asked.

"Mister Reggie?" the nurse said. "He went AMA."

On the ninth day, I approached a bored-looking staffer and told her I wanted out.

"You're aware that you're leaving against medical advice?" the woman said.

"I am," I said. They let me go upstairs and gather my beauty products, underwear, Payne Whitney journal, and apartment keys. I threw everything in a clear garbage bag and slung it over my shoulder, hobo style. Then I was out on the sidewalk in Westfield. Freedom! *Vive la pillhead*, as they say in France.

It was warm for November. There was even a lovely drizzle, like God Himself was spritzing my face with Jurlique Calendula Calming

Mist. I walked to a New Jersey Transit station and bought a ticket. The sun came out while I waited on the outdoor platform. A Manhattan-bound train—a double-decker—arrived ten minutes later. I snuggled into a seat on the upper level and looked out the window. I kept thinking about my job at the magazine. I had a strange feeling that I'd never had before: I wasn't sure that I could come back from all of this. But I had to try.

Forty-five minutes later, I was at Penn Station. I took the subway downtown and then walked back home through the East Village. My apartment looked like it had been ransacked by cat burglars—that is, just like I'd left it. I found my Adderall bottle twisted in my duvet right away. I didn't want to sleep that night. It felt too good to be home with all of my things.

I called Jean's line in the morning.

"Jean Godfrey-June's office," Simone answered.

"Hey," I said. "It's me."

There was a brief silence.

"Cat!" Simone said. "How are you feeling?"

"Much better," I replied. "Thanks."

"Good," Simone said.

"Can you tell Jean I'm coming back today?"

Another pause.

"Why don't you—" Simone started.

"Thanks," I said, and hung up. I threw on my white Alexander Wang jeans, a glow-in-the-dark plastic rosary, and my white Helmut Lang leather straitjacket. I stood in front of the dirty mirror and looked myself straight in the eye for a second. Then I was out the door.

Chapter Nineteen

I SHOULD HAVE GRACEFULLY ADMITTED DEFEAT when I returned to *Lucky* in the third week of November. Instead, I stuck around. Everyone treated me with kid gloves; Jean Godfrey-June was particularly protective as always. She told me to take it easy, gave me minimal writing assignments, and repeatedly pulled me into her office to check in, and to tell me to believe in myself. That I was talented. That I was creative. That it wasn't going to always feel like it felt today. But I could no longer hear her.

I'd returned to drugs the same way I'd gone back to work: quickly, and without thinking too much about it. My weeks-long abstinence had been a very nice holiday, but now that I was back in my regular life, I was taking a big, soul-flattening daily mix of pills just like before. Then I was deep inside my addiction again. Was it obvious? Probably. I wasn't engaged with people when I talked to them. My affect was flat as a flounder. I was popping in and out of the office to smoke like a drunk girl at a bar. I wasn't interested in the thank-you Sprinkles cupcakes that arrived from Pantene. I sat at my desk chair picking at my scalp and staring into space. You know. Little things! But they all add up. And my boss had to observe this stuff every day and—I imagine—figure out what exactly she was going to do about me.

I wasn't allowed to attend events anymore.

"For now," Jean said.

It was the height of the holiday season. Now there wasn't much for me to do but open gifts. I kept attending invite meetings, making things awkward for everybody. My coworkers would divide the dinners, press trips, and mascara launches three ways while I sat there with my eyes as glazed as a Krispy Kreme. I had no one to blame but myself, but still, it hurt my pride.

And *then*. Talk about adding insult to injury! With Cristina and Simone doubling down on events, *I* was assigned both weekly production meetings: Tuesday *and* Thursday mornings. And these would go about as expected.

"Beauty Spy Three?" Regan, the managing editor, would ask.

"Ummmm . . ." I'd say.

I started calling in sick—a lot—for the first time in my career. I'd always shown up for work before my second disability leave: I showed up high, I showed up bloody, I showed up crying and hid in the beauty closet all day, but I showed up. Not anymore.

"I can't come in," I'd mumble to Simone or Cristina from bed. I never called my boss directly. "Tell Jean." Then I'd hang up, turn my ringer off, and not check e-mail all day. It was sneaky and avoidant, and don't think everybody didn't know it.

"If you're going to stay home, you must speak to *me*," Jean would ream me out the next day. "Is that clear?"

I'd nod. Then three days later, I'd leave a message with the intern.

Despite all this, my boss kept trying to keep my career—and

me—afloat. After Christmas break, JGJ told me that she had great news. Everyone loved my once-a-week luckymag.com posts *so* much that they wanted me to blog three to five times a day! It was an obviously made-up position that played to my strengths and also kept me at my desk, where JGJ could keep an eye on me. I tried to be grateful. I gave it a shot, but nothing I wrote was clever or witty. My spark was gone. And I was too tired to fake it.

My addiction was beating me like a rug. It became harder and harder to get out of bed at Avenue C. I started oversleeping, arriving forty minutes late. Sometimes I didn't come in until noon.

"Golden Globes Beauty: Cameron Rocks the 'Cat Marnell Is Late for Work' Look" I wrote of a messily coiffed Ms. Diaz on January 20, 2010. Another post from this time alluded to sitting down in the shower. I was giving up.

By late January, I'd lost the ten pounds I'd put on eating French bread pizza and psych-ward bagels. Then I lost five more. I'd bring a stir-fry back to my desk and eat two water chestnuts before I lost interest. *Thump!* I'd throw it away in my trash can. Often Jean lifted her eyes and saw me doing this. And I saw her seeing me.

I'd stopped sleeping again, too. One afternoon when Jean, Cristina, and Simone were all out, I was sitting at my desk when I saw it: tissue paper *moving* at my feet. Something alive was in there!

"*AAUGHHH!*" I *sprung* out of that chair so fast that I careened into the beauty closet.

"*There's a rat under my desk!*" I cried to the intern. "HELP!" Intern put down the Rodin Face Oil she was about to file and let me drag her back to my cubicle. She got on her hands and nubile teen knees to investigate.

"There's nothing here," Intern said, pulling out sheets of designer tissue paper. I went to the Condé Nast nurse's office for a rest after that. I'd been up for two straight days.

The following Monday, I pulled another all-nighter. I was still wavy when I sat down for the Tuesday-morning production meeting.

"Beauty Spy One?"

"I dunno . . ." Ray glared at me.

"Beauty Spy Four?"

"Dunno . . ." I slurred through the whole thing like I was Johnny Depp at the Hollywood Film Awards.

Word got back to Jean, of course. I'd sobered up by the time she called me into her office that afternoon. It was gray outside the windows of 4 Times Square, with a fluffy flurry swirling around.

"I'm just depressed," I lied—as I always did. "It's not drugs or alcohol."

"You *must* do better," Jean said—as she always did.

"I know," I said. "I just . . . don't . . . know . . . what is wrong . . ." I met Jean's eyes. "With me."

We both sat there.

"What else can we do to help you?" For the thousandth time.

"I'm just going through a rough patch," I said.

I returned to my cubicle and sat down. Jean resumed editing with her blue pens. I started opening messenger bags with my numb hands.

Then I stopped. It was silent in the beauty department. Cristina wasn't there; neither was Simone. It was just my boss and me.

I stared at the gray carpet for a long time.

"I can't do this anymore," I blurted out.

What are you doing? someone screamed inside of me.

"*Hmm?*"

"I can't do this anymore," I repeated.

"*What?*" Jean looked up from her work.

"I quit," I said. I was still slumped in my desk chair. "I quit my job."

"Come in here!" she said. I obeyed and then resumed slumping, this time in a chair opposite her. Jean shut the door. "Look at me!" I lifted my eyes. "There are still so many options. You don't have to do this! Talk to me. Tell me how we can help you."

I stared at her. I was very tired. I thought about telling her the truth all over again: that it was drugs and alcohol, that I had been lying ever since I got back from Silver Hill.

"No," I said. "I have to go."

"You don't have to do this," Jean kept saying. "We *want* to help you. Let us help you!"

But I didn't want help. I was so tired of the fight inside of me.

"I can't have a job anymore." I shook my head. "I am so sorry, Jean."

My ambition and my addiction had been duking it out like two boxers in a ring for years. My ambition was bloodied, bruised, and—finally, now—defeated. *Ding ding ding.* That is supposed to be a bell. Addiction won. I didn't want to be an editor in chief or a creative director or a beauty director anymore. I just wanted to go to bed.

And that was that. I officially terminated my career at the greatest media company in the world in February 2010. I wish I could tell you how it felt to say good-bye to Jean, Kim, and all of my colleagues. I want to tell you how it felt as I packed up my desk, loaded everything into a taxi, and drove away from the dream. But I don't remember. Or maybe I'm confused. Maybe I *do* remember—it's just that by that point, I wasn't feeling anything at all.

I wanted to put my blackout curtains at Avenue C right up, go to sleep, and stay that way forever, but there was one last push I had to make. I'd been given a month's pay and—more crucially—one more precious month of health-care coverage. Over the next thirty days, I tore through my usual Upper East Side psychiatrist circuit like I was on *Supermarket Sweep.* I filled a few months' worth of Adderall, Adderall XR, Vyvanse, Xanax, Klonopin, Valium, Ambien, and Lunesta. Each script was only five or ten dollars with my Aetna card.

When my insurance ran out, I officially bowed out of the game of life. I was all alone. No more Condé. No more alarm clocks, no more F train. No more iced coffee. No more beauty events; no more desksides;

no more production meetings; no more editors in chief. No more dead-lines. No more pedicures; no more haircuts. No more Internet—I'd only used that at work. No more outside world. No more getting dressed. No more effort. It was all over.

It was just me.

I slept through March. When I woke up at strange hours—time didn't matter anymore—I'd turn on my side to stare at the wall I'd been collaging ever since I moved in.

HELP, Jack Pierson scratched out on one drawing of a mascara wand.

FUCK THIS LIFE, the artist Weirdo Dave told me in another one.

LIFE IS A KILLER, it read over a photo of William S. Burroughs.

INSANE! the Britney-on-a-gurney *Star* cover read.

WAS IT MURDER? That was the headline of the Anna Nicole Smith *New York Post* front page I'd tacked up. All of this toxicity com-forted me. It made me feel less alone.

But I wasn't even there—inside my body. One day I looked in the mirror and hardly recognized myself. I was so pale, with an inch and a half of black roots. Eye makeup was smudged all over my face. The bathroom was crusty with clothes and a broken Essie nail polish bottle stuck to the floor. Glass pieces stuck up like stalagmites. When I sat down to pee, I saw blood in my underwear. I'd forgotten about periods. I'd forgotten I was a woman.

Swamp Thing snoozed through April. Did I worry about money? No. I shut off that part of my brain (drugs helped: I was always either high or unconscious). I ordered grilled cheese every day just to barf it up. When my bank account hit zero, I stuffed bags full of all the de-signer stuff I've been namedropping like a brat this whole book—A.P.C. dresses, Prada cashmere cardigans, YSL T-shirts—and hauled them to Buffalo Exchange. I sold it all. Marco's things, too. The swag Christmas presents from beauty companies fetched the most.

Of course, a hundred bucks here and there didn't pay the

two-thousand-dollar rent. So neither did I. I kept waiting for someone to bang on my door. My apartment seemed just like my job—something I was bound to lose.

Months later, people *did* come pounding on my door, but it wasn't rent money they were after. It was early spring.

BANG BANG BANG.

What? I jerked awake to the racket. It was a sunny afternoon in May. I was on my sofa, wearing a leopard-print chiffon slip by Mischen. It was sheer and very short, with a lace hem. What was going on?

Then I remembered that I was overdosing.

Yup. I'd run out of both money *and* Adderall, and I'd decided to die. I'd taken every pill in the house—let's say twenty Xanax bars and twenty Ambien—and washed them down with Diet Snapple.

My mom had texted me just as the pills started kicking in.

I a0e24jeust took an overdose bbkfbal, I'd texted back. Then I'd started shutting down.

And now here I was, still on the couch, slipping out of consciousness. Trying to, anyway. *BANG BANG BANG.* The noise kept bringing me back into focus.

"POLICE!" a man was shouting. *BANG BANG BANG.* They were jiggling at the knob. "OPEN UP!" Yeah, right. I crawled over to the door and sort of . . . collapsed against it, and put my ear up to everything.

"*We need to go through your window!*" someone was hollering over the din . . . at my next-door neighbor?

"What's going on?" She was *hollering* back. Then I heard *thump-thump-clang-thump-clang*: firefighters, with their tanks on their backs. Oh God. I didn't want to listen anymore.

I slid down to the floor and curled up in a ball.

My eyelids were *so* heavy . . .

GRRZZZZZZZZ! I woke up to drilling.

But then I went under again. *Mmm.*

BANG BANG BANG BANG. I opened my eyes. *GRZZZZZZZZZ-ZZZZ.* That drill!

Then I heard a familiar voice.

"CAITLIN," it was screaming. "UNLOCK THE DOOR!"

My big sister was out there! I tried to lift my head, but it was like I had a broken neck.

"EMILY!" I moaned from my fetal position. "EM-I-LLY!"

"SHE'S AWAKE!" Everyone started freaking out—and *banging* harder than ever. *BANG BANG BANG BANG BANG BANG!*

"*CAITLIN!*" Emily was shouting.

"EMM-I-LLLY!" I wailed. "*EMM-I-LLLY! HELP MEEE! I'm scared of the police!*"

"I'm right here!" Emily shouted. "*I'M RIGHT HERE.*"

My sister pleaded with me through the door for twenty-five minutes. *GRRZZZZZZZZ. BANG BANG BANG.* The commotion wouldn't stop. Finally—and after a few false starts—I reached for the bottom lock. *Click.* Then I flipped the top lock. *Click—*

BOOM! A mob *barged* in and *snatched* me up by my ankles and my elbows. I was four feet in the air before I could even *try* to slump back onto the ground! It was like an episode of *Lockup: Raw.* Don't worry, I handled the whole thing like a lady.

"FUCK YOU," I spat, and thrashed at the cops and paramedics as I twisted around in the air. "LEMME GO!" I kicked one of them. They were struggling to strap me onto a gurney. "GET OFF ME!"

"RELAX, MA'AM!" the cops were shouting at me. "RELAX!"

I was being wheeled into the elevator when I spotted my sister. Her face was practically purple; she was crying so hard.

"EMILY!" I howled. She started crying harder. "*EMILY! EMILY!* HELP ME! EMILY!" I started thrashing around again. Two female cops were trying to hold me down. My slip was coming off. "FUCK YOU! GET YOUR HANDS OFF ME! NO! NO! EMILY! *HELP ME, EMILY!*" My sister was crying even harder now. They rolled me onto the elevator.

"LEMME GO. FUCK YOU!" I was still struggling. "EM-IL-YYYY!" I screamed for her the whole ride. "*EM-IL-YYY!*"

Ping. The elevator opened into the lobby. The paramedics rolled me out onto East Second Street. Fire trucks and police cars were everywhere: they'd closed the whole block off. The people gathered outside stared as I was put in the back of the ambulance. Suddenly, I was *very* tired.

"Where am I going?" I murmured to the EMT. Then I passed out.

I woke up the next day—for real—on a stretcher in the hallway of a psych ward. I was clammy all over, and my skin smelled bitter. I guess Xanax was coming out of my pores. I was starving, so I begged some chocolate puddings off a nurse and wolfed down three in a row. Then it was time to get out of there.

I called my sister at her PR firm.

"I'm in Bellevue," I greeted her. "Long story. Can you come sign me out?"

"I'm busy," she said.

"*Busy?*" I said. "I'm in the hospital!" She didn't say anything. "Do you have any idea what I've been through in the past twenty-four hours?"

Emily hung up.

What's her *problem?* I thought.

But my sister came through. An hour later, I was following her out into the bright Murray Hill sunshine. She was silent as she hailed a taxi. I tried to climb into the backseat after her, but Emily slammed the door shut.

"Wait!" I cried. "I don't have any money!"

The cab drove away.

It was a long walk to Alphabet City—especially in that see-through leopard-print getup and no bra. Guys in trucks kept honking at me, and I was *so* thirsty. I felt pretty sick from all those pills, too. I was mad at Emily. Why was she being such a bitch? It wasn't until I got home and stood in my hallway again that I remembered my big sister had been there the day before, screaming and screaming. Trying to save my life.

Marco was circling again. I could feel it. I hadn't seen him since Payne Whitney, but he still had a key to the building—on my neon-yellow lanyard. Some nights I jerked upright in bed, convinced I heard him at my apartment door, fiddling with the lock. One day I noticed his signature in spray paint on a wall on Avenue B—right by my house. Had it always been there? A few days later, I spotted another autograph on a lamppost on my block. I felt sick—and vulnerable. It had been a mistake to steal his clothes. I was always on edge.

It was just a few weeks after I'd landed in Bellevue, and I wasn't sure I could handle another showdown with my ex–best friend. So when the DJ from LA—the guy who'd followed me home from that coke party, re-member?—told me he was returning to New York and asked if he could crash for a few weeks, I said yes. Marco preyed on girls and wimpy gay guys (sorry, Trevor) but feared grown straight men.

The DJ from LA arrived at four o'clock on a Tuesday afternoon.

"Why aren't you at work?" he said. The last time he'd been in town, I'd gotten up every weekday morning and left him behind in my bed.

"Oh," I said. "I quit my job." I could tell he wasn't pleased to learn that I'd be around.

The DJ from LA was nice enough for the first few days. He and his friend Soupy even called Marco from my phone.

"I'm staying here now!" he barked. "And if you come around, we'll fucking kill you!"

"Yeah!" Soupy snarled. "We'll kill you!" As far as I know, it worked. I didn't see Marco again for years.

But I had a new jerk on my hands. After a week or so, the DJ from LA started acting really awful.

The DJ from LA was in a dark place, too—a downtown-nightclubs and after-hours schedule. He wanted the apartment to be like a cave.

So I climbed up on my radiator with a mouthful of thumbtacks and pinned up sheets and beach blankets like blackout curtains.

"Left," he directed me. He didn't want a single sliver of light. "Down." Then I stacked books and magazines on the windowsill to cover any holes. We left it like that for weeks. I couldn't ever tell what time it was. But since I was only getting out of bed to take baths, I didn't mind.

He'd get in from the clubs at eight in the morning and watch the video for "Estranged" on my laptop, on the sofa in the dark, coming down on coke.

"*Alone . . .*" Axl Rose would whisper through the blackness. The DJ from LA would crack open a can of beer. Sometimes he'd do bumps. All I could see was the red cherry of his cigarette. He smoked constantly, even with those sealed windows. I never said anything.

"How was your night?" I asked one morning when he came in at eight o'clock. I was always awake when he got home—and it irritated him.

He pretended not to hear me, even though we were in a studio, and sat down on the sofa.

"Hello?" I said.

He stared straight ahead.

"Okay . . ."

"I may be staying here, but I don't want to talk to you," he finally snapped. "We're not friends. Got it?"

But no matter how terrible the DJ from LA was, I let him stay. That's how low my self-esteem was when I was twenty-seven and a half.

I was zonked, anyway. My mom had given me cash to see a psychiatrist after the overdose, and I had a half dozen pill bottles on my bedside table again. Late at night, I'd take my sedative and sleeping pill and Seroquel, and the DJ from LA would watch from the sofa. He liked when I was stoned. Half an hour later, when my eyelids got droopy and I started acting all wonky, he'd come over from the sofa. He was mean during sex, too. I'm no prude; believe me, I can get down with a lot of stuff. This was not a good time. But I kept doing it. And when he pulled out his thirty-five-millimeter camera and took XXX pictures with flash, I let him. I was out to the ball game, as the song goes—too gone to care if I ever came back.

Weeks went by. One day I was wearing a white T-shirt from a Los Angeles company called Fucking Awesome. The letters were black, and there was a noose hanging from one of them.

HOW TO MURDER YOUR LIFE, it read.

The DJ from LA did a double take.

"Where did you get that shirt?" he said—like he was accusing me of something.

"eBay," I replied.

"But *I* used to have that shirt," he said.

"So what?" I was confused. He looked disgusted.

This would be the most pleasant conversation we had all day. The DJ from LA and I were getting into horrible fights. He'd say such ugly things! So I stopped having sex with him. He tolerated this for about a week. Then he started . . . just trying to *take* sex from me. One afternoon I tried to sit down on the sofa next to him and watch *Christiane F.* David Bowie was on-screen singing "Station to Station" when the DJ from LA reached over, grabbed the back of my head, and pushed it into his lap! I hadn't noticed him take his dick out.

"Hey!" I cried. "Stop!"

"Suck it," he was saying. "Suck it!" It was five o'clock in the afternoon! He wouldn't let my head up.

"NO!" I yelled. Now he was tearing at my clothes. He grabbed my arms and held them behind me. "Fuck you!" I struggled to get away from him. "GET OFF ME!"

"You know you like it." He was still trying to pull my sweatpants down.

"LET ME GO!" I screamed. I was still fighting to break free. "I'M SERIOUS! THIS IS RAPE!" He kept laughing. Finally I escaped his grip. I beelined to my bathroom and locked myself inside. I'd played sexy games before. That wasn't what this was. I got in the shower and stayed there for twenty minutes, shaking. Then I got dressed in the clothes I'd just taken off.

"I need you to go," I said. "I need you to get your stuff and leave my keys"—I'd given him a set, of course—"and go. I don't want to see you ever again."

The DJ from LA smirked.

"Whatever," he said. He grabbed his duffel bag and handed over the keys. "It's fucking depressing here, anyway."

A few days later, I was soaking—half sleeping, really—in a bath at five in the morning when . . . *BZZZZZZZZZZZZZZZZZZ.*

I opened my eyes to darkness. The candle I'd lit had gone out, and the water was cool. I turned the faucet to get hot water. Then I got out of the tub and wrapped my dirty Bambi towel around my body.

"Hello?" I mumbled into the intercom.

"It's me." The DJ from LA was very drunk.

"You can't come up here," I slurred. "I'm through with you."

I stumbled back into the dark bathroom and into the tub. The hot water was still running. I slid down and submerged my head. I closed my eyes.

BZZZZZZZZZ. BZZZZZZZZZZ.

I came up for air.

This time I went to the intercom naked.

"I SAID NO!" I screamed into the speaker, holding down the talk button. My body felt like rubber. "GO AWAY!"

Then I wobbled back to the slippery, dark tub and sat down hard. *Splash.*

BZZZZZZZZZZZZZZZZZZZZZZZZZZZZZZZZZZZZ. He was leaning on it.

I got out of the bath again.

BZZZZZZZZZZZZZZZZZ.

My life was on repeat, like Marco's *Eyes Wide Shut* DVD. I knew the man outside was bad. I buzzed the bad man back up.

Then it was June, and suddenly the DJ from LA was around less, anyway. I wouldn't see him for days at a time, and when he was there, he ignored me and slept on the sofa. I guessed that he'd found another girl to torture.

Good riddance! I needed to focus on my *new* freelancing career, anyway. After the Bellevue fiasco, suicide was officially off the table—which meant I had to make some money. I'd reached out to someone I knew at *Self* beauty and had been assigned four items: on the "gray" makeup trend, high-tech eyelash serums, and . . . well, I forget the other two. But it wasn't anything too tough. The pay was twenty-eight hundred dollars! Geez! I felt hopeful for the first time since I quit *Lucky*. Maybe I could make this drug-addict-who-works-from-home thing happen after all.

I had four weeks. I spent the entire month high and only started writing three days before everything was due. Then I sat at my desk for days, abusing speed with forty open windows on my desktop. Same old me.

Stormy shades are storming the runway, I wrote. No, that wasn't any good. *Storm-cloud colors. Concrete-colored manicures* . . . My mind was mush. Why couldn't I think of things that were gray? *Smoke.* I was so burned out. *Ash. River stones.* My face was swollen from not sleeping. I pressed it down with my fingers. *Gray goose.* My nose was running; my eyes were watering. *Gray mice.*

I'd been up seventy-two hours straight when I finally turned in the stories. Not only were they days late, they were awful. *Self* had asked for expert advice and quotes from research labs about the latest beauty technology. I hadn't delivered any of that; plus, the sentences were choppy and screwy and weird from my incessant cutting and pasting. It was "Secret Ingredient: Goat's Milk" all over again.

I couldn't deal with it anymore. I just wanted to be unconscious. I went to bed with my Xanax and Ambien bottles under my pillow. I barely moved for three days. Every time I woke up, I knew I should check my e-mail to get feedback and edits from *Self*. But I didn't want to. So I'd take another pill, and things would go back to black again.

And then I had company.

I woke up and the DJ from LA was on top of me. He hadn't been home since the previous week. And now he was inside of me.

"Don't," I mumbled. I tried to push him off. My mouth felt like it couldn't talk—like the thing that happens in bad dreams. "Stop!"

The DJ from LA thrust a few more times. I tried to push him off.

"Get off me!" I said. "Stop!"

Then he came inside of me. I started to cry. He pulled out and rolled over. My shorts were still down around my ankles. I couldn't believe what had just happened. I lay in the dark on the bed, sniffling and shaking. The DJ from LA pretended to sleep.

I kicked him out of my house for good the next day. He left without a fight. Then I stayed in bed another few weeks. It was beautiful outside, but I hardly ever went out. I just lay there reading celebrity gossip on the Internet and sleeping with the air-conditioning on.

Eventually I just knew I was pregnant. Was it from *that* encounter? I wasn't sure. It didn't matter. The test I peed on was a formality: it was positive as a proton. I booked an abortion. It was for ten days later.

I lay in bed for ten days.

Then I got up and went to my appointment. It was at one of the clinics hidden around Madison Square Park. I changed out of my white Daisy Duke shorts and McQ by Alexander McQueen rib cage baby tee and into a gown.

"Do you want to go under?" the nurse asked me. You bet, lady.

It was over in a snap. I woke up surrounded by other girls coming out of anesthesia. But only I was strapped to a stretcher.

"You were screaming and thrashing around," the doctor said.

The nurses took me out of my restraints. I went into the bathroom. My hands trembled as I applied my lipstick.

I didn't have anyone to take me home, so they just let me go. I walked out onto the street and put my headphones on. *It's Britney, bitch.* It was a gorgeous early evening. I'd been in the abortion clinic for hours and hours. The sky was turning pink over Union Square. I pulled a thirty-milligram Adderall out of my pocket and crunched it between my teeth. *Ahh.* Then I put a piece of Trident pink bubble gum in my mouth. Britney and I sauntered down Park Avenue South. I knew there was a blood streak on the waistband of my white cutoff shorts but I didn't care.

Chapter Twenty

SELF NEVER ASSIGNED ME ANYTHING AGAIN. So much for my hot freelancing career. I was broke as a joke. An eviction notice for nonpayment of rent got taped to my door not long after my abortion. I pulled it down so the neighbors wouldn't see. Then I called my mother.

"I can't help you anymore," she said. (I think it should go without saying that she was paying my Sprint bill.)

There was only one other person I could think of.

"*Hell-oo?*" Mimi answered. I hadn't heard her singsong voice since I'd called from Italy.

"It's Caitlin," I said.

There was a long pause.

"Caitlin *Marnell*?" my grandmother goofed.

At the time, Mimi was living in one of several town houses she owned near UVA. I took a seven-hour bus down to Charlottesville and arrived in the middle of the night. Mimi was out cold with the TV blaring. I went to bed but couldn't sleep, so at dawn, I got up and poked around. Her living room was the same as it always was: full of crystal balls, family Bibles, mother-of-pearl opera glasses, arrowheads, and Civil War bullets. Treasure everywhere.

And photographs in frames. I picked one up and stared at the little kid with dark brown hair: Caitlin.

You're in for it, I told her.

I wandered into the dining room and over to an antique bureau. The top drawer was full of my cringe-inducing first clips from *Nylon* ("This powder compact pops open like the trunk of a sleek Italian sports car"), a (humiliating) page from *Glamour* where I'd "outrageously" curled my eyelashes in high-end boutique windows, my first *Lucky* business card. There were even two *Beauty Queen Magazines* from 1991—and a familiar issue of *Vogue* from 1997. I'd forgotten all about my Courtney Love letter to Anna Wintour.

I was still poring over everything when Mimi came in wearing one of her signature kimonos. We hugged for a long time.

"I'm so glad you're here," she said.

"Me too."

My granny did *not* much care for cooking, so we hit the Villa for grits and fruit salad. I showed her my eviction notice and the ambulance bills right there in the booth.

"I didn't mean for this to happen," I said. "I really, really wanted to be successful." I started to cry. "I *really* wanted it. I really tried."

"I know you did, *sugah*," Mimi said. She put her hand on mine. She knew all about my drug problems. "I know."

"Can you help me?" I said.

"Let me think about it," she said.

Mimi's life coach and financial advisor, Vanessa, lived across the street, so she went over there after breakfast. They returned together two hours later and told me their decision. Mimi would support me until I got back on my feet. Until then, I'd live in Charlottesville half the time, working for her—and meeting with Vanessa four times a week for therapy and career counseling.

"Perfect!" I said.

"You're going to have to work *really* hard with me." Vanessa wagged her finger. That afternoon we put a check in the mail for the nine thousand dollars in back rent I owed. God bless grandmothers.

Mimi and I got into our routine right away. I'd get up every morning at approximately eight fifteen to sunshine streaming in through the window and birds being all cheepy outside in the garden. Then I'd scamper into Mimi's room to watch television. Little Jasper, Mimi's cockapoo, would be curled up at her feet like a black-and-white croissant. He'd wake up when I came in and stretch his front legs and wiggle around, saying hello. I'd sit on the floor and sneak a peek or two to make sure my grandma was breathing. I know that's morbid, but . . . octogenarians *are* sort of like junkies, you know? You can never be too confident that they're going to make it through the night.

Mimi always opened her eyes eventually. *Phew.*

"Morning, darlin'," she'd say sleepily. "Can you take out the baby?" Yes, ma'am. I'd put Jasper on his leash and stick on a pair of UGG boots, which Mimi was wearing back before all the girls in Bonnie Fuller–era *US Weekly* (I guess that's nothing to brag about). Jasper had to stop and sniff at absolutely *every* single plant, but I didn't mind. It was always mountain-air fresh and lush outside in the mornings—dewy, dewy, dewy, as JGJ would say.

Then I'd come back to set the table and make breakfast. We each had an earthenware mug full of piping-hot Nescafé Clásico instant coffee, half a grapefruit from Kroger's, and some lovely oatmeal cooked just the way Mimi liked it—with plenty of salt, and served on a plate, not in a bowl. Mimi would put a dollop of Greek yogurt on top of everything.

"Dr. Oz eats Greek yogurt *every* morning," Mimi would declare—every morning. I'd be reading the Charlottesville paper, which was full of murdered girls.

"Did you take your pills, Mimi?" I'd ask. She'd take out her sheet cake–size plastic grid full of meds. I'd already taken it upon myself to Google every pill in there, just in case someone was trying to poison my grandmother or something. I mean, elder abuse is very serious.

And then it was time to work! The house Mimi wanted to sell was stuffed like a turkey full of boxes, and it was my job to clean the place out. Mimi saved everything, which I thought was wonderful (my mother would disagree). It was all wrapped in newspaper from the midnineties.

"Ooooh," I'd say to Jasper as I unwrapped a cantaloupe-size glittery geode or something.

Mimi did not like me to throw anything away without her permission, but a lot of that stuff just had to go. I'd secretly lug massive trash bags to the Dumpsters until noon. Then it was time for lunch! We'd hop into Mimi's red Honda van. It had "MEMS" vanity plates because "MEEMS"—my brother's nickname for her—was taken.

"We'll have three tacos, and one senior tea," Mimi would say into the drive-through intercom at Taco Bell. That iced sweet tea was *complimentary* for customers over sixty-five and heaven help the newbie at the register who didn't know it. Sometimes we'd park by the UVA athletic fields and eat our tacos. Jasper was allowed exactly one taco.

Then it was time to run errands, though sometimes we would get a teensy bit sidetracked.

"Oh, please!" I'd cry when we passed the ASPCA. "*Please*, Mimi!"

"Oh . . ." Mimi would say. "Well, *all right*." Then she'd make a sharp left, and we'd look at the kittens and the puppies. Otherwise, we'd park outside of Rite Aid and I'd run in and pick up her prescriptions, something I was very good at. Or we'd visit Martha Jefferson Hospital, where a doctor would check on Mimi's . . . I don't know *what* it was, exactly. You know! Her heart thingy. It was a strange bulge that had been . . . *implanted* in her chest, as though by aliens.

When we got home, I'd go across the street to Vanessa's house and talk about why I had failed at my "dream career" as a Condé Nast beauty editor.

"Drugs," I always said. She wouldn't accept that answer. She really believed there was a science to career happiness. She gave me tons of homework: personality assessments, career quizzes. It was all very serious.

Back at Mimi's, it would be cocktail hour! She'd pour gin into her Ensure shake or something. While she mixed her signature "martinis," I'd light candles and heat up two Lean Cuisines and announce that dinner was served.

"This meat loaf is *delicious!*" Mimi would say. "Are you telling me you made this in the *microwave?*" She'd be a little drunk. After dinner we'd sit and talk. Mimi would be on the sofa, sipping an O'Doul's non-alcoholic beer spiked with Smirnoff. I'd be at her feet on the apricot carpet, with photos spread all around.

"Tell me about my mom's anorexia," I'd say, leaning my head on Mimi's knee.

"Oh, it was so terrible . . ." Mimi would say. She'd reach down and rub my neck. "We got a call from her college. She weighed eighty-five pounds . . ." Eventually she'd doze off, and I'd lead her to her bed. Then I'd go downstairs and take a bath and read John Updike's S. Maybe try on an old wedding dress.

I worked very hard with Vanessa, who was a highly practical, organized, and money-minded life coach. She had very little interest in my addiction; she just wanted to understand how *much* I spent every month on drugs. She made me print out six months' worth of bank statements.

"Are you out of your *mind?*" she said when we added up my withdrawals from sketchy Avenue C ATMs. But she didn't judge. She just took everything into consideration as she worked on a budget.

One night Vanessa came over to Mimi's house all excited. She told me she'd tallied my results from a big test that I'd taken over several days.

"You're off-the-charts creative!" she crowed, showing me a pie chart she'd printed out. "Look! Now, according to studies, if you satisfy the *creative* part of your brain, it will lead to . . ." And so on. I tuned out, because I am also off-the-charts ADD.

"I've *always* known Caitlin was creative," Mimi said, taking a slurp of her martini.

"Now we're going to figure out a way for you to make money!" Vanessa beamed.

"Great!" I said. I thought the whole thing was insane. Mimi wobbled over and posted the pie chart on her refrigerator with a big magnet, like it was an acceptance letter to Harvard.

Charlottesville was like rehab. The longer I was there, the better I felt. I started jogging alongside grad students and doing laps in the tiny housing community pool—or trying, anyway. Jesus, swimming was hard! I was out of breath so fast. Must have been all that freebasing with Marco.

After a month, I was lean, tan, glowy, and drug free. I was full of energy. I even had a fresh head of highlights from a salon at the Barracks Road Shopping Center. I decided I could handle going home for a while.

"I'll be back in two weeks." I gave Mimi a smooch. She gave me some cash. Swag! I mean, now I could afford Adderall again.

On the train back to New York, I thought about my new, *mega*important goal: a social life. Some *friends*. I didn't have a job and I was feeling healthy after all that time at Mimi's. There was no reason for me not to go out. I *had* to push myself to get out there. No more isolating! Recluses get weak, as Jenny Holzer said. At home in my apartment, I pulled on a see-through white mesh slip dress by Patrizia Pepe that brought out my Blue Ridge Mountain tan and decided to hit the town that very night. Carpe diem, right?

And I knew just who to call. SAME—aka Jacuzzi Chris, aka MA-CHINE, aka Mr. Menthol—went out six nights a week. I met up with him and Alden in a warehouse-cum-club on Bond Street. SAME was dressed in head-to-toe Newport cigarettes–brand gear and was even more handsome than when I'd met him at Alex's side almost ten years ago. I danced with his friend, a beefcake in his lavender Polo shirt. He looked like an NFL player, but he was actually a famous graffiti writer, REMO. I met OJ, aka SLUTLUST, and another graffiti writer, SHAUN RFC, and the artist duo Mint and Serf (aka the Mirf). Afterward everyone went to a Ludlow Street rooftop. I was in a fantastic mood—talking and talking to my new friends. I bounced over to SAME, who was off to the side, watching everyone as he sipped a forty.

"I'm having so much fun!" I told him.

"Good." The sun was rising. The night was almost over.

Suddenly, I felt a little desperate.

"SAME?" I said. "Can I go out with you guys again soon? It's been a really rough time for me." I got a little *weepy*, if you must know. "I've been through . . . a lot . . . I don't have a career anymore—"

"I got you," SAME interrupted, not so much to comfort me as to shut me up (weakness makes SAME sick). When he put his arm around me, he was so tall that I was literally taken under his wing.

And just like that, my life changed. I started partying with SAME's crowd all the time. Marco had played at graffiti, but these guys were the real deal: born and raised New Yorkers with funny nicknames—their "tags" (sorry, I know I sound extremely corny)—who'd been arrested approximately one million times each. A unit of the NYPD called the Vandal Squad was even after SAME, which I thought was terribly exciting even if SAME decidedly did not. I loved trailing along as these guys prowled the streets. They were so physical and graceful and fantastic doing their big fill-ins. And they could climb fire escapes like monkeys! They'd skulk away from their crime scenes with paint on their hands like blood on a murderer's. Sometimes *I* even got to be the lookout when they peed in phone booths.

"We can go back to mine," I'd offer when everyone spilled out of the clubs at four twenty in the morning. Back at 252 East Second Street, we'd do coke on the roof for hours. The graffiti writers would discuss their strange politics—who had beef, who was sitting in the Tombs. When the seasons changed and it started getting cold, I moved the after-hours indoors to my studio. It was a rough crowd, but anyone SAME told me to let up, I let up. My kitchen sink would clog with cigarette butts; I was always on my knees with paper towels, mopping up beer; party girls took their purses to the bathroom and stole every eye shadow compact with a Chanel logo on it—but I didn't care. You know me. Derelicts, DJs, and dealers slept on my floor and in my bathtub, and when we all woke up the next day I'd go out and buy everyone empanadas and the *Post*.

I continued to split my time: two weeks in Alphabet City, two weeks recuperating in Charlottesville. Back in the city, I hardly ever got a chance to isolate anymore. *BZZZZZ.* People would come by even on nights we didn't go out. They'd dump their plastic deli bags full of clanky spray-paint cans by the door and settle on my sofa with appalling forty-ounce bottles of malt liquor. I'd be sitting in bed collaging or something.

"So," I'd say. "What's the hot gossip? What's the 4-1-1?" We'd dish and laugh for hours. As the months passed, many of my new party friendships turned into *real* friendships—authentic, drama-free ones— that I cherish to this day.

But no matter how stimulated I was by my new life, I couldn't get over the one I'd left behind. One night I popped into the deli next to Lit to buy cigarettes and saw, for the first time, an issue of *Lucky* I hadn't worked on. My stomach flipped: it was like running into an ex on the street too soon after a breakup. I scanned the unfamiliar cover lines. *Lucky* had just . . . gone on without me. It looked good, too.

I avoided newsstands after that. Magazines had been the love of my life, but now I wanted to pretend they didn't exist. I also stopped reading the media columns in *WWD* and *The Daily Front Row*; I stopped checking Mediabistro and Ed2010 Whisper Jobs. What was the point? I was an addict; I was unemployable. I didn't want to know what was going on in publishing anymore. Thank God for my new buddies, who thought a Takashi Murakami–designed *POP* magazine with Britney Spears on the cover was just another thing to write on.

Winter arrived. Graffiti writers *live* for blizzards, blackouts—any disaster that means empty, unpatrolled streets—and watching them vandalize the city in the snow was so much fun. Plus, running around in scribbly, sticker-covered boy-world was a terrific distraction from the fact that I'd flunked out of *my* world—girl-world. I'd spent the past three and a half years with Jean, Cristina, Simone, Ray, and Kim. Now the only woman I talked to was the NA chairwoman. Not long after the Charlotte Ronson show, I'd figured out that "Lesley" was Lesley Arfin, the *Vice* columnist ("Ask Barf") and author of *Dear Diary*, a memoir I'd read several times. In it, *Vice* sends her to rehab at Betty Ford for heroin addiction. I'd never heard of anyone who worked in magazines *and* identified as an addict before I read that book.

I'd admired Lesley forever without actually knowing her (she was even an editor in chief for a while, at *Missbehave* magazine), and the universe had thrown her into my path—twice! I'd wondered if I would ever encounter her again after that crazy "lightning crash" moment at Fashion Week. And then it happened once more. One night, on yet another rooftop, I was talking to SAME, and he mentioned his ex, Lesley. They'd just broken up.

"Lesley who?" I knew the answer before it even came out of his mouth.

SAME gave me her number, which I'd lost. I'd hit her up, and now she and I were in touch all the time. We became friends. We talked on the phone, we talked on the computer. I gave her advice about SAME and the breakup, and she helped me with my drug problems.

Why am I telling you all this? Because it was Lesley Arfin who, in January 2011, sent me a link to a *New York Observer* story titled

"Jane Pratt and Tavi Gevinson Now Hiring for Your Dream Job." I was still avoiding media news—so I didn't see that people were freaking out about the return of the legendary editor in chief of *Sassy* and *Jane*, who had mysteriously left her namesake title in September 2005 and hadn't been heard from since. Well, until now, at least. Jane Pratt was back! And she was launching a website. It was a big deal.

Once, I would have been excited. I'd followed Jane Pratt my whole life. But in the wake of my flopped career, I just felt stabby pangs in my stomach as I skimmed the headline. I mean, I didn't get to have a "dream job" anymore.

A few weeks later, Lesley called. Her friend Amy Kellner was leaving *Vice* to be managing editor of JanePratt.com.

"Do you want me to tell her about you?" Lesley said. "They're going to need a beauty editor."

I laughed bitterly.

"I can't work for Jane Pratt," I said. "I can't work for anyone. I can't even freelance." I told her about the *Self* stories I'd screwed up. "I'm sick."

"You can't think that way," Lesley said. "You should at least try." But I didn't want to.

Meanwhile, Vanessa wanted me to do something creative, even if it didn't make any money. One night that winter, I had an idea. It came to me at the nightclub Kenmare, where I'd been watching party girls apply black eyeliner and check their noses for coke residue in the bathroom. I'd shared mirror space, drugs, and Trident gum with chicks like this for half my life . . .

"Why couldn't I share *beauty advice* with them?" I brainstormed out loud to Vanessa at our next session in Charlottesville. "Like . . . 'edgy' beauty advice for girls who stay up all night and sleep all day?"

"Would you *like* doing that work?" Vanessa said.

"Omigod, yes!" I said. "But I'd have to do it online. Magazine beauty is all goody-two-shoes!"

"Then you're onto something," Vanessa said. We decided I'd start my very own website. I even had a name: BEAUTYSHAMBLES—after Pete Doherty's band Babyshambles.

Now I just had to become a master of technology. Mimi drove me to Barnes & Noble and sat in the car while I charged *Blogging for Fame & Fortune*, *Blogging for Dummies*, and *The Idiot's Guide to Blogging* on her MasterCard. But reading the books back in Mimi's basement just made me feel worse. I'd never heard of WordPress or anything. Once I bought a domain name, what would I do with it? It was very frustrating.

I spent months "working" on that stupid site! Meaning I wrote down story ideas in notebooks and let my grandma keep paying for my life.

"You'll figure it out, sugar," Mimi said, handing over another check for ten thousand dollars. She was three SlimFast-and-Beefeaters in, watching protesters get tear-gassed in Cairo on CNN. "What *is* this program?"

Weeks passed. One night, I was sitting in Mimi's basement in my usual nest of blogging manuals, wanting to weave a noose out of my own hair extensions and hang myself when I happened to scroll through Twitter on my BlackBerry. That's when I saw the Tweet from Lesley's friend Amy Kellner that would change my life.

"We're looking for a health writer for janepratt.com—but so far all of the applicants have been too . . . healthy. Does anyone know of an un-healthy health writer?"

It was like it had been written exactly for me! *I* wasn't healthy. And beauty and health were always tied together in the magazines. I had *experience*. Should I apply?

But then the negative self-talk began: *You're an addict. You can't handle it.*

Right.

I put my BlackBerry down—on top of one of the open blogging books I knew I'd never understand. Ugh. I thought of how the universe had sent me Lesley Arfin in that lightning-strike moment at Fashion Week.

You have to try, Lesley said in my head.

Fuck it. I then opened my computer, typed and typed and typed, and finally, at dawn, e-mailed Amy my résumé and a long list of "un-healthy" story ideas. Then I crashed.

When I woke up at noon, I had an e-mail from Amy: Jane Pratt wanted to meet me.

"Mimi!" I catapulted upstairs. "MIMI!"

That night, I was on a train back to New York.

Say Media headquarters were in a loft building in the Flatiron District—practically on top of the Museum of Sex, and right around the corner from Le Trapeze. The latter was a swingers club with two floors, food, drinks, couches, a large orgy room, and private locker rooms with showers. It smelled vaguely of sweat and tears, and the action was nonstop. Couples were upstairs! Couples were downstairs! If you saw a couple you liked, you could lie down next to them and start gently stroking the woman's leg, arm, wherever, and—if she didn't say no—go *further* and further until before you knew it, you were having sex with her.

What?! Fine, those are not *my* memories; I have paraphrased a bunch of reviews from Yelp! I've never been to Le Trapeze. These "how I got my job" chapters are extremely fucking boring to write, you know. I'm just trying to keep it saucy for all of us.

Anyway. Say Media—the place I am actually *supposed* to be telling you about—*was* right around the corner from Le Trapeze. The company was San Francisco–based and also owned a site called Dogster—the first social networking site for dogs. Oh, and Catster. That would be the first social networking site for cats. The New York office was okay looking and cheerful, with bright walls and . . . you know, I don't really remember it too well. It had lots of conference rooms! I met with HR in a different one every time.

But I'm getting ahead of myself.

In February 2011, I was running late for my first-ever JanePratt .com editorial meeting. A girl in a polka-dot blouse and Bettie Page bangs signed in after me; she was late, too. We got on the elevator together, then smiled as we reached for the same button.

"Are you here for Jane?" she said. That was Emily McCombs. She told me she was there to write sex and relationships.

"I'm supposed to be writing health," I said as the elevator rose. "But I'm hoping I get to do beauty, too!"

Emily McCombs and I *rushed* into this office—okay, actually, first we *rushed* to this glass door and we didn't know the pass code; we had to wait to be beeped in. *Then!* We *rushed* into this office. An assistant escorted us to a conference room. The door was closed. Behind it—I knew—was the legend: the Anna Wintour of the alternative nineties, the woman who'd put Courtney and Kurt on the cover of *Sassy*; *Adweek*'s 2002 Editor of the Year, the publishing icon who may or may not have scissored with Drew Barrymore.

The assistant swung open the door . . .

"Welcome!" a shrimpy tween in a flannel shirt, a vest, and glasses said. She was about three feet tall with no makeup and blond hair that appeared to have been recently washed in the East River. Was that a *Dora the Explorer backpack* at her feet? I looked around the table. "Have a seat."

It was Jane Pratt. I blinked a few times.

"Sorry . . . we're late," I said. I felt very disoriented. Jane didn't look anything like an editor in chief was supposed to look!

I got over it soon enough. Like most people who willfully dress like Keebler Elves, Jane seemed impish and full of mischief. No idea was too wild for her. She had a distinctive, cackling laugh; weird pitches delighted her. She told us how much she liked pranks—"inappropriate" stuff. The meeting was energetic and fun, and I took lots of notes. My ears pricked up when Jane mentioned bringing back "Makeunders"—*Jane* magazine's signature beauty story. They were flattering, stripped-down portraits of typically high-maintenance celebrities, along with how-to beauty text. I'd read those stories every month for years. I even remembered how they'd been written and laid out and everything!

I raised my hand tentatively.

"I could be in charge of those." *Please please please please please.* I *really* didn't want to be stuck just writing health. "I did beauty shoots at *Lucky* . . . I'm good at them."

"Great." Jane nodded. "Pitch me some people." I was thrilled. This was gonna be just like working in print! I was already thinking of candidates to pitch when something else made me tune in again.

"*Vice* has a guy drug writer," Jane was saying. "I'd love to find a *woman* like that."

I looked around the room. No one was volunteering.

Screw it. I'd already sunk my magazine career. What did I have to lose?

I raised my hand again.

"Uh," I said. "I could write about drugs as well."

"Really?" Jane looked skeptical.

"I'm . . . qualified," I said.

Everyone in the room giggled. Then we all started having sex with each other. No, just kidding.

SAME had a dust dealer that looked like a chola. Her name was Laura. She had two kids and lived in the projects downtown. The first time we met, she pulled up to East Second Street and we climbed inside her SUV. I sat in the back. SAME was groomed to kill with his perfect deep-dish side part haircut that his friend Chaz had given him on a bench in Hamilton Fish Park; I was full-on homicide-victim chic in a Tsubi minidress covered in laser-cut stab holes and fake bloodstains. It was March 2011.

"This is my girl Cat," SAME said. Laura nodded.

"You want bags or dips?" Laura said.

SAME glanced into the backseat. What did I know? I'd never smoked PCP.

"One dip," SAME said. Dips were twenty bucks. "Four bags." Those were ten dollars each.

Laura dipped a Newport into a little vial. The stuff *seeped* up the cigarette, tainting all of the tobacco. This was the "dip." Then Laura gave us four ten-dollar baggies of brown flakes that had been drizzled with phencyclidine, then left out overnight to dry. I could smell the chemicals through the plastic.

Back in my apartment, SAME split open a White Owl cigar and dumped out the guts. Then he rolled up the angel-dusted tobacco into a long, brown cigarette and lit it up.

"Ahh." SAME pulled on it, then passed it to me.

What does angel dust feel like? Well . . . my gosh. It is truly a . . . a *transmogrifying* experience, to borrow a word from *Calvin and Hobbes*. Your whole body inside feels like a fluffy baby chick or something, and your face gets very slack, so when you look in the mirror you get . . . *disoriented*, and you have extremely glassy eyes. It feels like you are in a science fiction movie, and that you could float up and away and be on a boat under the pink sky, and then you *are* on a boat and it is *chugging* along up the East River, and your friends are on the boat and they are talking to you. And then you are in Sardinia on a patio with flat stone panels, and you're looking out at a vineyard and blue water beyond that, and then the patio falls out from under you. And you fall deeper and deeper into the earth, but it's not the earth, exactly, it's this series of . . . *lofts* built into the earth like underground *tree houses*, right, and *another* floor falls out from under you, and then you are on a different floor of the world, and you are starting to accept that things will never be the same. And there you are curled up in a nest, and that's when you realize you're in a forest—a *jungle*—and there are tigers and big cats hiding in the plants like in a Rousseau painting, and leopards are *stalking* you and you have to . . . sneak away, but vines are all wrapped up around you—you are *twisted* in vines—and you keep *twisting* and struggling, but you cannot break free! You can't see through this *curtain* of jungle foliage hanging in your face either . . . and you are *still* twisting . . . Wait. *What?*

And I came out from my psychotic break.

"Cat," someone was saying. "Cat!"

"I can't . . . see . . ." I rasped.

"She's bugging," a different someone said.

"That's your hair." SHAUN RFC—I recognized his voice now—reached out and pushed the curtain of dense jungle foliage out of my face.

I sat up. I was in bed, twisted up not in jungle vines but in my dirty Kathy Ireland for Kmart sheets. My apartment was full of graffiti writers drinking Heinekens, and I hadn't even heard any of them come in. SAME was totally channeling Terri Schiavo over on my busted Eames recliner, looking all comatose with his mouth wide open. Jesus! Now *that's* what I called a drug.

I started "getting dusted" all of the time. Well, at night, anyway. During the day I wrote stories for JanePratt.com: "I Spent Two Weeks in a Mental Institution, but I Left with Better Hair" was about the Davines NouNou Conditioner I'd brought to Payne Whitney; "The Art of Crack-tractiveness: How to Look and Feel Hot on No Sleep" was my *Lucky* morning grooming routine. "I have skipped more nights' sleep than any beauty editor that has ever lived," I wrote. "I used to be something of a party girl, you see." Jane required us to use photos of ourselves in all of the stories, so I had fun staging those, or finding old ones. I could put random videos in my posts, too.

But the very best part? I could talk about literally anything going on in my life—and in *my* voice, not magazine-speak. I hadn't written that way since *Alterna-Teen Retard*! (R.I.P.) I still refused to call myself a "blogger," but whatever I was doing, it was creative work, and I was enjoying it. Maybe Vanessa had been right after all.

Chapter Twenty-One

OOH, I JUST LOVE SOCIALITES—DON'T YOU? My first JanePratt.com Makeunder subject was Tinsley Mortimer, the girl-about-town known for her devotion to fuchsia Oscar de la Renta dresses ("I love a pouf," she told me), platinum ringlets, and Barbie doll lipstick. We stripped her bare-faced, roughed up her hair with a little Bumble salt spray for that "just-fucked at Gibson Beach" je ne sais quoi, and shot that fox on the terrace of her Fur District loft wearing a vintage AC/DC shirt I'd lamely bought back in the day to "fit in" at *Nylon*. Her vaguely famous Chihuahua, Bambi—his name runs in bold on Page Six, you know— *skittered* into my ankles the whole shoot. Tinsley loved the pictures by Blossom Berkofsky, and Jane did, too.

Days were for writing. Nights were for PCP and parties. I think my favorite was at the Gansevoort Hotel on Park Avenue South. SHAUN RFC and I arrived dusted at dawn. I was wearing Wayfarers and a tie-dye mini by Madonna Material Girl for Macy's. We walked through the huge duplex suite with floor-to-ceiling windows that the Kardashians stayed in—you know, that time Kourtney and Kim took New York?—surveying the wild scene. It was all stunning black people in slinky clothes, but no one was dancing or anything. Everyone was *lying* around. They were in the beds together, and out on the terrace on chaise longues. They looked half-dead! And very attractive.

Then I noticed something else. The coffee tables, the dining room table—*all* the flat surfaces—were covered in giant diamonds, or things cut to look like diamonds. Whatever they were, they were as big as grapefruits.

Suddenly, it was *very* clear what was going on.

"Shaun." I clutched my friend's arm. "This is . . . *an Illuminati party.*"

"Shhh." He led me over to the wall (I wasn't walking particularly well, I must admit). We stood there for a few. That's when CHRIS BROWN appeared right next to me. I nudged Shaun.

"Chris Brown!" I mouthed. When I turned back around, Chris Brown was gone.

"Let's sit down," Shaun said. He marched me to the living room, where the aforementioned sexy, glassy-eyed people were draped all over each other on the long sofas. I squished in between them.

"Hey, guys!" I chattered. "Did you guys see Chris Brown? Do you mind if I sit here?"

"*Shh,*" SHAUN RFC whispered. "That wasn't Chris Brown. You're bugging." Gorgeous people stared at me. *I* stared at the coffee table covered in softball-size diamonds.

"I am going to take one of these diamonds and put it in my bag!" I announced, and helped myself. They were so heavy! "Actually . . . I am taking *two* diamonds." I shoved another prism into my silver D&G tote. "I AM TAKING THREE DIAMONDS!" SHAUN RFC *marched* me away again, but I mean, nobody really cared that I took their Illuminati diamonds. I still have them.

Meanwhile, back in fascinating website-launch world, changes were afoot! For one, the site wasn't going to be called JanePratt.com anymore. Since jane.com was taken, we were now . . . xoJane.com. Jane wasn't thrilled; she thought it was too precious. I thought it was fine. It grew on all of us.

The second change was that Tavi Gevinson cut ties with Say Media—and thus with xoJane—telling WWD she wanted "full control" of her debut website. Jane seemed chill about it. Back on Avenue C, SAME told me he was going to skin Tavi and wear her to Fashion Week. The PCP was making him . . . aggressive.

The *third* change was that Amy Kellner quit! Her BFF Ryan Mc-Ginley had nabbed her a sexy photo editor job at the *New York Times Magazine*. Oh, I was so upset. And worried! I'd been trusting Amy's *Vice* pedigree as I cranked out story after story and essentially tethered my career to a site I'd never seen. Now I wasn't so sure what I was getting into. Emily, the sex and relationships writer, took Amy's place as Jane's second-in-command—the showrunner, if you will. I liked her, but she didn't have a magazine background—only online.

The fourth change, I didn't see coming at all. I was chilling with Jane in her office. She was telling me how Emily was one of two Say Media official hires; I wasn't really listening.

". . . and we'd like to bring *you* on staff in the other role."

I snapped out of my day-after dust fog.

"Wait," I said. "*WHAT?*"

"We want to hire you *and* Emily," Jane said, grinning. "Full-time."

Absolutely not. Full-time? It was a terrible idea. I was *not* going to put myself or anyone else through the whole "addict in the workplace" nightmare again. I was going to remain a *contributing writer* at xoJane, just as planned. I was *not* going to deal with Human Resources again. I was *not* going to set myself up to fail by attempting regular office hours when I knew I wanted to smoke PCP and party all summer. I was going to refuse right then and there—and save everyone a *lot* of trouble.

Then again . . .

"Would I get health insurance?"

"Of course."

Take the job, my addiction hissed.

I took the job.

Then it was almost launch, and I was nervous. Remember, I was a magazine-snob careerist. I may have hated myself, but I loved my print-only résumé, from the *Vanity Fair* fashion closet all the way up to *Lucky*. Was becoming a founding editor at a website the right move?

I wasn't sure, but there was no backing out now. *WWD* named me as beauty editor (a title I'd demanded from Jane); the *Los Angeles Times* ran a photograph of Emily, Jane, and me at Say. I wondered if Jean Godfrey-June was seeing everything.

Ultimately, though, my insecurities about online were assuaged by the fact that my new boss was *the* Jane Pratt—one of the Greatest of All Time, as Kanye would say. I wanted to know everything about her life, and I wanted to know *yesterday*.

"Are you a Scientologist?" I asked the day I met her.

"Oh, no," Jane said. "But I do have a Scientology sauna in my apartment. In my daughter's room. [Celebrity Friend] went in there when he was detoxing, and when he wiped the sweat off with a towel, it was all different colors . . . the dye from the pills, you know?" This was a typical Jane Pratt anecdote. She was a total weirdo!

Jane and I had lots in common. Her parents had been Duke professors; my dad went to Duke. We'd both left Condé Nast during periods of terrible distress (yes, I know why she really left *Jane*—but that's her story to tell). Jane had been a suicidal boarder at Phillips Academy in Massachusetts; I'd been a pregnant, self-destructive teen at Lawrence, twenty-eight miles and twenty-three years away. Jane was superclose to her grandmother, who lived in Charlottesville; I had Mimi in the same town. Crazy, right?

And we both loved *magazines*. Paper ones! Jane only got short-tempered with me once in my time working with her: when I swiped an Australian fashion magazine from her office to take to the airport and she'd spied it in a photo on my social media.

"That was *mine*," she almost-yelled when I returned from Miami. "You had no right!" (This is true. Sorry, Jane.)

What else? Jane's wee daughter Charlotte had "celeb-spawn" play-mates that you would recognize from *People* magazine. She and Jane regularly flew out for long weekends at Courteney Cox's Malibu compound, where they'd barbecue with Jen and Justin, play tennis with Sia, and sing around the campfire with Ed Sheeran. Jane had the same publicist as Julia Roberts; Jane used the same *makeup artist* as Julia Roberts and Anna Wintour. Jane had dated at least one major talk show host, plus a very appealing male movie star. Jane wore Michael Stipe's hand-me-down Dior Homme T-shirts to work. She had a two-bedroom loft in Tribeca, her own SiriusXM radio show, and expensive-looking Pilates Reformer abs. Her male assistants—all of whom, it seemed, had an X-rated Anderson Cooper story—popped umbrellas open over her head when it was drizzling à la Fonzworth Bentley and P. Diddy.

Still, no matter how interesting Jane was . . .

"You're nothing like my old boss," I'd tell her sometimes, glumly. Sometimes I even called Jane "Jean."

"I know, sweetie," Jane would say. "Sorry."

I obviously missed JGJ—and our close relationship—terribly. It didn't help that talking to Jane Pratt about beauty was like putting your head in a fucking blender! I'm still recovering from the conversation we had about the eyelash-growing serum Latisse, which my new boss had recently given a try.

"It *was* working," Jane said. "But it made my eyes red, and so now it's just sitting at home and I don't know what to do with it."

"Throw it out," I said.

"I was going to," Jane continued. "But it's a very expensive prescription. So then I was wondering, should I give it to a bald man? Why don't men use it for baldness?"

"Ha." I thought she was joking.

"No, for real," Jane said, toying with one of the pigtails her daughter had styled for her that morning. "I want to find a needy bald man and give him my Latisse."

I assure you I am not making any of this up.

"A *needy bald man*?" I said. "What are you *talking* about? And what *size* needy bald man? Those Latisse brushes are tiny! They're like paintbrushes a Barbie would use!"

"Oh," Jane said. "I didn't think of that." Seriously?

Part of Jane's glamour was that she was infuriatingly *un*glamorous—and it used to drive me nuts. Take this conversation we had before the launch.

"Do you want to see Dr. Brandt?" I asked. Beauty editors always hook up their editors in chief: Jean had done it for KF. "For Botox, a peel—anything? You're going to be doing so much press."

"Oh," Jane Pratt said. "I've been thinking about it . . . but I just feel like . . . all that stuff on me, it's . . . a lie."

"A lie?" I said.

Jane shook her head.

"All I really need is my 'instant glow' stuff," she said. "You know. The silver oxide that I drink?" I didn't, but whatever.

"So . . . nothing before the launch party?" I said.

"We-llll . . ." Jane leaned back in her desk chair. "I guess I *would* like a pedicure. But one that lasts and lasts!"

"Salon AKS has a new high-tech pedicure like that," I said. "Want me to call?"

"Actually, you know what?" Jane changed her mind. "What I *really* want is a product that makes my toenails not grow so quickly."

"I think we're done here," I said, and left her office. I gave up on talking beauty with Jane Pratt after that. She was impossible.

I guess Jane drank her silver oxide before the xoJane.com launch party on May 17, 2011, because she looked beyond, with fresh highlights by Kyle White of Oscar Blandi Salon (who also did Tinsley's and Mariah Carey's color, *dah-lings*), red carpet–worthy makeup by Genevieve Herr, and a canary-yellow Marc Jacobs floor-length gown with cap sleeves. I was rocking a sleazy sequined tunic I'd bought last-minute at AllSaints in Soho; Emily McCombs looked darling in her little mint-green number; and Eric Nicholson—ex-*Jane* magazine senior fashion editor, now xo freelancer—was nautical chic in a navy blazer and white pants that matched his shiny teeth. The four of us posed for pictures and took questions from the media. I felt a little famous. What a trip!

The party was at the Jane Hotel, of course. Eric and I were outside sharing a Parliament when a black Lincoln pulled up. A doorman opened the car door and . . .

"Omigod." I dropped the cig and clutched Eric's arm.

It was Courtney Love, looking more Courtney Love–like than one could ever want Courtney Love to look: platinum hair, white satin gown.

"Is someone going to hold my arm?" she said—to Eric and me! And then I took my favorite rock star's beautiful pale elbow and helped her up the hotel steps.

Inside, Courtney sat squished on a sofa with Jane and Michael Stipe, smoking Marlboro Lights and throwing them into the fireplace.

The site launched that week, and people loved the beauty stories I'd been writing all spring. Emily posted one of mine per day; she'd run out soon enough, though. The pressure was on! I wasn't coming into the office much. Later, when things fell apart, Emily would point out that I didn't show up for my first official hire day at xoJane. But what was the point of working for online if you couldn't do it from anywhere? I focused better from home, where I could hunch over my laptop and stay frozen in an amphetamine spell until dawn. I'd file the story around sunrise. Then I'd go meet my friends.

It was an enchanted summer. Each illegal after-hours party was more fantastical than the last. One was on Elizabeth Street in Noho, across from Planned Parenthood. It was down a rabbit hole—or it felt like it, since you descended a ladder into a lair with dirt floors. It was very kooky! Everyone was in there. It was full of drug dealers and NYU girls in American Apparel. Another spot was through a normal-looking Brooklyn deli. You walked past the register, the cat food, the SunnyD, and the Four Loko—straight to the back. The shopkeepers wouldn't stop you; they were in on it. You'd pass through a storage room, and there it was: a secret enchanted garden. Special lights made everyone twinkle: my friends looked like they were covered in fireflies. Prince Terrence would be DJ-ing, and you could stay until ten in the morning.

But my *very* favorite after-hours was inside an abandoned movie theater. It was hotter than a crack pipe in there, and everyone danced in the steam. There was always a movie like *Gia* on the screen, and the dancing people would be silhouetted against Angelina Jolie in Kabuki makeup or whatever. So rad.

After long early mornings out, SAME and I would go back to my house and watch *The World According to Paris*. I always thought I was *inside* that show when I was dusted—and SAME told me recently that he experienced the exact same thing! Television on PCP is far out. My friend would crash around seven in the morning, but I couldn't if I hadn't yet completed an xoJane story. I was usually too faded to write, but I wrote anyway. I would turn on the TV as background noise, but sometimes I would get . . . *sucked* in.

"Zoos are finding creative and effective ways to keep their animals cool and comfortable despite the rising mercury," the anchor said one morning. "One of the most interesting? The 'bloodsicle.' That's right. Popsicles made of blood!"

I looked up at the screen, slack-jawed. There was a *tiger*—just like the ones I hung out with all dusted in the jungle that time—slurping on a . . . a . . . an icy treat—made of gore and meat!

"SAME," I whispered. "SAME!"

"*Urgghrhghh . . .* " He was facedown on the couch.

"Is this real? SAME!" I grabbed his clammy hand. "Am I hallucinating or is this real?"

"*Bloodsicle*," SAME moaned.

I scrapped a short post together and sent it to Emily McCombs. She called my cell right away.

"What *is* this?" my managing editor said.

"I know it's a mess, but can you fix it up for me?" I begged. "I'm too high!"

"Fine," Emily sighed. The "piece"—titled "GOOD MORNING, BLOODSICLES: How the Chicest Furs Are Keeping Cool This Fashion Week"—ran later that afternoon. I didn't send Emily McCombs a photo of myself like I was supposed to, so she just ran one of a tiger.

I turned twenty-nine two days later, on September 10, 2011. That night, I smoked dust at four, left the after-hours—this one was in a synagogue—without telling anyone, and got lost in my own neighborhood for two hours. Alphabet City looked like it was made by Pixar—like an abandoned, waste-covered earth from the future! And *I* was a robot; and I could make all these robot sounds, like "*Eee-vaaa*." I was lurching around on wheels! All of the streetlights were Day-Glo with neon laser beams shooting out of them, and then there was a glow-in-the-dark baby deer—*Bambi*, like Tinsley's Chihuahua—racing alongside me, flickering like a lightbulb. Then I didn't have wheels anymore, just sneakers that weren't on all the way; I was shuffling along in my *WALL-E* world, and I was lost and I just wanted a mother. I knew I'd never find my friends again; I couldn't remember where I lived. And just when I was about to give up, I sat down in front of a building and then I realized it was *my* building, and the people in front of it were . . . my friends.

"Where you been?" REMO asked, extending his arm. I hung like a

Fendi baguette from his He-Man muscle. He took me to the deli to buy a quart of whole milk. I sat on the floor at home and chugged it until I gagged and milk spilled all over my face and shirt. That's how you come down from angel dust: you pound whole milk. Weird, right? Don't ask me how it works, but it does.

The following Monday, I cabbed uptown for my first-ever meeting with Say Media Human Resources.

"We're concerned about your drug use," a very nice operative said.

"*Mmm*," I . . . *hummed*—not only because I had the "dust stutters" but because half of my face was paralyzed like I'd gotten an injection or something.

Jane was in there, too, but I wasn't worried about my job. My irreverent beauty stories were becoming *hugely* popular, after all. The HR person told me to take it easy, and then she left me and Jane alone.

"What's wrong with your face?" My boss laughed. I told her the truth. I always did! And not just about drugs.

It was around this time that I started holding my new boss hostage in her office with the door closed, ranting and raving. I wasn't happy with the site. It was nothing like a magazine! Where were the unattainable physical ideals? Where were the aspirational fantasies?

Instead, xoJane was largely body-positive, inclusive, and "real"— *too* real, I thought. I particularly hated the gross-out stories and embarrassing bodily function–centric "It Happened to Me" essays.

"Why don't you just hire a full-time *yeast infection editor*, Jane?" I'd bitch—for, like, forty minutes straight. Once I got going, I couldn't stop. "A *nipple hair* columnist? A tampon director!" Her assistant would knock with a phony appointment, but I'd ignore it. I knew all the assistant tricks. "You were a Condé Nast editor in chief, for God's sake! You need to *control* things better!"

Control, control, control. I'd been obsessed with controlling things my whole life: my image, my weight, my moods. But I couldn't control what went up on the site, and this made me absolutely mental. Jane told me to bring in fashion and art contributors to match Emily McCombs's real-girl contributors, but I had drugs to do, you know?

What I *could* control was "my" beauty section. I wanted it, if nothing else on the site, to be great looking and glam.

So imagine my *outrage* one Friday afternoon in September when I hit up the site and saw not only that the "hero"—or lead, up-all-weekend story—was a *vile* "IT HAPPENED TO ME: ACCUTANE MADE MY BUTT BLEED" story, but that it was "tagged" (online-speak for "categorized") as "Beauty."

"*AUUUUUGGHHHH!*" I screamed.

I got Jane's assistant on the phone faster than you could say "anal leakage." He told me she was in Malibu with Courteney and Coco and wouldn't be available until—

"I DON'T CARE IF SHE'S ON MARS WITH MATTHEW *FUCKING* PERRY!" I roared. "TELL HER TO CALL ME BACK OR SHE DOESN'T HAVE A BEAUTY DIRECTOR ANYMORE!" And this was the first time I almost quit xoJane.

My threats worked. Jane returned my call; then she had Emily change the hero. I'd gotten my way, as usual.

Still, I kept acting like a jerk.

"I'd sooner sleep with a relative," I sneered when asked to have my midriff photographed for Emily McCombs's slideshow, "The XOJane 'Real Girl' Belly Project." ("Flat, flabby, hairy, pregnant, scarred, pierced, and tattooed—we've got bellies!") "At Condé Nast"—Emily McCombs shook her head—"you're not even allowed to *write* about your belly button! Because prisoners will use the images you create for their own masturbatory fantasies!"

"What are you *talking* about?" Emily McCombs said. I wasn't entirely sure, to tell you the truth.

But still—"real girl bellies"? I hadn't been making myself throw up for over ten years so I could be roped into *that* mess. Instead, I pitched a lighthearted, vaguely pro-ana-ish column called "Eating Disorder Corner," then consumed several Kleenex for appetite suppression and wrote a story about it. But it wasn't enough.

I needed a shallow ally—a Kylie to my Kim. I demanded Jane hire Julie Schott, my gorgeous, emaciated, stylish former intern from *Lucky* (she'd also interned in *Teen Vogue* beauty under *the* Eva Chen), who I knew lived on macrobiotic seaweed wafers. Whatever was underneath her Rag & Bone sweaters was as far from a "real girl belly" as it got. Julie was practically concave! She was perfect.

"You work for *me*," I reminded my new assistant three times a week. "Not *them*. Understand?" Jean Godfrey-June used to say that to me.

You know what JGJ never said to me? The word "sex." In all my years at Condé Nast, I'd never had a conversation about sex. No one wrote about sex; no one talked about sex. So at xoJane, I never wrote about sex—until I did. One time. Drunk! And of course it went fucking viral.

It all went down one early October morning after I left Gold Bar, the skull-lined nightclub on Broome Street. I still had my OneTeaspoon miniskirt and black-on-black eye makeup on—not to mention a buzz—when I got home. I hadn't posted in days, and I'd sworn to Emily McCombs that I'd have something for her. I scrolled through the photos in my phone. I had to have *something* in there I could write about.

Aha! I found a funny photo I'd snapped of a "PLAN B IS OUT OF STOCK" sign at Duane Reade. Great. I put it in the system; then I rambled on about my own (generally unprotected) sex life until I had a sufficient-feeling word count. The post—which I titled "EVERY PHARMACY IN NEW YORK IS OUT OF PLAN B!"—sucked a million proverbial dicks, but whatever; it was done. And it had only taken me twenty-five minutes. I put that bitch in the system, tagged it "health," and hit the sack.

I woke up that afternoon and hustled uptown for the two o'clock staff meeting. When I walked in—late—there was a weird energy.

"What's going on?" I said. "Why are you all looking at me like that?"

"You didn't see it?" an assistant said.

"See what?" I said.

"Gawker." Emily McCombs turned her laptop around. And there it was: a post titled "Ranting Lady Blogger Hates Birth Control, Only Uses Plan B."

"*LADY BLOGGER?!*" I shrieked.

"It's not that bad," Madeline said. Oh, but it was. Everyone read Gawker.

"This is *your* fault!" I screamed at Jane all afternoon—in her office, with the door shut. The comments on my article kept climbing: from three hundred to four hundred to five hundred. "I got caught up in all this *sex talk* and *oversharing*! I don't want to work here anymore!" That was the second time I almost quit xoJane.

But no matter how many times I threatened to walk, my boss always knew how to reel me back in. In December, Jane announced a series of stories called "Occupy: Courtney." Select staffers would be accompanying her to Ms. Love's town house all month to interview her and photograph all her beauty products and rock-star clothes. Suddenly, I was sweeter than a promethazine snow cone. Loyal, too. Quit? Who, me? Never!

On a Friday afternoon, I met Jane in the West Village and went into Courtney-land. I was *so* excited. The house was stunning—Zen and ultrafeminine. Right when you entered, there was an altar covered with crystals and seashells and packs of Marlboro Lights. This was Courtney's chanting room.

Jane led me upstairs into an unbelievable sitting room that looked like it cost a million dollars! There was baby-blue wallpaper, baby-blue sofas, and a Damien Hirst butterfly-kaleidoscope print on the mantel. Family photographs of baby Frances and Kurt, playing with Christmas tinsel, leaned against the mantel. Cupcakes and sugar cookies towered on pretty stands under glass (Courtney wanted to be the girl with the most cake, remember?). There were hunks of crystal everywhere, and exotic fashion magazines and books like Keith Richards's *Life*. I couldn't believe I was there.

Courtney wasn't home yet, so we talked to Hershey, one of the two housekeepers she'd poached from the Mercer Hotel. She told us Courtney loved avocados. Wow! So did I!

And then . . .

Courtney swept into the room like fucking Hedda Gabler or something! She was dressed "period drama" in a long skirt that sort of *swooshed* everywhere, low heels, and a high-necked sheer blouse. She was braless (swag), with cool blond highlights. Her pale, perfect skin looked even more expensive than her living room. I nudged my filthy Gucci tote behind the sofa with my foot.

The next two hours were . . . how do I even put it? I have no words. Courtney talked and talked and sipped her cappuccino and lit cigarettes and talked and talked. She ignored me, but Jane kept shooting me reassuring smiles. It was dark outside when the two of us got up to leave. Courtney walked us to the stairwell.

"What's today?" Courtney said.

"Friday," Jane answered.

That's when Courtney Love looked straight at me for the first time in hours.

"I have to chant, but I really want to curl up in bed and read chick lit and watch *30 Rock*," she said—and *reached out and touched my arm*. I almost passed out.

Two weeks later, it was Christmas Eve. I was feeling lonely, so I went shopping in Soho and then hit up Jane. She invited me to her loft on Desbrosses Street. I'd never been. It was on a high floor, with views of the Hudson and the River Lofts building, where all the movie stars lived. I met Jane's dog, Balloon, and saw the famous Scientology sauna, which was predictably gargantuan and ridiculous. An Andy Warhol electric-chair print hung in the living room. The Christmas tree had FedEx boxes piled under it—Charlotte's gifts from Santa.

"Jane!" I said.

"They're *sort of* wrapped, aren't they?" Jane shrugged. "They're in FedEx boxes."

Jane's daughter was running around like she'd just snorted meow-meow. She cackled maniacally as she opened the little presents I'd brought. Then Char wanted . . .

"DORRITTT-OOOOOOS!" The bag was on top of the fridge. "*DORRR-ITTTOOOS!*"

"All right, all right!" Jane said as the kid started climbing her like a jungle gym.

I sat on the sofa for half an hour, trying to talk to Jane. But Balloon kept yapping; Charlotte kept . . . *caterwauling*, and I kept laughing. What a fab, funny little family Jane had! I looked around at her life and wished I could stay forever.

But of course, I couldn't. It was Christmas Eve and they had things to do.

"I guess I should go," I finally said, and stood up from the sofa.

"Okay, honey," Jane said in her warm way. Charlotte raced over to say good-bye. She looked like she had on YSL Rouge Volupté no. 17—a bright coral—but upon closer inspection, I realized it was Nacho Cheese Doritos powder.

She ran away. I'd zipped up my LaROK parka and was almost out the door when I remembered something.

"Could you give this to Courtney?" I pulled a roll of Kiki de Montparnasse bondage tape out of one of my shopping bags. "It's just a silly gift . . . because she likes lingerie . . ."

Jane looked up from her phone.

"Why don't you bring it to her yourself?" she said. "She's over there now."

"Uhhh . . ." I was holding the elevator door. "You mean . . . go without you? Alone?"

"Sure," Jane said. "I'm texting with her right now. I'll let her know to expect you."

"Uh," I said. "Are you sure?"

Charlotte ran out of her bedroom, screaming and hooting: "DON'T GO, CAT! DON'T GO DON'T GO DON'T GO DON'T GO! DON'T GO!"

"Just go on over, honey," Jane shouted, restraining her monkey. The elevator door finally closed.

Well.

I went down to the street and hailed a cab and took it to Courtney's house. I got out on Hudson Street and went to Starbucks and got myself a venti coffee misto. I carried it up to Courtney's house, climbed the steps, and knocked on the door. Hershey opened it, and I stepped into the foyer. Courtney was sitting right there cross-legged at her altar with her eyes closed.

She opened one eye when she heard me come in—and stopped chanting when she spied my coffee.

"Is that for me?" Courtney Love said.

I nodded. I mean, I hadn't taken a sip or anything.

As I handed her the cup, I read the tattoo on her upper arm:

LET IT BLEED

I hadn't noticed it before.

Courtney resumed chanting, and Hershey led me upstairs. The sitting room was full of downtown girls in all black. They were talking and doing their makeup in little mirrors. They looked at me curiously.

There was a little tree glowing with gold fairy lights in the corner. I put my gift under it. Then I wasn't sure what to do, so I sat on a couch and didn't talk. What was I doing there? I didn't know, but *wow*. I closed my eyes and tried to send the halo of white light over the tree to young Caitlin Marnell—like a visit from the Ghost of Christmas Future.

Half an hour later, Courtney came up. It was time for her and her friends to go to the Waverly Inn for dinner. I didn't want it to seem like I was trying to get invited or anything, so I slipped downstairs and said good-bye to Hershey as everyone was putting on their coats. And then I was back outside, on the cobblestone street.

It was very beautiful in the West Village: everyone had trees in the windows. As I walked along, I suddenly felt overcome. I started to cry. It had all been worth it, hadn't it—all of the things I'd gone through to get to this point, and not having a family I was close to to spend holidays with? This was better than being normal, wasn't it? I'd been through such dark times, but look at me now! I remembered being eighteen on the Fourth of July, walking on this same street in the Village and hearing the fireworks and not having any friends, and going home to vomit up my ice cream cone. I'd come so far since then. I had a ton of cool new friends, I worked for Jane Pratt, *New York* magazine wanted to write an article on me (more on that in a second), and I'd just gone to Courtney Love's house on Christmas Eve!

I kept walking east, past all of the Christmas trees in the windows. I took an Adderall or two.

But . . . if everything in my life was so good, why did I still feel so bad inside? Why did I always feel so lonely? Would it ever end?

I kept sniffling. My friends texted me; I ignored my phone.

When I got home to Alphabet City, I called my favorite dealer, Amazing Andy. He came down from Spanish Harlem and offered me everything he had for two hundred dollars. It was all pills: Oxycontin and ecstasy.

"Ugh," I said, and bought it all anyway.

Then I switched off my phone and holed up for six days. Ecstasy and Oxycontin decidedly do *not* mix; I mixed them anyway. On Christmas Day, I called Jean Godfrey-June, but I was crying so hard and she sounded so alarmed that I had to hang up. I didn't go out with my cool new friends for the New Year.

Chapter Twenty-Two

BY JANUARY, I WAS *RIDIN' FOR A FALL,* as Mimi's granddaddy used to say: I'd been getting too high, and now it was time for a long, nasty, deep low. Addiction is *rather* cyclic, you know. I let my prescriptions run out and hid in my apartment ordering from the Devil's website: Seamless. Do you know what that is? It's like Amazon 1-Click ordering, except you get French toast and cheesesteaks instead of books. Then you eat everything in bed and stay there all day watching *TMZ Live* on a loop on your laptop, fishing in the plastic delivery bags for any butter squares or ketchup packets you might have missed. Fine, maybe that's just me.

The depression lasted five weeks. Sometimes I'd post to xoJane. Sometimes not. When the gloom finally cleared—it always does—and I finally felt like leaving the house again, none of my clothes fit. Fucking skinny jeans! They are really contributing to this *Adderall culture*, I swear. Anyway, that was it for me. I went uptown to Dr. X. and walked out with a veritable *stack* of prescriptions. It was time to play *The Biggest Loser*—Cat Marnell style: zero exercise, triple amphetamine.

On Saturday, February 11, 2012, I was slouched in a chair waiting for my man (the night pharmacist) to fix me up at my favorite drugstore, the twenty-four-hour place on the Lower East Side, when I read that Whitney Houston had died in the bathtub at the Beverly Wilshire Hotel. I was gutted. I'm telling you, I was such a fan of Whitney that I once crawled under a food cart after the Gay Pride Parade to snatch a fan that said "I'm a Fan of Whitney" on it! Back at home, I ate speed, fanned myself with the aforementioned fan, and wrote my first serious, long-form piece about addiction. It was called "On the Death of Whitney Houston: Why I Won't Ever Shut Up About My Drug Use."

"When Whitney died, I wasn't surprised: women are using drugs all around you, and I'm one of them," the dek, or subheadline, read. "Now why aren't I allowed to talk about them again?" I was speaking not only to the xoJane commenters who kept kvetching about how often I referenced narcotics in my stories, but also to women's media and to the world at large. Social stigmatization of crackheads and all that. It was a strong essay, and after it posted on Monday, the feedback was incredible. Gawker even ran an item titled "Jane Pratt's Resident Angel Dust Aficionado Wrote the Best Piece on Whitney Houston's Death." That was a huge compliment from such a scary website—I am very grateful to the writer Danny Gold—and it did big things for my career. A major publishing house even reached out to talk to me about writing a book!

This positive attention reinvigorated my ambition—briefly. My *top* concern was still losing weight. I don't think I ate for a month! Instead, I guzzled bottle after bottle of something called the Ritual Cleanse that Julie ordered for me. Have you tried it? It's about seventy-five thousand bottles of expensive juice, and you sort of feel like you're drinking gazpacho, and if you take Vyvanse with it you actually stick to the diet. That's a tip. I mean, you're not even allowed to have a macchiato; the big treat is the mealy cashew sludge and you sort of *gag* it down, you know, but it's all worth it, because if you do it fifteen days in a row, your legs absolutely start to look like arms. That's what happened for me!

After a few weeks of cleansing, I was a bit *woozy*, of course—I practically passed out at the Wu-Tang show at Milk Studios during Fashion Week! But so what? Oh, and I guess I was also acting a tad . . . *batty*.

"I want a month's worth of holy water!" I barked at Julie over the phone. "To wash my face with!"

"Uh—" *Click.*

I started wearing my sunglasses indoors, and I bleached my hair platinum blond—that is, Zoe Weipert at Bumble did—and I couldn't stop listening to "Walk Like an Egyptian" on my headphones.

I also felt like returning to work—full throttle! After a six-week absence, I *stormed* off the Say elevator at three o'clock on a Tuesday afternoon in February clutching an iced Americano with half-and-half from Eataly, ready to whip my beauty section into—goddammit!—I still didn't know the code. Why was this place locked down like the fucking Pentagon? I banged on the doors until someone let me in.

Then I commenced storming over to the xoJane area.

"What are *you* doing here?" Julie said.

"I work here!" I snapped. There was a pile of unopened boxes on the floor next to my desk. "Would it kill you to open these once in a while?"

"Good to have you back, Cat," Madeline the editorial assistant said.

But she was just being polite: it was *not* good to have me back. When you don't eat, you always pay the price, and so does everyone around you.

"*I'm* the beauty director." I berated the entire staff when I found Emily McCombs had "made under" the porn star Belladonna—"without telling me." (I'd actually ignored a month of e-mail correspondence about the shoot.) "*I* pick the Makeunder subjects! *I* do the shoots!"

"But you weren't here!" Emily said. "You're never here! You don't even answer your phone!"

"I'm nocturnal!" I screeched. "A lot of people are! Half of Saudi Arabia is because it's so hot outside!"

"This isn't Saudi Arabia!" Emily said.

"A porn star?" I spat. (Belladonna is fabulous, by the way—I was just being vicious and hadn't yet heard of her.) "They'd never shoot a porn star at Condé Nast!"

"This isn't Condé Nast!" Emily said for the zillionth time.

The more weight I lost, the more awful I acted. I didn't whine to Jane behind closed doors anymore. Now I'd throw a rude fit right there in the staff meeting when I hated a pitch for a slide show. I knew I was being hurtful—I could see it in my coworkers' eyes—but I couldn't contain the stabby rage I felt inside. Or maybe those were hunger pains.

"This isn't fashion forward! This isn't trendsetting! This isn't anything!" I'd get hysterical. "It's Internet garbage!"

After a few weeks of this, Emily McCombs and I were barely speaking. Even though we shared an office. It was tense. Finally, one night, we started arguing about how I didn't want to contribute to something called "Say Something Nice Day."

"It's a dumb idea," I said. "I hate it!"

"Why do you always have to be so . . . *mean*?" Emily said.

This escalated into a screaming match so violent that we closed the office door to have it out. I felt high and wild as I eviscerated my colleague. By the end, Emily was crying, and I felt so disgusted that I was dizzy! Or maybe that was my low blood sugar.

I had to get out of there. I grabbed my jacket and opened the door. The assistants were sitting at their MacBooks, their eyes as wide as little owls'.

"What are you looking at?" I snarled. "Mind your own business!" But of course, I was making my toxicity everyone else's business, all of the time.

By March, I was in terrible shape—mentally, psychologically, physically, spiritually. But I fit into my size 25 Imitation of Christ jeans—*and* I was attracting attention to the site. As I mentioned, a reporter from

New York magazine had been hitting me up for an interview. Now a writer from the *New York Times* wanted to talk, too. It had all started after my Whitney Houston piece.

I forwarded all the requests to Jane and started leveraging for money, honey. Then I sweetened the pot with traffic-generating stunts like snorting a huge line of Napoleon Perdis jasmine bath salts off a mirror at the office—a joke on "bath salts" the drug, then trending worldwide—while my delighted boss filmed me on her iPhone. A week later, Say gave me a twenty-thousand-dollar raise. Lean in, bitches!

After dark, I was back in the clubs. I don't want to go into it, but let me just say that if you ever find yourself at a table at Le Baron with Lindsay Lohan and the Yahoo girl—you know, the one they call "the lesbian Don Juan"?—do *not* give the male model sitting next to you a puff of your e-cigarette! LL will be up in your grill in two seconds flat, all flashing eyes and floating hair like the demon in "Kubla Khan," demanding you leave before she personally has your "disrespectful" ass thrown out onto Mulberry Street by security—and you will obey, because that hot bitch owns the night. I'm not saying it happened to me, just . . . FYI.

Let's just say, I had a rough night. I was trying to sleep it off the next morning, but a Say Media number kept calling my cell.

"*Auuugghh*," I finally answered.

"There's a reporter from the *New York Times* here," Madeline whispered. She sounded very anxious. "She's been waiting for half an hour!" The interview had been scheduled for ten o'clock. I'd forgotten. The interview was about "female confessional bloggers" or something; I wasn't too thrilled about that, either.

"I'll be there in a few," I muttered. Then I fell asleep again.

I showed up at Say at eleven forty-five wearing my Pete Doherty FUCK FOREVER T-shirt.

"I'm *so* sorry," I . . . *tried* to coo. Instead I sort of croaked.

"No problem." The reporter grimaced. I took her into the office I shared with Emily. Ooh, I was so cranky and out of it! I couldn't even turn on the charisma (and that *never* happens). Madeline brought me a coffee. I gave terrible answers. I looked for the piece later, but it never ran.

Oh well. I had more pressing concerns—like getting skinnier! I had Julie arrange for me to get a complimentary fat-freezing treatment at a plastic surgeon's office on the Upper East Side. CoolSculpting! Let me tell you *all* about it. You sit there for hours as a machine freezes your belly fat and your . . . *flanks*, I guess the nurse called them; then the fat cells die, and you pee them all out later. And you can't cough; if you do it's just agony; the machine is already *gripping* your body, you know, and when you cough it grabs your skin *harder*; that's when you wail, believe me. I kept beeping for a nurse to come in and hand me my pills and my phone. I was heading to Los Angeles the next week to shoot MTV's *The Hills'* Audrina Patridge for Makeunder, and I had *very* important calls to make.

"I want to shoot Audrina by a *Dumpster*, do you hear me?" I ranted on speakerphone to the staff meeting. I was wearing Stella McCartney tortoiseshell sunnies that made me look like a giant bug. "Tell her people!"

"Are you sure you can handle this by yourself?" Jane said.

"Of course I can!" I answered. I was particularly looking forward to staying at the Chateau Marmont—the greatest party hotel in the world—and hitting the Hollywood clubs. "Who do you think I am?" The treatment ended and I lurched out onto Park Avenue with a frozen section of fat like a stick of butter over my abs.

The day before the trip, I found out that fucking Julie was being sent along to babysit (an experience she has since compared—incidentally—to the Jonah Hill–Russell Brand movie *Get Him to the Greek*).

"WHAT?" I screamed.

"Don't be mad," Julie said. I hung up on her. I wanted to kill Julie! Then Jane. How dare they treat me like a child? I sulked and sucked on strawberry-flavored Klonopin wafers the whole flight to LA.

Once we landed and got into a taxi, I got another surprise. We weren't staying at the Chateau Marmont, or anywhere near the Sunset Strip. Instead, we were booked at Shutters on the Beach in Santa Monica, one of the most luxe, picturesque hotels in the world. It's *the* place to party—if you're Diane Keaton.

"*WHAT?*" I screamed when Julie told the driver our destination.

When we arrived, the pop singer P!nk was in the Shutters lobby, bouncing a baby on her knee as she gave an interview. Couples rode by outside on the hotel's signature Kate Spade bicycles, rekindling their marriages. It was a complete nightmare. Julie and I had adjoining rooms with views of the glittery Pacific Ocean, but I was barely speaking to my traitorous assistant.

"Look how beautiful it is." She came to my windows and opened the . . . *shutters.*

"SHUT THEM!" I screeched, paging through the room service menu. "There's not even *champagne* here, Julie! It's just fucking prosecco!" I charged a bottle to Say anyway and sprawled out on the bed in Ray-Ban Wayfarers and a bathrobe, listening to Julie interview Carmen Electra on speakerphone. Carmen said she used to slather her body in butter and lie out in a cornfield to tan. Could this possibly be a real memory? I was really out of it. The next day we shot Audrina at Pier 59 with two baby braids hanging in her face, à la *The Face*–era Kate Moss. There were a bunch of waste-management-themed murals outside the studio, so I got my Dumpster shot after all.

By April, I looked like Nicole Richie when she had that mysterious wasting disease—that is, incredible! I was as abusive, entitled, and openly intoxicated at the office as ever, but Jane and Say kept on letting me get away with it. Until one day, they didn't.

Two weeks after I returned from LA, I e-mailed in "dope sick" to work. You know how it is: some graffiti kid leaves piles of skag on your coffee table and the next thing you know you're high and listening to the *Contagion* soundtrack in your underpants for six straight hours. I'd offered to pop by Oscar Blandi Salon in the morning to meet a reader who had won a hair makeover, but . . .

Ugh I did heroin last night and now I'm sick, I e-mailed Jane. *Throwing up. Sooo sorry.*

Well. You know how in *Meet the Parents* Ben Stiller is all, "You can't say 'bomb' on an airplane?" I guess same goes for writing "heroin" in a work e-mail, because *right* after I sent that—like, within twenty-four hours—I was summoned by Say Human Resources.

Here we go again, I thought, thumping on the glass door. I still didn't know the damn pin code!

I got in and went to a conference room.

"Where's Jane?" I asked as the HR chick closed the door behind us.

"She's not coming," she said.

"Okay . . ." That was weird. Jane always came to my meetings with Say. "So . . . what's going on?"

"We are very concerned about your drug use," the HR person said. "And we are putting you on disability leave." (Or something like that. Surely I am phrasing it all wrong—HR people are way formal.)

"*What?*" I said.

"We want you to get treatment," the HR woman said.

"Is this because of the bath salts?" I asked. "That was a beauty product, not the drug. Jane *wanted* me to do it! She filmed me! It was funny! Bring her in here! Ask her!"

"Jane's not in the office today."

"Why not?" I was getting upset.

"The content of your stories can be very troublesome," the HR woman said.

"I don't understand this company!" I exploded. "I literally just got a raise based on the strength of a piece about never shutting up about my drug use! It went viral on the Internet! I have a boss who encourages brutal honesty, and I write about addiction, and then it's used against me in Human Resources meetings and I get put on disability?"

"We care about you," the HR person said. "And—"

"It doesn't *feel* that way!" I said. "No offense, but it *feels* like you guys are covering your own . . . whatever, you know, so if anything happens to me, the company can't say they didn't try to help me!" Where the *fuck* was Jane? I worked for *her*, didn't I? Not for these people! "I need to talk to *Jane*. Where is *Jane*?"

But Jane never showed. I didn't get answers. Without them, my mind raced; my feelings tangled up. I felt *extremely* unloved. Abandoned. Betrayed! And also: paranoid. Was Say reading our e-mails? Where was I going to go to rehab, anyway? My salary had been cut in half until I returned to work. And I'd just gone back on drugs—I didn't want to go off them again.

I was very shaky in the taxi home. I called Jane about eight times, but she didn't answer. I left her a voice mail.

"I was just put on disability and told I have to go to rehab, so I guess I'll see you in a month," I said. "I don't understand why you're not answering my calls. I don't understand why this is happening all of a sudden. I don't understand what changed between today and two weeks ago when we were celebrating my raise. Was it the heroin e-mail?" Who had seen it? The Say dudes in San Francisco? Had someone reported me to HR? Jane's assistant? (This is still my guess to this day.) Was this out of Jane's hands? Or was it in them? "Oh, and the *New York* magazine interview is tonight, by the way. Bye."

I hadn't slept, so I went home and took a nap. I woke up to two missed calls from Jane. She *did* care! I called her back in the cab en route to my seven o'clock appointment with *New York*. This time, she answered.

"Hi," I said.

"Hi, sweetie," she said. "I just . . . We wanted to make sure you didn't say anything too crazy in the interview."

"*That's* why you called?" I squawked. "Who's this *we*?"

"I—" I hung up on her.

The piece was supposed to be about my writing, so I didn't want to tell the *New York* reporter about the drama until the end. I met her outside a Dunkin' Donuts in Tribeca.

"They want me to go to rehab!" I blurted out while we were waiting in line. So much for that. Then I spilled my coffee on the reporter.

The interview got worse from there. I ranted and raved about Jane Pratt, Say Media, and why I hated working for online. I was so mad at the whole company. The whole situation I was in. And somewhere— deep inside, at my core, when you peeled back all of the defensive rage—I was upset at myself for being there. On disability. Because of addiction. Again.

I didn't leave town for rehab. Instead, I enrolled in the intensive out- patient program at the Realization Center in Union Square—where I'd gone (briefly) after Silver Hill. I stayed clean for a month, but every time I handed over my debit card to pay the lab fees or got *urine* on my hands taking a drug test, my resentment toward Jane and Say grew.

You don't even care about this job! my addiction—that naughty sab- oteur—hissed. *Fuck those people!*

At home, I was agitated and isolated, pacing my apartment. I wasn't "allowed" to contact Jane or anyone else at the site. I felt like I'd been quarantined. The whole thing was embarrassing. The bouts of shame came and went every hour. Bad memories of *Lucky*, too.

I was still on leave on April 15 when the *New York* magazine pro- file, "142 Minutes with Cat Marnell," ran. It wasn't as bad as it could have been—I'd called the writer and begged her to go easy—but . . . it wasn't great: " 'On our site we run stuff like, "Can you wear white pants when you have your period?" and I flip out,' " I was quoted. " 'It's like, *Shoot me in the fucking mouth.*' " Then I compared Jane to Slimer in *Ghostbusters*: " 'She's always smiling and hovering and saying "I love you, honey." ' " I don't know what I meant by that either. One thing was for sure: xoJane.com was the reason I was getting press in *New York* magazine in the first place. And still—again—I'd failed to simply say something nice.

Whether I deserved it or not, the profile received heaps of attention. Jezebel ran a story called "Cat Marnell Is Fucked Up and Fascinating"; I got e-mails from reality show producers, talent agents, and publishing houses—all of this while I was on disability for addiction. Surreal. Even my psychiatrist saw the story—and he was eighty years old! Dr. X. was *not* happy. He'd prescribed the Vyvanse that I'd popped in front of the reporter (who'd described me as "clearly high"). At our next appointment, Dr. X. cut my prescriptions in half! Thank God he was overprescribing me to begin with.

I still had enough "medicine" to return to work on May 15, 2012. I was cool and stiff as I greeted Emily McCombs and the xoJane assistants. I dutifully met with Jane, HR, and a new managing editor, but I was a million miles away. I knew I wasn't going to stay at xoJane; I wasn't going to quit using. I wasn't fit to work. Besides, it was weird being there now.

I stuck with it for a few weeks. Then one Friday in May I left the office late. I hadn't slept in two nights, so at home, I finally went to bed. I'd forgotten my phone at the office and my Internet and cable had been turned off.

No Signal. The words on the blue screen on my VIZIO television set bounced around. *No Signal. No Signal. No Signal.*

I didn't get up until my sister came and banged on my apartment door the following Thursday. The next day, I went into Say—who hadn't heard from me in a week—and then immediately into Jane's office. When we saw each other, we just sort of laughed. I personally believe Jane would have kept me around forever, but she had bosses and employees to answer to. I'd put the final nail in the coffin for myself, and we both knew it. It was over.

Jane and I hugged and sat down with Human Resources to hash out the end. I received a month's severance and health insurance, for which I was very grateful. It was all positive vibes from then on. There has been speculation over whether I was fired or whether I quit; the truth is, when an addict leaves a job, it really feels like neither.

I'd predicted things at xoJane would end as they did. But I never could have predicted what happened next. I left the office and went home to crash for a few days, just as I had when I left my last job. Unlike what happened when I quit *Lucky*, this time I woke up to an e-mail from the most powerful gossip column in the world. Was Page Six seriously interested in why I couldn't hold down my job? I responded to the reporter's questions the only way I knew how—with pizazz!—and went back to sleep.

Later that week, I went to the deli on Avenue C, flipped open the *New York Post*, and there it was:

Drugs More Fun Than Work

Cat Marnell, the drug-addicted beauty columnist for Jane Pratt's Web site xoJane.com, has parted ways from the site after refusing to get clean. Marnell chronicled her drug use on xoJane.com, and was profiled by New York magazine in April, the day before she entered rehab, as ordered by xoJane.com publisher Say Media. But sources say Marnell never stayed clean, with one suspecting she even worked high. "I'm always on drugs," she wrote to us in an unapologetic e-mail. "Look, I couldn't spend another summer meeting deadlines behind a computer at night when I could be on the rooftop of Le Bain looking for shooting stars and smoking angel dust with my friends and writing a book, which is what I'm doing next." Marnell, formerly a beauty editor at Lucky, admitted she's not fit for the 9-to-5. "Drug addicts undeniably bring editorial black magic to the table like nobody else, but obviously we make the worst staffers," she wrote us. "We can fake it [for a time] . . . before we turn into coddled emotional vampire nightmares."

If *New York* magazine had put my name into orbit, this rocketed it into the damn stratosphere. Everyone wanted to interview me. And I could barely get out of bed. I couldn't keep up with all of the e-mails. I'll never forget groggily opening my laptop in bed and seeing the headline "Cat Marnell Needs to Get Some Sleep Before She Can Talk About Leaving xoJane.com" on *New York* magazine's "The Cut." They'd just reported my e-mail, blowing them off. I was that big of a story. What the *hell* was going on?

I was so sick that I'd been put on disability and dismissed from my job, yet my career was on fire. I was a mess just like I'd always been, but now everyone loved it. Magazines and websites were contacting me not only to talk but to ask if I'd write for them. I'd worked in media too long not to cash in on the moment (plus, I was about to be broke). But where? For whom? I thought of Lesley Arfin and chose *Vice*. I made myself leave my apartment-cave for lunch in Williamsburg with the editor in chief, Rocco Castoro. He offered me great money to do whatever I wanted.

Now, what did I want to write? My media brain also knew to switch things up—to do something drastically different. I decided to get weird. Back at home, I climbed back under my duvet and cranked out my first of eleven dissertations on race relations in America today. No, I wrote about coke sex and Art Basel. The dark, druggy vignettes were beauty product–free, and less accessible than anything I'd ever done. I called the series "Amphetamine Logic," like the Sisters of Mercy song. These columns turned out to be such a big hit that they began eclipsing my work at xoJane! Kids stopped me in the street to tell me they loved my writing on *Vice*. I signed with a literary agent that Charlotte knew and started piecing together an outline for a book.

The press kept coming. The *Daily Beast,* the *New York Observer, Page Six* magazine—you name the title, they wanted to talk to me or have a photographer follow me around for a night. I was literally walking home from an interview with the *Wall Street Journal* ("I'm going to be the bald Britney Spears of the literary world!" I told them) when I got a call from a fact checker from the *New York Times Magazine*. Huh? I hadn't spoken with anyone from the *Times* yet. Had I? Or . . . Oh, man.

> "Umm, O.K.," said Cat Marnell, who was an hour and a half late for our scheduled interview last spring. "I basically overmedicated myself this week." She explained that she was taking new sleeping pills, although PCP is her drug of choice. "I'm using drugs very heavily this week, O.K.? And it's screwed up my whole body."

That's an excerpt from a two-page essay about my "spectacular meltdown" that ran that weekend—not merely in the paper but in the fucking Sunday *New York Times Magazine*! It was by the woman I'd practically stood up after the Lindsay Lohan night; she, too, was savvy enough to capitalize on the media circus. Sitting in the stairwell at Avenue C and reading about my shitty drug problems in this prestigious publication—which I fished out of my neighbor's *Times*—was the craziest feeling. To borrow a turn of phrase from the YouTube sensation David After Dentist: *was this real life?*

After the *Times* piece, the foreign press wanted to talk to me! My trajectory toward "celebrity" had a life of its own; it required zero effort from my end. Sometimes I did a phone call or met a writer at a café, but that's it. I woke up every day to e-mails from all over the world. "Cat Marnell, 'the beauty editor who smokes crack'[. . .]" the *Telegraph* captioned my photo. "[S]he refuses to conform to the sanctioned narrative of contrite, recovering addict [. . .]" the *Guardian* wrote, essentially praising my inability to get sober. "Le Jolie Junkie Du Net!" *Grazia France* declared. "Drug Addicts *Can* Wear Makeup!" [I'm not sure who said they can't], the *Grazia Australia* headline declared. And everyone wanted to put me on television! I negotiated with (but ultimately turned down) *Anderson Cooper 360°*, *Dr. Phil*, and ABC's *20/20*—even after Chris Cuomo personally and repeatedly called my cell. I *did* actually agree to smoke dust on the National Geographic

Channel's *Drugs, Inc.*, but I backed out at the last second. (That producer still hits me up.)

I was too sick to be a media star. It was all too much. I started refusing to be photographed for the big interviews I gave (sorry, the *Telegraph*); then I'd stop responding to the editors' e-mails. My agent was pressuring me to do a book proposal, but I could barely string sentences together. We sent a gibberish writing sample to an editor, and it was returned quietly to us, along with advice to yank it off the market. Eventually I couldn't even handle my once-a-week *Vice* column. The last ones were so druggy and incoherent that they rhymed—badly ("The Boom Boom Room was full of doom . . ."). Still, people loved it: *Rolling Stone* put me on their 2012 Hot List alongside Riff Raff and the Ying Yang Twins and called me "Hot Bukowski." I could do no wrong. *Vice* even sent me to a glamorous rehab in Thailand and then made me editor-at-large—I signed the contracts and everything—but I didn't show up my first day, and then never again.

It took me until spring 2013—almost a year after my career really popped off—to get a decent proposal together. But I finally did. Then I got a book deal. And now—two more rehabs, one overdose, two boyfriends, another pregnancy, two apartments, and approximately fifteen *thousand* fucking years later—here *you* are, holding that very book in your chic little hands.

Afterword

HOW DID THE CRAZY BLOND DRUG ADDICT get through the forest? She took the psycho path! If it took three days and a near-psychotic break for me to complete one paragraph about goat's milk, can you imagine what my ass has put myself through to finish this fucking memoir? I can't even go into it; that's a whole other book. For now, just know that in April 2013, I signed my contract; my deadline was April 1, 2014. In September 2013, I overdosed on heroin; by December, my agent was sending a ghostwriter over to gather my "notes" and piece everything together for me (I scared him away); by February, I was suicidal—texting with dealers to buy Oxycontin. I know, right? I'm the worst.

In March 2014, I did what all despondent addicts who are about to be sued should do: bought a one-way ticket to Bangkok. No, seriously! When *Vice* sent me to the Cabin Chiang Mai rehab a few years earlier, I'd met a fantastic addiction specialist named Simon Mott (who also treats Pete Doherty, FYI). Simon was about to open a new treatment center called Hope Rehab on the eastern seaboard of Thailand, and when he heard about my troubles, he invited me out for an open-ended stay. I arrived looking like a DUI mug shot and yakked just from being out in the sunshine, but three weeks in, I started writing. I began this book on the day it was due at a little desk in the main house, which was surrounded by jungle and built on a hill overlooking the sea. Simon is a big believer in "get up before your addiction," so it was still dark outside when I typed my first coherent sentences in years. My head was so clear before dawn. Who knew?

I stayed two months, feeding bananas to dirty monkeys by the railroad tracks and swimming in the ocean and feeling very far away from New York. I went to bed at eight o'clock every night, then woke up at four to write. I was also counseled heavily about my delusional devotion to ADHD drugs. They were hurting me, not helping me, Simon said. Did I understand that? Yes. Two weeks later, I had the first chapter to send off to my editor—the one I couldn't complete for an entire year. Then, a few *more* weeks later, I e-mailed yet another chapter to New York. My brain was focusing all by itself! I could hardly believe it.

Have you ever heard that Andy Warhol quote "I never fall apart because I never fall together?" Well. I *wish* I could say that. ADHD drugs *did* make me fall together when I was fifteen. I'd felt like such a failure getting those terrible grades—then I took Ritalin and everything changed. I went from loser to winner so fast! I guess I should put "winner" in quotes. As Charlie Sheen, Lance Armstrong, Lamar Odom, and I can all attest, when you're "winning!" on performance-enhancing drugs, well . . . you're actually sort of losing the whole time.

How so? Because instead of learning to push through my helplessness and overcome obstacles, I'd learned that I could chemically alter my brain. But the medicine never worked as well as it did in the beginning. After I initially "fell together" sophomore year, I used more and more pills to keep myself that way—an ill-fated strategy if there ever was one. I've been stuck in a gnarly cycle of "performance-enhancing" drug abuse followed by completely falling apart ever since. What happened my senior year was the first go-round; *Lucky* was the second; xoJane was the third. God knows what the fourth will be. As my addiction has continued to progress, I've stopped trusting my brain to do *anything* on its own: relax, fall asleep, stop eating.

You're going to do it wrong, my addiction snips—not unlike an impatient Condé Nasty to an intern. *It's easier if I just take care of it.*

I sure didn't trust my brain to finish this book. I came home from Thailand in May 2014 focused, positive, and—most important—*really* tan. No, most important, I was obsessed with writing. But every time I had trouble concentrating (i.e., every ten minutes) . . .

This would be so much easier if you were on speed, my addiction would whisper in my (very tan) little ear.

It didn't help that I was back in the eating-disorder matrix. I always am when I go off stimulants. And bulimia is hell! If you've ever tried to bang open a can of cranberry sauce with a hammer in the dead of night, or wept and vomited at the same time . . . you know what I'm talking about. In Thailand, I was breaking into the kitchen at three in the morning to steal yogurts and ketchup packets. Back in New York, it was even worse: I was at 7-Eleven four times a day, buying Gatorade and Hostess cupcakes. It had to stop. But I knew that instead of getting therapy or going to Overeaters Anonymous, I could go doctor shopping for the quick fix: appetite suppressants.

And eventually, of course, that's just what I did. There's a bottle of Adderall right next to me on Mimi's peacock feather tray as I sit writing this, in fact. It has always been my "mostly companion," as Eloise would say. It still is.

I guess that's the bad news.

The *good* news is that I'm so, so much healthier than I was. Happier, too! And I owe it all to this book. Finishing it may have taken years, but it has totally straightened out my life. While I worked, everything got better, though I was so distracted that I didn't even notice. I'd get up every day and drink a banana smoothie with a skinny little straw just like I did in Thailand; then I'd sit down and write. Then it would be nighttime, and I wouldn't go out. The next day I'd do it all again. My moods stabilized; I didn't hole up for days, not answering my phone. I started exercising to relieve the stress.

Flash-forward a year and a half. I am typing this now at thirty-three years old, sitting in my white-on-white apartment in Chinatown, which overlooks the Manhattan Bridge. I have a rainbow machine and crystals and sheepskin rugs and strings of electric-blue bulbs that I bought on the Bowery; my art books and my magazine collection are arranged just so. I have a potted tree that I water every day—even though the pot is *extremely* leaky—and a large conch shell that Simon bought me in Thailand. So I pick that up sometimes and listen to the ocean.

I may be back on speed, but I take *way* less than I used to—and I feel like a totally different person. I sleep eight hours every night. My home doesn't look like a drug den anymore. There aren't any Adderall collages climbing the walls. I don't walk around high all of the time. Ask anyone! I do take Ambien at night—but so does TMZ's Harvey Levin, and I can't think of anyone more successful and together than him, can you? And I'm trying to be successful, too. I quit drinking. I quit heroin, PCP, cocaine, and ecstasy. I don't touch benzos—Xanax, Klonopin—or painkillers. I quit cigarettes. I even quit graffiti writers!

I don't go to nightclubs anymore. Every morning I go to Dunkin' Donuts for an *extra*large coffee. Then I come home and write, take a break at noon for a Pilates Reformer class on Howard Street in Soho, and then I come home and write some more. I take long walks underneath the FDR Drive, listening to Louise Hay's affirmations: *I am grateful for my life. Only good lies before me.* I pray every day around sunset and thank God for everything I have, and for helping me through some very rough times. I know the God stuff weirds people out, but . . . spirituality is so dope. It's such a great relief to get on your knees and talk to someone and just . . . *believe* that if you do that, then things will be okay. Honestly, I don't know why everyone doesn't do it.

After I pray I edit for a little while, and then I go exercise *again*, at Barry's Bootcamp in Noho. Have you heard of it? There's this trainer Noah Neiman there, and he's so hot and healthy; omigod. Working out with him is better than heroin—and I've done, like, *unbelievable* heroin. Noah makes us kiss our biceps at the end of every class, and I tell my body that I love it. I go there with Julie and when we leave and walk down Lafayette Street, I'm babbling like I just freebased; I can't shut the fuck up. Runner's high is so crazy! Especially when you boost that shit with a little nibble of Adderall just before you hit the treadmill.

I'm supertight with my family now. Can you believe it? They've been so incredible as I've struggled to keep it together and finish this book. My mom helps me with literally everything; she lets me order FreshDirect on her credit card, and once even sent me a chic little red Nespresso machine—you know, the ones George Clooney tells you to buy? And I have a heart murmur, so she tries to make me go to doctor's appointments and things like that. And the dentist. I'm also so grateful for my sister, Emily, who has been there for me again and again—and still is. She's still living in Gramercy Park with her beautiful brindle boxer, Mason—he is so *wiggly*—and my new brother-in-law, Jack. Emily is pregnant! *I* thought of the baby's name. I'm *so* excited for this child! I may have been the worst sister ever, but I want to be a stupendous aunt. I'm gonna drape my new niece in sequins and dab lipstick on her like she's Suri Cruise.

As for my little brother . . . he wasn't in my life—or this book—much because I was a self-absorbed jerk who never bothered to look out for him after I left for prep school. But we've reconnected a teensy bit: I went hiking in the Dolomites with him and my dad over the summer, and we played Ping-Pong surrounded by all these snowcapped mountains and wildflowers. He is the sweetest person. He is funny and smart. And a talented writer, too. (FYI—he is looking for love in the DC area, ladies. Get it.)

Then, of course, there's Dr. Dad. Our relationship has come *so* far. Recently he came and visited me in New York. We sat out on my fire escape eating lychees, rode Citi Bikes along the East River, and went to the new Whitney Museum, where we got separated for a while. I found him in front of Willem de Kooning's *Woman and Bicycle*. It's, like, the most shambolic portrait of a female ever: red lipstick, strappy sandals, crazy eyes, sleazy outfit, crimson slashes over her belly, chaos swirling all around.

My dad—a Cloisters man—looked a little scared.

"I don't know what to make of this at all," he said. "But . . . I love it!"

"Ha-ha," I said. "Dad! That painting is me!" He frowned . . . and then he laughed. Fifteen years ago, he wouldn't have cracked a smile. What happened to me in high school—the pregnancy, the expulsion, the second-trimester abortion . . . well, there wasn't anything funny about it. That mess disturbed my father even more than it traumatized me! But at least I got to move to Manhattan and fuck the pain away. My dad—my mom told me—stayed up nights obsessing over his failures as a father. The chasm between us got wider as time passed; this distance from my family allowed me to go off the deep end undetected. Years later, when my addiction came to light . . . my dad must have been destroyed all over again. We've never talked about it, but I can't imagine that he hasn't blamed himself at least a little for my problems with ADHD drugs. He wrote my refills all those years and all. *I* sure don't blame him, though. My dad was a psychiatrist, not a psychic! He didn't know I was gonna abuse friggin' Ritalin like Michael Vick abused dogs. You can form your own opinions.

Actually, no! If you are sitting there reading the end of this book all "Cat Marnell's dad was such a careless doctor and a shitty parent for refilling her Ritalin and Adderall all those years," then you can't form your own opinion. I forbid it! You have to understand: no one on this planet is more strict, responsible, and anti-drug than my father. No one! He is hardcore, man. If he'd found out that I was doing coke at boarding school, he would have sent me to lockup on Jupiter! And he is an ill physician (chiefs of psychiatry are like editor in chiefs, I say!), and the smartest person I know! That's why it's so crazy that it never occurred to him something was up. But you know what? Maybe that speaks to a larger problem these days: kids are put on Ritalin by doctors and parents—my dad happened to be both—like it's nothing. And it changes the whole direction of the kid's life, maybe. I guess I can only speak for myself. And that's sure what happened to me.

But I don't think it matters anymore, anyway. The past is the past, isn't it? What matters is the present—and today, my dad and I are *good*. He is so supportive; he got me a tax attorney for Christmas so I can start working with the IRS and all that boring stuff you do when you clean up. We talk on the phone absolutely *all* of the time. Nearly twenty years after he destroyed my zine, he's so excited for me to be publishing this messy tell-all. It is . . . crazy. He even tells me to make sure that I come to the Midwest on my book tour! That's where my dad lives now. Isn't that awesome? He quit the DC grind and moved to a loft apartment overlooking a famous river. He's a changed man: relaxed and happy. I think it has a lot to do with his girlfriend, K. I met her for the first time a few years ago at my grandmother Nanny's funeral in Philadelphia. Everyone was walking out of the cathedral after the service. I barely knew her, but K. took my arm and leaned in like she wanted to tell me a secret.

"*I think it's just despicable how the Catholic Church treats women,*" she whispered in my ear.

There was no way I'd heard her right.

"Sorry?" I whispered back.

K. repeated herself. Oh, I'd heard her right—and you could have knocked me down with a feather! Had *my* father . . . found true love . . . with a *feminist*? Well I'll *be*.

I know you're all, "But Cat, where are they now?" about every single *other* person in this book. No, you are not like that at all, but I'm going to dish on everyone anyway. I never talk to anyone from boarding school. Can you blame me? What happened there was so harrowing that I just wanted to forget it forever. When I was at *Lucky*, I realized a girl from my class at Lawrence was a publicist at Aveda, and I never called Aveda ever again! Nicky and I follow each other on social media, which . . . means nothing. I dream of seeing Greta T. again; she's still so hot and German in her Facebook photos. Alistair died in Los Feliz a few months after I returned from Thailand. He was an addict. We were very close the year before he died. I went to his funeral in New York.

I'm still tight with Alex—I just love him. He lives near me on Canal Street and is part owner of Whitman's in the East Village, where I particularly enjoy the crispy kale. At the time of my writing this, he has been dating Julie—my former assistant—for almost a year. They met at my thirty-second birthday dinner at Lil Frankie's. Julie is currently a hotshot beauty and fitness editor at Elle.com. (*I* puppetmaster her career, you know.) I don't even emotionally abuse her anymore or anything! Though I have zero regrets about doing it back then. Josh is obviously hugely successful as "the Fat Jew." Every time I turn on the television, Brooke Shields is shouting him out on *Watch What Happens Live* or something. Even his dog is famous! *The* Eva Chen put Toast on the cover of *Lucky* after she became the editor in chief in 2013. Small world.

SAME is still being dashing and running around causing trouble. I can't get into details . . . but let's just say that no Jeff Koons retrospective is safe as long as he's around. I'll always be grateful for how he took me under his wing after I quit Condé. REMO is awesome; he has a baby daughter now. SHAUN RFC still insists that wasn't Chris Brown at the party, but I know what I saw. Like I said, I don't see my graffiti-writer buddies much anymore, but they'll always be my family. They brought me back to life! It was their world, though—not mine. I think everyone understands why I had to step away.

Who else? Shabd is the ill tie-dye artist here in New York. Dr. X. is still kickin'. I haven't seen Dr. Jones with the great legs since right after Silver Hill, but I'd love to again (maybe someday I'll be able to afford her). Cristina lives out in California and has a baby. Dawn is still happily married. Simone is a senior beauty editor at *Glamour*, though Felicia and Mary aren't there anymore. Charlotte is great; she's working for online. We talk all of the time. Eva has since moved on to Instagram; I saw her recently. I think she's going to be the next editor in chief of *Vogue*, but hey, what do I know? *The* Chrissie Miller is pregnant—due the same month as my sister! Lesley Arfin just got married out in Los Angeles. I still think that God intervened to help me find her again—in that "lightning crash" moment at Fashion Week, the day after I went to that NA meeting on my twenty-seventh birthday. If I hadn't met Lesley, I never would have landed at xoJane, and I wouldn't be writing this book. I'm sure of it.

Lucky folded in 2015. A lot of things folded that year! Print isn't doing so great. Whatever; I still miss magazines—the great love of my life. All the book deals in the world won't feel as good as my name did on my first-ever Condé Nast masthead. But of course, I used drugs to "fall together" at 4 Times Square, too—so it was only inevitable that I'd fall apart. I walked into the building a twenty-year-old *Vanity Fair* fashion closet intern. The external glamour and flash of magazine publishing had made me feel better about who I was on the inside—initially, anyway. But then, over the next seven years, my addiction became so powerful. By the time I realized my dream of being an editor, I felt like a zombie disaster trying to pass for human in a world where women didn't even have split ends. I became more and more self-destructive as I realized I wasn't cut out for the life I'd imagined for myself.

Still, I was in denial for such a long time. I thought my ambition—to be a beauty director, a creative director, an editor in chief—would always be stronger than my illness. And it just wasn't. But God bless my first real boss, Jean Godfrey-June. She tried to help me right until the end—to keep me there, close to her, with a job, as long as she could. Some of the loveliest memories of my life are of being tucked away in her office, with snow falling outside in Times Square, playing with new makeup and gossiping about Tom Cruise and Katie Holmes (JGJ went to a Sting concert with them once, you know). For years, I couldn't talk about JGJ without crying. Leaving her behind when I quit *Lucky* was devastating: she was everything to me. At the time, I made a deal with myself that when and *only* when I had three months clean, I'd ask my former boss to lunch. So I never saw her again.

She seems to be doing well, though. As I was writing this book, *Page Six* announced that Jean had been appointed beauty director over at Gwyneth Paltrow's goop website. There was a photo and everything! (JGJ looked *very* dewy.) No one has had a greater impact on my life and the way I think about myself. I still keep the letters she sent to Silver Hill close to my bed, though I've read them so many times that I don't really need to anymore. I can just close my eyes and see her words scribbled in blue felt-tip pen:

> *You are so full of imagination and brilliance and humor, and those things will shine out even brighter as you take care of yourself. Think of how you will RULE!*

Jean planted seeds of self-love and positive thinking in my brain. She shut down my negative self-talk again and again and insisted that I believe in my talent and my future. I was too sick to believe the things she told me back then, but over the years, they have grown like flowers—bright thoughts along the psycho path that I can pick and gather when the forest feels too dark.

> *It's not always going to feel like it does today.*

You were right, Jean. Thank you for everything. I love you.

Being high all of the time was like being in a bubble: there was always a chemical barrier between myself and other people. The only guys I let into the bubble . . . well, they weren't good for me, to say the goddamn least. One of the hardest things to write about was how badly I let men treat me when I was deep into drugs. I was used, degraded, robbed, and assaulted, and I didn't think I deserved better. Of course, the way I was treated was just a reflection of how I treated myself: like shit, all day, every day. I had no self-respect; I abused my body and my brain; I trashed my property. Why did I expect better from anyone else?

Which brings us to Marco. Whatever happened to him? Well.

In the years following my best friend's . . . *metamorphosis*, I discovered a book by Dr. Sam Vaknin called *Malignant Self-Love*. It was about malignant narcissism—a particularly sinister type of narcissistic personality disorder (NPD). A malignant narcissist sucks a victim in by mirroring her ("I thought I'd found my soul mate," survivors recall): this is the honeymoon period. Once the victim's hooked, the narcissist vampire feeds off her for his own "supply" until he inevitably finds another victim who he believes is a better source. Once victim number one is devalued in his mind, the malignant narcissist is free to drop the angelic act and to openly degrade and exploit her—and in doing so, reveals himself as the greedy, destructive, aggressive and sadistic predator he truly is.

Omigod, I thought, reading all this.

Yo. *Malignant Self-Love* might as well have been titled *The Idiot's Guide to Marco*! Every question I ever had about my ex–best friend was addressed somewhere. Why had I only noticed Marco's narcissism after he started dating Carly? Because he'd hidden it from me while I was still his "primary source" of supply. What was up with those penis stickers? Dr. Vaknin's discussion of "phallic narcissists" told me more than I ever wanted to know. Why did Marco turn on me right after we returned from Trevor's parents' house? According to the book, I exposed my disgusting sexuality and pathetic vulnerability (malignant narcissists hate women) to Marco when I slept with him, and he never respected me or my boundaries again. That's when the overt theft and violence started.

Of course, I can't say that Marco is a malignant narcissist. I'm not a doctor. It's just my opinion. I read *Malignant Self-Love* again and again over the next few years. The book helped me resolve my anger, hurt, and grief. It also made me understand my part in everything. Malignant narcissists go for easy prey: the sick, the elderly, the young. When I was using drugs so heavily in my twenties, isolated from my family, relying on pills instead of people, I was one of the weak ones—a target.

"He's going to kill you!" Jean used to say. I always thought she was being dramatic. Only now do I realize how lucky I was to have escaped that relationship (relatively) unharmed.

As I was writing this book, Trevor called me with some news: Marco was in court-ordered rehab, after a stint in jail. Around the time that my *Vice* column was popping off, he'd had a violent altercation with his elderly dad. I don't know the details, except that Marco allegedly locked his dad in a room during the alleged attack. According to Trevor, his dad had his cell on him, so he called a relative, who called the police. Marco was arrested and charged with kidnapping and threatening to kill. His father, who had already been ill, was taken to the hospital. He died a few months later. A police escort brought Marco to the funeral in handcuffs.

I was horrified, obviously—especially for the family. I never wanted to see Marco again. But I did.

It was late spring 2013. I was packing up my Avenue C trap/house. I got a call from him, as I often still did. But for the first time in years, I answered. He had a key worth three hundred bucks to the building I was leaving behind.

"Let's smoke an L," he said—casual as hell.

"Okay," I said. "I'm moving out of Second Street. If you bring my keys, I'll see you." He agreed. He probably wouldn't even show up.

But he did, in his dad's Fiat. He looked awful—extragreasy. I gave him a half hug.

"I really miss you, Cat," Marco said.

"I bet." I pulled my keys from around his neck. They were still on the neon-yellow lanyard, just like when he'd stolen them. We stood in the glow of the gas station light on Houston Street. "How was jail?"

"You heard about that?" Marco said.

"Yup," I said. Then: "I gotta go."

"You don't want to smoke?" Marco said.

"Good luck, babe," I said. I was done.

So what can all you pretty young addicts learn from this? Beware. Unhealthy people attract other unhealthy people—and girls on drugs attract bad guys like a wounded baby deer attracts vultures. When you're high every day, you are vulnerable every day. You are making your judgment all screwy. You will let bad people into your life. They will steal from you and manipulate you, and possibly fuck you while you are sleeping. They will take advantage of your disorientation and messiness. They will take advantage of your numbness—that you aren't feeling what one should when one is treated atrociously. They will tell you that you look amazing when you're malnourished. They will shoot you up. They will encourage you to stay on drugs: they want you woozy, emaciated, and addicted so they can keep exploiting you.

Strong, healthy people just don't interest the sickos of this world as much. You want to be one of the strong, healthy people—which is basically impossible when you're using. I'm telling you all this in case you are young. It took so long for me to figure it all out! Now that I'm thirty-three—officially a woman—I'm finally getting there. Guys still buzz my apartment, but I don't always let them in. Marco doesn't know where I live. I've got a hot career, a clear head, and an ice pick in my kitchen in case I need to *Basic Instinct* a bitch, and nobody fucks with me anymore.

I live near Jane Pratt now, but I never see her. I never pop by xoJane or anything. I feel too embarrassed by how I behaved there. Jane had no idea what she was in for when she hired me. When I left 4 Times Square forever, my self-esteem was even lower than when I was asked to leave boarding school. I'd escaped in graffiti-writer world for a while, but starting at xoJane brought the bad feelings all back—and I took it out on everyone around me. It wasn't Say Media's fault that they weren't Condé Nast. It wasn't Jane's fault that she wasn't Jean Godfrey-June. It wasn't Emily's fault that she didn't have a print background. The problem was always me. My addiction was a wrecking ball in my life. It knocked down everything my ambition built. *It* was the reason I didn't work in magazines anymore.

But even though I knew all this, I wasn't ready to let my addiction go—and we protect the things we want to keep. So when Say ordered me to go to rehab, I went on the attack, blaming them for my "creative unhappiness." I deeply regret trashing the site to *New York* magazine. I am so sorry to my coworkers (especially Emily McCombs) and to Say Media. I was so ungrateful. It was despicable behavior, but because it was an online spectacle, I got rewarded for it. My career took off when it should have flopped. But as Jane would say, "That's the Internet, right?" Needless to say, I don't hate on "online" anymore. As for me and Jane—we'll always be tight. We had a really special connection. If I ever return to work, it would be for her. Jane's the best. And the site is doing great: xoJane was just purchased by fucking Time Inc.! Talk about your A-list publishing companies. Now Jane and her staff are in Time's new company headquarters on the West Side Highway, sharing glamorous elevators with editors from *People*, *InStyle*, *TIME*, *Entertainment Weekly*, *Real Simple*, *Sports Illustrated*, *Essence*, *Wallpaper*, *Travel + Leisure*, *Fortune* . . . I should stop; I'm getting too aroused. *All* those top-tier titles—in one building? You know, I might just *mosey* on over one of these days and visit my old friend Jane after all.

I'm a little lonely, but that's okay. I used to be so despondent about having "no friends," but the truth is, I kept myself out in space, instead of down on earth with the humans. Ground control to Major Tom and all that. And forget intimacy. I couldn't get close to anyone—much less Netflix and chill, or whatever couples do these days. I couldn't even engage in television! Sometimes I worry that no matter how much I've cleaned up, I was in so deep so long that I am too weird, and no one healthy is ever going to want me. I don't know how to cook, and I don't know how to fall asleep. It all feels like too much to work through . . . and I think, *Just stay by yourself.* Then I remember that that's my addiction talking. It wants me to be alone! It doesn't want me to put myself out there—to courageously become unstuck and leave it behind.

So I can't think that way. Someday I'll find a man who treats me right—but I know I have to treat myself right for a while first. I have a ways to go, though, so for now, I sort of keep to myself. But I *do* believe I can change, don't you? I'm changing all of the time! After I get out of Barry's Bootcamp, I wander home past all of the bars on Orchard Street, and I'm so tired I don't want to go into them. I get home at ten thirty and eat my little chicken sausage and watch *Vanderpump Rules* or whatever. Then I run my bath. I pour the Epsom salts right in the water without snorting any of them. Then I take off my clothes and put them in the hamper, not on the floor, and I get in the tub. Louise Hay tells you to paint the life you want with a paintbrush in your head. So that's what I do when I'm soaking. I paint my boyfriend; I don't really know what he looks like. All I know is, I go to restaurants with him. Like a *normal* woman. And to the movies, too. I paint myself getting pregnant and being happy about it. And then we'll have kids; I'll name the girls after famous editors in chief and the boys after punk rockers, and the two of us will raise them all over the world à la Brangelina. *Only good lies before me.* I see it all in my dumb mind.

Yes, my addiction is still very much part of my life—distracting me with cravings, obsessive thoughts, and negative self-talk. Yes, I see my Chinese night pharmacist more often than I see my pregnant sister. Yes, I was recently "caught" doctor shopping on the Bowery and wound up getting a stupid flu shot instead of sleeping pills. Yes, my annual carbon footprint from orange plastic pill bottles alone is worthy of its own Al Gore documentary. Yes, I'm keeping my disease active as long as I'm not in recovery. By keeping away from AA or NA, I remain in the danger zone. Things could—and probably will—get bad again. Real talk!

But the fact that I am writing this afterword means that my ambition is fighting back—against my addiction, against my self-destructive tendencies, against my death drive. And this gives me so much hope. I am so grateful for this book project, which has forced me to clean up and totally turn my life around. It was the best thing that ever could have happened to a zero like me. I am so incredibly fortunate. I am so grateful to be in the friggin' *New York Times*. I can't believe this happened to me. Thank you so, so much for reading my book. Most addicts don't get the chances that I have been given, obviously. I should be in the damn gutter. Or at least in Mimi's basement.

Instead, here I am in the city of dreams. Still going! And getting better all of the time. Now that I'm finally done writing this thing, I almost don't even know what to do with myself. I guess I'll go outside and take a long walk. You know what's great? Condé Nast isn't at 4 Times Square anymore—it's down at the new World Trade Center. And I live downtown, too! And the Freedom Tower skyscraper looms over my neighborhood. Every time I walk out my front door, I see it.

Hiii-ii! I tell the greatest company in the world. *I love you!*

But listen to *this*. You won't fucking believe it. As I was writing this book, I read that there are actual rats in the new Condé Nast offices—*creeping* around at *Vogue*, and everyone is worried they are going to go in the fashion closet and eat the couture. When I read that story in the *Post*, I was all, *I could not have handled that*. So maybe things worked out for my career when they should have after all.

Then I started thinking. Maybe there aren't *really* rats at Condé Nast, you know? Maybe the person reporting the rat sightings is another drug-addicted, ambitious beauty assistant, hallucinating things under her desk—a girl like I used to be. Did you ever think of that? Honey, if you're out there: it's not always going to feel like it does today. Or maybe my theory is crazy . . . but so many girls *do* take Adderall these days! So really, you just never know.

Acknowledgments

Thanks to my addiction counselor and friend Simon Mott of Hope Rehab Thailand, who gave me so much incredible insight into the disease of addiction. His influence is all over this project.

Thanks to my family, who have been so unbelievably supportive and kind throughout these difficult past few years. You're all in my heart.

Thanks to my agent, Byrd, at Waxman-Leavell—I know it is not always easy working with me.

Thanks to Simon & Schuster and my first editor, Sarah Knight—I'll never forget the lovely letter you sent when I started to give up, and thanks to my second editor, Emily Graff. You're sharp as a syringe, my dear—I'm very lucky to have you.

Thanks to all the incredible people in publishing I ever worked with and/or for, from the *Vanity Fair* fashion closet all the way to *Vice*.

Shout out to all of my downtown friends, who keep the magic glittering in between my ears. Thank you for all the inspiration, drink tickets, travel, and laughs. I adore you all.

ACKNOWLEDGMENTS

Thanks to Jason Dill of Fucking Awesome clothing, from whom I lifted "HOW TO MURDER YOUR LIFE" from a shirt.

Thanks to Chris Habib for those insane days of final edits when I couldn't talk, read, or process what was being read aloud to me.

Thanks to Christos Katsiaouni for the author photo.

And thanks to Britney Spears and Pete Doherty. I love you guys!!!

About the Author

Cat Marnell is a Condé Nast dropout and a former beauty editor at *Lucky* magazine. She wrote the Amphetamine Logic column for *Vice*, and was a founding editor of xoJane.com. She lives in downtown New York City. *How to Murder Your Life* is her first book.